Insight and Innovation in International Development

Edited by International Development Research Centre
Ottawa, Ontario, Canada

Titles in this series:
Göransson, B., Brundenius, C., eds., Universities in Transition

D1293035

For further volumes:
http://www.springer.com/series/8850

Bo Göransson • Claes Brundenius
Editors

Universities in Transition

The Changing Role and Challenges
for Academic Institutions

 Springer

International Development Research Centre
Ottawa • Cairo • Dakar • Montevideo • Nairobi • New Delhi • Singapore

Editors
Bo Göransson
Research Policy Institute
Lund University
Lund, Sweden
Bo.Goransson@fpi.lu.se

Claes Brundenius
Research Policy Institute
Lund University
Lund, Sweden
Claes.Brundenius@fpi.lu.se

A copublication with the
International Development Research Centre
PO Box 8500
Ottawa, ON, Canada K1G 3H9
info@idrc.ca/www.idrc.ca
ISBN (e-book) 978-1-55250-505-2

ISBN 978-1-4419-7574-4   e-ISBN 978-1-4419-7509-6
DOI 10.1007/978-1-4419-7509-6
Springer New York Dordrecht Heidelberg London

Library of Congress Control Number: 2010938620

Printed on acid-free paper

Springer is part of Springer Science+Business Media (www.springer.com)

Foreword

Universities in Transition investigates the evolving interaction between higher education institutions and society. While the university was once described as an "ivory tower," a new metaphor is emerging as the institution becomes more embedded in society. Universities, governments, and industries are now described as the DNA strands of a "triple helix," forming the dynamic building blocks of the knowledge economy. When the strands are healthy and interconnected, the helix produces the knowledge, know-how, and technology of prosperous societies. With this recognition comes new pressure on the university – provide specialized training to more students; develop and transfer technologies to industry; and respond to numerous societal needs.

Despite the importance, we still have only a partial view of why the triple helix expresses itself so differently across countries, leading to different development outcomes. We are therefore indebted to the 34 authors who have investigated the relations that universities have with civil society, government officials, and entrepreneurs across the 12 country studies presented in this book. The selected countries have different political and economic systems, and together these countries account for a significant portion of world enrolment in higher education. Interestingly, we do not see a genetic predisposition toward an embedded or isolated university sector. Rather, the authors have done a great service by identifying the internal dynamics and external forces that have influenced the way universities contribute to social and economic development, helping to explain why some countries advance while others lag.

In the chapters on Brazil and South Africa, for example, political change has directed the university sector to increase access to previously marginalized groups while at the same time called for greater commercialization of university research. The adjustment has neither been easy nor uncontroversial, as universities struggle to adapt basic research to meet market needs, and to accommodate a larger student body while retaining the quality of education. Experiments in widening access to higher education demands special attention, as too many aspiring university graduates are denied the opportunity.

The transformation of the university sector in Cuba and Russia is an illustrative comparison. Soviet and Cuban socialist revolutions were at the same time scientific revolutions, with governments placing considerable attention on higher education.

Emerging from virtually illiterate societies, both countries attained stunning technological accomplishments in relatively resource poor environments. With the demise of the Soviet Union, Russian higher education institutions ceased to be the engines of technological development they once were. Moreover, it has taken considerable time to reform university governance and curricula to respond to the new political and economic realities. By contrast, Cuba's university system – having experienced more continuity than change since the revolution – has managed to provide a fairly consistent level of support to the productive sector and society. The explanation for divergent pathways is both economic and political but choices remain that can make a difference. In pointing out the choices and their consequences across numerous country studies, the book provides an invaluable resource to inform future debates.

As editors Bo Göransson and Claes Brundenius note in their introductory chapters, the multinational collaboration that went into the publication had a goal beyond advancing understanding. Unlike many books that create the space for authors to educate the reader, the editors and their UNIDEV network used this book to create the environment for chapter authors and policymakers to exchange views on trends affecting higher education in their countries, and the opportunity to situate their context in a comparative setting.

For both the process involved and for highlighting the factors that influence how universities contribute to the wealth of nations, this is a highly appropriate book to inaugurate the International Development Research Centre's new book series – *Insight and Innovation in International Development*.

For four decades, IDRC has supported research that brings to light new ways of looking at social, economic and environmental issues, and technological solutions. A significant amount of this work has been conducted at universities in developing regions of the world with strong linkages worldwide. IDRC has challenged researchers to inform academic debates and to share knowledge beyond academia – with communities, policymakers, and entrepreneurs. We see this as an innovative research process that delivers ideas and options needed for people to make informed choices. Not only does this book discuss innovations in university governance and how research spurs social and industrial innovation, but it also provides insight into how research enhances public understanding.

David M. Malone
President, International Development Research Centre

Acknowledgments

During the 4 years of research work carried out by the UniDev network in preparation of this book, numerous persons from different walks of life have been involved as participants either in the national workshops or in other project activities. They are too numerous to be listed here but we would like to thank them collectively for their enthusiastic contributions which provided valuable insights as to how representatives of the nation state, industry, academia and civil society view different aspects of the evolving role of academic institutions.

For financial support we thank the Department for Research Cooperation (SAREC) at the Swedish International Development Authority (SIDA) in Sweden and the International Development Research Centre (IDRC) in Canada. The dedication and wholehearted support of their program officers greatly facilitated the project work. Finally, we would also like to give special thanks to Sylvia Schwaag Serger who was directly involved in the project in its initial phase and has since provided insightful comments on various drafts of contributions to this book.

Contents

Contributors

Anda Adamsone-Fiskovica
Centre for Science and Technology Studies, Latvian Academy of Sciences, Riga, LV, 1524, Latvia

Jan Ågren
Research Policy Institute, Lund University, Lund, Sweden

Rodrigo Arocena
Universidad de la República, Montevideo, Uruguay

Mats Benner
Research Policy Institute, Lund University, Lund, Sweden

Claes Brundenius
Research Policy Institute, Lund University, Lund, Sweden

Tran Ngoc Ca
National Council for Science and Technology Policy (NCSTP), Hanoi, Vietnam

Bitrina D. Diyamett
Commission for Science and Technology, Dar es Salaam, Tanzania

Aurora Fernández González
Ministry of Higher Education, Cuba

José Luis García Cuevas
Ministry of Higher Education, Cuba

Leonid Gokhberg
Higher School of Economics, Moscow, Russian Federation

Bo Göransson
Research Policy Institute, Lund University, Lund, Sweden

Birgitte Gregersen
Department of Business Studies, Aalborg University, Aalborg, Denmark

Jørgen Gulddahl Rasmussen
Department of Business Studies, Aalborg University, Denmark

Nguyen Vo Hung
National Institute for S&T Policy and Strategy Studies (NISTPASS),
Hanoi, Vietnam

Wang Haiyan
Chinese Academy of Science and Technology for Development (CASTED),
Ministry of S&T, Beijing, Peoples' Republic of China

Janis Kristapsons
Centre for Science and Technology Studies, Latvian Academy of Sciences,
Riga 1524, Latvia

Tatiana Kuznetsova
Higher School of Economics, Moscow, Russian Federation

Anne-Marie Maculan
Universidade Federal do Rio de Janeiro, Rio de Janeiro, Brazil

Rasigan Maharajh
Institute for Economic Research on Innovation,
Tshwane University of Technology, City of Tshwane, South Africa

José Manoel Carvalho de Mello
Universidade Federal Fluminense, Niterói, Brazil

Luis Félix Montalvo Arriete
University of Havana, Havana, Cuba

Enver Motala
Institute for Economic Research on Innovation,
Tshwane University of Technology, City of Tshwane, South Africa

Burton L.M. Mwamila
College of Engineering and Technology, University of Dar es Salaam,
Dar es Salaam, Tanzania

Jorge Núñez Jover
University of Havana, Havana, Cuba

Isarelis Pérez Ones
University of Havana, Havana, Cuba

Prasada Reddy
Research Policy Institute, Lund University, Lund, Sweden

Thiago Borges Renault
Universidade Federal do Rio de Janeiro, Rio de Janeiro, Brazil

Mario Scerri
Institute for Economic Research on Innovation,
Tshwane University of Technology, City of Tshwane, South Africa

Ulrich Schmoch
Fraunhofer Institute for Systems and Innovation Research, Karlsruhe, Germany

Judith Sutz
Universidad de la República, Montevideo, Uruguay

Erika Tjunina
Centre for Science and Technology Studies, Latvian Academy of Sciences,
Riga 1524, Latvia

Inga Ulnicane-Ozolina
Centre for Science and Technology Studies, Latvian Academy of Sciences,
Riga 1524, Latvia

Zhou Yuan
National Research Center for S&T for Development, Ministry of S&T, Beijing,
Peoples' Republic of China

Stanislav Zaichenko
Higher School of Economics, Moscow, Russian Federation

Part I
The Context

Chapter 1
Background and Introduction

Bo Göransson and Claes Brundenius

In recent decades, a number of structural changes frequently described in terms such as globalization, the information age, and the rise of the knowledge-based economy are significantly transforming the way we acquire, disseminate, and transform knowledge. Among other things, these structural changes, to which one could add the demise of the linear model of the innovation process and an accelerating pace of change, have resulted in knowledge production becoming closer and more directly linked to economic competitiveness. It could be argued that today knowledge and competencies play a more critical role than ever before in national economic growth and welfare creation.

The above-described developments put new and urgent demands on academic institutions[1] to adjust to the changing needs of society and economy. In particular, there is growing pressure on the institutions of higher education and research in developed economies to find and affirm their new role in the national innovation system, while their counterparts in developing economies need to define their role in supporting the emerging structures of the innovation system.

Consequently, there is a global tendency toward reforms of universities and education systems. While there is a general trend, the emerging role of universities in different countries on different levels of economic development will of course vary. In this book, we will examine the role of universities and national research institutes in social and economic development processes. Moreover, we will highlight general patterns in developed as well as developing countries, and also distinguish and take into account country-specific conditions. In other words, we recognize that there is no generic or best way to organize academy–society interaction and that there exist good opportunities for learning from each other's experiences.

---

[1] In this book, academic institutions refer not only to the university as such, but also to its extensions as well as other forms for public knowledge production such as research institutes and academies of sciences.

B. Göransson (✉)
Research Policy Institute, Lund University, Lund, Sweden
e-mail: Bo.Goransson@fpi.lu.se

B. Göransson and C. Brundenius (eds.), *Universities in Transition:*
The Changing Role and Challenges for Academic Institutions,
© International Development Research Centre 2011

The same argument is applicable to the concept of innovation systems. In its current understanding, innovation systems refer mostly to highly developed countries, with strong institutional capabilities in education, research, finance, training, and infrastructure. In these countries, the main policy challenge is to develop stronger cross-sectoral interaction (especially between academic institutions and industry) and broadly accepted visions of technoeconomic development. In most developing countries, on the contrary, the evolution of innovation systems is a much more complicated issue, because a number of basic social institutions are rudimentary or perhaps even nonexistent. Hence, innovation systems in many ways have to be "created," either on the basis of existing sectors (e.g., a knowledge-based agricultural sector), or on emerging technologies and sectors (for instance, locally customized ICT). In this creation process, universities tend to be important players, given a number of specific features, such as their potential global integration into technological and scientific networks, their tradition as relatively autonomous organizations, their relationship to international diasporas, etc. Hence, in the development process, universities are not just one of many important institutions, they are potentially one of the most important.

There is thus a growing consensus, first, that universities and research institutions play a key role in national innovation systems, and, second, that their role is changing significantly. Universities have become key players of the innovation system, both as providers of human capital and as incubators for entrepreneurial activities. The ability of countries to grow and prosper will, thus, depend critically on the ability of their universities and university systems to adjust to their new role.

The notion of the increasingly important, and significantly changed, role of universities is not only important to highly developed economies, but is also a relevant and topical issue for countries in all stages of economic development. More specifically, universities play multiple roles in the development/transition process by:

- Creating (potential) nodes in global knowledge networks. This process that is also driven by the expansionist tendencies of universities in developed countries, seeking new engagements and roles outside their home base (i.e., MIT in China, Stockholm School of Economics in the Baltic states, Harvard's Dubai Initiative, and Copenhagen Business School in St. Petersburg)
- Developing a basis for social capital, i.e., as a "neutral" meeting ground in countries perhaps torn by corruption, lack of integrative mechanisms, and lack of stable relations between state and industry, and between companies
- Providing a source of entrepreneurship in countries with a lack of entrepreneurial traditions
- Offering nodes to international diasporas – personal connections and potential networks between developed and developing countries.

The responsiveness of universities, and of the university system, varies considerably among institutions and countries. Universities in many regions of Europe can currently be described as being in a state of crisis, which is partially caused by the inability to respond to the changing conditions. Thus, many universities in Europe currently suffer from some of the same maladies as their counterparts in developing countries; an acute lack of funding, problems with maintaining quality of research and education, and with providing knowledge and education that meet the changing needs of their surrounding society and economy. In addition, there is a significant generational shift in university staff and a growing need for alternative sources for education and research. All these external and internal pressures for change impelled Burton Clark to declare over a decade ago that "[T]he universities of the world has entered a time of disquieting turmoil that has no end in sight" (Clark 1998: xiii). If anything, the development during the following years has added to the plight of the university system in the developed countries as well as in the developing world.

1.1   Universities in Development

There is emerging literature on the role of universities in development and transition processes. Many of the studies have been pursued under the organizational umbrella of Triple Helix conferences, where proceedings have included case studies of the role of the academic system in low- and middle-income countries, both for countries with only a rudimentary system (mainly developing countries) and those with a highly developed system challenged by brain and resource drain during the last decades (mainly transition countries, a few examples include Sutz 2003; Etzkowitz et al. 1998). The literature also covers the expansion of science globally and its role in local technoeconomic development. Historically, two frameworks have dominated the understanding of the role of science in development. The first is the view that science is an instrumental element in universal societal modernization (modernization theory), and the other is that science functions as an instrument of dominance (dependency school). With the growth of more sophisticated models of the role of science in development, a more nuanced understanding has emerged. It is pointed out in the models that science is a global institution, playing an increasingly important role in almost all societies in the world. This seems to be the case partly because of the role of policy diffusion agencies such as UNESCO, partly because science is seen as having an impact on environmental protection, economic development, societal rationalization, etc. (Drori et al. 2001; Paytas et al. 2004).

These studies suggest that there is a potentially large role for the academic system as a source of capabilities – ranging from social to intellectual and industrial – but that the role of the academic system as an engine of development has been seriously neglected, in favor of other policy measures ("quick fixes"). The gains of science and technology policy – as well as of innovation policy more broadly – are long term rather than short term, diffused rather than concentrated and visible, but nevertheless probably essential if the goal is to develop an economy built on the capacity to generate and exploit knowledge. One reason is that knowledge, while often freely available, cannot be understood and adapted to local conditions without a large degree of tacit knowledge. This tacit knowledge can only emerge through local research capabilities. However, the global knowledge system should be linked to local conditions if it is to play a role in the development process. Ideally, universities function as a bridge between global flows and science and technology on the one hand, and local conditions for economic development on the other.

1.2   The UniDev Project

The empirical findings and theoretical considerations presented in this volume
have been produced in the UniDev project.[2] This project was conceived in 2005
as a response to the need for examining the changing conditions within which
the universities of the world define their roles. The importance of this topic and
its relevance to all countries, regardless of the size or level of development,
made it a unique and ideal subject for initiating international policy dialog and
learning among different regions and countries. By examining the changing role
of academic institutions within the contexts of innovation and economic growth
and development, the project has aimed to establish a new and important conceptual and policy link between the work of development agencies, and the
methodologies and approaches of national innovation policy and innovation
agencies.

The overall objectives of the project were, first, to contribute to a better understanding of the changing role of academic institutions in national contexts, and,
second, to contribute to initiating a process of policy learning and exchange
between countries in different stages of economic development. Furthermore, an
important aim of the project was to start public discussions and policy process on
this issue and on the policy implications both within countries and in international
fora and organizations.

The research undertaken in the project consisted of both a positive and a normative element. In the first instance, we endeavored to analyze and gain a better
understanding of how universities and research institutions function, and what their
role is, within

- Different economic systems (ranging from liberal market economies to socialist
  economies)
- Different national innovation systems (small vs. large countries, countries with
  strong vs. weak national innovative capacities, etc.)
- Different local contexts
- The local/global interface (that is, how are universities operating in an age
  where, in what might appear to be a paradox, both globalization and local context seem to be increasing in strength and importance)

To this end, 12 countries were selected as case countries, representing the diversity
described above. The countries were Brazil, China, Cuba, Denmark, Germany,
Latvia, Russian Federation, South Africa, Sweden, Tanzania, Uruguay, and
Vietnam. This cross-section of countries accounts for a substantial share of total
world production of goods and services as well as the resources devoted to higher
education and R&D. In terms of GDP, the 12 countries account for over 23% of

---

[2]Financial support for the project from the Swedish Agency for Research Cooperation with
Developing Countries (Sarec) and the International Development Research Centre (IDRC) is
gratefully acknowledged.

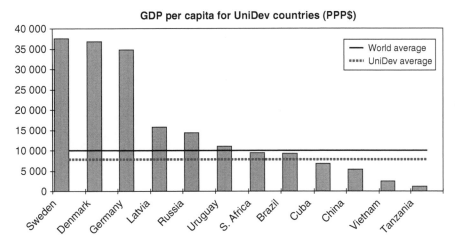

Fig. 1.1 Constructive modules to characterize the Uruguayan NSI

total world GDP (Table 1.1 of Appendix). The average GDP per capita of PPP$7,853 for the UniDev countries is slightly lower than the world average of 9,947 (Fig. 1.1).

Furthermore, the UniDev countries account for a substantial share of world population (29%), of the total number of students enrolled in tertiary education worldwide (31%), of the global gross expenditure on research and development (22%), and of the number of personnel engaged in research in the world (Box 1.1).

Each country case study is presented as a separate chapter in this book. Based on the insights gained from the analysis of the country case studies, we have ventured to provide some conclusions on how universities should function within different contexts in order to fulfill their role and potential as anchors of economic development and national innovative capacity.

The research was structured around the following issues:

1. Universities and research institutions within the general economic and social context, and their role in national and regional innovation systems

   - *Linkages and cooperation* (Triple helix models)
   - *The "entrepreneurial university"*: Universities as incubator, innovator, networker, neutral arena, etc.
   - *Knowledge production*: The profile of universities in relation to the local environment and to the international scientific and technological trends

2. "Internal" dynamics, structures

   - *Organizational structures*, especially the balance and connections between research and teaching, between knowledge fields, and between knowledge refinement and societal interplay, and how is innovation "internal" to the organization

Box 1.1 UniDev Countries' share of selected indicators

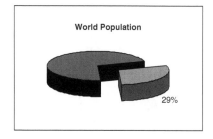

World Population

29%

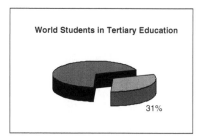

World Students in Tertiary Education

31%

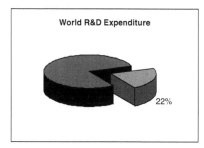

World R&D Expenditure

22%

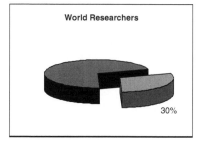

World Researchers

30%

Source: Table 1.1 in Appendix

- *Funding*, especially the interaction between local, national, and international funding streams
- *Management structures*, especially the role of international influences and steering
- *Issues of inclusion*, especially how universities, both individual and as a sector, are handling and promoting gender and other equality issues such as women entrepreneurship and ethnic diversity as sources for strengthening innovative capacity
- *The "Third mission"*, or extension activities, of the university in its relations with the surrounding society[3]

In exploring these issues, we have employed a comparative, multistakeholder, and multilateral approach. The project has worked in close collaboration with national networks of researchers and policymakers in selected countries and organizations. In each country, the aim has been to engage one research organization and one policy-making organization as main partners in the research. The interaction between the researchers and policy makers during the project has taken place

---

[3]For some of the findings of the UniDev project on the Third Mission of universities, see the special issue of Science and Public Policy (2009).

through national policy workshops organized by the UniDev network members. The workshops have provided a platform for discussion between researchers and policy makers – for ensuring an agreement on the relevance of the research for policy making as well as for firmly anchoring the project work in relevant policy-making bodies in preparation for discussions on research results.

The UniDev project deals with change processes. The evolving role of universities and the complex interplay between stakeholders in academia, politics, and civil society are at the core of the project. Such processes are inherently difficult to monitor and evaluate. Nevertheless, it is our hope that the project has contributed to the identification of "good" practices for policy prescription and to facilitate constructive dialogues between national policy makers, representatives from the entrepreneurial sector, and the research community. Furthermore, we hope that the results from the project work presented in this text will provide useful insights for international and development organizations in the formulation of development strategies in the support of knowledge for development.

1.3 Organization of the Book

This book is organized in three parts as follows. Part one provides a background and introduction to some salient features of the changing role of universities in today's societies. In the next two chapters, we will take a global view on the governance of research as well as how universities in different countries organize their linkages with industry and society. In the analysis, the experiences of the 12 case countries are commented upon and contrasted with each other. In the second part, the country case studies are presented, providing a wide range of experiences and solutions to universal problems, or in other cases, problems relevant only for countries with similar organizational structures or levels of development. Finally, in part three, a synthesis of the country experiences is provided together with policy considerations.

Appendix

Table 1.1 UniDev in relation to world: some basic data

	Population (million) 2007	GDP (b. PPP$) 2007	GDP (PPP$) per capita 2007	Students in tertiary education (000) 2007	GERD (m. PPP$) 2007	Researchers (FTE) 2007
Brazil	191.6	1,775.6	9,270	4,880	19,709	124,882
Cuba	11.3	77.4	6,876	865	317	3,142
Uruguay	3.3	36.6	11,020	159	161	1,158
Denmark	5.5	2,01.0	36,800	232	5,105	29,572
Germany	82.3	2,857.7	34,740	2,279	72,300	279,800
Sweden	9.2	343.0	37,490	414	12,451	55,729
South Africa	47.9	452.3	9,450	760	4,297	18,572
Tanzania	40.4	48.7	1,200	55	235	2,755
Russia	142.1	2,036.5	14,330	9,370	22,809	469,076
Latvia	2.3	35.9	15,790	129	158	4,223
Vietnam	85.2	215.4	2,530	1,928	883	15,484
China	1,318.3	7,150.5	5,420	27,195	106,542	1,123,756
UniDev	1,939.4	15,230.6	7,853	48,266	244,781	2,126,749
WORLD	6,610.3	65,752.3	9,947	154,251	1,137,900	7,100,000
UniDev as % of World	29.3	23.2	78.9	31.2	21.5	30.0

GERD gross expenditure on research and development; *FTE* full-time equivalents
Sources: Tables 16.1, 16.2 and 16.11 in Chap. 16

References

Clark, B (1998). *Creating Entrepreneurial Universities: Organizational Pathways of Transformation*. Pergamon.

Drori G, et al. (2001). *Science in the Modern World Polity*, Stanford U.P.

Etzkowitz H, Mello JMC, Terra, BRC (1998). When Path Dependencies Collide: The Evolution of Innovation Policy in the State of Rio de Janeiro-Brazil. *Science and Public Policy* vol. 25, no. 6.

Paytas J, et al. (2004). *Universities and the Development of Industry Clusters*, Carnegie Mellon.

Science and Public Policy (2009). Volume 36, number 2, March 2009. Special Issue on the Third Mission of Universities.

Sutz J (2003). Inequality and University Research Agendas in Latin America. *Science, Technology & Human Values*, vol. 28, no. 1.

Chapter 2
In Search of Excellence? An International Perspective on Governance of University Research

Mats Benner

2.1 Introduction

A research policy doctrine characterized by resource concentration to fewer universities and areas selected on the basis of their scientific excellence is emerging worldwide. The doctrine is based on the assumed contributions of high-quality research environments to industrial innovation. The foundation of the governance model is a fusion of the linear model – stressing academic self-organization – and the innovation systems model, emphasizing the systemic interaction between academic research, and the economy and significance of clusters around leading universities and research environments. This chapter traces the emergence and rise to prominence of this policy paradigm in several OECD countries. It is discussed, on the basis of the material from the UniDev country case studies, if this model is transferable to developing countries.

2.2 The End of Basic Research?

Postwar research policies in Europe and North America were based on the so-called linear model, postulating that basic research – evaluated by scientific peers – would eventually lead to industrial applications and economic growth. The model made legitimate a radical increase in spending on academic research, mainly channeled through university bloc grants or through research councils' appropriations (Elzinga and Jamison 1995).

It has been claimed that basic research in this format no longer holds a privileged position in research governance, primarily due to rising costs to the government without corresponding returns on investment (Nowotny et al. 2003). "Excellence,"

M. Benner (✉)
Research Policy Institute, Lund University, Lund, Sweden
e-mail: Mats.Benner@fpi.lu.se

B. Göransson and C. Brundenius (eds.), *Universities in Transition:*
The Changing Role and Challenges for Academic Institutions,
© International Development Research Centre 2011

as determined in collegial procedures, has been replaced by "social robustness" evaluated in broad-based processes, as the prime goal for research policy. The governance of academic research should accordingly be based on interest mediation rather than intra-academic priority setting (Gibbons 2001). This implicates that research and innovation govern in a more open and flexible manner – involving more actors and operating through broader agenda setting.

A more careful reading of research governance will reveal that the picture is less clear-cut and that the linear ideals still matter in research governance. If anything, the relative autonomy of the academic system has been strengthened. We argue that research governance in Europe and North America is still very much "excellence driven," with a stress on quality criteria and peer review procedures for the allocation of resources. The model is tailored on the form and function of the US research system. The rapid growth of the US economy in the 1990s resulted in a reconsideration of research policies worldwide, as the growth pattern was attributed to the strength of the research system and, in particular, the US university system (Pavitt 2000). Research governance has targeted excellence-driven milieus as an essential underpinning of a dynamic economy. Such research milieus are expected to attract other growth-enhancing institutions such as venture capitalists, science parks, technology-based firms, service providers, and so on. Hence, excellence-driven academic milieus are viewed as strategic elements in the emergence of knowledge-intensive economy; hence, the model has gained worldwide prominence and attraction.

2.3 Explaining Research Governance: An Analytical Model

Research governance takes place on three levels: on a macro level (policy), meso level (funding), and micro level (laboratory organization). Most studies of research governance focus on the meso level and, in particular, the interaction between funding agencies and researchers in the selection, monitoring, and evaluation of publicly funded research (e.g., Geuna and Martin 2003). Microlevel studies on the governance of research stress the negotiated practices in academic organizations, in laboratory work, in interaction pattern, and in writing and communication (Knorr-Cetina 2000).

This paper deals primarily with the macro-governance of research, articulating goals for public research and its role in relation to the political and economic systems, although it also covers some aspects of meso-governance (such as research funding and models for university–industry interaction). It sets the framework for both meso- and microlevel governance by identifying overarching goals and priorities, and by regulating funding streams and research practices (Elzinga and Jamison 1995). There are stable systemic differences in the macro-governance of research systems, for instance, with respect to the funding and regulation public research organizations (Whitley 2000). These differences are mainly based on institutional variations in the relationship between states and universities. Even if governance trajectories are relatively stable over time, and national institutional differences tend to prevail over short-term policy trends, there are tendencies toward policy convergence as well, not least driven by the apparent "success" of certain institutional models (Drori et al. 2003). The Humboldtian research university became a global model in the late nineteenth century, spreading from Europe to USA (and further, through colonialism, to Latin America and Asia); in recent years, a reverse policy transfer has taken place where the North American "entrepreneurial" university has become the beacon for university reformers worldwide (Marginson 2006).

2.3.1   Comparative Aspects

In the first three decades after World War II, economic growth was based on economies of scale. The centrality of national political and economic space and of the national regulation of the mode of growth led to the emergence of many different institutional configurations in this period. The contrasts between national production systems were stark, with the Anglo-Saxon countries organizing their economies along competitive lines, with few coordinating mechanisms. As a contrast, Nordic and Continental European countries developed a broad range of coordinating mechanisms (Hollingsworth and Boyer 1997). In a similar vein, rather idiosyncratic research governance models emerged: in USA and the UK with a strong emphasis on universities as the key arena for research, whereas many Continental European countries developed a large institute sector (often in correspondence with dominant industrial sectors), while the Nordic countries combined elements of both the Continental and Anglo-Saxon models (Clark 1983; Ronayne 1984).

The period since the early 1970s has been characterized by the search for a new growth model with institutions that can support the transition toward a knowledge-based economy (Jessop 2002). In science and technology policy, there has been a shift toward the creation of "knowledge infrastructures" relevant to business development. In this process, the university has emerged as an important source of company formation but and of linkages with existing and emerging industrial sectors (Martin 2003).

However, transforming research governance is a complex process. Institutional change emerges in a dialectic process of path dependence and adjustments to changing conditions and power constellations (Thelen 2004). We would therefore assume that governance systems are relatively stable over time, although new functions can be added to the original institutional set up. Several experiments with the institutional structure of research governance have taken place recently, where novel funding models and organizational structures have been introduced. Many of these experiments have been inspired by the evolution of the US research and innovation system and have been added to existing institutional structures. The focus of this paper is to explore the forms and content of these adjustments.

The ambitions henceforth are twofold: to study the rise and dissemination of the excellence-driven governance model and to analyze its diffusion across countries. This is done through a survey of research policy priorities in a number of OECD countries in the recent decade. The analytical dimensions include the structure of support, the policy discourse, and the prescribed role of academic research in innovation systems. The analysis is comparative, searching for possible variations of research governance models in different socioeconomic systems. The analysis will then proceed to a critical discussion of the impact of such concentration policies on the fabric of higher education and the possible lessons for higher education policy in developing countries.

2.3.2   Anglo-Saxon Research Governance

The US economy was, at least until the fall of 2008, portrayed as a global role model in debates on economic growth. Among the institutions that were singled out as core elements in the US growth model are the research universities and the risk capital market (Powell et al. 2003). From such a perspective, US economic prosperity and innovation dynamics build upon the combination and concentration of advanced technology, talented people, and social diversity, resources that are highly dependent on universities, in combination with public and private actors with complementary resources. The US research system has become a magnet for talented scientists worldwide, which contributes to the concentration of leading knowledge and innovation centers to North America (Cooke 2004). These centers tend to be organized around not only a limited number of "star scientists" with a high profile in research but also tight connections to the market (Darby et al. 1998). This concentration process has been reinforced by the aggressive recruitment strategies of leading research universities, which have resulted in the clustering of prominent scientists to a small number of institutional settings (Geiger 2004). This process is reflected in and has been further reinforced by the concentration of support from the dominant funding agencies. Hence, a limited number of universities have reinforced their position in the research system on the basis of aggressive managerial strategies to recruit leading scientists, large endowments, and strong position in the highly stratified funding system.

The research governance model has emerged not by design but as a result of an uncoordinated evolution of different policy spheres. One such sphere is the research laboratory system, which accounts for about a third of total public R&D expenditure in USA. The laboratories combine a high level of scientific activity with a mission-oriented role, if only indirect. The National Institutes of Health (NIH) and Department of Energy laboratories perform basic research, although they are nominally mission oriented. In a similar vein, government laboratories in agriculture and defense also conduct a large share of basic research (Bozeman and Dietz 2001).

Many of the pillars of US research policy tend to be based outside a policy for research per se. Whether this lack of a coordinated policy approach is an advantage or a disadvantage is a debated issue; it has even been claimed that the productivity and visibility of US science can be explained by the very lack of policy integrative mechanisms (Savage 1999; Stokes 1997). The civilian part of the funding system is heavily biased toward the biomedical area: while resources for many other areas are growing slowly, or even decreasing (for instance in energy), support of biomedicine grew dramatically in the 1990s and the beginning of this decade, and now represent about half of federal research funding (AAAS 2005). The strength of biomedical research in USA has been further reinforced by the rich supply of private funding. The US research system is therefore marked by resource concentration to a limited number of research organizations, intense competition for funding, a rich supply of relatively undirected research support (with allocation criteria mainly based on scientific quality), and a marked focus on the biosciences.

The US political economy is often viewed as the ideal typical example of a liberal market economy, with few strong binds between actors and organizations, but a large degree of flexibility based on the flexible deployment of resources, a vigorous capital market, and a vivid culture of entrepreneurialism. The mechanisms for integrating the research system with the market are, therefore, exceptionally well developed in USA if compared with that in the European countries. First, the universities are often based in an entrepreneurial tradition and are accustomed to operating according to market or quasi-market conditions (Etzkowitz 2001). Second, academics have historically been subject to many incentives to combine traditional academic tasks with entrepreneurial activity, without necessarily having to depart from their academic positions (Mowery et al. 2004; Etzkowitz 2003). Third, the infrastructure for science-based entrepreneurship is highly developed, with a rich flora of venture capitalists, organizational brokers, university patenting, and licensing organizations surrounding the academic centers (Mowery 2001).

As a result, the research system has emerged as an integrated part of the development, dissemination, and exploitation of new knowledge. Key aspects in this institutional set up include the mobility of scientists, the amount and scope of policy initiatives to support academy–industry linkages, the openness of research organization to scientific change, and the importance of integrative mechanism between academics and entrepreneurs.

However, knowledge interplay is less well developed outside the science-based sectors where investments in skills tend to be marginal, and networks and systemic interaction between institutions and organizations are much weaker. Several attempts were made in the 1980s and early 1990s to mimic the institutional structure of the European countries to remedy some of these shortcomings, with public technology transfer programs to increase competence accretion in the manufacturing sectors and in strategic fields such as microelectronics (Gulbrandsen and Etzkowitz 1999). Due the continued resistance against direct state interventionism in the economy, these policy initiatives were never fully institutionalized and now play a marginal role in the policy mix.

While USA is the premier example of this type of research governance, similar institutional structures have emerged in other Anglo-Saxon countries. Canada has taken steps to support the concentration of research activities into "networks of centers of excellence" combined with support of individual researchers with a strong scientific track record. The ultimate goal of this radical increase in government spending on research – with a special focus on excellence-driven activities – is to reinforce the country's position in a new economic landscape (Bernstein 2003).

Funding of academic research in the UK has been more competitive than that in most other European countries. The introduction of resource allocation on the basis of the Research Assessment Exercise, together with the program-based structure of research council funding, has fostered competition and concentration in the research system (Georghiou 2001). Furthermore, the importance of private sources of funding has increased rapidly. UK research governance is similar to the US model, with a highly competitive funding regime, a premium placed on scientific excellence but with many incentives for academic–industrial collaboration (PREST 2000). This indicates that several governance instruments are in operation in parallel and that the successful research environments are those that can fulfill several different roles at the same time: scientific excellence, the concentration of resources to larger and multidisciplinary research programs, and industrial collaboration. The UK research system is marked by an increasing concentration of both academic research and industrial activities to a relatively limited number of settings (Riccaboni et al. 2003).

The UK political economy shares many of the characteristics of USA, with its dual structure of the economy, consisting on the one hand of a highly competitive science-based sector (notably in pharmaceuticals and chemistry) and on the other, industries such as mechanical engineering and manufacturing with much weaker performance (Rhodes 2000).

To sum up, the governance of research in the Anglo-Saxon liberal market economies is based on resource concentration via competitive funding programs. The strong focus on resource concentration has been accompanied a rich institutional structure for the commercialization of public research, either directly or through dense networks between academic environments and companies (Pavitt 2001). Hence, there seems to be no necessary trade-off between "excellence" and "relevance," but rather a reinforcing relationship, at least in many areas. It has, obviously, resulted in the hegemony of academic institutions in USA – and to a lesser extent in UK and Canada – in the global research system.

2.3.3 Research Governance in Continental Europe

Despite the historical origin of the modern research university in Germany, Continental European universities function primarily as educational organizations, whereas research institutes are the dominant organizations for basic as well as applied research (Meyer-Krahmer 2001). Universities perform far less than half of public sector research in France and Germany. Studies of the development of science-based areas indicate that the large Continental European countries follow a policy trajectory of resource concentration to one or very few organizations, mainly research institutes (Riccaboni et al. 2003). Furthermore, universities and other public research organizations play a marginal role in R&D collaboration, a role instead played by larger firms (Ibid: 179–181).

Continental universities with their tradition of rigid career structures and professorial hierarchies have had difficulties in adapting to a more fluid and flexible knowledge-producing system. The university system is considered inflexible, segmented, and too overloaded to be able to provide a strong infrastructure for top-class research (Krull 2003). Continental universities have suffered from an overburdened education component and have had difficulties in exploiting the dynamic local interactions that characterize leading universities in USA and UK.

Research governance in the Continental European countries has traditionally focused on the interests of existing industrial strongholds. This is the case not least for the applied research institute sector where rich ties and networks have strengthened the corporate capacity for technological upgrading and renewal (Becker and Dietz 2004).

To counteract some of the imbalances, several of the Continental European countries have pursued institutional reforms in science and innovation policy. In Germany, in the absence of a developed venture capital system, the government has fuelled the development of a biotechnology sector, for instance through efforts to support university spin-offs, a total investment of over €150 million annually (Kaiser and Prange 2004: 402). Another aspect has been increasing spending on research, especially the biosciences. The German Research Council expanded its support of biotechnology research rapidly in the 1990s and 2000s, and a similar adaptation pattern is found in France (Kaiser and Prange 2004: 404; Larédo and Mustar 2003: 21). The funding basis and the organizational standing of universities have also been reinforced. Recently, the German government announced major initiatives to modernize its academic system, by adding more resources but at the same time pressing for a concentration both among universities and research constellations, to so-called excellence clusters. A similar transformation of research governance has taken place in France, where money has been reallocated from the research institute sector to universities, to address the dismal performance of French universities in international ranking exercises (Laredo fc.). Hence, resource concentration and a competitive allocation of resources are an emerging phenomenon in many Continental European countries; however, as noticed by Schmoch in his contribution to this volume, the signals are mixed, as university governance in Continental Europe strongly emphasizes the contribution of universities to technology transfer (see Chap. 13).

The exceptions to the pattern of weak university performance in Continental Europe are the Netherlands and Switzerland. Dutch research governance is similar to the model that has emerged in USA, with a university system taking a lead in both research and innovation networking (Van der Meulen and Rip 2001: 318). The issues of resource concentration and support of excellence-driven research milieus have also been addressed by the Dutch political system with strings of programs to support "top-class research groups at the universities" (Dutch Ministry of Education, Culture and Science 2004). A similar pattern can be found in Switzerland, where public resources are concentrated to a small number of actors – actors which operate in relative autonomy from public regulation (Braun and Benninghoff 2003).

The background to the reforms of research governance in Continental Europe can be found both in the inertia of the academic system and in the search for new innovation policy instruments. Traditional instruments for supporting economic growth and innovation have become increasingly obsolete, as indicated by sluggish growth, especially in science-based sectors. In France, the importance of large governmental programs for technological development has waned during the last decades, due to a more stringent financial policy, deregulations, and changing ideological commitments (Schmidt 2002). The German model of a coordinated structure to manage industrial and technological change has also been weakened in the 1990s. The German political system has struggled with structural reforms for well over a decade, but the strong institutional regulation in employment, welfare, and economic development has hindered the development of alternative sources of growth and employment (Streeck 2008).

In the light of these rigidities and the obsolescence of traditional policy instruments, and with ubiquitous references to the "American challenge" in basic research and in science-based sectors, state support of excellence-driven research milieus has come to the forefront in Continental European research governance as have state-initiated programs to improve the supply of venture capital. This represents both continuity and change in research governance. The break lies in the radical reforms of the research system, with a partial dethronement of the professoriate and a parallel strengthening of the universities within the research landscape – also at the expense of the traditionally very powerful institute sector (which has responded vigorously to the political challenges; Laredo et al., fc.). The strengthening of universities and academic research is therefore seen as a necessary part in the renovation of the innovation system of the Continental European countries, even at the price of a confrontation with embedded interests.

2.3.4   A Nordic Model of Research Governance?

The Nordic countries are usually singled out as a group of their own in comparative studies of political institutions and economic development. They are often labeled as social-democratic, indicating the strong legacy of social democratic values in their commitments to general welfare and full employment, enabled by a historical compromise between the labor movement and the organized business interests. Their economies are institutionally embedded, as in the case of the Continental European countries, with highly advanced systems of investment regulation, labor market interaction, and social protection. On the contrary, the countries have been open economies, already from an early stage developing mechanisms to adapt their economies according to changes in world markets and to technological dynamics (Scharpf 2000).

Traditionally, research governance in the Nordic countries was based on bloc grants to universities together with a relatively small competitive funding layer in the form of research council funding (Skoie 1996). The countries also established relatively large institute sectors, funded by both the state and industry, mainly performing near-market R&D. This governance model has been partially transformed in the last decade. The dominant parts in the reform process have been the proliferation of competitive funding, the concentration of resources in the form of larger and excellence-oriented programs, and the relative decline of the institute sector.

Hence, a convergence of research governance has taken place, based on resource concentration and a growing share of funding exposed to peer-reviewed competition, together with institutional reforms to reap the benefits of growing spending on R&D (Kim 2002). The Research Council of Norway has been restructured due to the instability of the interdisciplinary and cross-organizational agency established in the early 1990s (Skoie 2000). The reformed council has adopted a governance structure based on role differentiation, with earmarked support for basic research projects and for large center support. Along similar lines, the Danish funding system has been amended by a basic research foundation and also by a program to establish centers of excellence. Another striking feature of research governance has been the reorganization of the university system – including state-initiated mergers and detailed "contracts" between the state and universities (see Chap. 14). While universities have been empowered and have seen their resources for basic research increase, they have at the same time been re-regulated and enmeshed in ever more complicated negotiations with the state. In Finland, a center of excellence initiative was devised in the early 1990s, operating in parallel with a large technology-driven program and with several support mechanisms for regional science-based development (Lemola 2004). In Sweden, the process of concentrating resources to a more limited number of institutions begun more recently, partly explained by the large number of funding agencies and the limited interaction between them (Benner 2008).

Despite the convergence in research governance mechanisms, the countries show variations, especially in their levels of R&D expenditure – variations that primarily reflect the different compositions of their economies, where raw materials- based sectors and SMEs are more significant parts of the economy in Denmark and Norway than in Sweden and Finland. These variations aside, the countries have all increased funding to university research organized in larger constellations and evaluated according to scientific quality criteria. This excellence orientation in research governance has then been accompanied by initiatives to bolster the interaction between universities and industry. As a result, many Nordic universities have evolved along similar lines as their US and UK counterparts, taking on entrepreneurial roles involving licensing and firm formation (Jacob et al. 2003).

This has corresponded with the growth of technology-based firms, many with a background in academic research. By European standards, the risk capital markets are relatively well developed as are the mechanisms for integrating academic research and market actors (Henrekson and Rosenberg 2001).

The Nordic countries thus seem to be mimicking the US research governance model, with strong position for universities, a high profile in growing research areas, and strong ties between the research system and high-technology firms and sectors. Contrary to the development in USA and the UK, however, this governance model has been combined with a strong public support of research areas with connections to low-technology industries and to mature industrial fields such as food, engineering, and the transport industry. Furthermore, the drive to concentrate resources to fewer recipients and fields has been balanced by regional considerations: the Nordic countries, with the partial exception of Denmark, have all made major investments in peripheral universities. Hence, the Nordic countries face the challenge of combining policy goals: resource concentration and adaption of the research system to economic and regional interests.

2.4   Discussion – Where Is Research Governance Going?

Research governance in the Nordic countries, Continental Europe, and the Anglo-Saxon countries has converged around a pattern of resource concentration to fewer field and fewer recipients. Universities have become the most important instrument for securing a position in the globalized knowledge-based economy – by securing scientific visibility and by fostering networks of innovators and innovating sectors around them. These processes are assumed to develop in parallel, where scientific visibility is supposed to be related to innovative capacities. Hence, universities are subject to dual steering signals, on the one hand relating resources to scientific impact, and on the other, directing resources to maximize their interaction with the market. The new global policy is clearly tailored on the US experience, in and particular the very strong emphasis on a select number of universities as engines of scientific visibility and innovation activities. Universities are being highlighted as engines of economic development, and research policy is empowering a small number of elite institutions. The expectation is that these will become nodes in global research networks. From a global perspective, we find trends toward resource concentration.

How, then, are countries outside the European–North American model responding – is the emerging governance model emulated also outside Europe and North America? Generally speaking, most countries have fostered at least one leading national university, although these universities have neither always been the foci of research activities, nor have they always taken on broader roles in economic development. Some of these national, "flagship," universities are extremely large by international measures, and are therefore more cumbersome to reform. The general view seems to be that universities in developing countries are large (in terms of student intake), weak (in their research profile), and rigid (in their management). Nonetheless, a recent survey of university politics and research governance in Asia and Latin America indicates a trend not only toward empowering universities but also toward a more stringent evaluation of their performance, to make them more responsive to the dynamics of research and to the socioeconomic demands (Altbach and Balán 2007). The case studies conducted within the UniDev project also point to the slow and uneven emulation of the university-centered model – focusing public support to a limited number of universities that are expected to increase the visibility of the national scientific fabric and the connections to global knowledge networks.

Again, there are marked variations along this theme. The Cuban experience is telling, with universities being responsive to the demands of the domestic economy, but obviously at the price of research with a more long-term perspective – with the exception of biotechnology (see Chap. 6). A similar pattern is found in Tanzania, where universities still focus, and increasingly so, on near-market issues rather than basic research. In both these countries, severe economic conditions limit the possibilities of developing full-fledged research universities; universities still plays an intermediary role as providers of education for a selected elite and performing applied research with the national firms and sectors in mind (see Chap. 9). Even Russia, historically a scientific powerhouse in its own right, has seen a deteriorating position for the universities with sliding state appropriations for research and a general political neglect of the university system (see Chap. 12). China is the most obvious contrasting case, where various policies have been devised to elevate select parts of the Chinese university system to a level of international eminence, while at the same time, the contribution of universities to technological upgrading and organizational networking (for instance through spin-offs and technology transfer) has been stressed (see Chap. 8). The rapid transformation of Chinese universities, some observers argue, will create a more multipolar research system, dethroning European and (in particular) US universities from the currently hegemonic position in virtually all scientific fields (Hollingsworth et al. 2008). In a similar vein, the Vietnamese universities have taken on a much more proactive role in the economy (see Chap. 7). In both of these cases, universities have a broad function, acting as midwives (in the relative absence of high-technology-based firms) for technological development and as a complement (and in some cases a replacement) of the academies as the center of public research activities.

2.5 Conclusions

While the political and economic centrality of universities has increased dramatically and has fostered more autonomy for universities in stark contrast with a tradition of often coercive state steering, it has also created overly optimistic expectations on the university system, and a search for "quick fixes" in the form of a simplified emulation of a US-styled governance model. This does not necessarily fit very well with existing institutional structures or with the socioeconomic conditions surrounding universities; it might instead create "islands of excellence" with global connections but limited interaction with broader social and economic interests. It can also overshadow and marginalize developments toward a new type of "indigenous university." In this respect, Arocena och Sutz (see Chap. 5) points at the emerging role of a developing university, a new species that neither resembles the old-style "flagship university" nor the global, US-style university but a university that connects local interests with global research dynamics. This is not a theoretical excursus, as the experience in many countries such as South Africa and Brazil both exemplify a more ambitious and original approach to tailor and adapt the generic university concept – modeled on the USA style governance mechanisms – to indigenous needs (see Chaps. 4 and 10). In particular, a more comprehensive overhaul of governance mechanisms – to rid the universities of hierarchical, etatist, and racist sediments – has been combined with a leading role for national economic and social development and the ambition to play important roles in global knowledge networks. If realized, this model is in itself a most important contribution to policy formation in developing and developed countries alike, and an attractive alternative to the current hegemony in university governance.

References

AAAS (American Association for the Advancement of the Sciences) 2005 AAAS Analysis of R&D in the FY 2005. Washington, DC: AAAS.

Altbach PG, Balán J, eds. (2007). *Transforming Research Universities in Asia and Latin America: World Class Worldwide*. Baltimore: Johns Hopkins University Press.

Becker W, Dietz J (2004). R&D Cooperation and Innovation Activities of Firms – Evidence for the German Manufacturing Industry. *Research Policy* 33: 209–223.

Benner M (2003). The Scandinavian Challenge: The Future of Advanced Welfare States in the Knowledge Economy. *Acta Sociologica* 46 (2): 132–149.

Bernstein A (2003). Canadian Institutes of Health Research Budgetary Dilemma. *Canadian Medical Association Journal* 169: 6.

Bozeman B, Dietz JS (2001). Research Policy Trends in the United States, in Larédo P, Mustar P, eds. *Research and Innovation Policies in the New Global Economy*, 47–78. Cheltenham: Edward Elgar.

Braun D, Benninghoff M (2003). Policy learning in Swiss research policy – the case of the National Centers of Competence in Research. *Research Policy* 32; 10: 1849–1863

Clark BR (1983). *The Higher Education System*. Berkeley: University of California Press.

Cooke P (2004). Biosciences and the rise of regional science policy. *Science and Public Policy* 31; 3: 185–198.

Drori GS, et al. (2003). *Science in the Modern World Polity*. Stanford: Stanford Universty Press.

Dutch Ministry of Education, Culture and Science (2004). *Science Budget 04: Focus on Excellence and Greater Value*. Downloaded at: www.minocw.nl/english/doc/2004/sciencebudget.pdf.

Elzinga A, Jamison A (1995). Changing Policy Agendas in Science and Technology, in Jasanoff, Sheila, et al., eds. *Handbook of Science and Technology Studies*, 572–597. London: SAGE.

Etzkowitz H (2001). *MIT and the Rise of Entrepreneurial Science*. London: Routledge.

Etzkowitz H (2003). Research Groups as 'Quasi-Firms': The Invention of the Entrepreneurial University, *Research Policy* 32; 1: 109–121.

Geiger R (2004). *Knowledge and Money: Research Universities and the Paradox of the Marketplace*. Stanford: Stanford University Press.

Georghiou L (2001). The United Kingdom National System of Research, Technology and Innovation, in Larédo P, Mustar P, eds. *Research and Innovation Policies in the New Global Economy*, 253–296. Cheltenham: Edward Elgar.

Geuna A, Martin BR (2003). University Research Evaluation and Funding: An International Comparison', *Minerva* 41: 277–304.

Gibbons M (2001). Governance and the New Production of Knowledge, in de la Mothe J, ed. *Science, Technology and Governance*, 33–49. London: Continuum.

Gulbrandsen M, Etzkowitz H (1999). Convergence Between Europe and America: The Transition from Industrial to Innovation Policy. *Journal of Technology Transfer* 24 (2–3): 223–233.

Henrekson M, Rosenberg N (2001). Designing Efficient Institutions for Science-Based Entrepreneurship: Lessons from The US and Sweden. *Journal of Technology Transfer* 26 (2): 207–231.

Hollingsworth JR, Boyer R, eds. (1997). *Contemporary Capitalism: The Embeddedness of Institutions*. Cambridge: Cambridge University Press.

Hollingsworth JR, et al. (2008). China: The end of the science superpowers, *Nature* 454, 412–413.

Jacob M, Lundqvist M, Hellsmark H (2003). Entrepreneurial Transformation in the Swedish University System. *Research Policy* 32; 9: 1555–1568.

Jessop B (2002). *The Future of the Capitalist State*. Cambridge: Polity Press.

Kaiser R, Prange H (2004). The Reconfiguration of National Innovation Systems – The Example of German Biotechnology. *Research Policy* 33 (2004): 395–408.

Kim L (2002). *Lika Olika*. Stockholm: Högskoleverket.

Knorr-Cetina K (2000). *Epistemic Cultures*. Cambridge: Harvard University Press.

Krull W (2003). Toward a Research Policy for the New Europe: Changes and Challenges for Public and Private Funders. *Minerva* 42: 29–39.

Larédo P, Mustar P (2003). Public Sector Research: A Growing Role in Innovation Systems. *Minerva* 42: 11–27.

Lemola T (2004). Finnish Science and Technology Policy, in Schienstock G ed. *Embracing the Knowledge Economy*, 268–286. Cheltenham: Edward Elgar.

Marginson S (2006). The Anglo-American university at its global high tide. *Minerva* 44: 65–87.

Martin BR (2003). The Changing Social Contract for Research and the Evolution of the University, in Geuna A, Salter AJ, Steinmueller W, eds. *Science and Innovation*, 7–29. Chaltenham: Edward Elgar.

Meyer-Krahmer F (2001). The German Innovation System, in Larédo P, Mustar P, eds. *Research and Innovation Policies in the New Global Economy*, 205–252. Cheltenham: Edward Elgar.

Mowery DC (2001). The United States National Innovation System after the Cold War, in Larédo P, Mustar P, eds. *Research and Innovation Policies in the New Global Economy*. Cheltenham: Edward Elgar.

Mowery DC, et al. (2004). *Ivory Tower and Industrial Innovation*. Stanford: Stanford University Press.

Nelson RR (2004). The Market Economy, and the Scientific Commons. *Research Policy* 33 (2004): 455–471.

Nowotny H, Scott P, Gibbons M (2003). Introduction: 'Mode 2' Revisited: The New Production of Knowledge. *Minerva* 41: 179–194.

Pavitt K (2000). Public Policies to Support Basic Research. *Industrial and Corporate Change* 10(3): 761–779.

Pavitt K (2001). Why European Union funding of academic research should be increased: a radical proposal, *Science and Public Policy*, 27(6): 455–460.

Powell WW. et al. (2003). The spatial clustering of science and capital. *Regional Studies*, 36(3): 299–313.

PREST (Policy Research in Engineering, Science and Technology) (2000). *Impact of the Research Assessment Exercise and the Future of Quality Assurance in the light of Changes in the Research Landscape*. Manchester: PREST.

Rhodes M (2000). Restructuring the British Welfare State, in Scharpf FW, Schmidt VA, eds. Welfare and Work in the Pen Economy, Vol. 2, 19–68. Oxford University Press.

Riccaboni M, et al. (2003). Public Research and Industrial Innovation, in Geuna, A, et al. *Science and Innovation: Rethinking the Rationales for Funding and Governance*, 169–201. Cheltenham: Edward Elgar.

Ronayne J (1984). *Science in Government*. London: Edward Arnold.

Savage JD (1999). *Funding Science in America*. Cambridge: Cambridge University Press.

Scharpf FW (2000). Economic Changes, Vulnerabilities, and Institutional Capabilities, in Scharpf FW, Schmidt VA, eds. *Welfare and Work in the Open Economy*, Vol. 1, 21–124. Oxford: Oxford University Press.

Schmidt VA (2002). *The Futures of European Capitalism*. Oxford: Oxford University Press.

Skoie H (1996). Basic research – a new funding climate. *Science and Public Policy* 23: 66–75.

Skoie H (2000). Diversity and Identity: The Merger of Five Research Councils in Norway. *Science and Public Policy* 27, 2: 83–96.

Stokes DE (1997). *Pasteur's Quadrant*. Washington, DC: Brookings Institutions Press.

Streeck W (2008). *Re-Forming Capitalism. Institutional Change in the German Political Economy*. Oxford: Oxford University Press.

Thelen K (2004). How Institutions Evolve. (Cambridge: Cambridge University Press)

Van der Meulen B, Rip A (2001). The Netherlands, in Larédo P, Mustar P, eds. *Research and Innovation Policies in the New Global Economy*, 297–324. Cheltenham: Edward Elgar.

Whitley R (2000). Divergent Capitalisms. Oxford: Oxford University Press.

Zucker LG, Darby MR, Armstrong J (1998). Geographically Localized Knowledge. *Economic Inquiry* 36, 65–86.

Chapter 3
The Evolving Role of Universities in Economic Development: The Case of University–Industry Linkages

Prasada Reddy

3.1 Introduction

For the last decade and a half, the role played by universities in economic growth, particularly through university–industry linkages, has been occupying the minds of policymakers and academics equally. The direct influence of university research in economic development is, however, not new. Since their inception, more than a century ago, agriculture universities through their research on new varieties of seeds, disease resistant crops, etc., have played a vital role in increasing the agricultural productivity and farmers' incomes. Extension services provided by the agricultural universities, through which they transferred new technologies and associated knowledge to farmers, have been the main channels through which university research has been commercialized.

In USA, the Morrill Acts of 1862 and 1890 created the "land-grant universities" (also called land-grant colleges or institutions). These Acts funded educational institutions by granting federally controlled land to the States to develop or sell such land in order to establish and endow "land-grant" colleges. These institutions' mission is to focus on the teaching in agriculture, science, and engineering. The mission of these institutions was expanded by the Hatch Act of 1887, which led to the establishment of a series of agricultural experiment stations under the direction of each state's land-grant college to diffuse new information, especially in the areas of soil minerals and plant growth. This outreach mission was further expanded by the Smith–Lever Act of 1914 to include cooperative extension – the sending of agents into rural areas to help transfer the results of agricultural research to end-users.

In Brazil, the Agricultural Company (Embrapa) played a vital role in the development of Brazilian agriculture, whose research projects were designed to improve seeds and livestock as well as to protect against plant and animal diseases. The results of these research projects were rapidly disseminated through industrial

P. Reddy (✉)
Research Policy Institute, Lund University, Lund, Sweden
e-mail: PrasadaReddy1@gmail.com

B. Göransson and C. Brundenius (eds.), *Universities in Transition:*
The Changing Role and Challenges for Academic Institutions,
© International Development Research Centre 2011

agriculture and were responsible for a substantial increase in the grain harvests and excellent performance of agribusiness exports (see Chap. 4).

Similarly, in Vietnam, in many traditional sectors, such as agriculture and forestry, academic institutions play a vital role in bringing technical solutions to farmers. For instance, in the Mekong River Delta, more than 80% of the rice varieties in use have been bred by the Rice Institute of Mekong River Delta (a public research organization (PRO)). The Institute of Southern Fruit Trees is also very active in identifying quality parent trees for breeding, in developing advanced cultivation methods for different types of fruit trees, and in disseminating technical knowledge to farmers (see Chap. 7).

The linkages between universities and the industry, on the contrary, have historically not been that strong when compared with agriculture. Part of the reason for this may be that unlike the farmers in the agriculture sector, industry tends to have equal or superior competence when compared with universities in developing new technologies. Moreover, universities tend to conduct basic research of generic nature, whereas industry is more interested in specific application technologies. Converting basic research results into specific technologies is time and resource consuming with uncertain outcomes. Therefore, the university–industry linkage was mainly confined to the issue of training of corporate human resources.

This does not, however, mean that there were no university–industry linkages in the areas of research and innovation. Although no consolidated data are available, university–industry collaborations in research have been taking place for a long time in certain fields such as chemistry, medicine, and engineering. Such collaboration encompassed a range of activities from simple activities such as testing of machinery and materials to full-fledged technology development projects. For instance, in USA such collaboration began during the late nineteenth century, when a formal research funding system was lacking for subjects other than agriculture. This compelled academicians to take initiatives to obtain resources from the industry to support university research (Etzkowitz 2003, p. 109).

With the emergence of new science-based technologies such as electronics, bio-, and nanotechnologies, university research has come to play a greater role in industrial innovation. Added to it, the perceived notion of "knowledge economy" made the policymakers to think that university research and innovation are indispensable for industrialization and economic development. Consequently, governments have started fine-tuning their policies to promote university–industry interaction. Stemming from the industrialized world, particularly Europe, this idea is fast spreading to developing countries, as discussed in the previous chapter.

Universities, today, are not only collaborating with the industry through technology transfer, but are also undertaking entrepreneurial activities themselves. This has generated a heated debate on the "pros and cons" of university's direct participation in industrial innovation and its potential impact on knowledge generation and welfare. Some critics suggest that financial rewards that accrue from research results may bias and distort the judgments and actions of academicians with respect to problem choice and research direction (Krimsky 1991) and in the long run may draw scientists away from basic research.

As the country case studies in this volume show, the organization of research differs considerably from country to country. In some countries, research activities are concentrated in universities, along with higher education. In some other countries, universities are mainly involved in educational activities, with major research being carried out in specialized national research institutes. For the purposes of this paper, university research includes all academic research including the ones performed by the national research institutes.

The objective of this chapter is to study and analyze the university–industry collaboration in practice across the participating countries in the UniDev project. This chapter is organized into six sections: Section 3.1 analyzes the driving forces behind the new university–industry collaboration; Sect. 3.2 reviews the existing literature on the subject; Sect. 3.3 describes the conceptual frameworks in which the topic is analyzed; Sect. 3.4 analyzes the university–industry collaboration across the countries involved in the project; Sect. 3.5 analyzes different forms in which the university–industry collaboration takes place; and Sect. 3.6 concludes the chapter.

3.2   Driving Forces for New University–Industry Collaboration

Today, the university is seen as providing the most conducive environment for innovation due to its specific features that include a high turnout of human capital in the form of students, who are a major source of ideas. A university also acts as a natural incubator by providing support structure for teachers and students to initiate new ventures. It is also an ideal platform for new interdisciplinary scientific fields and new industrial sectors, each cross-fertilizing the other. The overlapping networks of academic research groups and start-up firms, intersecting with the alliances among large firms, universities, and the start-ups, reflect the emerging pattern of academic–industry relations in biotechnology, computer science, and similar fields (Herrera 2001).

In Europe, the beginning of formalized university research can be traced to the establishment of University of Berlin in the early nineteenth century based on Humboldt's concept. The concept was oriented toward fundamental or basic research and was curiosity driven, with no consideration of application of such research results. This first academic evolution made research into a mission of the university in addition to the traditional mission of teaching (Veysey 1965). A few years later, a second academic evolution integrated the university tasks into a teaching, research, and economic development. In USA, this change initially took place through the industrial activities at the Massachusetts Institute of Technology (MIT), which was founded in 1862 as a "land-grant" university (Etzkowitz 2003).

In Europe, the integration of teaching with research has not progressed as effectively as in USA. Differences in education systems, especially on the higher education level, exist across Continental European countries. The present enthusiasm for university–industry collaboration worldwide, particularly in Europe, seems to be driven by the supply-side factors without much consideration for the demand-side factors. In Europe, the university–industry collaboration emerged recently as a "top-down" phenomenon in order to bridge the perceived innovation gap between USA and Europe (Soete 1999).

The current interest in university–industry linkages is mainly fueled by two factors: (1) emerging knowledge economy and (2) the governmental interest in getting a return on its investment in research.

The notion of the knowledge economy and competitiveness as the new framework for policymaking calls for the promotion of innovation on a national level. National research or science policy has been identified as a key policy mechanism for achieving innovation through integration between knowledge infrastructure and economic structure. Following this, research policy has progressively come to be integrated with innovation policy. Innovation policy, at least in the leading EU Member States, is said to have gone through two phases: the first being the linear model and the second being the collaborative model. According to the linear model, universities contribute to innovation primarily through the conduct of basic research and teaching. University research opens up new opportunities for innovation that are subsequently exploited by firms. Teaching provides skilled graduates to be employed by companies. Therefore, in the linear model, there were no overt efforts to induce collaboration between universities and industry or any other partners. The present approach of integrating research policy with the innovation policy in order to meet the perceived requirements to compete in the knowledge economy led to, in some respect, a further revision of the social contract of scientific research in favor of direct steering of science for economic and social reasons. The most immediate expression of this is reflected in the mechanisms for promoting collaboration between universities and other PROs, and the wider society (Jacob and Orsenigo 2007, pp. 22–26).

The changes in a number of factors contributed to the need for alternative approaches to science policy. Innovations in new technologies are increasingly dependent on scientific research, resulting in new science-based technologies. In these new technologies, the time lag between invention and innovation is very short. Moreover, the boundaries between basic science research and application technologies have blurred in the new technologies such as ICT and biotechnologies (Mansfield 1998; Rosenberg and Nelson 1994). Furthermore, the information and biotechnologies have raised the knowledge requirements for entry-level workers and created a need for continuous upgrading of the skills of the employees (Piore and Sabel 1984). Such changes called for a closer interaction between industry and other knowledge producers such as universities and other firms (Reddy 2000).

In order to make university research more productive and promote industrialization, in USA, the Bayh Dole Act was enacted in 1980. The Bayh Dole Act refers the enactment of P.L. 96–517, The Patent and Trademark Law Amendments Act, and amendments included in P.L. 98–620 enacted into law in 1984. This legislation gave universities and small firms the right of ownership of inventions made under federal funding and to become directly involved in the commercialization process. This right of ownership also includes exclusive licensing. This has spurred the enthusiasm of policymakers around the world to adopt their own versions of legislation for the intellectual property (IP) generated by their universities and mechanisms for commercialization of this IP.

A few studies by organizations such as the OECD suggested that Europe lagged behind USA and Japan in innovation. European policymakers began to address this as "innovation deficit." These studies indicated that although the European countries spend considerable resources on R&D, their innovation output is low. On the contrary, USA and Japan have better ratios of innovation outputs for the amount they spend on R&D. Potential implications of this innovation deficit for future economic growth provided the European countries to adopt a new policy doctrine. The key points of this doctrine have been summarized by Jacob and Orsenigo (2007, pp. 27–28) as follows:

(a) Universities should contribute more directly to industrial innovation and to (local) economic growth.
(b) Science's natural tendency is to promote its own interest and therefore policy will have to intervene to facilitate the development of a more positive climate in universities toward more applied concerns.
(c) The speed of technological development suggests that national competitive advantage can only be developed and maintained through linking the sources of the production of knowledge directly to those that create wealth.
(d) As a consequence of a, b, and c, most countries have put into place a matrix of collaborative policy instruments aimed at promoting and securing closer links between industry and PRO of all kinds (OECD 2003).
(e) Additionally, universities must be encouraged to not restrict themselves to providing knowledge to existing firms but to engage in the commercialization of knowledge themselves.
(f) It is the responsibility of the government to support the development of the support institutions that would assist universities in moving toward a more systematic set of policies and institutions for the commercialization of knowledge.

3.3 University–Industry Linkages: Some Theoretical Considerations

In the discussion about university–industry collaboration, it is necessary to consider the differences between types of universities. Most studies on commercial and outreach activities of universities have focused on elite universities in such activities. Turk-Bicakci and Brint (2005) point out some distinct differences between the top-tier and the middle- to low-level performers in university–industry relations. The latter may not earn substantial revenues from such linkages, but there are other benefits coming out of their interaction with the industry, for example, contribution to local social, cultural, and economic development. Owen-Smith (2005) also points out that not all universities can act in the same domain of innovation. Distinct first-mover advantages are conferred on universities that entered into the patenting game early, resulting in a stratified system. Increasing returns accrue to the first movers, whereas very limited opportunities exist for the large majority. Certain commercialization activities do not have the same value to all universities. A majority of the universities may have to create a value base through more indirect means, for instance, by building local social capital and achieving broad knowledge transfer, rather than technology transfer in a narrow sense (Hellstrom 2007).

The concept of commercialization in the context of a university refers to the activities in which a university is involved, at some point, in selling to a customer for profit. These activities include the usual forms of industry collaboration, when industry pays for direct or indirect knowledge transfer, licensing of proprietary knowledge owned by the university, and taking and exchanging equity in licenses or spin-off firms. Commercialization, however, may also involve other forms of profit-seeking activities. The university may engage in more mundane commercial ventures on campus, for example, running shops, or conferences for businesses in the surrounding areas (Clark 1998) and selling consultancy hours (Rappert et al. 1999). Commercialization of this type involves very concrete and outcome-oriented actions, aimed at increasing the university's revenue. Such activities may be referred to as entrepreneurial, because at every stage they build on a commercial rationale (Hellstrom 2007).

The concept of "research commercialization," on the contrary, is narrower and more closely connected to technology transfer. It can be defined as the "process of turning scientific discoveries and inventions into marketable products" (Harman and Harman 2004, p. 154). From a policy perspective, however, the concept may also encompass as much as "the process of transforming ideas, knowledge and inventions into greater wealth for individuals, businesses and/or society at large" (Prime Minister's Science, Engineering and Innovation Council 2001, p. 9).

Bozeman (2000) points out that the concept of university technology transfer may encompass all movement of ideas and knowledge from the university to wide groups of users in society, including public departments and nongovernmental organizations, as well as across nations, e.g., in the form of development aid. Also, from a societal perspective, graduates from universities carry knowledge into firms; faculties provide knowledge on a consultancy basis; and industries, as well as public sector actors, consume scientific publications in their respective domains of activity. An "entrepreneurial university, among other things:

– Responds to varying students' needs and circumstances;
– Takes account of labor market requirements and employer needs;
– Embeds entrepreneurial skills and ethical values in course offerings;
– Develops application linkages for research;
– Undertakes collaborative research with industry;
– Employs flexible staffing strategies" (Gallagher 2000, p. 2).

Hellstrom (2007, pp. 483–486) in his analysis of the Swedish universities' strategies for commercialization of their research results arrives at the following categories:

(1) *Support infrastructure for commercialization* – This category deals with the creation of special infrastructure for commercialization within the organizational structure of the university. These include new units and dedicated administrative functions such as technology transfer offices (TTOs), and professional advice and support functions. The most important infrastructural platforms for commercializing research seem to be the stand-alone business development units: university holding companies and science parks. These units are intended to become intermediate proprietary platforms through which new discoveries and inventions can be identified, funded, and commercialized.

(2) *Internal knowledge building and cultural change* – The second strategy relating to commercialization activities deals with processes rather than products. These processes consist of a set of interrelated activities aimed at knowledge building and transforming the university culture to promote entrepreneurialism and outreach. The most prominent of them are education and knowledge dissemination on commercialization. Such activities have three aims: (a) general increase of knowledge regarding academic entrepreneurship; (b) direct support for commercialization activities; and (c) the formulation of new flexible models for spin-off creation. The second type of processes deals with the generation and harvesting of ideas. The most important activity here is the business plan competition. This group of strategic actions has a third subcategory, which involves the creation and stimulation of strategic research activities. The university sponsors research programs and projects in specific areas in order to encourage research in an attractive field and further obtain additional funding. This type of initiative reflects an entrepreneurial spirit set within a more traditional academic frame of reference.

(3) *Outreach and sectoral cooperative activities* – This category concerns strategic activities aimed at linking the university to the surrounding society. Such activities are generally directed toward contributing to the growth and innovation in the municipality and the region where the university is located. The first type can be referred to as focused bridging activities. One such activity is the joint university–industry projects, which are often established as part of state and university initiatives, and cofinanced by strategic research funding organizations, e.g., attracting funding for national competence centers for long-term industrial cooperation. Another activity under this general heading has been the strategic/open-ended bridging activities to create bridges between the university and other sectors of society. One recent trend in this area has been the strategic intention of placing business representatives on university bodies, as an open-ended way of providing new directions for the university on various levels of organization (Hellstrom 2007, pp. 483–486).

There are several reasons for weak linkages between the university and the industry. One perception of the public has been that the universities engage in too much basic research and consume scarce resources on issues with little or no relevance to economic development, particularly the industry. Part of the reason for weak linkages between the university and the industry lies in the existence of cultural differences between university and industry, in terms of different orientations and value systems governing academic and industrial research. Innovation in university-based research is measured in terms of criteria such as (1) an advance in knowledge; (2) providing new means for further research; and (3) improving or deepening understanding of processes (know why, how, and what). Commercial innovation, on the contrary, is defined in Schumpeterian terms, i.e., it is market success rather than originality or newness that is the predominant value (Jacob and Orsenigo 2007).

University scientists are mainly motivated by the rules of "open sciece" and by the "publish-or-perish" principle (Dasgupta and David 1994), whereas the industry relies on proprietary knowledge. Moreover, university researchers take pride in engaging in big scientific issues concerning nature and matter, whereas industry is engaged in more mundane activities of converting existing knowledge into tangible products and services. Therefore, university scientists may need to be motivated to engage in research relevant to industry. One of the most popular policy measures to creating such motivation has been to increase the need for public research to seek industry funding by reducing the government funding. This is often accompanied by the removal of the legal and bureaucratic impediments to the university's engagement in industry-sponsored research. As an incentive to the individual researchers to link up with the industry, the researchers are encouraged to patent their research results and license the know-how to the industry for royalty. Furthermore, another perception has been that academic research results require a lot of developmental efforts to make them useful to industry. Therefore, there is a need for creating bridging institutions to take responsibility for conversion and diffusion of academic research results.

Some scholars are of the view that engaging in industry-oriented research may be counter-productive in the long run to upholding the values, such as open communication that would lead to better diffusion of knowledge into society, that sustain the system of knowledge production at universities (David et al. 1999). Nelson (2001) also argued that the increasing commercial orientation on the part of individual university researchers combined with universities' growing dependence on revenues from research output may weaken the traditional commitment to publish in the open domain and contribute to public science. A few other studies conclude that an increased emphasis on technology transfer and linkages with the industry often leads to significant delays in the publication of research findings by the researchers and creates constraints in openly discussing their research issues with other faculty and students (Blumenthal et al. 1997; Stephan 2001).

Many scholars believe that history, trust, and clearly defined demands are important prerequisites for closer university–industry linkages. Rosenberg and Nelson (1994) point out that US universities have a long tradition of interaction with local firms on issues of practical concerns in practically oriented disciplines, such as engineering, medicine, and agricultural sciences. The existence of long-standing relations and above all of a strong demand by industry, especially at the local level, are necessary for establishing healthy ties between the universities and the industry. An additional factor has been the proactive role that many US universities play in seeking employment opportunities in the industry for students (Adams et al. 2005).

The university–industry collaboration tends to be stronger in certain fields than that in the others. For instance, the recent spurt in university–industry relations in USA is closely linked to and concentrated in the new booming technologies such as information technology and biomedical research (Mowery et al. 2001). The US firms, it is argued, mostly use university research that is performed in high quality research universities, published in quality academic journals, funded publicly, and cited frequently by academics themselves (Pavitt 2001; Narin et al. 1997).

A firm's ability to collaborate successfully with the university depends on the firm's own experience and ability to absorb and integrate new knowledge into its operations. For effective acquisition of academic knowledge, the firm should have at least three types of competences: (a) knowledge seeking capacity, which is the capability to explore an expanding set of opportunities (through closed links with the scientific community); (b) absorptive capacity, i.e., the capability to absorb new knowledge created outside the firm (Cohen and Levinthal 1989; Iansiti1997); and (c) integrative capacity, which is the ability to integrate different new and old scientific disciplines (Iansiti 1997).

3.4   Conceptual Frameworks

The concept of university–industry collaboration is mainly policy driven. There are no strong theoretical explanations or large empirical studies for the better understanding of the concept. Furthermore, there are very few studies explaining the magnitude and nature of such collaboration, the circumstances in which such interaction takes place, or the economic impact of such collaboration. However, there are three conceptual frameworks – Systems of Innovation (SI), Mode 2 Production of Knowledge, and Triple Helix – that provide some understanding of the nature of such interaction.

3.4.1   Systems of Innovation

The SI framework comes under a new school of thought known as "evolutionary economics." The discussion about SI can be traced back to the work of Friedrich List (1841) who introduced the notion of national systems of production and learning. The concept of "national systems of innovation (NSI)" as an analytical tool was first used more or less independently by Freeman (1987), Lundvall (1988), and Nelson (1988). Freeman (1987) attributed Japan's successful development over the postwar period to certain key and distinctive elements in its national system of innovation. He defined the concept as "the network of institutions in the public and private sectors, whose activities and interactions initiate, import, modify and diffuse new technologies" (p. 1).

Lundvall (1992) defines the concept at two levels, where the narrow definition of an NSI includes the organizations and institutions involved in searching and exploring such as the R&D departments, technological institutes, and universities. The broader definition encompasses "all parts and aspects of the economic structure and the institutional set-up affecting learning as well as searching and exploring – the production system, the marketing system and the system of finance present themselves as subsystems in which learning takes place" (p. 12).

The view that an innovation system is confined to the national boundaries, however, did not appeal to many scholars. Over the years, several scholars have started to use the concept "systems of innovation" to explain the developments at international, regional (subnational), and sectoral or technology levels. Carlsson and Stankiewicz (1995) used the "technological systems" approach to explain that innovation systems can be specific to particular technologies and/or sectors. Edquist (1997, p. 14) defines SI as "all important economic, social, political, organizational, and other factors that influence the development, diffusion and use of innovations."

Carlsson et al. (2002, p. 234) note that the systems comprise of components, relationships, and attributes. Components are the "operating parts of a system" and they can be actors or organizations such as individuals, business firms, universities, banks, etc., and groups of them. Physical and technological artifacts as well as laws, regulations, etc., are considered as system components. Relationships, the second key constitutive element of an SI, are linkages that bind the components. SI components are highly interdependent, with strong linkages among them. Technology transfer and acquisition are considered to be two of the more important relationships in an SI. Relationships are also the source of interaction and ultimately feedback into the system. The third element is described as attributes. Attributes characterize the system and are the results of the interaction between components through the relationship among them. The function of an SI is the generation, diffusion, and utilization of technology.

The essence of an SI framework is as follows:

(a) Firms do not innovate in isolation. Innovation has to be seen as a collective process involving other firms as well as a number of other key actors/organizations such as universities, research centers, government agencies, etc.
(b) Firms' capacity to innovate is further shaped by institutions, including policies, laws, and regulations (Lundvall 1992; Edquist 1997).
(c) Learning and interdisciplinarity are key determinants of innovation (Edquist 1997).

3.4.2 Mode 2 Knowledge Production

The Mode 2 framework deals with the conditions for the organization and production of knowledge at the microlevel. The argument of what is now familiarly known as the Mode 2 thesis has been outlined in the New Production of Knowledge (NPK) (Gibbons et al. 1994). According to this framework, in today's world, a new mode of knowledge production is emerging. This mode, called Mode 2, has five distinguishing features:

- Transdisciplinarity
- Knowledge produced in the context of application
- Quality control
- Social accountability and reflexivity
- Heterogeneity and organizational diversity.

The first feature, transdisciplinarity, is a departure from the previous Mode of Knowledge Production (Mode 1) in which the source of ideas for knowledge production was the discipline. Although multidisciplinary research has been in existence for a long time, the transdisciplinarity in Mode 2 goes beyond the group of scholars from different disciplines working together on the same problem, but from their respective disciplinary background. Transdisciplinarity, on the contrary, is based on the development of a distinct framework intended to guide problem-solving efforts. The final result is an integrated systemic effort and not traceable to any single discipline. Mode 2 has an independent set of theoretical structures, research methods, and modes of practice. The channels for communication of knowledge also differ from Mode 1 in that results are communicated to group members during their participation itself. Thus, the diffusion occurs in real time. Subsequent diffusion occurs through the mobility of the team members rather than through reporting results in professional journals or at conferences. An important feature of Mode 2 is that the knowledge is produced in the context of its application. In Mode 1, it was pointed out that research was conducted almost exclusively in universities, whereas in Mode 2 collaborative partnerships between stakeholders are the key factors of knowledge production. Researchers deal with problems identified by practitioners or a group of practitioners and scientists, and knowledge is generated in the context to which it will be applied. Since knowledge is produced in the context of application, issues of validity and quality assurance are defined in terms of social utility and other criteria of validity which may suit the needs of users.

A number of the institutional innovations that took place in the science policy are reflections of Mode 2 types of knowledge production. Prominent among them is the concept of "centers of excellence," a form of organizing research that embodies the Mode 2 principles for the organization of knowledge production. Centers of excellence are usually problem oriented and transdisciplinary. Another important feature common to centers of excellence is that they are intended to achieve critical mass in a particular area of endeavor by building networks that span several sites (Jacob and Orsenigo 2007).

3.4.3 The Triple Helix Framework

The Triple Helix framework was introduced by Etzkowitz and Leydesdorff in 1997. In the framework, there are three main actors – university, industry, and government – playing the major roles in innovation. The core proposition of the triple helix is that the universities play an enhanced role in innovation in the knowledge-based societies. The university–industry–government relations are considered to be a triple helix of evolving networks of communication (Etzkowitz and Leydesdorff 1997, 2000). The framework seems to attach equal role to all the three actors in innovation, which mainly takes place in the enterprises. It also does not take into account sectoral differences and the proportional contribution made by each of the actors.

According to Jacob and Orsenigo (2007), there seems to be two distinct strands within the triple helix tradition, Triple Helix I and II. The focus of Triple Helix I is the entrepreneurship in universities and the emerging infrastructure for promoting entrepreneurship, such as incubators, liaison offices, and other similar structures. The thrust of the argument outlined is similar to that of the Mode 2 concept in that it posits that the university is undergoing a process of change. Mode 2 emphasizes social utility and the organization of the production of knowledge at the microlevel, whereas Triple Helix I is concerned with turning knowledge into wealth. Triple Helix I presents a stylized model of history of the evolution of the university in which academic entrepreneurship is depicted as the latest stage (Etzkowitz et al. 2000). The emphasis is on institutions rather than individuals, and on the way in which roles, rules, and knowledge are transformed as a result of this tripartite coalition. Triple Helix II is an effort to construct a narrative that coheres with the Mode 2 and SI perspectives. Triple Helix II is less concerned with entrepreneurship and more with the questions of evaluation and the criteria for the validity of knowledge (Leydesdorff and Meyer 2003).

3.5 University–Industry Collaboration: A Cross-Country Analysis

An overview of the cross-country scenario shows that in most countries the university–industry collaboration is still at a nascent stage. There continues to be a separation of activities between the universities and the industry. This is partly because the universities themselves carry out little research or tend to do research that is of little relevance to the industry. Another part of the reason lies in the lack of demand from the industry, mainly because either the industry depends on technology transfer from abroad or its operations require only solving minor technical problems and is not interested in upgrading the technological capacity.

For instance, in the 1950s, Brazil established a number of new public and private universities. By 2005, there were 2,165 institutions of higher education, of which 173 were classified as universities. Research is undertaken only among the public universities and in some research institutions linked to specific ministries (Health, Agriculture, Mines, and Energy). Only the institutions of higher education that are categorized as universities are required to undertake research activities, and less than 10% of the institutions of higher education (173) are considered to be universities. However, the systems of higher education, research, and industrial production developed rapidly for three decades but without much interconnection among them, each following its own path (see Chap. 4).

In China, from the beginning, research institutions constituted the core of the national innovation system. Inspired by the Soviet Union system, the Communist government of China established a complex system of research institutions, among them the most important one being the Chinese Academy of Sciences (CAS). The government directly organized a range of S&T plans and programs, and directly administrated the research institutions. Much of the research was military related and few research results were applied to industrial production. The research institutes, university, and enterprise were separated from each other, and academic researchers had few linkages with industry (see Chap. 8).

In Germany, universities are only one of several types of PRO. The most important among PROs are the Max Planck Society, the Fraunhofer Society, and the Helmholtz Centers. The Max Planck institutes conduct excellent basic research in physics, biology, and chemistry. Although it is basic research, Max Planck's research results are increasingly becoming useful for industrial application. The Fraunhofer Society distinctly focuses on applied research and is primarily funded by external financing, especially from industrial enterprises. The main means of technology transfer to industry is the "contract research," which accounts for 40% of the Fraunhofer's activities. All the Fraunhofer's institutes have a special technical focus covering the areas of ICT, life sciences, microelectronics, surface technology and photonics, production, and materials. The Helmholtz centers began with nuclear research and now their research has been extended to fields such as aeronautics, computer science, and biotechnology. Their activities include basic research requiring large research facilities; large projects of public interest requiring huge financial, technical, and interdisciplinary scientific resources and management capacities; and long-term technology development, including prototype building (see Chap. 13).

During the Soviet Union period, almost all the research was conducted in the national research institutes, with universities focusing on education and the industry on producing goods and services with no linkages among them. In the 1990s, after the collapse of the Soviet Union, there was a disintegration of large departmental institutions and those that were under the Russian Academy of Sciences became smaller entities. Today, the isolation of Russian higher education institutions from industry has been mainly due to the lack of research financing and the focus of newly established private higher education institutions on educational activities only. As a result, less than 38% of higher education institutions are currently engaged in research activities. Under the conditions of the economic isolation in the Soviet Union, science had to contribute comprehensively to the economic and social development, production growth, and defense capacity. Such system required vast resources and was not economically viable. But, successful research results in one area were applied immediately even in other areas, and this led to generation of considerable synergetic effect. However, such break-through results were implemented primarily not in the civil, but in the military sphere and in the fields that were important for the national prestige (such as the space). Among the most highly developed fields of science and technology in Russia where both basic and applied sciences are equally well-developed are physics, mathematics and ICT, space research, research in chemistry and materials, medicine, biology, and the Earth study (see Chap. 12).

The innovation system of Tanzania lacks linkages between the universities and other R&D organizations and the productive sector. However, there are difference between sectors and subsectors. A study of three sectors, viz. agriculture, industry, and health, showed better linkages in the health sector followed by agricultural sector, especially the cash crops subsector sector. The situation in the manufacturing sector is the weakest, with very little connection between R&D and the manufacturing industries, with the exception of some consultancy projects with few firms. The large industries are not interested in the universities' R&D results, as most companies claim that such R&D is irrelevant to their activities as most of the innovative activities are those of learning by doing and using. On the contrary, small-scale industries consider R&D organizations as their competitors. In the advent of economic liberalization and government budget cuts, most of the industrial R&D organizations have faced budget cuts. In order to survive, such R&D organizations turned themselves into small-scale manufacturing firms (see Chap. 9).

In Uruguay, the public policies aimed at supporting innovation have historically been relatively weak. Several important policy instruments like technology and industrial extension services, government technology procurement, etc., have either been lacking or weak. Other policy instruments such as subsidies to firms to innovative activities have usually been underutilized as a result of complicated application procedures. Strong specialized technology centers to support productive sectors have existed only in the agriculture sector. In recent years, however, new institutions related to software are fast emerging and other institutions such as technology incubators have been established (see Chap. 5).

In Vietnam, the lack of demand for technology services provided by universities and other public R&D organizations seems to be related to the nature of innovation services provided by them. Firms seem to perceive that the PROs do not or cannot provide the type of technology services required by the industry. The capability of PROs, including universities, is below the expectations of the firms, particularly in technology consulting field, where they are not able to provide sophisticated and advanced services. For their innovation activities, firms depend on their in-house teams or sometimes collaborate with other related firms (see Chap. 7).

Not withstanding such lack of enthusiasm among the actors, governments across the countries are persisting with the efforts to promote university–industry collaboration. Such efforts range from broader policy initiatives to specific micro-level measures in the form of funding of joint research programs and projects.

During the military regime, between 1968 and 1980, Brazil pursued a policy of self-reliance and self-sufficiency through State companies that served a dual purpose: to guarantee the production of primary raw material and industrial inputs (steel, minerals, and hydroelectric power) and to create R&D centers to diffuse technological advances to strategic sectors (nuclear power, aviation, and data processing), e.g., Petrobras, Eletrobrás, Telebrás, Nuclebras, and Embraer. The University Reform Law of 1968 was enacted to make the system more responsive to the market demand for an educated labor force and to support the process of industrialization through the development of graduate studies and academic research. The National Fund for Scientific and Technological Development (FNDCT) was established in 1969, with substantial resources in relation to the size of the scientific community. A portion of public funding was made available to the industrial sector for innovation, but the impact was limited due to the lack of demand from industry, which preferred transfer of technology from abroad rather than investing in own R&D. Therefore, industry's collaboration with universities or research institutions was very limited. Companies seldom purchased the results of research from other local institutions.

In the 1990s, some leading universities in research adopted new strategies for the dissemination of research results and the transfer of technology. Several initiatives were undertaken to facilitate the creation of spin-off companies around academic research projects. The number of "business incubators," technology transfer offices, and technological parks multiplied. The first company incubators were created at the end of the 1980s and by 2003, there were 70 university incubators in operation. The Innovation Law (No.10.973) adopted in 2004 was enacted after extensive consultations with the civil society. This law is designed to legalize the initiatives of the universities regarding commercialization of research results, including the rendering of services, the formation of partnerships with companies in research projects, creation of technology companies, and patenting and licensing (see Chap. 4).

In early 1979, the Chinese government decided that the key universities should also become research centers, which marked that research formally became a mission of Chinese universities. In 1980s, the number of research institutions established by the universities grew rapidly, and the achievements in R&D field became one of the important indicators to evaluate a university. In 1985, the Chinese government reformed the S&T system, decentralized fiscal and managerial control, and encouraged establishment of linkages between research institutes and industry. The government drastically reduced the financial support to research institutions and universities, and forced them to search for other sources of funding. Some research institutions began to offer graduate education, and the universities started to undertake research projects, but there was still a lack of interaction between universities and research institutions, and the enterprises were still relatively separated from the academia.

In 1992, the Chinese government initiated the project of "enterprise–university–institution cooperation" to encourage collaboration among the enterprises, universities, and research institutions. Contribution to economic development and promotion of advancement of S&T officially became missions of the university. The Chinese universities began to set up their own enterprises. These university-run enterprises provided urgently needed finances for the universities and also directly contributed to the economic development, creating a perception among people that the universities could be growth engines in the knowledge-based society (see Chap. 8).

In Cuba, the government introduced changes in its science and technology policy in the mid 1980s. They include the reorientation of university research, toward more applied research; the definition of new priority areas for S&T development (i.e., biosciences, biotechnology, pharmaceutical industry, and high-tech medical equipment); and the creation of the productive scientific parks – networks of integrated collaboration where research, creation of technologies, production, and commercialization of products are part of a continuous process led by unique strategies, the enhancement of the S&T Forum. This is a unique Cuban experiment aimed at increasing social participation in the S&T development and its applications (see Chap. 6).

In Denmark, during the past years, the role of universities in knowledge and technology transfer has been increasing. In addition to teaching and research, the so-called third mission of knowledge diffusion and technology transfer has become an important goal of the universities. This role did not emerge as a joint initiative of university–industry or due to the government support, but through different research groups in specific departments. As a result, all the Danish universities have now established TTOs, Patent Offices, Network Centers, Incubators, Knowledge Ambassadors, etc. Now these activities have explicitly been incorporated into the University Act and the activity contracts that the universities have to enter into with the Ministry (see Chap. 14).

In South Africa, research and development takes place in the 23 public institutions for higher education as well as in PROs (Science Councils). The White Paper on Science & Technology envisages promotion of competitiveness and employment creation; enhancement of quality of life; development of human resources; work toward environmental sustainability; and promotion of information society. The Council of Scientific and Industrial Research (CSIR) is the largest performer of R&D in South Africa among PROs. It carries out directed and multidisciplinary research, technological innovation, and industrial and scientific development to improve the quality of life of people. Its science and technology services and solutions support various stakeholders. The Parliamentary grant accounts for 40% of CSIR's income and the rest is generated through research contracts, royalties, licenses, and dividends from its IP and other commercial operations (see Chap. 10).

In Sweden, since the late 1990s, the system for higher education has been assigned the so-called Third Mission. It means that in addition to the two traditional tasks of education and research, the universities and other academic institutions are now also officially obliged to interact with surrounding society and economic life. Formation of research consortia is the main mechanism through which university–industry collaboration is envisaged. Funding agencies that support the consortia tend to act as intermediaries between the academia and the large firms. This reflects the traditionally strong relations among the State, industry, and university in Sweden. The State plays an important role as the conductor or facilitator of academy–industry collaboration through various research funding schemes. In recent years, a bottom-up entrepreneurial model, where universities and academics themselves take on the role of entrepreneurs, is complementing these highly organized forms of interaction (see Chap. 15).

In Tanzania, the College of Engineering and Technology (CoET) contributes significantly to achieving the national socioeconomic advancement through proper selection, adoption, adaptation, and further development of technological solutions as well as the development of appropriate and sustainable technologies. It involves all academic disciplines of the CoET in prototype development and technology transfer. Technology brokerage and the subsequent transfer to industry are being coordinated by the Technology Development and Transfer Centre (TDTC). It is felt that a broker approach to innovation and technology transfer has greater potential impact on socioeconomic development in Tanzania. It is imperative to ensure efficient absorption and adaptation of imported technology to national priorities and resources. This requires that the CoET has arrangements for exchange of technological information with, at least, some leading international technology transfer centers (see Chap. 9).

In order to promote university–industry collaboration, most countries have adopted very specific microlevel measures, such as the establishment of TTOs, clusters, and science parks.

In China, the first university S&T Park was set up in the Northeast University in 1991. Later, Peking and Tsinghua Universities set up their own university S&T Parks. Presently, there are 50 national university S&T Parks in China. According to provisional statistics, the 42 national university S&T Parks together had 5,037 enterprises in incubation, and 1,256 graduated enterprises at the end of 2004 (see Chap. 8).

In Cuba, the sectoral system of the biotech-based medical-pharmaceutical industry is considered a success story in the knowledge-based economy. It is based at Havana's West Pole, a cluster with more than 40 institutions and 12,000 workers, 7,000 of whom are scientists. These institutions operate in a "closed cycle": research, design, product development, and product manufacturing and marketing. This sectoral system of innovation incorporates other actors such as universities, research institutes, the healthcare system, and, very importantly, the government. The system works under the leadership of the state (see Chap. 6).

In Latvia, the industrial sector is dominated by the small and medium enterprises (SMEs) with low innovation capacities. In order to strengthen the technological capacity of the enterprises, the government is taking several measures. A new Department of Science, Technologies and Innovations was created in 2006 within the Ministry of Education and Science. The Innovation Division was established in 2003 at the Industry Department of the Ministry of Economics. In recent years, the Ministry of Regional Development and Local Government is also playing a proactive role. The innovation and business support organizations form the expanding component of the NSI. They include a growing number of industrial parks, technology centers, risk capital funds, consulting companies, and various other intermediaries. These are expected to strengthen the enterprise sector by assisting established companies and facilitating formation of start-ups and new technology-based companies (see Chap. 11).

In Sweden, due to the perceived benefits associated with a range of so-called agglomeration economies, the concepts of Innovation systems and clusters have attracted the interest of the research community and policy makers wanting to promote innovation and competitiveness in industrial growth sectors such as biotechnology and telecommunications, as well as to support local economic development in disadvantaged localities and regions. The concept of clusters has been promoted mainly not only by the ministry of industry, from a growth perspective, but also by the ministry of education due to the links between universities and industry, and also by the foreign ministry as a way to promote FDI, mainly through the Invest in Sweden Agency (ISA) (see Chap. 15).

In Tanzania, the Tanzania Gatsby Trust (TGT), a nongovernmental organization, was established in 1992 to support the SMEs through credit provision, training in marketing, and technology transfer. Since 2001, CoET and TGT have been collaborating in the field of technology development and transfer (TDT). Technology/business incubation and brokerage are among the other strategies for university–industry collaboration in technology and applications of research results. The CoET–TGT collaboration has technology incubation as one of the areas for cooperation. The activities being undertaken include

- analysis of the respective local economy;
- assessment of the prevailing technology levels;
- specification of basic incubator design features;
- assessment of available support for alternative incubator options; and
- preparation of business plans for both the incubator and tenants (see Chap. 9).

Many governments and universities have fine-tuned their intellectual property rights (IPRs) regimes to encourage researchers to commercialize their research results by themselves or license the technologies to other firms.

In terms of patenting activity, Brazil has not been very active. Its companies file for fewer patents than the universities. Between 1999 and 2003, the largest number of patent applications originated from the University of Campinas (UNICAMP) and of the 20 largest patenting institutions, 5 were universities and 2 were development agencies. At the US patent office, 106 patents were granted to Brazil in 2004, representing 0.6% of the patents registered that year, while Brazil's share in the world production of scientific articles was three times greater (see Chap. 4).

In Sweden, the IP ownership of results of the university rests with the researchers participating in the project. A "professor's or university teacher's exemption" from employment contracts, which gave ownership to the employer, was enacted in a 1949 law. Ownership, however, is notional rather than a real incentive to transfer technology, without financial resources to do the follow-up research to produce a prototype. Since the existing firms are often unwilling to license discontinuous inventions, a source of seed or venture capital is required to form a firm to further develop the technology and move it toward the market. As a result, individual academics seldom have the knowledge and resources to realize benefits from their formal ownership rights (see Chap. 15).

3.6   Different Forms of University–Industry Collaboration

University–industry collaboration in innovation takes place in several different forms that include the following.

3.6.1   Consulting Services

Consulting services are provided by individual faculty members to the enterprises. Such collaboration takes place at the microlevel on a project to project basis both formally and informally. University–industry interaction usually begins at this level and progresses to other forms of collaboration, once the history, trust, and confidence in capabilities are established through this process of consulting services.

For instance, for many Swedish academics, the interaction with firms takes place through their regular academic role. The usual relations have involved transferring different inquiries to people who are best suited for answering them and dealing with matters concerning students. "The traditional form for commercial involvement has, therefore, been as *consultants*. Restrictions on their professorial role have largely limited their involvement with professorial firms to part-time, one-person consulting operations. The type of involvement is therefore relatively limited in terms of time and financial support, and it seldom develops into long-term interaction with customers. Thus, there is a clear separation between consulting activities and academic work" (see Chap. 15).

3.6.2   Technical Support Activities Extended by Universities to the Industry

In general, academic research contributes to the solution of technical problems through a variety of ways (Klevorick et al. 1995; Sequeira and Martin 1996; Pavitt 1996): (1) Instruments and techniques for engineering programming, including the creation of models and simulation, in addition to theoretical prediction; (2) the provision of instrumentation, e.g., the cathodic tube and more recently the "gene sequencing" techniques; (3) background knowledge – often industrial researchers are less interested in the context of publication than in the experience and tacit knowledge of the authors of these articles; and (4) participation in professional networks at the national and international levels – scientists and engineers provide "knowledge of knowledge" to the solution of technical problems, i.e., they know that they can rely on the skills of other colleagues for specific problems. Enabling personnel mobility between and within sectors is the most efficient and effective means of diffusing knowledge in society. Knowledge flows largely occur through the mobility of people and teams across organizations and through the labor market (Breschi and Lissoni 2001).

3.6.3   Sponsorship of Research/Establishment of Chair
Professorship in Universities by Enterprises

Enterprises sponsor such research/chair professorships in universities in order to
ensure that research progresses in an area in which the enterprise is interested,
but is not in a position to take up the research by itself for various reasons.
Such reasons include the lack of resources or expertise in basic research methodologies, and/or the area falls outside the firm's immediate areas of operations.
For example, the AstraZeneca, the Swedish–UK pharmaceutical multinational
corporation established a Chair Professorship in the Indian Institute of Science,
India (Reddy 2000).

3.6.4   Joint R&D Projects Between the University
and the Industry

Such joint R&D projects involve each partner contributing its area of competence.
Due to the confidentiality issues involved, this form of collaboration takes place
only after the industrial partner develops trust and confidence in university's
capabilities. In recent years, in order to promote university–industry collaboration,
some governments have initiated and funded such joint R&D projects. For instance,
in the past, the Chinese enterprises did not have much R&D capability and had to
seek help from the research institutes for technical help and technologies. The joint
research activities between universities and enterprises in China began in 1980s.
The universities not only provide professional training to the employees in
enterprises, but also collaborate with enterprises through research projects to solve
practical technical problems. "With the implementation of the 'enterprise-universit
y-institution cooperation' project from 1992, the cooperation between the enterprises and the universities were strengthened. The enterprises funds given to universities for R&D increased from 3.6 billion Yuan in 1998 to 7.45 billion Yuan in
2004. Nowadays, the enterprise-oriented technology transfer is an important source
of R&D funds for universities" (see Chap. 8).

3.6.5   Transfer of University-Generated Technologies
to the Industry

Transfer of technologies from university to industry, traditionally, faced the
constraint of requirement for huge developmental costs to convert them into
tangible products. But, in the new science-based technologies, the boundaries
between basic research and product development are blurred and do not necessarily
require much resources in terms of developmental costs.

For instance, in Brazil, the importance of patenting the knowledge generated at the university increased after enactment of the new IP law in 1997. The objective was to create interest among the companies to license the patents of the universities, which would allow them to obtain supplementary resources. TTOs were established to deal with the offer of technological services, negotiation of contracts, patenting, technology commercialization, training of human resources, and technological diffusion. Presently, there are 30 such offices in operation in the university system. The Innovation Law passed in December 2004 strengthened these options and forced the universities to create a specific administrative structure – Offices for Technological Innovation – NITs – to manage the activities for the commercialization of knowledge (see Chap. 4).

3.6.6 Outsourcing of Complete R&D for Industrial Product to Universities

This type of collaboration occurs when there is a higher level of confidence on the university's competence and its ability to meet delivery schedules and budgetary discipline. For instance, the National Chemical Laboratories in India developed a catalyst called "zeolite," which is used in the oil industry, for the Netherlands-based multinational Akzo (Reddy 2000).

In addition to these university–industry interactive activities, universities are themselves becoming entrepreneurial by directly participating in business activities. Such activities include investing in university spin-off companies through holding companies, and undertaking manufacturing activities themselves.

In Sweden, in 1994, the Swedish Parliament gave a right to universities and university colleges to establish holding companies to procure, hold in trust, and sell shares in project and service companies engaged in R&D. Later, they were also given a right to have companies with the purpose of arranging commissioned education. Such holding companies have so far been established at 14 universities and university colleges. According to *Vinnova* (Vinnforsk VP2003:1), the Swedish research institutions already have sufficient funds to support and strengthen the incentives for the commercialization of research results. The primary weaknesses in the system are rather insufficient financial resources in the holding companies and somewhat negative attitudes of the faculty toward commercialization of research results (see Chap. 15).

The reform of the S&T system in China in 1985 drastically cut down the government fund support for universities. Therefore, many Chinese universities decided to run their own enterprises to earn revenues and improve the conditions for teaching. However, the Chinese university-run enterprises in the 1980s were all profit-oriented enterprises, such as printing house, publishing company, and some service business. In 1990s, more universities directly entered the market by establishing their own enterprises. A major change was that many Chinese universities began to set up S&T-based enterprises. The development of university-run enterprises, especially the university-run S&T enterprises, became an important criterion to evaluate a university. With the support of the government, university-run S&T enterprises are increasingly growing larger and stronger. Many university-run enterprises have taken the leading role in Chinese high-tech industry, such as Tongfang, Founder, and Dongruan. The Chinese university-run enterprises are quite different from the spin-off enterprises. A spin-off enterprise by definition is an economic entity of academic origin that becomes an independent entity, while a university-run enterprise is an economic enterprise that remains part of the administrative structure of the university (see Chap. 8).

3.7 Conclusions

Until recently, the university–industry relationship was not as strong as the relationship between the university and the end-users in the agriculture sector. This was partly due to the equal or sometimes even superior technological knowledge base of the industry when compared with that of the universities. But, with the emergence of new science-based technologies, the distinction between basic research, applied research, and technology development is blurred. Furthermore, the new technologies also require inputs from several different disciplines, compelling firms to collaborate with other firms and universities. This has set the basic platform for increased collaboration between universities and enterprises in certain technology fields. This can be called the demand-side factor for university–industry cooperation. The governments worldwide, wanting to improve the competitiveness of their industrial sectors, started taking policy measures such as envisaging a "third mission," of supporting the society through knowledge diffusion, for their universities in addition to the earlier missions of teaching and research. Such policy measures also include changes in the IP law, enabling universities to patent results of the publicly funded research, and licensing these technologies to the industry.

In certain technologies, such as biotechnology and ICT, university researchers saw the potential to convert their research results into products. As a result, they started their own spin-off firms to develop products based on their university research and commercialized their innovations either through alliances with large firms or sometimes on their own. Realizing the potential of university research for regional development in the form of spin-off firms and entrepreneurship, several governments started developing science/technology parks, establishing incubators and business service organizations. These developments have fostered closer university–industry cooperation in certain industrial fields. However, the university–industry cooperation in a large number of industrial branches (e.g., engineering) is still limited.

It is also clear that stronger university–industry cooperation is not a panacea for all the weaknesses of the industry. There are still no conclusive studies, other than anecdotal illustrations, that the university–industry cooperation or the measures to encourage such cooperation such as the establishment of science parks have led to significant economic benefits either regionally or nationally.

References

Adams, J,D., Black, G.C., Clemmons, J.R., Stephan, P.E. (2005). 'Scientific teams and institutional collaborations: Evidence from U.S. universities, 1981–1999,' *Research Policy* Vol. 34, No. 3, pp. 259–285.

Blumenthal, D., Campbell, E.G., Andersson, N. et al. (1997) 'Withholding research results in academic life science: evidence from a national survey of faculty', *Journal of the American Medical Association*, Vol. 277, No. 15, pp. 1224–1228.

Bozeman, B. (2000) 'Technology transfer and public policy: a review of research and theory', *Research Policy*, Vol. 29, pp. 627–655.

Breschi, S. and Lissoni, F. (2001) 'Knowledge spillovers and local innovation systems: a critical survey', *Industrial and Corporate Change*, Vol. 10, No. 4, pp. 975–1005.

Carlson, B. and Stankiewicz, R. (1995) 'On the nature, function and composition of technological systems', in B. Carlsson (ed) *Technological Systems and Economic Performance: The Case of Factory Automation*. Dordrecht, Kluwer.

Carlson, B., Jacobsson, S., Holmen, M., and Rickne, A. (2002) 'Innovation systems: analytical and methodological issues', *Research Policy*, Vol. 31, No. 2, pp. 233–245.

Clark, B.R. (1998) *Creating Entrepreneurial Universities: Organizational Pathways of Transformation*. Oxford, IAU Press/Pergamon.

Cohen, W. and Levinthal, D. (1989) 'Innovation and learning: the two faces of R&D', *Economic Journal*, Vol. 99, No. 397, pp.569–596.

Dasgupta, P. and David, P. (1994) 'Toward a new economy of science', *Research Policy*, Vol. 23, No. 5, pp. 487–521.

David, P., Foray, D., and Steinmueller, W.E. (1999) 'The research network and the new economics of science: from metaphors to organisational behaviour', in A. Gambardella, and F. Malerba (eds) *The Organisation of Economics of Innovation in Europe*. Cambridge, Cambridge University Press.

Edquist, C. (1997) 'Systems of innovation approaches, their emergence and characteristics', in C. Edquist (ed) *Systems of Innovation: Technologies, Institutions and Organizations*. London, Pinter.

Etzkowitz, H. (2003) 'Research groups as 'quasi-firms': the invention of the entrepreneurial university', *Research Policy*, Vol. 32, pp. 109–121.

Etzkowitz, H. and Leydesdorff, L. (2000) 'The dynamics of innovation: from national systems and "Mode2" to triple helix of university-industry-government relations', *Research Policy*, Vol. 29, No. 2, pp. 109–123.

Etzkowitz, H. and Leydesdorff, L. (1997) 'Introduction to the special issue on science policy dimensions of the triple helix of university-industry-government relations', *Science & Public Policy*, Vol. 24. No. 1, pp. 2–5.

Etzkowitz, H. and Webster, A. et al. (2000) 'The future of the university and the university of the future: evolution of ivory tower to entrepreneurial paradigm', *Research Policy*, Vol. 29, No. 2, pp. 313–330.

Freeman, C. (1987) *Technology Policy and Economic Performance: Lessons from Japan*. London, Frances Pinter.

Gallagher, M. (2000) 'The Emergence of the Entrepreneurial University'. Paper Presented at the Institutional Management in Higher Education (IMHE), General Conference of the Organization for Economic Cooperation and Development (OECD), Paris, September 11-13.

Gibbons, M., Limoges, C., Nowotny, H., Schwartzman, S., Scott, P., and Trow, M. (1994) *The New Production of Knowledge: The Dynamics of Science and Research in Contemporary Societies*. London, Sage.

Harman, G. and Harman, K. (2004) 'Governments and universities as the main drivers of enhanced Australian University Research Commercialisation Capability', *Journal of Higher Education Policy and Management*, Vol. 26, pp. 153–169.

Hellström, T. (2007) 'The Varieties of University Entrepreneurialism: thematic patterns and ambiguities in Swedish university strategies', *Policy Futures in Education*, Vol. 5, No. 4, pp. 478–490.

Herrera, S. (2001) 'Academic research is the engine of Europe's biotech industry', *Red Herring*, Vol. 108, pp. 72–74.

Jacob, M. and Orsenigo, L. (2007) *Leveraging Science for Innovation: Swedish Policy for University–Industry Collaboration 1990–2005*. Stockholm, Swedish Centre for Business and Policy Studies.

Iansiti, M. (1997) 'From technological potential to product performance: and empirical analysis', *Research Policy*, Vol. 26, pp. 345–365.

Klevorick, A., Levin, R., Nelson, R., and Winter, S. (1995) 'On the sources and significance of inter-industry differences in technological opportunities', *Research Policy*, Vol. 24, No. 2, pp. 185–205.

Krimsky, S. (1991) 'Academic-corporate ties in biotechnology: a quantitative study', *Science Technology and Human Values*, Vol. 16, pp. 275–287.

Leydesdorff, L. and Meyer, M. (2003) 'The Triple Helix of university-industry-government relations', *Scientometrics*, Vol. 58, No. 2, pp. 191–203.

Lundvall, B-Å. (1992) 'Introduction', in B-Å. Luvall (ed) *National Systems of Innovation: Toward a Theory of Innovation and Interactive Learning*. London, Pinter.

Lundvall, B-Å. (1988) 'Innovation as an interactive process. From user-producer interaction to National Systems of Innovation', in G. Dosi, C. Freeman, R. Nelson, G. Silverberg and L. Soete (eds) *Technological Change and Economic Theory*. London, Pinter.

Mansfield, E. (1998) 'Academic research and industrial innovation: an update of empirical findings', *Research Policy*, Vol. 26, Nos. 7/8, pp. 773–776.

Mowery, D.C., Nelson, R.R., Sampat, B., and Ziedonis, A. (2001) 'The growth of patenting and licensing by US universities: an assessment of the effects of the Bayh-Dole Act of 1980', *Research Policy*, Vol. 30, No. 1, pp. 99–119.

Narin, F., Hamilton, K., and Olivastro, D. (1997) 'The increasing linkage between US Technology and Public Science', *Research Policy*, Vol. 26, No. 3, pp. 317–330.

Nelson, R. (2001) 'Observations on the Post-Bayh-Dole Rise of Patenting at American Universities', *Journal of Technology Transfer*, Vol. 26, No. 1, pp.13–19.

Nelson, R.R. (1988) 'Institutions supporting technical change in the United States', in G. Dosi, C. Freeman, R. Nelson, G. Silverberg and L. Soete (eds) *Technological Change and Economic Theory*. London, Pinter.

OECD (2003) *Main Science and Technology Indicators*. Paris, OECD.

Owen-Smith, J. (2005) 'Trends and transitions in the institutional environment for public and private science', *Higher Education*, Vol. 49, pp. 91–117.

Pavitt, K. (2001) 'Public Policies to Support Basic Research: What Can the Rest of the World Learn from US Theory and Practice? (and What they Should not Learn)', *Industrial and Corporate Change*, Vol. 10, No. 3, pp. 761–780.

Pavitt, K. (1996) 'National policies for technical change: Where are the increasing returns to economic research?', *Proceedings of the National Academy of Sciences United States of America*, Vol. 93, No. 23, pp. 12693–12700.

Piore, M.J. and Sabel, C. (1984) *The Second Industrial Divide: Possibilities for Prosperity*. New York, Basic Books.

Prime Minister's Science, Engineering and Innovation Council (PMSEIC) (2001) Commercialisation of Public Sector Research. Paper Presented at the PMSEIC Seventh Meeting, June 28. (http://www.dest.gov.au/sectors/science_innovation/publications_resources/profiles/commercialisation_research.htm)

Rappert, B., Webster, A., and Charles, D. (1999) 'Making Sense of Diversity and Reluctance: academic-industrial relations and intellectual property', *Research Policy*, Vol. 28, pp. 873–890.

Reddy, P. (2000) *Globalization of Corporate R&D: Implications for Innovation Systems in Host Countries*. London, Routledge.

Rosenberg, N. and Nelson, R. (1994) 'American Universities and Technical Advance in Industry', *Research Policy*, Vol. 23, pp. 323–348.

Sequeira, K. and Martin, B. (1996) 'The Links between University Physics and Industry, Science Policy'. Report to the Institute of Physics Research Unit, University of Sussex.

Soete, L. (1999) *'The Challenges and the Potential of the Knowledge Based Economy in a Globalised World'. Background paper of the Portuguese Presidency of the European Union.* Maastricht, MERIT.

Stephan, P. (2001) 'Educational Implications of University–Industry Technology Transfer', *Journal of Technology Transfer*, Vol. 26, pp. 199–205.

Turk-Bicakci, L. and Brint, S. (2005) 'University–Industry Collaboration: patterns of growth for low- and middle-level performers', *Higher Education*, Vol. 49, pp. 61–89.

Veysey, L. (1965) *'The Emergence of the American University.'* Chicago, University of Chicago Press.

Part II
Country Case Studies

Chapter 4
Brazilian Universities and Their Contribution to Innovation and Development

José Manoel Carvalho de Mello, Anne-Marie Maculan, and Thiago Borges Renault

4.1 Introduction

Brazilian higher education institutions (HEIs) have been established since the first half of the nineteenth century under the format of colleges of medicine, law, or engineering. Brazilian universities (HEIs with a poly-disciplinary structure), however, were established more recently. The first university was created in 1920, in Rio de Janeiro, by the Federal Government and, in 1934, the State of São Paulo created its own university, which remains a Brazilian landmark of teaching and research.

In the 1950s, in parallel with the process of intensive industrialization, the creation of higher education institutions and, in particular, of public and private universities began to intensify. In 1980, Brazil had 882 HEIs, of which 65 were universities.

The institutionalization of research mission at the universities came by the end of the 1960s, associated with the creation of postgraduate courses. Besides universities, some research institutions have been created linked to specific ministries (Health, Agriculture, Mines, and Energy).

Public policies for science and technology (S&T) were developed during the 1970s. The difficulties in achieving planned goals for technological autonomy generated great frustration in the academic and scientific community because of the difficulty in achieving the ambitious goals they held.[1]

Brazil's industrial capability is relatively recent. The process of industrialization began in the 1950s based on three elements: multinational corporations, the state, and the embryonic national enterprises. Each of these three factors was assigned a specific role: the first was charged with bringing capital and technology, the second

---

[1] I, II Plan for Scientific and Technological Development (PBDCT), II National Development Plan (PND).

J.M.C. Mello (✉)
Universidade Federal Fluminense, Niterói, Brazil
e-mail: josemello@pq.cnpq.br

B. Göransson and C. Brundenius (eds.), *Universities in Transition:*
The Changing Role and Challenges for Academic Institutions,
© International Development Research Centre 2011

with obtaining international financing to compliment insufficient domestic saving, and the third with preparing technologically to develop the domestic market – preferably in association with foreign companies.

The systems of higher education, research, and industrial production developed rapidly for three decades but without much interconnection among them, each following its own path. During the 1980s, the so-called lost decade,[2] because of the heavy external debt and the hyperinflation that was not controlled until 1994, these three systems entered into crisis.

Beginning in 1990, profound changes were introduced in the economic structure of Brazil: the economy was opened to foreign investment, a number of public service companies were privatized, monetary stabilization was imposed, and the organizational structure of large companies was modernized, all tending to increase Brazilian companies' quality of production and ability to compete. Since then, the articulation between higher education, research, and industry has been viewed as a major challenge, in order to improve the private sector's ability to innovate, an element that is seen as a key factor in competition.

The object of this study is to analyze the changes that have occurred to provide a context for the current discussions of the new missions of the University, and in particular, with regard to its contribution to local economic development, technological training for the business community and for the generation of entrepreneurial opportunities.

The study begins with an analysis of the functions of the university vis-à-vis the characteristics of the process of industrialization, which is presented in the first section. This is followed by a detailed examination of the ability of the university system to meet the demands for the formation of human resources, which speaks essentially to its teaching mission. Later, the development of research activities and their contributions to the process of innovation are examined, with particular emphasis on the discussions of the Innovation Law. Finally, the essential points of the discussion about the social context of university activities are discussed in succinct fashion.

4.2 The Socioeconomic Context

4.2.1 Rapid Industrialization Heavily Dependent on Foreign Technology

Access to technological progress and new production technologies has been the great challenge of the Brazilian economy since the beginning of industrialization. The separation of universities and the business community, between research and

---

[2] In the political arena, this period coincided with the return to democracy and the adoption of the new constitution in 1988.

innovation, is rooted in the historic characteristics of a delayed process of industrialization.

Before the Second World War, Brazil was essentially an agricultural country. The 1950s marked the beginning of a policy of delayed but intense industrialization. Under the influence of the studies of unbalanced economic growth done by the Economic Commission for Latin America (ECLA), Brazil opted to pursue a process of industrialization known as "import substitution." The development of the more dynamic industrial sectors would be left to the large multinational corporations that brought capital and technology.[3] State companies were concentrated in sectors such as generation and distribution of electric power, telecommunications services, mining, and production of basic industrial goods (steel, petrochemicals, etc.). Funding for these activities would be guaranteed by the State and companies would rely on contracts for the transfer of technology and know-how to organize their productive activities. Other sectors were left to local companies, with limited financial capacity and precarious and limited access to technology. This industrial policy, guided by the development of the domestic market would come with strong protectionist orientation.

From 1952 to 1980, Brazil followed an import substitution industrialization strategy with a large presence of state-owned companies in primary sector industries (steel, mining, and petrochemical) and in concessions for public services. There was also growing participation by multinational companies in the consumer goods sector. The industrial sector developed behind high tariff and nontariff barriers that protected domestic, state, and multinational companies from international competition.

During the military regime, between 1964 and 1980, a succession of governments intensely pursued a policy of industrial and technological self-sufficiency through State companies that served a dual purpose: to guarantee the production of primary raw material and industrial inputs (steel, minerals, hydroelectric power) and to create centers of research and development (R&D) to spread specific technological advances to strategic sectors (nuclear power, aviation, data processing). There are numerous examples: Petrobras, Eletrobrás, Telebrás, Nuclebras, and Embraer. An important role was also played by the Brazilian Agricultural Research Company (Embrapa) in the development of Brazilian agriculture and whose research projects were designed to improve seeds and livestock as well as to offer protection against plant and animal diseases. The results of these projects were rapidly disseminated through industrial agriculture and are at the root of the substantial increase in the grain harvests and the extraordinary performance of agribusiness exports during the last 10 years.

The period from 1950 to 1980 is when Brazil's industrial base was formed, with high rates of growth and a considerable degree of diversification. During

---

[3] Automobile, pharmaceutical, capital goods and equipment, and cement industries.

1970–1979, Brazil experienced an average annual rate of growth in GDP of around 8.4%, but this rate of growth was not linked with technological development of the same magnitude. The desired articulation between industrial autonomy, through import substitution, and technological autonomy, through the substitution of imported technology with endogenous technology, simply did not occur.

During the decade of the 1980s, a crisis occurred in the Brazilian economy as it began to confront two negative effects of the growth model it had adopted: the rapid growth of external debt that helped to feed extremely high levels of inflation on the one hand, and low levels of productivity that left Brazilian industry unable to compete in international markets on the other. The 1980s are referred to as the lost decade. Inflation was not brought under control until 1994.[4] It was a decade marked by a significant reduction in government funding for science and technology.

4.2.2 Research and Training Human Resources: The Dual Mission of the University

The most significant feature of the policy of industrialization and technological development was revealed in the ambitious plan for training human resources at the graduate level linked to the implementation of institutional research activities. This was an attempt to integrate university research with the training of highly qualified human resources for the production sector (Table 4.1).

Table 4.1 The process of industrialization and university functions

	Features of industrialization	University functions
1920–1950	Heterogeneous industrialization, with offshore technology incorporated in imported equipment, and the immigration of foreign technicians	Few institutions of higher education (schools of engineering)
1950–1970	Import substitution industrialization, with the creation of subsidiary companies for production by multinational corporations and state-owned companies in primary and public services sectors	Training of human resources (engineering) as part of the process of industrialization
1970–1990	Diversification of the industrial base. Leading edge Industries based on endogenous technology and an increasing number of Brazilian employees at the managerial levels of multinational corporations	Training of specialized human resources and research scientists for the apprenticeship process

Source: Maculan (1996)

---

[4]Between 1980 and 1994, the annual rate was above 100% with rates greater than 1,000% per year between 1988 and 1994 and reaching 2,700% in 1993 (see http://www.ipea.gov.br/ipeadata, accessed 21/11/2006).

This view was based on a linear conception of the process of innovation and the belief that there would be a natural overflow of research to companies. While the utopian ideal of technological autonomy failed to materialize, and domestic companies proved to be technologically passive, there was, however, a real process of learning that was marked by the progressive mastery of the technology of production that took place in a manner much like that described by Bell and Pavitt (1993).

Public policy for S&T during the 1970s was characterized by the adoption of programs directed to the creation of an infrastructure for research with a reasonable degree of installed capacity and important human resources. The principal policy instrument was the creation of the National Fund for Scientific and Technological Development (FNDCT) created in 1969.[5] The fund had significant resources compared with the size of the scientific community.

A portion of public funding was made available to the productive sector for innovation; but the impact was limited because of the lack of demand on the part of companies that, rather than investing in internal research, gave priority to the transfer of technology from abroad – the standard option at the time. The internal funding allocated by private companies for R&D did not amount to more than 3% of total government funding available and was concentrated in a few state-owned companies.

The availability of public funding at the time was nearly always associated with the "developmentista" policy of import substitution. Furthermore, there were various external loans coming from the Inter-American Development Bank, devoted specifically to scientific and technological development or to higher education. During the 1970s, a growing volume of government funding became available. The fund was created and conceived to be quite flexible, and could use budgetary resources, based on loans from financial institutions or other organizations, tax incentives, contributions and donations from public and private organizations, and other sources. By the beginning of the 1980s, an important loan was being negotiated with the World Bank for the area of S&T – the PADCT,[6] signed in 1983.

The most visible sign of the role of the FNDCT in the process of the institutionalization of scientific and technological research during the 1970s was the growth in the number of postgraduate courses, which increased from 125 in 1969 to 974 in 1979. A complex institutional system was created around the federal agencies promoting postgraduate and research activities, which allowed the creation and financing of laboratories for postgraduate education, the creation of scholarships for students at the MSc and PhD level, and the evaluation of the quality of these courses. This system – unique among the countries of South America in the 1970s and 1980s – attracted numerous researchers and students from neighboring countries, particularly from Argentina and Chile.

During the decade of the 1980s, because of the imbalance in public accounts, difficulties with servicing the foreign debt, and the decrease in direct foreign

---

[5] According to Decree Law no. 719 of July 31, 1969.

[6] Guimarães, 1995.

investment in productive activities, the FNDCT suffered a violent reduction in the amount of available funding for the most important research projects as well as in the importance of S&T in general in governmental policy. The model for the institutionalization of academic research began to collapse. New guidelines began to appear that placed pressure to reduce the financing of basic scientific research and shift it to research in applied technology (Guimarães 1995) that was more in tune with the objectives of III PBDCT (1980–1985).

4.2.3   Technological Training, Industrial Technological Capability

Beginning in the 1990s, the Brazilian economy was subjected to a series of profound changes that altered its growth path. The new directions for the economy were the result of the interaction of various factors: deregulation (telecommunications, water, electric power distribution), the privatization of the large State mining companies, and the opening of various industries to foreign investment (energy, petroleum, finance). New management models and a new wave of organizational innovation and modernization spread through Brazilian companies as they adapted to new standards of performance that were essential to their participation in globalized economy.

Successive governments redefined the goals of industrial policy emphasizing the need to increase the competitiveness of Brazilian companies, so that they would be able to integrate with the offshore market. The use of new technologies (particularly data processing technology) was considered essential and spread throughout Brazilian industrial companies. Training in technology was now understood to include the ability to find, use, and master new technology and became the principal goal of industrial and technological policy.

The challenge was to get companies to become more engaged in the effort of modernization and to assume innovation as a central part of their strategy. The process of technological training and the acquisition of the ability to innovate were now seen as the goals of industrial policy, but to achieve them the cooperation of the universities was required. There was an urgent need to shed the passive acceptance of technology of the recent past. Various policy instruments were used, but with the economy still plagued by instability, although with inflation almost under control, investment and modernization of the productive sector took time to reach a significant volume. The new model of Development, however, was unable to return to the rates of growth of the earlier period, reaching an average annual level of 1.7% between 1990 and 1999 and of 3.6% between 2000 and 2008 (see Fig. 4.1).

The broader objective of technological education began to replace the goals of expansion of production capacity and the search for technological autonomy. But government funding for S&T, although slightly higher than that during the previous decade, did not reach the levels obtained in the 1970s. The FNDCT in particular remained at a very low level. The new development model was not able to provide

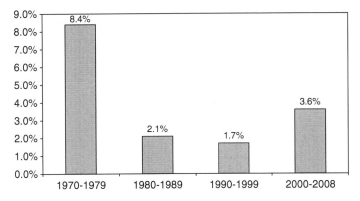

Fig. 4.1 Annual GDP growth average. *Source*: IPEADATA (2008)

technological dynamism to Brazilian industry. The introduction and incorporation of new technology, and the modernization of all business technology after the "opening" of the economy were much less than had been expected.

The lack of technological dynamism and the limited capacity for innovation can be clearly seen in three reports, PINTEC[7] for the years 2000, 2003, and 2005 (IBGE 2002, 2005, 2007). The latest edition of the survey analyzed the nature of innovative activities in 93,301 companies with more than ten employees, most of them from industrial sector (91,055), but for the first time it also included companies from the service sector: telecommunications (393), computer science (3,811), and R&D (42). The surveys show the differences in innovative behavior according to sector and size.[8] The last survey showed that about one-third (34.4%) of the companies surveyed did innovative activities, that is, developed products and/or implemented processes that were technologically new or substantially improved during the period 2003–2005. However, those innovative activities were characterized essentially by the acquisition of machinery and equipment, of which the largest part was imported. The preference for mature technology, tested and incorporated in capital goods, remained strong and the trajectory of Brazilian industry continued to be heavily dependent on external sources of technology. Brazilian companies continued to be essentially receivers of technologies developed by others, generally outside the domestic production system (Maculan 2005).

In general, the innovations that took place resulted in a modest improvement in the technology of the production processes. Important changes in the technology of production were rare and innovations in products were even rarer. The lack

---

[7] PINTEC is the Brazilian Technological Innovation Survey.

[8] According to the "Cadastro Central de Empresas 2004" (IBGE 2006), Brazil had 5,371,291 active firms, including private businesses, government agencies, and other private not-for-profit entities. Of this total, only 9.2% correspond to manufacturing industries.

Table 4.2 Brazilian exports of industrialized products by technological intensity 2000–2007 in percentage

	2000	2001	2002	2003	2004	2005	2006	2007
High technology intensity products	14.8	14.6	12.2	8.8	8.5	9.3	8.7	8.4
Medium technological intensity products	50.0	46.7	48.5	51.4	53.3	55.0	55.6	55.9
Low technological intensity products	35.2	38.7	39.3	39.8	38.2	35.7	35.7	35.7

Source: MDIC/SESEX (2009)

(or insufficiency) of demand for new products appears to have originated outside the decision making of the individual company. It was a characteristic of the domestic economic environment that was still unable to understand fully that technological education, innovation, and knowledge were the new parameters of competition.

Companies invested very little in inhouse R&D activities, collaborated infrequently with universities or research institutions, and rarely purchased the results of research performed by other institutions. In the latest survey (PINTEC 2005), 6,168 companies said that they invested in internal R&D activities, 58.6% of these performed R&D activities on a continuous basis and 86% of these were large companies. The survey also showed that 1.3% (83,944 people) of employees work with R&D activities in full-time (1.7%) and part-time (0.38%) regimes.

The effects of the lack of technological dynamism in industry during this period can also be seen in the low productivity of the labor force and by the composition of exports. Industrial productivity, which grew rapidly during the 1960s and 1970s, remained essentially stagnant during the following decades, in sharp contrast to what occurred in countries like Korea and Taiwan, which also industrialized during this time. Productivity in Brazil that reached a high of 35% of the US productivity today corresponds to 25% of it. Brazil, like Mexico and different from the Asian countries, appears not to have been able to expend the effort to learn and assimilate the technology it received from abroad (Viotti et al. 2005). The broadening research base appears to have had little impact on the process of absorption, mastery, and improvement of technology.

The composition of the exports is another indicator of the lack of Brazilian technological dynamism. Brazilian exports of industrialized products grew by 138% from 2000 to 2007, but their composition in terms of technological content remained quite constant along those years, with a small share of high technological intensity products and a dominance of medium technological intensity products, as showed in the table above (Table 4.2).

4.3 The System of Higher Education

The system of higher education, although relatively new, grew rapidly. But this expansion occurred in an unorganized manner, accumulating countless problems and distortions. Today, the image of the whole is filled with contrasts.

The first HEIs were created at the beginning of the nineteenth century, with the arrival of the Portuguese Court in Brazil in 1808, anatomy and surgery courses in Rio de Janeiro and Salvador in 1808, and the Military Academy in 1810. More than one century later, the first universities were created, starting with the University of Rio de Janeiro, founded in 1920. This first university was created through the merger of three autonomous colleges: law, medicine, and engineering. During the following years, several State and Federal universities were created, among them was the University of São Paulo that distinguished itself by pursuing excellence as measured by the standards of European universities.

The first attempt to organize higher education and universities dates back to 1931, during the first government of Getulio Vargas, as evidenced in the "Statutes of Brazilian Universities." The objective was to "raise the level of general culture; encourage scientific investigation [...] and facilitate the exercise of activities that require higher technical and scientific training." This goal was the responsibility of the University system and autonomous institutes. In addition to teaching activities at the undergraduate level, the Statute anticipated extension activities that would take the form of courses, and educational or utilitarian conferences to aid the spread of useful knowledge to individuals and communities, provide solutions to social problems, and assist in the spread of ideas and principals that support higher national interests.

During the 1950s, universities and other institutions of higher learning were exclusively involved in the preparation of human capital at the undergraduate level. The demand from the productive sector for skilled human resources was quite modest, mainly due to the low level of industrial development at the time. A limited number of research activities were performed by independent researchers in institutions such as the National Institute of Technology, the Butantã Institute, and the Oswaldo Cruz Institute.

By 1962, when the Federal University of Brasília was created, the importance of the relationship between higher education and research had become evident. In subsequent years, the need for universities devoted to graduate studies and research activities to have a new organizational and legal framework became clear. In 1968, the federal government sanctioned this new organization of universities through the so-called University Reform Law (Law 5.540) that was designed to meet the new demands for training skilled human resources and the generation of scientific and technical knowledge required for the process of industrialization. Graduate studies and research completed the triad (undergraduation, graduate studies, and extension services). Extension activities were reemphasized in this Law as a means of providing services to society. Universities were given this task, in addition to the teaching and research that was taking place in graduate courses based on the "Sucupira Opinion."[9] The university administration was then structured around Undergraduate, Graduate & Research, and Extension activities.

---

[9] Opinion no 977/65, C.E.Su, approved. December 3, 1965. Definitions of graduate courses published 03/12/1965.

According to the present statute, HEIs are classified in three categories related to their organization and academic prerogatives: universities, university centers, or colleges (MEC 2004). All have to be certified by the National Education Council, an autonomous regulatory agency, after being approved by the Ministry of Education (MEC). These institutions may be public (created, maintained, and managed by public authorities) or private (managed by private individuals or corporations).

Universities should generally have a poly-disciplinary structure, with a regular offering of at least 12 undergraduate courses in at least three different disciplines, all recognized and having a positive evaluation from the MEC; graduate programs with at least three fields of study at the master levels and one course at the PhD level, all evaluated by the MEC; institutional extension programs; at least 33% of the teaching faculty working full time; and at least 50% of the academic faculty with a master's or PhD degree. Among the higher education institutions, only those considered universities are required to develop research activities.

4.3.1 A System in Expansion, Marked by Contrasts

Higher education institutions nearly doubled in number from 2000 to 2007, reaching 2,281 institutions of which 8% (183) achieved the requirements to be considered as universities (Table 4.3).

Enrollment of undergraduate students increased by 81% from 2000 to 2007, reaching 4,880,381 enrollments, of which 2,664,187 (54.6%) were in universities.

Table 4.4 reveals the continuous expansion of enrollments in private higher education institutions, from 67% in 2000 to 74.6% in 2007. All together, Tables 4.3 and 4.4 reveal, for the year 2007, that although the universities represent only 8% of the HEIs, they encompass 54.6% of the undergraduate student enrollments, showing the relevance of the universities. Moreover, 52.5% of the universities are public ones and they encompass 40.6% of the enrollments in universities.

Enrollments in undergraduate courses in 2007 were heavily concentrated in certain areas of learning: 42% in social sciences, business, and law, and only 17% in science and engineering. The distortions in the distribution by area of knowledge

Table 4.3 Brazilian higher education institutions (2000–2007)

	2000	2001	2002	2003	2004	2005	2006	2007
HEIs (Total)	1,180	1,391	1,637	1,859	2,013	2,615	2,270	2,281
Public	176	183	195	207	224	231	248	249
Private	1,004	1,208	1,442	1,652	1,789	1,934	2,022	2,032
Universities	156	156	162	163	169	176	178	183
Public	71	71	78	79	83	90	92	96
Private	85	85	84	84	86	86	86	87

Source: INEP (2009)

Table 4.4 Enrollment of undergraduate students 2000–2007

	2000	2001	2002	2003	2004	2005	2006	2007
HEIs	2,694,245	3,030,759	3,479,913	3,887,022	4,163,733	4,453,156	4,676,646	4,880,381
Public	887,026	939,225	1,051,655	1,136,370	1,178,328	1,192,189	1,209,304	1,240,968
Private	1,807,219	2,091,529	2,428,258	2,750,652	2,985,405	3,260,967	3,467,342	3,639,413
Universities	1,806,989	1,956,542	2,150,659	2,276,281	2,369,717	2,469,778	2,510,396	2,664,187
Public	780,166	816,913	915,902	985,465	1,022,923	1,042,816	1,053,263	1,082,684
Private	1,026,823	1,139,629	1,234,757	1,290,816	1,346,794	1,426,962	1,457,133	1,561,503

Source: INEP (2009)

Table 4.5 Undergraduate students' enrollment per field of knowledge

Field of knowledge	2000	2001	2002	2003	2004	2005	2006	2007
General programs	–	1,570	1,314	1,858	2,022	2,626	572	706
Education	584,664	653,813	757,890	838,102	858,943	904,201	892,803	860,513
Humanities & arts	88,559	99,926	114,870	135,413	150,517	156,888	165,662	170,231
Social sciences, business and law	1,122,142	1,265,861	1,448,445	1,621,879	1,735,105	1,852,373	1,962,369	2,050,282
Science	233,726	262,207	299,530	333,559	360,059	377,818	392,930	414,600
Engineering sciences	234,497	254,398	279,716	301,158	319,175	344,714	371,502	417,448
Agriculture and veterinary	63,260	67,533	73,058	80,454	87,215	97,280	105,758	113,630
Health & welfare	323,196	363,466	424,383	483,997	556,505	622,464	694,103	753,015
Services	44,201	61,980	80,707	90,602	94,192	94,792	90,947	99,956
Total	2,694,245	3,030,754	3,479,913	3,887,022	4,163,733	4,453,156	4,676,646	4,880,381

Source: INEP (2009)

are directly related to the predominance of private, for profit, institutions offering a large number of courses requiring little investment in equipment (Table 4.5).

4.3.2 Regional, Social, and Racial Inequalities

Although the number of students enrolled in undergraduate studies increased in absolute terms from 2000 to 2007, the percentage of youths between 18 and 24 years of age enrolled (that is, the net enrollment rate) practically remained unchanged, around 10%, a very modest performance.

Inequalities are reflected in the geographical distribution of universities and HEIs in Brazil. Half of the HEIs are located in the southeastern region. In terms of gender, most of the enrollments are female: 2,193,246 as opposed to 1,693,776 males. But the gender inequality is reversed when the concentration by area of knowledge is considered: in engineering and the exact sciences 80% of the students are males.

Finally, as far as the racial (color) issues are concerned, we may see that the distribution of Brazilian population according to color during recent years has been approximately equal among whites and blacks plus browns (Table 4.6). The percentage of white students between the ages of 18 and 24 years enrolled in any school at any level is more than the double for black and mulatto students (Table 4.7).

Table 4.6 Distribution of Brazilian population according to color in 2004–2007 in percentage

Year	White	Black and mulatto	Asian, indigenous and undeclared
2004	51.4	46.0	2.6
2005	49.9	49.5	0.6
2006	49.7	49.5	0.8
2007	49.4	49.7	0.9

Source: IBGE Síntese de Indicadores Sociais 2005, 2006, 2007, 2008

Table 4.7 Enrollment of white and black and mulatto students (ages 18–24 years) at higher education institutions in percentage

	% White	% Black and mulatto
2004	46.6	16.5
2005	51.6	19.0
2006	56.0	22.0
2007	57.9	25.4

Source: IBGE Síntese de Indicadores Sociais 2005, 2006, 2007, 2008

4.3.3 University Graduate System

In terms of performance, graduate programs show dynamism and quality. In 2006, the university system provided 2,410 programs in graduate studies (master's and doctorate), 86% were in public institutions and 14% in private institutions.[10] The public segment is responsible for 82% of the master's courses and 90% of the doctoral courses.[11] But universities in the private segment increased their offer of graduate courses, from 87 to 346 courses in the master's degree program and from 44 to 96 courses in doctoral programs between 1996 and 2004.

In 15 years, the number of enrollments in master's degree programs doubled, while enrollments in PhD programs increased five times. The average annual growth in master's degree programs was 12.9% and in PhD programs, 15.4% from 1987 to 2003. The number of master's degrees increased by 757% and PhD degrees by 932% during the same period. But by 2003, Brazil was only awarding 4.6 PhD degrees per 100,000 inhabitants (see Fig. 4.2).[12]

In 2003, 41.6% of the students receiving advanced degrees were concentrated in applied social sciences, the humanities, linguistics, and arts and letters, with 31.6% of the students receiving degrees in the exact sciences, biology, and engineering.

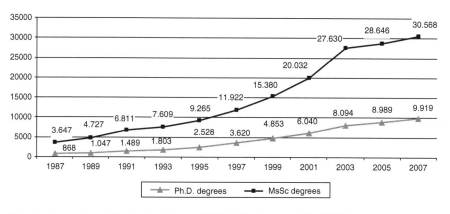

Fig. 4.2 Expansion of Graduation System 1987–2007. *Source*: MCT (2008)

[10] See Sinopse da Educação Superior – 2004 http://www.inep.gov.br/superior/censosuperior/default.asp e www.edudatabrasil.inep.gov.br.

[11] http://www.capes.gov.br: National Plan for Graduate Studies 2006–2010.

[12] A rate much lower than that of Germany which graduates an average of 30 PhDs per 100,000 population, South Korea with 13.6 or Japan with 12.1. In 2003, the number for South Korea was three times that of Brazil.

4.3.4   New Proposals for the Higher Education System

The system of higher education developed very rapidly, but without a clear government strategy to follow and with no explicit social objectives. Expansion took place in a laissez-faire context under the influence of the market interests of private groups. The need to correct the most obvious distortions and create conditions to promote social inclusion, reduce social inequalities, and expand the through-put capacity of the system became obvious. The University Reform Law of 1968 was based on adapting the system to the demand for an educated labor force to support the process of industrialization – and the chosen path was the development of graduate studies and academic research.

The government of President Luiz Inácio Lula da Silva that took office in 2003[13] attempted to reduce Brazil's social deficit, i.e., citizens without access to universities and whose exclusion was based on ethnic and social factors. The Government's proposals for university reform, like other complementary measures, were designed to promote the expansion of a democratic, multiethnic, and poly-cultural university. The reforms were based on the need to adapt the system of higher education to the needs of a sovereign democratic country, able to foster social emancipation with a view of a radical modernization that would allow the entry of wider segments of the population that had so far been excluded from the university population and higher education in general.

Two measures in particular should be discussed in view of the controversy that surrounded them. One was the offer to provide scholarships for students who did not have the ability to pay the tuition and student fees. The other was the reservation or "earmarking" of positions in public universities for students with specific ethnic or social backgrounds (quotas), based on the primary and secondary schools that the candidates attended.

4.3.5   Social Inclusion and "Positive" Racial Discrimination

The MEC created a program called University for Everyone (ProUni) to assist low-income students. ProUni[14] provides scholarships for students who were educated in the public school system, those with physical disabilities than those who identify themselves as black, mulatto, or of Indian descent. The percentage of scholarships offered by the State is determined by the proportion of black, brown, or Indian descent in the total population as shown in the IBGE census for each state. The first year ProUni offered 112,000 scholarships in 1,142 institutions of higher education. In the next 4 years, 400,000 new scholarships will become available.

---

[13]The Government of Luiz Inácio Lula da Silva was inaugurated in 2003 and reelected in 2006.
[14]Medida Provisória no. 213/2004 e Lei no. 11.096 January 13, 2005.

The implementation of ProUni, combined with the creation of 10 new federal universities and 42 new campuses, significantly increased the number of openings in higher education and completes a system of free public education, reducing regional inequality and allowing greater integration of new universities with the regional social and economic objectives.

The measures adopted revived heated debates and the assumption of opposing positions. In the society at large, there is a consensus that a large part of the population of indigenous or African descent is in fact marginalized in all segments of social life. But the ProUni program was criticized because it reserves space for individuals who *declare themselves* to be black, brown, or of Indian descent, using the argument that this introduces criteria that are explicitly racial in direct opposition to the supposition of the equality of rights of the individual.

The academic community disagreed with the policy of reserving places for students from lower levels of society who studied in public schools, arguing that this would represent a threat to the quality of instruction in public universities. In fact, basic (primary and secondary) public school education for the least favored social classes is considered to be totally deficient in quality. The students who are trained in this system are unable to qualify for the leading public universities in terms of quality higher education. These students are only able to qualify for enrollment in private institutions where education is expensive and of limited quality (and where entrance requirements are low). Students who are socially disadvantaged do not attend public universities because they cannot qualify through the selection process, and do not enroll in private universities because they cannot afford to pay the tuition.

The academic community argues that facilitating the enrollment of the students will have a negative impact on the quality of public higher education and research. Since the basis of exclusion is the quality of primary instruction, it is there that governmental action should be invested in the improvement of teaching and teachers. The former Minister of Education Cristovam Buarque points out that selection for study in the university system was always intended for a smaller, select group of persons, because the majority of the population has not even completed high school.

The Brazilian Academy of Science believes that the racial prejudice that exists in Brazilian society cannot be overcome using criteria based on race as a substitute for an objective basis. This could leave space for distortions and a worsening of tensions that would be prejudicial to university life. The central issue is social inequality, a situation that affects individuals coming from a wide variety of ethnic and cultural groups. The important question, therefore, is how institutions of higher learning can reduce social exclusion and increase the social diversity of the student body without affecting the quality of instruction.

A group of well-known members of the university community, particularly anthropologists and sociologists, made a public declaration that rejected the selection based on racial factors, even when used as an instrument of "positive" discrimination. In addition to ignoring constitutional issues, this would have the perverse effect of creating "legal" racism. Despite obvious differences in opportunities that affect the poorer population, especially those of African descent, problems would arise in applying these rules to admissions, given the lack of clear racial categories in the Brazilian population. Finally, racial distinctions are difficult in a country whose population is the result of a historic mixture of indigenous, European, African, and Asian peoples.

4.3.6   University Autonomy

ProUni was also criticized as a threat to the autonomy of the universities. First, the academic community believes that the reforms by the Federal Government and the "affirmative actions" by the states in defining quotas for specific social groups in public universities[15] clash head on with the principle of university autonomy in terms of their selection criteria.

The second controversial aspect has to do with the autonomy in financing. There is a consensus regarding the role of the state in financing and consequently its right to establish goals for the public universities. But the question arises of whether the State is to be the sole supporter of the universities, or if the universities should be encouraged to generate their own revenues, offering paid MBA-type courses or based on payment for services rendered, more closely approximating the model of corporate administration.

Administrative autonomy has been guaranteed to public universities since the 1990s but few have shown serious interest in fully developing this potential. In fact, many have expressed the concern that autonomy might mean the suspension of government financing.

4.3.7   Teaching Quality

The subject of the quality of teaching and research is also addressed in the reforms. The disorganized growth of private higher education, which for many years was facilitated by the lack of clear regulation by the State, seems to have reached its limit. Several institutions are facing financial difficulties, leading to a trend of mergers and consolidations. Moreover, private international institutions[16] started entering the field. One of the consequences of this process has been the questioning of the quality of the teaching offered. The result has been a commercialization without quality in higher education, and an increase in supply that does not meet

---

[15]The State University of Rio de Janeiro was one of the first to introduce reservation of places for black students.

[16]A multiplication of corporate universities established by major corporations or banks is also occurring.

the needs of those who cannot pay and the economic or social requirement for preparing human resources. Courses in management, administration and education, law, and accounting sciences are the most common. With few exceptions, private institutions offer education of limited quality and do not carry out research.

In reviewing this situation, the Brazilian Academy of Science says that "the current panorama of higher education requires effective measures to improve teaching quality, encourage production of new knowledge and new academic models, control the autonomy and financing of federal institutions of higher education, and the expansion of education in areas important for the development of the Country. These objectives will only be reached by reinforcing and expanding public sector education which is where the largest numbers of enrollments in higher education are concentrated in all developed countries."

The government confirmed the need to evaluate the quality of teaching using several measures for this purpose, depending on the level of the teaching considered. There has been a significant resistance, but the practice is becoming established. A recent survey by the MEC found that 70% of the students want more rigorous evaluation of the teaching quality.

4.4   The University System and Innovation

In the context of reform, the ability of academic research to contribute to innovation and competitiveness of domestic companies and corporations is also in question. The National PostGraduate Education Plan[17] prepared by the MEC states that the educational system is a strategic factor in the process of socioeconomic and cultural development and represents an indispensable institutional reference for the formation of highly qualified human resources and invigoration of the national scientific-technological potential. The training of professionals capable of participating in different sectors of society and contributing to the modernization process of Brazil is a task that required graduate studies, because it is in the National Graduate Education System that essentially all of Brazil's scientific and technological research takes place.

Two other bottlenecks have been identified: First, an inadequate system of financing that still gives preference to the desires of individual researchers who work "over the counter" as opposed to the practices of scientific research through collaboration and networking, an organizational model indispensable for the generation of cutting-edge knowledge. The second bottleneck is the disparities in the level of scientific development among different states. From the perspective of the demands and the economic potential of a continental country like Brazil, scientific

---

[17]CAPES 2004b.

research needs a national policy for integrating the measures that would promote the structuring of research activities to meet the specific demands generated by the local economic development. The recent opening of new universities, new campuses, and advanced technical schools (CEFET) reflects the efforts of the current government to respond to these needs.

However, it is worth noting that in this set of measures to reform the higher education system, the efficiency of the generation and dissemination models for new knowledge in society and especially in the economy, or the lack thereof, was often overlooked. The reference model continued to be almost exclusively the formation of human resources, with little attention given to the subject of research and the generation of knowledge as input for the technological training of the companies and innovation.

4.4.1 University–Industry Relations

After the expansion of the graduate education system, the university is poised to move in the direction of an alliance with the corporate community through the formation of highly qualified human resources and knowledge generation.

In the 1990s, the most active universities in research initiated new institutional policies for the dissemination of research results and the transfer of technology, with the creation of institutional mechanisms such as technology transfer offices, technology parks, and incubators. University incubators, in particular, had a remarkable growth. The first university incubators were created at the end of the 1980s.[18] By 2003, 70 university incubators were in operation.

Under the entry into force of new legislation regulating intellectual property (IP) at the end of 1990s, associated with the launching of governmental programs to stimulate university–enterprise partnerships, an increased number of universities have joined the IP system, spreading innovation culture, increasing the awareness about the importance of protecting research results, and establishing guidelines for technology transfer.

Wishing to convert their work into transferable outputs to industry, many universities entrusted their existing (or created new ones) technology transfer offices within the acquisition of intellectual property rights (IPRs) and their licensing to private parties, largely impelled by the entry into force of the Law of Technology Innovation (2004), which requires that universities hold a sector dedicated to IP management.

A recent analysis showed that there were 54 such offices in operation in the university system by 2007. The performance of those new forms of action by the universities still needs careful evaluation.

---

[18]At the University of São Carlos in the State of São Paulo and at the Federal University of Santa Catarina.

On the contrary, the business community has shown limited interest in the university initiatives. The efforts and investments by the universities do not appear to be sufficient to open the way for a more systematic interaction with companies that would lead to more intense efforts toward innovation. It is probable that the companies still lack sufficient internal capacity to absorb and to benefit from the knowledge generated in the universities.

It has been noted that the generation of Brazilian patents is quite limited and that companies file for fewer patents than universities. Data from the National Institute of Intellectual Property (INPI) clearly reveal the lack of innovative activities on the part of Brazilian companies. Between 1999 and 2003, the largest number of patent applications came from the University of Campinas (UNICAMP) and of the 20 largest patenting institutions, five were universities and two were development agencies (Carvalho 2006). At the US patent office,[19] 106 patents were granted to Brazil in 2004, representing 0.6% of the patents registered[20] that year (Rezende 2005) while Brazil's share in the world production of scientific articles was three times greater.

These data confirm the strong scientific production of universities, the lack of innovative capacity of industry, and the fact that there is little interaction between research institutions and the productive sector within the innovation system. This situation seems to still resemble the same one of the industrialization process presented in the first section. According to Viotti (2006, p. 9), "the vast majority of Brazilian companies do not seem to have accumulated sufficient technological training to change into an active agent of the absorption process and generation of innovations."

According to PINTEC 2005 (IBGE 2007), only 34.4% of the Brazilian industrial companies made innovations between 2003 and 2005 and of this total, 34.122% engaged in R&D activity. It should be emphasized that the large companies are the more innovative but they represent only 1.71% of the companies surveyed.

The haphazard process of industrialization, mainly based on multinational companies, did not promote conditions for the generation of adaptive or incremental technologies for the companies. This failure did not allow the national system of innovation to develop in a complete and effective way, and was classified as an immature system (Albuquerque and Sicsú 2000) based on its passive role in learning, and the low propensity to transform knowledge into innovation (Viotti 2002). Brazil, like Mexico and unlike Korea or Taiwan, has a system of innovation that rewards the passive absorption of technology and underestimates the importance of the learning processes and adaptive innovations. Companies act in isolated fashion and have difficulty developing partnerships and cooperation, either among themselves or with research institutions. As a result of this culture, the production and innovation systems show little synergy, and interactions among the actors are insufficient to generate

---

[19] USPTO – United States Patent and trademark Office.

[20] The same proportion of the beginning of the 1990s.

innovations. Very few of the results obtained by R&D institutes flow directly into the productive sector, which remains distant from scientific and technological development (Rezende 2005). In other words, there is a serious lack of interaction between the productive structure and the scientific structure.

4.4.2 The Innovation Law

The final version of the Innovation Law,[21] adopted in 2004, was delivered after wide discussion in the civil society that was coordinated by the Ministry of Science and Technology. That law legalizes several university initiatives regarding commercialization of research results, including the rendering of services, the formation of partnerships with companies in research projects, the creation of technological companies, and the patenting and licensing of technology.

The Ministry of Science and Technology based its proposal on the assumption that the commercialization and licensing of technology is an "important collective interest, because its purpose is to provide society with the products and processes that guarantee improvement in the quality of life of the population. The productive sector... is the most interested party in the implementation of the measures... since it will derive direct benefits from the possibility of economic exploration of products and processes resulting from research lines."[22] Commercialization is not directly related to the primary activity of the universities, but is related to a secondary result from research activities and the economic exploration.

Industry associations declared themselves in favor of the proposal, though clearly noting the restrictive nature of the law. In fact the bill as voted is limited to regulating the activities of the academic sector, while an innovation law should actually focus on the business sector. The extensive debate in the scientific community was focused on the measures that break with the traditional view of academic research.

The Brazilian Association for the Progress of Science (SBPC) believed that turning the university into an institution to enter the market for technological development [is] a certain contradiction. "All indications are that one of the purposes of that project is to lead the university to self-sustainability based on the competition for investment in technological development... [with] the collateral effect of a decrease in its capacity to think about society [as a whole]."

Among the most controversial aspects is the proposed change to legalize the creation of "start-up businesses" through an incubation process in the universities. The law authorizes the shared use of university laboratories, equipment, material, and facilities for small businesses and companies in activities to promote technological

---

[21]Law No. 10.973, enacted in December 2004.

[22]From the statement of reasons for the draft of Law 2001.

innovation. The universities may authorize their researchers to form a company with the objective of developing innovations.

Another controversial issue concerns the legal system for the transfer or licensing of technologies developed at the university which is authorized "to enter contracts for technology transfer and licensing granting the right to use or exploit the creation developed there" with private companies. For this purpose, the universities will have to "provide a nucleus for technological innovation, whether own property or in association with other institutions of Science and Technology with the purpose of managing its innovation policy."

4.5   The Social Dimension of the University

To complete the analysis of the mission of the universities for the social development, a summary of extension activities needs to be presented. Referred to in the Academic Reform Law of 1968 as services rendered to the community, separate from the undergraduate and graduate education and research activities and more connected to participation of the teaching corps, extension services were taken to a new level, by force of the Constitution of 1988. The extension services were raised to the level of teaching and research activities and all three are considered to be inseparable missions.

The Deans responsible for extension activities in public universities[23] want to redefine the content of that mission. Extension activities are traditionally understood to mean services provided for disadvantaged social groups. They are supposed to represent the commitment of the university to overcoming situations of inequality and social exclusion. Today they seek to integrate those actions with areas of knowledge (communication, culture, human rights, education, environment, health, technology, and work) in the form of offers for training or economic opportunities.

However, in the last census done by the Ministry in 2004, extension services continued to be seen from the point of view of services rendered to the community. The importance of the services rendered to the citizenry is worthwhile recording: 180 million patients were treated in academic health units and 350,000 cases of legal assistance were provided by academic judicial units.

A novelty concerns the emergence of incubators for popular cooperatives, the first one being created in 1995 by the movement "Citizen Actions Against Hunger and Poverty and for Life." The experience of the technology-based incubator was adapted for the incubation of cooperatives; aiming to provide employment for people from the low classes. In 2005, 34 universities already had incubators of popular cooperatives, totaling 350 incubated cooperatives generating a total of 8,000 direct jobs (Etzkowitz et al. 2005).

---

[23] FORPROEX – Public Universities Extension Pro-rectors Forum.

4.6   Conclusions

Brazil has arrived at the twenty-first century with a complex productive structure and a reasonable research system, with respect either to the number of master's and PhD graduates or to its share in international scientific publications. These two systems, however, remain quite distant from one another. Companies continue to see themselves as having a limited capacity to absorb and to improve technology and develop innovations.

The use of research infrastructure installed mainly in public universities to raise the technological capabilities of the companies became the larger objective of the recent political changes. The universities are being strongly encouraged to exploit commercially the results of their research, to protect their creations, to patent the technologies developed, and to provide support to the process of entrepreneurship and the generation of companies of technological basis.

In the examination of those initiatives, two issues stand out. On the one hand, there are initiatives that fit into the university environment, but do not focus directly on companies. The contribution of the university continues to be confined to technological training and the innovative performance of the companies.

On the other hand, the economic value of research, and the patenting and licensing policy of the universities, as expressed in the recent Innovation Law, continue to raise concerns in a significant portion of the academic world.

Continuous monitoring and evaluation activities to determine how the universities are implementing these activities would seem to be useful, even indispensable. The Academic Reform Law, still under discussion in the Congress, is designed precisely to address these issues. But outside of graduate studies and research policies in the universities, the same political will is not there in relation to undergraduate teaching – which continues to be characterized by serious shortcomings.

Referencems

Albuquerque, E., Sicsu, J. (2000). "Inovação institucional e estímulo ao investimento privado". São Paulo Perspec. [Online]: vol. 14, no. 3, p. 108–114. Available at http://www.scielo.br/scielo.php in 04/10/06.

Bell, M., Pavitt, K. (1993). "Technological Accumulation and Industrial Growth: Contrasts Between Developed and Developing Countries" Industrial and Corporate Change, vol. 2, no. 2, p. 157–210.

Buarque, C. (2003). "The University at a crossroad". Paper presented at the World Conference on Higher Education + 5 at UNESCO. Paris, 23–25 June.

CAPES (2004b). "Plano Nacional de Pós-Graduação (PNPG) 2005–2010". Brasília: CAPES/MEC.

Carvalho, P. (2006). "O papel da propriedade industrial no estímulo à inovação – a experiência da UNICAMP". Seminário Transferência e Inovação Tecnológica. Curitiba: UFPR, 11/05/2006.

Cavalcante, C. (2005). "Educação e inovação: o papel e o desafio das engenharias na promoção do desenvolvimento industrial, científico e tecnológico". Parcerias Estratégicas, no. 21, Brasília.

CNPq website, www.cnpq.br – in 20-31/01/2006

Etzkowitz, H., Mello, J.M.C., Alemida, M. (2005). "Toward "meta innovation" in Brazil. The evolution of the incubator and the emergence of a triple helix". Research Policy, vol. 34, no. 4, p. 411–424.

Guimarães, R. (1995). "FNDCT: uma nova missão". In: Schwartzman, S. (coord.) "Ciência e Tecnologia no Brasil: Uma Nova Política para um Mundo Global" (II PADCT). Rio de Janeiro: Fundação Getúlio Vargas.

IBGE (2002). "Diretoria de Pesquisas Departamento de Indústria Pesquisa Industrial Inovação Tecnológica 2000". Rio de Janeiro: IBGE.

IBGE (2004). "Pesquisa Nacional de por Amostra de Domicílios 2004". Rio de Janeiro: IBGE.

IBGE (2005). "Diretoria de Pesquisas Coordenação de Indústria Pesquisa Industrial de Inovação Tecnológica 2003" Rio de Janeiro: IBGE.

IBGE (2006). "Cadastro Central de Empresas 2004". Rio de Janeiro: IBGE.

IBGE (2007). "Diretoria de Pesquisas Coordenação de Indústria Pesquisa de Inovação Tecnológica 2005" Rio de Janeiro: IBGE.

IBGE (2008). "Síntese dos Indicadores Sociais". Rio de Janeiro: IBGE.

INEP (2009). "Sinopse da Educação Superior – 2008". Available at: www.inep.gov.br.

IPEADATA (online) http://www.ipeadata.gov.br in 22/11/2006 and 28/03/2008.

Maculan, A.M.D. (1996). "From research to innovation: the Brazilian experience with business incubators". In: Universities and the global knowledge economy: A Triple Helix University-Industry-Government Relations, 1996, Amsterdam. Book of Abstracts. Universities and the global knowledge economy. Amsterdam: University of Amsterdam, vol. 1. p. 80–86.

Maculan, A.M.D. (2005) "Capacitação tecnológica e inovação nas empresas brasileiras: balanço e perspectives". Rio de Janeiro. FGV Cadernos EBAPE. BR. Special edition Management of Innovation Technology in the context of Emerging Economies: The Experience of Companies in Brazil.

MCT (2008). "Brasil": Alunos titulados nos cursos de mestrado e doulorado, 1987–2007.

MEC (2004). Anteprojeto de Lei – versao preliminar dezembro de 2004. Avaialble at: www.portal.mec.gov.br.

Rezende, S. (2005). "Ciência, tecnologia e inovação para o desenvolvimento nacional: o papel do MCT". [s.l.]: Science, Technology and Innovation Conference, Brasília, November 18, 2005.

Viotti, E. (2002). "National learning systems: a new approach on technological change in late industrializing economies and evidences from the cases of Brazil and South Korea". Technological Forecasting & Social Change, n. 69.

Viotti, E., Baessa, A., Koeller, P. (2005). "Perfil da Inovação na Indústria Brasileira – Uma Comparação Internacional". cap. 16 in Salerno, M. and De Negri, João (eds.), "Inovação, padrões tecnológicos e desempenho das firmas industriais brasileiras", Brasília, IPEA, 2005, p. 653–687.

Viotti (2006). "O crescimento da produção científica brasileira". Brasília: (mimeo).

Chapter 5
Uruguay: Higher Education, National System of Innovation, and Economic Development in a Small Peripheral Country

Rodrigo Arocena and Judith Sutz

5.1   Introduction

This chapter aims at describing some main relations between knowledge and development in Uruguay. Section 5.1 summarizes the historical evolution and actual situation of the small peripheral country with comparatively high levels of Human Development. Section 5.2 focuses specifically on the Uruguayan National System of Innovation (NSI); organizes the empirical elements in a theoretical approach to the study of Systems of Innovation (SIs) by means of "constructive modules"; and discusses some of such modules. Section 5.3 offers a preliminary mapping of the Uruguayan Academic System, discussing the modules of the Uruguayan NSI related to it; particular attention is paid to the University of the Republic (UR), by far the most important institution of Higher Education in the country. Section 5.4 describes the current debate in Uruguay about Higher Education and its external relations. Section 5.5 sketches main issues for future research, connected with the notion of Developmental University.

5.2   The Uruguayan Context

Uruguay is a small South American country, with a surface of 176,000 km^2 and a population slightly over 3.3 million inhabitants. As discussed in the following, it is also quite atypical in the Latin American context. Its insertion in the "center–periphery" system, as an exporter of primary products and importer of industrialized goods during the so-called outward growth period (circa 1850–1930), was early and quite successful. The country has been well placed in the "commodity lottery" (Bulmer-Thomas 1994: 15): its main exports are based on cattle raising, and such products have quite significant linkages – stimulating industry and

R. Arocena (✉)
Universidad de la República, Montevideo, Uruguay
e-mail: roar@fcien.edu.uy

B. Göransson and C. Brundenius (eds.), *Universities in Transition:*
The Changing Role and Challenges for Academic Institutions,
© International Development Research Centre 2011

urbanization – as well as relatively high international income elasticity of demand. These factors help to explain why Argentina and also Uruguay around 1900 were comparatively rich and growing quickly.

By that time, the Uruguayan population was almost a million, having grown from around 150,000 in 1850. A strong immigration from Europe was taking place. The integration of immigrants was facilitated by the early extension of public, free, compulsory, and secular elementary education. Illiteracy diminished quickly. After 1900 public secondary education was fostered, not only in Montevideo – the capital city, the main port, and the economic, political, and cultural center, where more than 40% of the population lives even today – but also in the rest of the country. Tertiary public education also grew significantly, but it was and still is essentially concentrated in Montevideo. Uruguay has traditionally been proud of its educational system, in spite of several flaws, some of them stemming from the low social and cultural valuation of manual work and technical activities.

Nevertheless, a century ago the country was ready for success. Immigration was fostering some degree of technical progress and an early industrialization. The introduction of well-known techniques for cattle raising and innovations related to the transport of frozen meat led to an export boom. Peace in rural areas became essential for business: the long history of civil wars came to an end. Urbanization advanced quickly, as well as public services, light industries, and mass politics. A liberal democracy emerged. Immigrants brought not only technical know-how but also trade unionism. Even if mainly concentrated in Montevideo, a quite "modern" set of social relations emerged, including a remarkable Keynesian social democracy *avant la lettre*.

When external income diminished abruptly in the 1930s, an important social and political turn took place, and the government became dictatorial for the first time in the century. At that time, Latin America was starting a new stage in its economic history, an inward-led growth period based on the import-substituting industrialization (ISI). In Uruguay, that type of growth already had a quite strong base. It acquired momentum in the 1940s, when the "commodity lottery" was becoming favorable once more, as it stayed up to the second half of the 1950s, mainly due to the external demand connected with the Second World War and the Korean War. Another reformist wave greatly expanded the state-owned productive sector and the Social Security System. Around 1950, Uruguay saw itself and was seen from abroad as a "model country": quite prosperous, pacific, and far less unequal than the Latin American average. Greatly idealized, that "model country" of yesterday is still highly influential today in the Uruguayan "collective imaginary."

The political history of Uruguay in the twentieth century can be divided in two periods of roughly 50 years each (Filgueira et al, 2003): the first one is characterized by the systematic expansion of the social and economic role of the state and the second one by a conflictive and contradictory process of decreasing state intervention. This second process was fostered by the limits to an inward industrialization in a small country, the lack of technical progress in Uruguayan agrarian production and the decreasing international prices for primary products. After 1960, Uruguay changed from a country of immigration to an emigration country while social unrest and repressive policies escalated. Step by step, a dictatorial government was built, culminating with the dissolution of Parliament in 1973; for more than 10 years, Uruguay lived under a military regime, by then a common situation in the South of Latin America. With the great debt crisis of the early 1980s, production fell abruptly and people below the line of poverty increased to 46%, an almost incredible figure in the Uruguayan context. Social opposition to the military increased; almost all the political spectrum demanded the end of the dictatorship; a difficult transition took place; and on March 1985, a democratically elected government took office.

It can be said that in the following 20 years, the main problem was how to combine a restoration of the welfare state – strongly demanded by the majority of the population – with the search of new sources of economic growth. That combination showed some possibilities, at least up to the late 1990s.[1] In the decade following 1985, poverty and inequality diminished. By 1995, Chile was the success story of South America in economic terms and of Uruguay in social terms. Uruguayan governments tried to implement a somehow weakened version of the Washington Consensus policies, which faced strong social and political resistance. The economic situation changed in the late 1990s. For Latin America as a whole, Economic Commission for Latin America and the Caribbean (ECLAC) asserted that 1998–2002 was a lost half decade. The crisis accelerated a political change already underway. A broad left wing coalition, the Frente Amplio – the Wide Front – became increasingly identified with the Welfare State tradition. In 2005, for the first time in history, a left wing government took office in Uruguay.

By then economic recovery was being fuelled by international trends, particularly the rising prices of commodities. Economic growth in Uruguay amounted to almost 40% of GDP in 2004–2008, quite a different situation than before the crisis of 1998–2002. During the last decades of the twentieth century, growth was slow in Uruguay. It averaged 0.9% in 1960–1998 in Uruguay and approximately 2% in USA, so "between 1960 and 1998 Uruguay's per capita income fell from 28.3% of the US average to 19.0%. [...] roughly speaking long run per capita growth has averaged about one percent which implies that the country has been growing less than the technological frontier over a long period of time." (Hausman et al. 2004: 7).

To discuss if the long-term pattern is being changed, the often overlooked distinction between economic growth and economic development must be recalled. In his "Theory of Economic Development," originally written in 1911, Schumpeter made the distinction between the mere growth of the economy, that reflects material and demographic growth, and [economic] development, that only exists when new combinations of productive means take place (Schumpeter 1957: 74–76). Such new combinations, or innovations, increase the knowledge content and the value added in the production of goods and services; this is the core of economic development. A related and fundamental assertion is that "As has been repeatedly observed over the last few centuries, the common problem faced by all catch-up economies is that the shift to higher value-added activities, which constitutes the key to the process of economic development, does not happen 'naturally'" (Chang 2002: 126).

---

[1] Concerning different aspects of the period 1985–2005, a good reference is the collective volume Caetano (2005).

Economic growth has been slow in Uruguay because investment has been low and because economic development has been very weak. Bértola and Bittencourt (2005) characterize the period starting in 1985 as "twenty years of democracy without economic development." After that, growth accelerated and investment rose significantly, while unemployment and poverty diminished. Up to now (September 2009), Uruguay is far from being one of the countries suffering most due to the global crisis. New support has been given to social and educational policies. The fundamental question is if, in the ups and downs of international indicators, Uruguay will be able to make a gradual turn toward a more knowledge-based and innovation-driven economy.

Here such a question is considered from the point of view of the potential contributions of universities to development. Now, universities can neither deploy their potentialities, nor transform themselves in isolation. What they can do depends both on their internal structure and on the world outside them. Their impact as providers of knowledge and knowledgeable people is highly dependent on the way the society as a whole interacts with knowledge. Consequently, "the role of higher education needs to be assessed in the wider context of the national innovation system and [...] higher education policy needs to be coordinated with a wider set of innovation policies" (Lundvall 2007). This is why we shall present some main characteristics of the Uruguayan SI, as a way to have a broader picture of the landscape in which the Uruguayan Higher Education system lives and evolves.

5.3 The Uruguayan National System of Innovation: A Characterization by Constructive Modules

Any useful characterization of an NSI needs to fulfill three requisites: first, to allow national specificity to be taken accurately into account; second, to allow meaningful comparisons with other NSI; and third, to be able to give account of the system's evolution. A methodological procedure to achieve this is to construct a "picture" of NSI by means of constructive modules, each of which helps to understand a key factor or situation; the combination of the different modules approaches the variety of the NSI (Arocena and Sutz 2000). The assessment of the linkages between the different modules completes the construction of the picture by showing to what extent we have an integrated picture or a set of more or less isolated parts. National specificity is reflected in the choice of the constructive modules; international comparisons can be built "bottom-up," from comparisons between the constructive modules that are considered in different characterizations. The evolution of the system, which is quite difficult to analyze as a whole, can be better explored by looking at the evolution of each of the modules.

Eight constructive modules were selected for the Uruguayan case as sketched in Fig. 5.1: five of them will be briefly discussed in this section and the other three, more directly related to the academic system, in the next one.

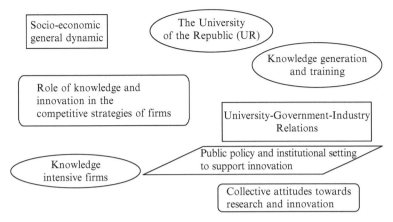

Fig. 5.1 Constructive modules to characterize the Uruguayan NSI

5.3.1 Socioeconomic General Dynamic

Three of the most salient characteristics of the recent Uruguayan socioeconomic dynamic have been (1) the low levels of productive investment, a figure that has been below 15% of GDP for the last decades; (2) little foreign direct investment (FDI); and (3) an export structure mainly based on the good endowment of natural resources with relatively low value added. The first two characteristics have been noticeably changing in the last 5 years: productive investment has rose to around 20% of GDP and FDI is growing rapidly, mainly around the forestry complex, given the big current investment on cellulose mills. The third characteristic is changing too, but at a slower pace.

The new government, mentioned at the end of the former section, introduced some significant changes regarding the socioeconomic general dynamic. The market fundamentalism of former administrations has been tempered; the need for some type of active policies to build a "productive country" has been recognized and put in place. An active industrial policy is fostering productive chains, the formation of industrial clusters, and other measures aimed at opening room for better industrial performance, particularly of the SMEs, which are more than 95% of all industrial firms and represent 25% of all industrial employment.

The good conjuncture in terms of international prices for commodities, in some of which – like meat and diary products – Uruguay excels, can be an opportunity to support a long-term investment in knowledge and innovation policies. If this is achieved, the universities will receive a stronger demand than ever, given the wide opportunities to apply new knowledge and to develop new technologies to add value to the traditional productive sectors and, even, to develop independent new industrial sectors.

5.3.2 Role of Knowledge and Innovation in the Competitive Strategies of Industrial Firms

An "aerial" view of this issue can be approximated by innovation surveys. The last industrial innovation survey, covering the period 2004–2006 (ANII 2008), indicates that 28% of all firms with more than five employees declare having undertaken at least one "innovation activity." The most popular by far of these innovation activities is the acquisition of capital goods, performed by almost 60% of firms; 22% of firms declare performing internal R&D.

To approximate the importance of knowledge in the competitive strategies of firms, two indicators can be especially important: the knowledgeable people employed by the firms, and the intensity of the links with diverse type of knowledge providers in the NSI that firms have. The first indicator shows a very difficult situation for the small firms, where more than 80% of firms (innovative and non-innovative alike) do not have a single professional with scientific or technical background. This proportions drops with the increasing size of the firms, with around 60% of medium firms without such knowledgeable professionals and slightly over 10% of the biggest firms in that situation. Given the quantitative importance of small firms in the Uruguayan industrial fabric, this is a worrisome situation. These figures correspond to the latest innovation survey, 2004–2006. Table 5.1 shows that this situation of structural knowledge weakness comes from long ago, suggesting that only strong and creative public policies could eventually lead to a positive change.

This situation reflects and partially explains the weakness of the knowledge demand from business firms: very few researchers work there. This leads to a mismatch between the capacities developed by young people and the opportunities they have to apply such capacities to productive endeavors, a worrisome trend leading to brain drain, heavily present in Uruguay.[2]

Table 5.1 Proportion of firms without university-trained technical staff, 1986 and 2003

1986 Innovation survey	>100 employees	51–100 employees	20–50 employees
% of business firms without engineers	21.9	50.3	73.8
% of business firms without computer analysts or programers	47.2	66.1	81.9
2003 Innovation survey	>100 employees	20–100 employees	<20 employees
% of business firms without engineers and other university graduates in science or technology careers	22.5	63.2	87.4

Source: Argenti et al. (1988) and Bianchi and Gras (2006). It must be taken into account that the last survey included the smallest firms, under 20 employees

[2]Connections between brain drain and Innovation Systems in the South are discussed in Arocena and Sutz (2006).

The linkages with the NSI are weak in relation to R&D activities but are relatively widespread concerning information gathering: around 20% of all innovative firms established linkages around R&D while three quarters did so for information purposes. Expectedly, suppliers and clients are the most required agents of the NSIs; the less required ones are the classical knowledge providers, such as universities, technical laboratories, technical training institutions, and R&D agencies.

It seems clear that knowledge demand in the Uruguayan industry has been and continues to be structurally weak. This is not a specific trend for Uruguay, as the following quotation demonstrates: "The Latin American and Caribbean production pattern on the one hand, induces private sector and enterprises to express a meager demand for knowledge, and on the other hand, leads domestic agents to mostly seek outward oriented linkages, privileging foreign companies and research laboratories that already have sound reputation and worldwide recognized experience in effective and efficient S&T efforts. Thus a mismatch ensues between demand side needs and supply side offerings, hampering policies' impact" (Cimoli et al. 2009: 43).

However, there are several truly innovative firms in the country that use knowledge as a productive force and strengthen their cognitive base by hiring and training highly qualified personnel. To what extent they can become a key vector of innovation for the whole economy depends on the strengths of the backward and forward linkages (Hirschman 1958) throughout the economy and society at large. We turn briefly to such firms next.

5.3.3   Knowledge Intensive Firms

A case study of the Uruguayan professional electronic industry (Snoeck et al. 1992) showed the role played by high-tech firms in the export capacity of the country: main private clients of the electronic industry were big exporters that needed ad hoc solutions to improve their competitiveness or to fulfill external requirements. Other example of this type relates to the meat industry, where locally designed biotechnological vaccines were able to fight efficiently against cattle diseases that hampered exports, such as the foot and mouth disease. That is, even if electronic or biotech firms are quite weak exporters themselves, they greatly contribute to exports in an indirect way. In more general terms, this can be seen in Table 5.2, where the exports of a sample of firms that include knowledge users and knowledge producers are depicted: more than 90% of all exports were done by the user firms. The big exception is the software industry, which exports fairly well; it is worth noticing the contribution of the biotechnology firms to the exports of their users firms.

It is interesting to note that for establishing linkages with knowledge providers firms, it seems that qualified personnel are needed: the proportion of qualified personnel of the knowledge-users firms was 15% in 2002, a much higher figure than the one for the general industry, around 3.5% at that time. This points to the key contribution, from the supply side, made by research universities to the absorptive capacities of firms.

Table 5.2 Exports by knowledge-based firms and by their clients, 2000 (%)

	Knowledge producers (knowledge-based firms)	Knowledge users (clients of knowledge-based firms)
Software	82.1	2.5
Biotechnology	6.1	43.2
Entrepreneurial engineering services	–	37.8
Environment	0.6	16.4
Pharmaceutical	11.2	–
Total exports by category	100	100
% of total exports in the sample	*8.5*	*91.5*

Source: Based on Pittaluga et al. (2005: 213)

5.3.4   Public Policy and Institutional Setting to Support Innovation

It is a shared understanding that public policies devoted to support innovation have been historically weak in Uruguay. First of all, the level of investment in R&D has been particularly weak, always below 0.3% of GDP. Besides this, some important policy instruments have also been weak or nonexisting, such as technological and industrial extensionism, government technology procurement, or the systematic elaboration of statistics and studies on science, technology, and innovation to better inform policy design. On the contrary, some canonical instruments, such as subsidies to firms for innovative activities coming from international loans, have usually been underused, mainly as a result of complicated application mechanisms.

Strong specialized centers of technology to support productive sectors have existed until now only in the agrarian sector, but new institutions related to software with encouraging prospects are emerging, and other institutions, such as technological incubators, have been put in place recently.

The current situation has greatly improved in terms of investment in science and technology (S&T). Even if not reflected in the proportion of the investment on R&D in the country's GDP, because of the great expansion of the latter, the number of different kinds of instruments as well as the amount of money devoted to fostering the knowledge production, particularly the academic knowledge production, is noticeable. In institutional terms, the most salient evidence of the renewed importance of the subject is the creation of an Innovation Ministerial Cabinet, integrated by the Ministries of Finance, Industry, Husbandry, Education, and Planning and the creation of a specific Agency of Research and Innovation to manage the resources devoted to the S&T policy. New important scientific institutions have been created, like the Uruguayan branch of the French Institut Pasteur, and important investments have been made in other academic and applied research organizations.

Regarding innovation, even if more money has been made available for competitive projects, the structural problem of weak innovative behavior and weak demand for knowledge has not yet been fully grasped.

5.3.5 Collective Attitudes Toward Research and Innovation

NSI and innovations develop in a cultural milieu. What people think about S&T sets the state where different innovative efforts take place. Several key attitudes can be traced back to public perception of S&T. The willingness of the youth to choose scientific and technical careers, how businessmen evaluate hiring highly competent personnel, and the drive of young professionals toward starting their own knowledge-based firms are a few examples of such attitudes.

These issues were studied in Uruguay in 1996 and again in 2003 (Arocena 2003). For instance, people were asked to choose between three "policy alternatives": (1) Uruguay can and must do research with public funds, because benefits will be greater than costs; (2) Uruguay can do successful research but should not do it, because costs will be greater that benefits; and (3) Uruguay cannot do successful research. In 1996, 55% of the population chose the first alternative; in 2003, during the most severe economic crisis in 2 years, 51% of the population still chose the first alternative. This implies that a fair proportion of the population truly sees research as a tool for national development that deserves public support. This result is in tune with the wide expectations that people put in the UR, the institution where research activities are concentrated (Bortagaray 2006).

In a new survey made in 2008, 80% of the population choose the option "Uruguay can do scientific research," 6% choose the option "Uruguay can do scientific research but it is not worth it," and 4% choose the option "In Uruguay it is not possible to do scientific research," with no answers of 10% (Bortagaray 2009). Interestingly enough, the average number of 80% of those who believe that Uruguay can do scientific research is not greatly skewed between the less and more educated part of the population: such answer reached 71% among people with primary school and 91% among people with university level (Bortagaray 2009). This spread conviction adds legitimacy to R&D policies.

5.4 Mapping the Academic System in Uruguay: An Overview

5.4.1 The University of the Republic

The only public university of Uruguay, the UR, is by far the most important Academic Institution in the country. The UR is a typical product of the Latin American Reform Movement which created a specific type of university in Latin America, with a strong but atypical influence in society (Arocena and Sutz 2005a). The autonomy of the university was conquered after long fights; the law passed in 1958, the "organic university law," consecrated as well the cogovernance of students, teachers, and graduates.

There exist some other tertiary institutes, including four private universities, the oldest of which is only 25 years old; their contribution to teaching and research is small but has been increasing. The UR has more than 80,000 students, above 80% of total tertiary enrollment.

In 1996 – when the last general Population Census took place – less than 9% of people above the age of 24 years had some type of tertiary education, while those who had completed some type of university studies were less than 5% (Boado 2005).

Concerning the preferences for knowledge areas among the new students of UR, the most striking figure is the low preference for agrarian studies, 3.5%, the same figure as that for arts; social sciences and humanities account for almost 45%, while S&T is chosen by slightly less than 20% and health (including Psychology) by around 30%. An important proportion of UR students work or need to work: 55% are employed and 21% are unemployed; around 33% work more than 30 h per week.

In UR, at an undergraduate level, gender is not really an issue: in recent years, female enrollment was almost 63% of total enrollment. However, the proportion of women in high academic positions is not so even: their participation in a special full-time regime designed to foster research activities is 40%. Additionally, the highest positions in an incentive scheme for researchers, the National System of Researchers, put in place in 2008, show an extremely skewed structure: more than 80% of men in the top level.

5.4.2 *Knowledge Generation and Training*

Uruguay exhibits a very concentrated structure of knowledge generation and training. As already pointed out, more than 80% of tertiary enrollment corresponds to the UR. Concerning researchers belonging to the recently organized National System of Researchers, almost 80% of them work in the UR, and 93% in the public sector.

Some main characteristics of the Uruguayan knowledge system have changed significantly in the last 20 years. In 1986, only 13% of all researchers had post-graduate studies and there were no national master or PhD programs (Argenti et al. 1988). Local postgraduate programs began to develop since the late 1980s, especially in basic sciences; diverse schemes of fellowships allowed unprecedented levels of people to study abroad. Some years ago, 80% of all the research groups in UR had already at least one member with either a master's or a PhD degree or following postgraduate studies (Unidad Académica de CSIC 2003).

The following figure shows the evolution of the UR research groups' formation in Uruguay; the positive effect of the democratic recovery since 1985 is clearly seen, as well as the early 1990s boost, due in part to the massive repatriation of researchers, to a very successful national program to foster the development of basic sciences, and to the creation of two new schools at UR: the Faculty of Social Sciences and the Faculty of Natural Sciences (Fig. 5.2).

Table 5.3 gives a comparative idea of the Uruguayan R&D situation in the international arena; it includes only small and medium countries.

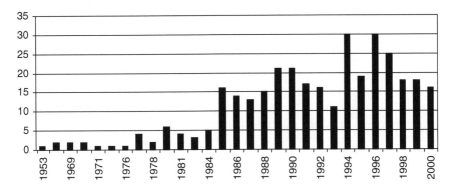

Fig. 5.2 Creation of research groups at UR. *Source*: Unidad Académica de CSIC (2003)

Table 5.3 Some indicators of research in selected countries

	Researchers in R&D/ million inhabitants (1)	GERD/GDP (2)	GERD U$S per capita PPP (3)
Argentina	720 (2003)	0.49 (2006)	59.2 (2006)
Bolivia	120 (2002)	0.28 (2002)	9.0 (2002)
Chile	444 (2003)	0.67 (2004)	76.5 (2004)
Costa Rica	81	0.37 (2004)	30.3 (2004)
Paraguay	79 (2002)	0.09 (2005)	3.4 (2005)
Uruguay	*366* (2002)	*0.26* (2002)	*18.4* (2002)
New Zealand	3.945 (2003)	1.17 (2005)	290.3 (2005)
Denmark	5.016 (2004)	2.44 (2006)	870.6 (2006)
Sweden	5.415 (2004)	3.82 (2006)	1,307.2 (2006)
Finland	7.832 (2004)	3.43 (2006)	1,134.1 (2006)
Netherlands	2.481 (2004)	1.69 (2006)	615.6 (2006)
Ireland	2.674 (2004)	1.31 (2006)	535.0 (2006)
Belgium	3.065 (2004)	1.85 (2006)	625.7 (2006)

Source for columns (2) and (3): UNESCO statistics, last consultation 09/2009. http://stats.uis. unesco.org/unesco/tableviewer/document.aspx?FileId=76. Source for column (1) World Development Indicators Data Base

5.4.3 University–Government–Industry Relations

The relations between the UR and the national government have been historically conflictive. These conflicts were usually connected to the university budget, always extremely tight, but they had a broader political nature. During the social struggles of the 1960s, the UR strongly opposed the authoritarian trends that led the way to the military dictatorship. The university was heavily attacked during that time, a process that reached its climax with its military intervention in 1973, which lasted until the end of the dictatorial rule; it caused massive faculty firings, as well as exile for many professors. After 1985, the situation changed for the better, in a mix of cooperative and conflictive relations with the new democratic governments. The government that took office in 2005 promoted important changes in policies for health, education, and research; those changes generated not only new possibilities for cooperation with the UR but also some disagreements. Nevertheless, nowadays UR cooperates with almost all important organizations of the public sector. That cooperation is particularly close in the realm of social policies fostered by the new Ministry for Social Development. Programs for research and innovation are being implemented by the UR and big public enterprises. Summing up, since 2005, cooperation expanded qualitatively and quantitatively.

Even if in general terms the university–productive sectors relationships are not particularly strong, there are important examples of very successful interactions showing excellent results, in almost all fields of knowledge and in several sectors, including bioengineering, wool production, veterinarian vaccines, pharmaceutical products, industrial automation, and environment.

From an institutional point of view, the UR has put in place many changes to favor stronger and more fluid relationships with production. Formal contractual arrangements between research groups and firms are allowed; researchers can get an increase in their salary for participating in such arrangements; a special commission has been created to deal with problems related to Intellectual Property Rights (IPR) in joint projects with industry; firms can be incubated in faculty laboratories; and some faculties have created special offices to encourage and facilitate the links between research teams and business firms. All this shows that what was left from the old academic antagonism toward involvement with business firms has been weakening at institutional level. Changes in ideological perceptions are partly responsible for such evolution; surely part of the explanation also relates to the growing financial difficulties that push research groups toward industry to be able to go on with their work and to keep their most talented researchers. It must also be stressed that in academic circles, an increasing attention is being paid to substantive problems of productive sectors.

Summing up, university–industry relations are stronger than in the past, institutional innovations were put in place to facilitate these relations, researchers are generally willing to participate in research commanded by business firms, and the ideological suspicions that these practices used to give rise to, have been eroded and even substituted, in some discourses, by an enthusiastic praise. However, the relations between university and industry continue to be weak: the university change of mood has not been accompanied up to now by a major productive twist, making industry more eager to rely on the university expertise. The last should not be seen as a minor issue: in fact, weak market demand for endogenously generated knowledge is a structural feature of underdevelopment. Only very specific and long-term policies can help to overcome such problem.

5.5 The Current Debate

Key questions driving public debate concerning the higher education system include the following issues:

(1) Levels of public investment, low salaries, and different sources of financial resources, including cost sharing, tuition, and fees;
(2) Quality assessment of teaching and learning;
(3) Access and success in higher education, related social and regional inequalities;
(4) Relations between public and private institutions;
(5) The social use of knowledge and the orientation of the research agendas; and
(6) New challenges regarding the role universities should play in society and how they should be inserted in the NSI.

5.5.1 Investment, Salaries, Free Access

Educational investment in Uruguay in relation with GDP has been comparatively quite low in recent times. On average, public spending in education has been around 3% of GDP and 0.6% in higher education. When it took office, the present government asserted that it would increase that spending up to 4.5% of GDP by the year 2009: this has been highly demanded within the leftist political coalition now in power. At this moment, it can be said that public spending in education is above 4% of GDP.

Salaries in higher education have been usually considered low if compared internationally and even regionally; they even compete badly with those offered to the technical staff by public enterprises and some other public institutions devoted to R&D or technical services. Nevertheless, salaries in UR rose 50% in real terms from 2004 to 2008.

Public education is free of charge in Uruguay, including the tertiary level. This issue has been much discussed. Some years ago, the Parliament passed a law that authorizes the UR to establish tuition fees, but the University decided not to do it. The General Law of Education passed in 2008 establishes that public tertiary education must be free of charge. Tuition is seen by a majority of university authorities, and particularly by the organizations of students and teachers, as something that harms educational rights and that would diminish the access to higher education, thus weakening the knowledge potential of the country, besides increasing inequality. Those who back tuitions say that they should exist (but be paid only by those who can afford it), to avoid the regressive distributional effect of having the whole population supporting the UR through taxes and at the same time the majority of students belonging to the middle and upper classes. Now, as already pointed out, 76% of UR students work or need to work. So charging tuitions would be complicated and give little amount of money and/or push out many students. The so-called Solidarity Fund charges graduates from public tertiary education with a fixed annual tax after 5 years of graduation. The money is spent mainly in fellowships for students with low income. The system has a quite positive impact. Critics stress that the contribution is almost not related with incomes, that is, graduates hardly earning their living pay as much as professionals with handsome revenues coming for their practice. If this system were to be bettered by making contributions proportional to earnings related to professional activities, it would be fairer and more efficient than tuitions.

Discussions about merits and flaws of free public higher education are connected with international migrations. Should foreign students benefit from such system? Students coming from Chile, where access to higher education is neither free nor easy, were accepted for many years in the same terms as the Uruguayan students, a norm that is being contested nowadays. Those who disagree remember that many Uruguayans now working in Uruguay – including a large number of researchers – have been able to study without charge in many countries, including Mexico, Venezuela, Brazil, Sweden, and others, particularly when they were not able to do it in Uruguay during the military government.

Not less relevant is the "converse problem" stemming from accelerating brain drain. Many capable graduates and postgraduates trained for free at the UR migrate, particularly to USA. In some sense, a small and comparatively poor country is subsidizing a very rich and powerful one. Is that a good use for scarce public monies? Addressing the problem is not easy.

The context of many of those problems has been changing with the expansion of private tertiary education, a comparatively new and slowly evolving phenomenon in Uruguay. Its regulatory framework is still weak. A law is being proposed in order to create an agency for assessing the quality of tertiary education.

Tuitions are only one aspect of the general debate around free access. In Uruguay, every person who has completed secondary education may enter the university to follow the path of his/her choice: very few careers limit the number of students or have admission examinations. Both types of requisites existed when the UR was governed by authorities appointed by the military government. The elimination of such requisites was an important claim of the democratization movement. It was immediately implemented when the autonomic governance of the University was restored. Nevertheless, some important political leaders and influential media demand limitations or admission examinations. On the opposite side, the UR and also public authorities related with education foster changes aiming to the generalization of lifelong advanced learning. Given that no more than 40% of young people finish secondary studies nowadays, such a goal requires important and lasting efforts and reforms.

5.5.1.1   The Social Use of Knowledge and the Orientation of the Research Agendas

To put in context the debate concerning the roles of universities, it must be recalled that the research university in Uruguay suffers from what can be called a "loneliness syndrome" (Arocena and Sutz 2001): the lack of social demand for endogenously generated knowledge leaves to a great extent the academic realm on its own. Voices can be heard claiming for "useful research," but the real demand is weak. This is one side of the coin: the other one is what researchers perceive as their real duty, that is, the products they have to deliver in exchange for being paid by the tax payers' money. This in turn has to do with the academic reward system, where publishing in international refereed papers is considered the hallmark of academic soundness. This is being challenged now: the debate around the specificities of the academic production in different disciplines and the need to provide diverse ways of measuring quality and productivity is producing changes. The thorny issue of "relevance" continues to be an important part of the discussions, adding a crucial dimension to the debate.

The loneliness syndrome and the current academic reward system shape a sort of schizophrenic situation: research should be useful for different stakeholders who however do not demand its results; according to this point, research should be rewarded by its relevance, but the academic system puts too high a prize in results measured in international rather than in national terms.

The debate around these issues has different axes: more emphasis in long-term or short-term research? Which is the right balance between the academic freedom to pursue knowledge and the duty to be responsive to pressing national problems? Should university research be oriented according to some priorities? If yes, at what level should a scheme of priorities be elaborated? Inside the UR, the debate is vivid but not fierce: nobody denies the key role played by research in basic sciences; nobody denies, either, that the humanities form integral part of what the university is and what it has to offer to society. The debate is more in terms of how to allocate scarce resources to research: some claim that funds should go to fields of knowledge where a direct contribution to national problems can be made, while others claim that the balance in terms of support for all types of knowledge should be maintained.

In a survey among researchers enjoying a competitive scheme of salary compensation for their full-time dedication to the university, conducted in 2006 around what should the priorities be for a National Strategic Plan on Science, Technology, and Innovation, some interesting things came out (Academic Unit, CSIC 2006). For instance, the willingness of researchers to devote their efforts to concrete problems of Uruguayan development was clearly stated. At the same time, researchers declared that for solutions to be implemented, the problems should not be invented by the researchers themselves: the problems need to be detected and communicated by a specialized body. Only in that way would problems related to development be able to influence the research agenda. On the contrary, some researchers feared that the setting of national priorities through the National Strategic Plan could give too much influence to those with voice and power, for instance, the few powerful agrarian sectors with high exports, narrowing the opportunities and support for addressing the problems of small producers. In more general terms, the main challenge to foster the concrete application of research results, as indicated by the researchers, was a better articulation and a better communication between university, production, and society. This is a different wording for what has been already said: the need to understand the work of universities in the wider context of the NSI.

Since then, several policy instruments have been put in place with the aim of achieving a better tuning between research agendas and societal and productive problems. We shall here mention only one of them: a small form that provides information for some hundreds of researchers about their field of research and for whom they believe that their research results might be of use. The forms that have been widely distributed among productive organizations, from industry, agriculture, and services, will be regularly updated and expanded.

5.5.1.2   New Challenges for the University and Insertion in the National System of Innovation

The higher education system in Uruguay and particularly the UR faces important challenges. Few students enter the system, less than 30%, while the average for the OECD countries is well above 50%; few students come from the countryside, where the university facilities are scarce and incomplete; and few students come from the by now wide part of the population that live in poverty or slightly over it. These are huge challenges that redefine the role of the university today: to foster social integration in the context of the learning economy. The challenge is huge because integration should be pursued among students who exhibit high disparities in terms of knowledge backgrounds and social capital: nothing less than inventing new teaching approaches and mobilizing diverse forms of solidarity within the university will do the job. Part of the challenge is fairly consensual, for instance, the need to transform the university into a more inclusive institution. Other parts of the challenge, though, are not so consensual, for instance, the need to have much more university students and university graduates. The latter relates directly to the enhancement of the NSI: only if the actual demand for knowledge grows, will the need to strengthen research and to have more university students be widely understood and supported.

It is worth mentioning two other challenges related to knowledge production and diffusion. One is to foster research on pressing social problems. Another challenge is to relate more deeply the historical third mission of the university, extension, with knowledge. It requires bringing knowledge closer to the people. This can only have sustainable social impact if it forms part of a wide transformation of the NSI. Such transformation should aim to relate knowledge directly with development concerns, particularly with social inclusion.

Finally, a big challenge for the university will be to find ways to foster and participate in a wide national debate on Science, Technology and Innovation policy.

This will help building the necessary consensus for a long-term knowledge commitment, a must to facilitate the university transformation and to allow the NSI to become much more integrated and strong.

5.6   Conclusions: New Development and Developmental Universities

Our major concern is underdevelopment, a main source of many of the most acute problems in the world today and the most relevant aspect of inequality. Underdevelopment is a dynamic phenomenon that combines continuity and changes. Some of the most important changes are related to the new role of knowledge in the economic realm and in society at large. Such an increasing role of knowledge creates new divides – the "learning divides" – that widen inequality between geographic regions and between social groups. The learning divide between North and South stems from the fact that, generally speaking, underdeveloped countries are weak in advanced capabilities – which are mainly obtained by learning at high-level institutions – as well as in opportunities for using such capabilities in knowledge-demanding contexts, thus learning by using, solving, and interacting.

So in the context of the global but very asymmetric knowledge economy, a new development is needed. For addressing the issue of capabilities and opportunities, in such a way that the quality of life is improved, a new development must include two main aspects:

(a) *Socially led innovation and productive upgrading*, the expansion of knowledge and innovation capabilities in every productive activity (including the so-called traditional sectors, in order to improve competitiveness), particularly those related to the attention of social needs.
(b) *Advancing toward a learning society*, based on the generalization of lifelong higher education, closely connected with the world of work (necessary in particular to "recover" those who have abandoned education).

Both are needed to diminish inequality by expanding individual and collective capabilities so inequality can be further diminished in the future, that is, proactive equality: equality that generates more equality (Arocena and Sutz 2003).

This perspective highlights the role of higher education in development processes; it is clearly connected with discussions about the "third role" of universities, and it leads naturally to the notion of developmental university.

The *developmental university* can be briefly defined by commitment to development as its third role. "Now, a more precise characterization can be proposed. [...] the Humboldtian project is not exactly defined by the adoption of research as a second role of universities, but by the joint practice of the fundamental missions of teaching and research. As suggested by [empirical evidence...], performing those missions is essential for the contribution of universities to innovative activities.

The conceptual reference is an actors-centered approach to development, directly connected with the Innovation Systems framework. Thus, the developmental university is characterized, in a neo Humboldtian perspective, by the joint practice of three missions: teaching, research and cooperation for development with other institutions and collective actors. That means that developmental universities can only exist as active partners in Innovation Systems" (Arocena and Sutz 2005b).

In order to know if this notion can be useful for research as well as for policy making, several issues must be explored. Some questions related to them are briefly sketched here.

5.6.1 Possibilities for Studying at an Advanced Level in Qualified Teaching Contexts

(1) How universities cooperate with other organisms to set a wide and diversified system of tertiary education that offers lifelong learning possibilities to the majority of the population?
(2) What efforts are being made, at practical and theoretical levels, to cope with the fundamental challenge, posed by lifelong education, of offering advanced education to people of different ages and backgrounds?
(3) To what extent tertiary education employs the human and material resources available in the best sites of socially useful production?

5.6.2 Evolution of the Humboldtian Project

(1) Which are the old and new ways of connecting teaching and research? Today it is even truer than when the Berlin University was created that such connection is beneficial for both activities.
(2) Which are the ways of connecting studying with problem solving? This is a key issue for preparing creative people, able to cope with the quickly changing problems and opportunities raised by the knowledge economy.

5.6.3 Academic Cooperation with Solving Social and Productive Problems

(1) What is the actual participation of academic groups in the solution of specific problems of productive sectors and those derived from the social situation?
(2) What is the priority given to such problems in research agendas?
(3) To what extent and how do universities and related institutions help students and graduates to get acquainted with said problems, and foster their participation in the search of solutions?

(4) In particular, how do they cooperate with external actors in expanding capabilities by means of new opportunities for using advanced knowledge?

5.6.4 The Evaluation System

(1) Given that the academic reward system is one of the main factors that shape actual research agendas, it deserves special attention in order to gauge priorities and possibilities of academic institutions.
(2) Does such system promote a high quality research with a broad scope?
(3) Does it foster paying attention to relevant cultural and scientific problems, pressing social needs, and economic development?
(4) Which types of external relations does it promote?

Several issues, including the above-mentioned ones, need to be studied in a comparative way in order to assess if the notion of Developmental University is useful, from an empirical point of view what is really happening today? – from a prospective point of view – which are the main possible futures? – and from a policy oriented point of view – what should be done?[3] As a working conjecture we assume that the notion of Developmental University is useful in relation to the third question, quite probably concerning the second one, and perhaps also for giving partial answers to the first.

References

Agencia Nacional de Investigación e Innovación (ANII) (2008): *III Encuesta de Actividades de Inovación en la Industria Uruguaya (2004–2006)*, Montevideo.

Argenti, G., Filgueira, C. and Sutz, J. (1988): *Ciencia y Tecnología: un diagnóstico de oportunidades*, Ediciones de la Banda Oriental, Montevideo.

Arocena, R. (2003): "La percepción ciudadana de la ciencia, la tecnología y la innovación. El caso de Uruguay", paper presented to the Workshop on Indicators of Public Perception: Scientific Culture and Civic Participation, University of Salamanca.

Arocena, R. and Sutz, J. (2000): "Looking at National Systems of Innovation from the South", Industry and Innovation, vol. 7, no. 1, pp. 55–75.

Arocena, R. and Sutz, J. (2001): "Changing knowledge production and Latin American Universities", Research Policy, vol. 30, no. 8, pp. 1221–1234.

Arocena, R. and Sutz, J. (2003): "Inequality and innovation as seen from the south", Technology in Society, vol. 25/2, pp. 171–182.

Arocena, R. and Sutz, J. (2005a): "Latin American Universities: from an original revolution to an uncertain transition", Higher Education, vol. 50, no. 4, pp. 573–592.

Arocena, R. and Sutz, J. (2005b): "Developmental universities: a look from innovation activities", paper presented to the GLOBELICS Conference in South Africa.

Arocena, R. and Sutz, J. (2006): "Brain drain and innovation systems in the south", IJMS: International Journal on Multicultural Societies. 2006, vol. 8, no. 1, pp. 44–61. http://www.unesco.org/shs/ijms/vol8/issue1/art3

---

[3]An electronic article on this topic (Sutz 2005) was published in paper with the subtitle "Developing countries should promote developmental universities."

Bértola, L. and Bittencourt, G. (2005): "Veinte años de democracia sin desarrollo económico", in Caetano director, *20 años de democracia. Uruguay 1985–2005: miradas múltiples*, Taurus, Montevideo, pp. 305–329.

Bianchi, C. and Gras, N. (2006): "Economic Behavior and economic performance in the Uruguayan Manufacturing Industry 2001–2003", paper presented in the Innovation Pressure Conference, Finland.

Boado, M. (2005): "La deserción universitaria en Uruguay: aproximación descriptiva y perspectivas", Comisión Sectorial de Enseñanza, Universidad de la República, Montevideo.

Bortagaray, I. (2006): UniDev Project paper: "Universidad de la República: case study".

Bortagaray, I. (2009): "Los uruguayos y su percepción sobre ciencia, tecnología e innovación. Datos de una encuesta sobre percepción pública de ciencia, tecnología e innovación 2008", Technical Report, ANII, Montevideo.

Bulmer-Thomas, V. (1994): *The Economic History of Latin America Since Independence*, Cambridge University Press, Cambridge.

Caetano, G. director (2005): *20 años de democracia. Uruguay 1985–2005: miradas múltiples*, Taurus, Montevideo.

Chang, Ha-Joon (2002): *Kicking Away the Ladder. Development Strategy in Historical Perspective*, Anthem Press, London.

Cimoli, M., Ferraz, J.C., and Primi, A. (2009): "Science, technology and innovation policies in global open economies: reflections from Latin America and the Caribbean", GCG Georgetown University, vol. 3, no. 1, pp. 32–60.

Filgueira, F., Garcé, A., Ramos, C.Y., and Yaffé, J. (2003): "Los dos ciclos del Estado uruguayo en el siglo XX", en El Uruguay del siglo XX. La Política, Ediciones de la Banda Oriental, Montevideo.

Hausman, R., Rodríguez-Clare, A., and Rodrik, D. (2004): "Toward a strategy for economic growth in Uruguay", Interamerican Development Bank.

Hirschman, A. (1958): *The Strategy of Economic Development*, Yale University Press, New Haven, CT.

Lundvall, B-A. (2007) "Higher education, innovation and economic development", Paper presented at the World Bank's Regional Bank Conference on Development Economics, Beijing.

Pittaluga, L. (coord.) (2005): "El Uruguay hacia una estrategia de desarrollo basada en el conocimiento", in UNDP Desarrollo Humano en Uruguay, pp. 149–315.

Schumpeter, J. (1957): *Teoría del desenvolvimiento económico*, Fondo de Cultura Económica, México.

Snoeck, M., Sutz, J., and Vigorito, A. (1992): *Tecnología y Transformación. La industria electrónica como punto de apoyo*, Trilce, Montevideo.

Sutz, J. (2005): "The role of universities in knowledge production", SciDevNet, Policy Briefs, April 2005. http://www.scidev.net/dossiers/index.cfm?fuseaction=policybrief&dossier=13&policy=59. Published also in Journal of Himalayan Science, vol. 3, Issue 5, January–June 2005, pp. 53–56.

Unesco statistics: http://stats.uis.unesco.org/unesco/tableviewer/document.aspx?FileId=76

Unidad Académica de CSIC (2003): *Grupos de Investigación en la Universidad de la República*, Montevideo.

Unidad Académica de CSIC (2006): "Pensando el Plan Estratégico Nacional en Ciencia, Tecnología e Innovación Elementos para la reflexión derivados de la Encuesta a Docentes en Régimen de Dedicación Total", http://www.csic.edu.uy/seminarios/doc_final/Informe%20encuesta%20DT.pdf

World Development Indicators Database: http://www.nationmaster.com/graph/eco_res_in_ram_per_mil_peo-amp-d-per-million-people

Chapter 6
Cuba: University, Innovation, and Society: Higher Education in the National System of Innovation

Jorge Núñez Jover, Luis Félix Montalvo Arriete, Isarelis Pérez Ones, Aurora Fernández González, and José Luis García Cuevas

6.1 Introduction to the Cuban Context

Higher education has been making significant contributions to the Cuban innovation system. In this chapter, we claim that such contribution does not come only from the research activity as such in the universities, but also from other activities performed by the universities. We also discuss issues such as the formation of graduates and the role of postgraduate studies, and the formation of university staff. These processes link the university to the innovation system.

This chapter begins with the presentation of the recent economic context in the country. This is followed by the description and analysis of the system of science and innovation that is established in Cuba, the main actors in it, and their roles. This section puts emphasis on the role of universities in the national innovation system. The concluding section deals with the main challenges.

6.1.1 The Economic Context

For Cuba, the early 1990s were featured by a very difficult economic situation called "Special Period" resulting from the demise of the Union of Soviet Socialist Republics (USSR) and the weakening of the commercial links established with the Eastern European countries.[1]

---

[1]The rupture of the longstanding relationships with those countries meant for Cuba a drastic reduction of more than 70% in imports, the loss of guaranteed markets for its products, quick decrease of the imports, and the impossibility of consenting to soft credits from international organizations. In these difficult circumstances, the continuity of the social and economic development that had been achieved by the end of the 1980s was at risk.

J.N. Jover (✉)
University of Havana, Havana, Cuba
e-mail: jorgenjover@rect.uh.cu

B. Göransson and C. Brundenius (eds.), *Universities in Transition: The Changing Role and Challenges for Academic Institutions*,
© International Development Research Centre 2011

The negative impact on the Cuban economy, as a consequence of the changes taken place in the East European countries, was reinforced by the effects of the growing globalization process and the permanency of the economic blockade imposed by USA, which was strengthened further through the implementation of Torricelli Law[2] (1992) and Helms–Burton Law[3] (1996). Under the influence of these external changes and the conditions that characterized the internal context, the government started a process of transformations to stop the decline of the economy and to put the country on the growth path, based on new conditions and resources.

In 1994, after a sustained period of economic decline,[4] Cuba began a slow process of economic recovery. In 2006, the economy achieved a growth rate of 12.5%, the highest since 1959. In 2007, however, the growth rate was only 7.5%, below the targeted 10.0%, mainly due to the negative impact of the climatic conditions on the construction and agriculture sectors (Rodríguez 2007a, b). During the period from 1990 to 2006, Cuba began transforming into a service economy, prioritizing activities that generate foreign currencies, save energy and reduce the energy dependence, utilize the talent of qualified human resources, and sell its products in dynamic markets. In 2006, the structure of the GDP performance by sectors was as follows: primary sector 4%, secondary 20%, and tertiary 76% (Rodríguez 2007a, b).

The recovery process started in the mid-1990s; it was accompanied by a diversification of the economic structure. Thus, the Cuban economy moved from an economy where the key factor of growth was centered in a specialization pattern in the production and export of goods featured as of low technological intensity[5] (sugar and tobacco) to an economy where the production of services with high added value prevails, such as those associated with health, education, and tourism. In 2006, the export structure of Cuba showed 30% of goods and 70% of services, of which 39% corresponded to professional services (Terrero 2006). Economic efficiency and productiveness has been severely criticized recently (Castro 2008) and a group of prioritized sectors has been identified for development: electro-energetic, transport, hydraulic development, social programs, feeding, and housing.

---

[2] The Law's objective is to impede Cuban trade with subsidiaries of US companies located in third countries.

[3] Law aimed at preventing foreign investments in Cuba and penalizing foreign companies that attempt to trade with formerly US-owned companies in Cuba.

[4] Between 1989 and 1992, technological supplies coming from USSR were interrupted. In three years, the imports decreased by 72% and the exports by 67%, the rate of investments decreased from 26 to 7%, the gross capital formation decreased by 60%, and the imports of oil fell by more than 50%. In 1993, the GDP declined by 35% when compared with the 1989 level.

[5] Kelly's typology conceives technological intensity as the relationship among the total expenses (current plus investment expenses) assigned to R&D and the value of the production of an economic activity. The critics of this typology point out some limitations, for instantce that an industrial branch can be classified as having a low technological density, while still being user in an indirect way of technologies generated in other branches by way of inputs. The followers justify the use of that classification based on empiric evidence, in many industries, between the intensity of the expenses of R&D and the technological complexity (Fernández 1994).

The economic recovery of the country and the structural transformations that should be carried out in the immediate period will heavily rely on the Cuban System of Science and Technological Innovation.

6.2   The System of Science and Technological Innovation in Cuba

In the mid-1990s, the Cuban Science and Technology Policy evolved toward the construction of a System of Science and Technological Innovation (SCIT),[6] similar to the concept of National System of Innovation. We will try to describe SCIT,[7] commenting on the main actors, the environment where the system operates, its priorities, some indicators, limitations, and observable strengths and weaknesses.

6.2.1   Main Actors of the SCIT

The entities of the Central Administration of the State take an important role (OACE). They are divided into two types: the ones of global reach and those of branch reach. Regarding SCIT, its functions are linked basically to the planning, financing, evaluation, and control of the science and the technology activities. The Ministry of Science, Technology, and Environment acts as a rector of the science activity and technological innovation. It is responsible for designing the policies of promotion and development of innovation according to strategic projections that optimize the available investments, as well as to regulate and facilitate the actions among the actors that intervene in the innovation process.

As the branch entities take charge of the guidance and management of one or several branches of the economy, they have two main functions related to SCIT: First, to appropriate the scientific and technological development for the continuous improvement of the economic efficiency in accordance with established policies and plans; and second, to evaluate the process of technological development and technology transfer.[8]

As stated earlier, an outstanding role is conferred on the enterprises producing goods and services. They play an important part in SCIT through their revenue

---

[6]CITMA (1995). "The System of Science and Technological Innovation". Basic Document. Havana, December, pp. 3–61.

[7]Here we assume the conception of "innovation" system as a "group constituted by the organizations, institutions, interactions among different collective actors and the social general dynamics that have a higher incidence in the capacities available for research, experimental development, technological innovation and the diffusion of productive technical advances" (Arocena and Sutz 2005, p. 96).

[8]Scientific and technological potential is considered (branch in this case) the total of resources available to investigate, innovate, and study the problems of national or international character outlined by the process of science, technology, and innovation.

generating activities and contributions[9] to the society, and as an important performer of the innovation activities. There are more than 3,000 enterprises in the country, of which 715 are subjected at the moment to a process denominated as the "Managerial Improvement."[10] The rest of the enterprises will be gradually incorporated into this process. The benefits of this process for the enterprise and the society are tangible.[11]

Universities play a decisive role in the creation, diffusion, and implementation of knowledge. They carry out an important part of the national scientific research; they form the graduate university students and have a decisive weight in the graduate degree education, particularly in the development of the doctorate level education.

The Entities of Science and Technological Innovation (ECIT), that is, research centers, centers of scientific–technological services and units of scientific–technological development, are essential in the system. Scientific research, techno-logical development, and the provision of scientific–technological services are the fundamental missions of these entities. The number of entities is considered to be more than 200 at present (OCCyT 2005:19).

The financial institutions have as their main mission in the system to offer financing through different modalities and to try to develop the key capacities of the actors in the system. At present, a group of institutions support the entities in that mission.[12]

The SCIT incorporates organizational forms and organizations whose objec-tive is to promote and integrate innovation efforts, especially to interconnect the

---

[9]Inputs are the total monetary contribution to the State, the generation of products and useful services to improve the people's life, job guarantee, organizational and technical contributions, the new products and services, the patents, innovations, and all that elevates the efficiency of the socialist society.

[10]Program of renovation of structures and work methods of the Cuban enterprises whose main objectives are to reorganize the production flows and services, and to modernize the productive processes with an economic rationality approach, looking for the maximum effectiveness, effi-ciency, and possible competitiveness and observing the necessary protection of the environment and a fair treatment to the labor resources.

[11]For example, in 2005, the enterprises in the system of improvement had a higher productivity by 54.55% than those that are not. The contribution in foreign currencies per worker was 1, 618.76 compared with 480,86 in other enterprises, and the utilities of the enterprises in that system were 14.50% greater than the remaining ones (Betancourt 2005). In 2007, the entities in improvement achieved a productivity 48% greater than the rest of the enterprises (Terrero 2008). The managerial Cuban panorama has enterprises that are able to be equalled to similar ones in the international envi-ronment from the point of view of their activity indicators, and others that need to change to respond to the demands of the economy and the Cuban society of gaining higher productivity and efficiency.

[12]The following ones are among them: *Cuban Central Bank.* Rector authority of the banking system, among other functions, proposes the monetary policy that allows the country to achieve the demanded objectives.

Investments Bank S A. It is guided to the provision of specialized financial services as regards investments, identifying and mobilizing available resources, so much in the national market as in the external one, guiding them to the more productive and prioritized sectors of the economy.

Trade International Bank S A. It offers a wide range of services to Cuban, foreign, and mixed entities. Their main activities include, among others, transactions related to the external trade and transfers from and toward Cuba.

Financial International Bank. It carries out operations in convertible foreign currencies with the character of commercial bank, and has a solid reputation and agent banks in several countries.

scientific and technological research with the productive sectors. It is the case of the Scientific-productive Poles, the National Science and Technology Forum, the National Association of Innovators and Rationalizers (ANIR), and the Technical Juvenile (BTJ) brigades.

Scientific-productive poles are coordinating and integrating instruments that have as main objective to link efficiently the results of the research and development entities with the necessities of the sector that produces goods and services. Fourteen poles work at the moment, two of them in the capital of the country and the rest distributed in the remaining provinces. Territorial poles are the stage of interaction for universities, research centers, productive sectors, government, and social organizations. The western pole is the most relevant scientific-productive

Simplified diagram of the innovation system in Cuba (after 1994)

Source: Elaborated by the authors from (Monreal 2005).

one, for its role in the creation of the new medical–pharmaceutical industry with biotechnological knowledge. It also promotes the interactions and the consensus among the actors linked to its development.

The National Science and Technology Forum is a movement that promotes a wide social participation in the innovation processes; it favors the interactions among key actors and allows dissemination of the results. The Forum facilitates the search for useful solutions to daily problems related to production and services, including the appropriate application of science and technology. It is organized from local to national level.

ANIR is an organization that embraces the whole productive fabric and whose members contribute through different ways to develop the technological management in the enterprises and the improvement of its efficiency and competitiveness. Its importance within SCIT resides in the fact that its activity inside the enterprises maximizes the use of tacit knowledge and the display of technological creativity.

BTJ is a movement of youths' participation in the search for solutions to problems that usually demand the employment of scientific and technological knowledge. Among its objectives are the substitution of imports and the creation of new exportable funds to influence in the introduction and generalization of the scientific results, as well as their popularization.

The mechanisms to define the research and formation calendars and their connection to the economic and social strategy of the country are not limited to the organizational forms and organizations mentioned. Diverse mechanisms of exchange exist among the highest government levels, ministries, enterprises, universities, and research centers, which generate several combined initiatives that influence the scientific research, the exchange of specialists, and modes of qualification. Let us look at some selected indicators of the System of Science and Technological Innovation.

The government has for many years made important efforts in promoting science and technology activities, S&T (ACT in Spanish), as illustrated below. Figure 6.1 shows how in 1995, despite financial difficulties, Cuba spent 0.87% of

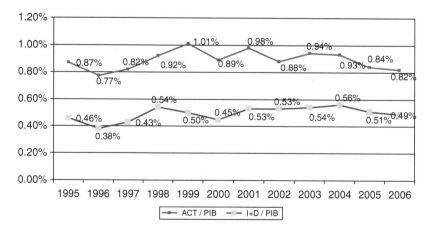

Fig. 6.1 Total expenditure on S&T and R&D as percentage of GDP. *Source*: ONE (2005a, 2005b) and CITMA (2006)

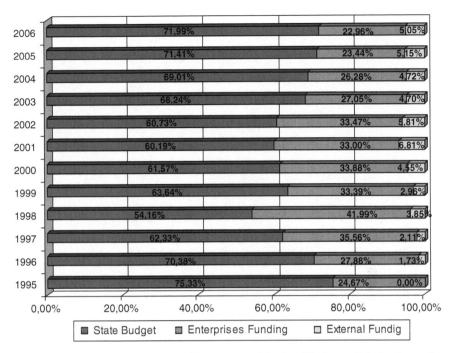

Fig. 6.2 Current expenditure in S&T (ACT) per source of funding (%). *Source*: Calculated according to CITMA information (Dirección de Planificación)

GDP on S&T, with a tendency to grow in the following years. After 2001, the percentage has a tendency to decline as a result of disproportionate investments in science and technology activities.

Figure 6.2 also shows the efforts in S&T (ACT), identifying the sources of finance. The government's relative participation, the enterprise, and the external financing in this effort are shown. As known, in Cuba the private enterprise has a limited reach; with the exception of areas with participation of foreign capital, they are enterprises with no development of ACT. So when speaking of managerial financing, it is in most of the cases State enterprises.

Finally, Fig. 6.3 depicts the number of researchers per 1,000 inhabitants of the economically active population (PEA). It should be noticed that by the end of 2005, the country reached 1.15, showing an important human potential for R&D (CITMA 2006). In 2003, according to RICYT data, if it is compared with countries such as Colombia (0.52), Panama (0.35), and Latin America and Caribbean (1.02), Cuba had an important potential of human resources for R&D (RICYT 2003).

The construction of the innovation system is still an on-going process. Numerous foundations have been created; there are advances, but the SCIT still has some limitations that restrict its effective operation.

As mentioned before, at the beginning of the 1990s, when the country entered the so-called Special Period, the productive sector suffered a disinvestment process.

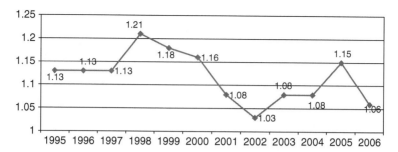

Fig. 6.3 Number of researchers per thousand inhabitants of the economically active population (EAP). *Source*: CITMA (Dirección de Planificación)

Many enterprises operated with obsolete technologies and mainly with a high density of materials and high energy intensity.[13] This situation still remains in many areas and influences the productive development and the innovation capacity.

The shortage of financing is another important problem. Cuban government's policy to preserve and support the activities of the R&D sector has propitiated that, despite the severe economic restrictions, the institutions have kept working with the existing resources. The State financial support to the R&D sector allows to guarantee basically the payment of salaries to the personnel dedicated to the activity, as well as to cover other executable expenses in national currency.

The most important problem of financing the R&D sector by the State is related to the supply of foreign currencies. The considerable shortage of foreign currencies made it imperative to assign those resources in a very selective way, to guarantee the appropriate operation of R&D institutions and specific sectors involved in highly prioritized works. The impossibility to meet the requirements of foreign currencies of all the institutes of R&D, universities, and enterprises, among other actors of the system, is the origin of considerable difficulties in obtaining materials, specialized resources, international mobility, and equipment, as well as in gaining access to national networks of information and the Internet.

Limitations of organizational character are added to the already mentioned. Despite the SCIT declarations, R&D continues to be, predominantly, external to the enterprises. The enterprises are not the center of the System. The technological management in the enterprises is unable to guarantee effective links between R&D and production. The entities specialized in interface services are concentrated on organizational development and have devoted less attention to technological management.

---

[13] The impact on the country in energy terms is illustrated by Figueras when pointing out that Cuba consumed in 1978 a total 1,111 energy kilograms (in terms of equivalent petroleum) per each million dollars of GDP. Due to the rationalization and economy efforts, by 1987 that cipher was reduced to 848 kg. However, in the mentioned years, the value of that indicator decreased in Spain from 407 to 323; in Italy from 322 at 259; and in Japan from 286 at 205 (Figueras 1994:46).

It is also likely that in some sectors the qualification of the workers, technicians, and professionals does not meet, to the necessary extent, the requirements for development of those sectors. The systematic mechanism of pursuit and assessment of SCIT has not worked optimally either. Even in some cases, there is lack of accurate information to support the decision making (OCCyT 2005).

The identified limitations indicate that the effective implementation of SCIT still requires a long and complicated process of improvement. The sociocultural and educational environment is favorable for SCIT. Cuba has an excellent educational system that guarantees the access with equality of opportunities for all and allows developing the continuous formation of human capital.[14] The literacy rate among the population between the ages of 15 and 24 years is 99.96%; the enrollment rate in primary education is 99.4% (98.5% reache the fifth grade), and the average level of education of workers is 10.8 grades (above Taiwan, Chile, China, and Brazil). The population with university instruction in the ages between 25 and 64 years is 11% (similar to France and over Italy and Portugal). Studies are obligatory up to the ninth grade.

According to UNESCO, the number of students per teacher in primary education and mid level is 14 and 12, respectively (in USA it is of 15 in both levels). In 2005, the television dedicated 62.7% of its transmissions to educational programming (Rodríguez 2005).

There are, however, sectors of the Cuban economy and society that constitute successful examples of innovative efforts of great social impact. There are, for example, very serious advances in the energy sector innovation, with significant transformations in the production and distribution of electric power and the use of nonrenewable energy sources. The innovation associated to the assimilation of technologies for nickel production has also been important.

The sectoral system of the medical–pharmaceutical industry with biotechnological base can be considered a successful case of knowledge-based economy (Lage 2000). Its foundation is the western pole of Havana, a cluster with more than 40 institutions and 12,000 workers, of which 7,000 are scientists. Those institutions work at "complete cycle": research, design, and development of products; production; and commercialization of the products.

The biotechnology industry operates with positive cash flow,[15] it has generated more than 900 patents, and its importance in the Cuban exports has grown. For example, in 2002, the external sales of medical and pharmaceutical products was

---

[14] In 2006, Cuba dedicated to the education 9.6% of the GDP and 24.6% of the domestic budget (Prontuario estadístico. MES 2008).

[15] In USA and Europe, 20% of the biotechnical companies are hardly able to be financed with its own sales of products. They depend mainly on venture capital and speculations in the stock exchange (Lage 2001). As can be appreciated, the experience of the Cuban biotechnology is radically different to the one that we find in USA and Europe. Maybe the crucial difference is in the regime of property. In Cuba, there is social property and the benefits are received by the society. Moral motives are fundamental in the performance of scientists and other social actors.

valued to be USD 50 million (ECLAC 2003:5) and in 2005, these sales were estimated to be between 100 and 200 million, thus becoming the country's second largest export item. Cuba is probably the main exporter of medicines in Latin America with exports to more than 50 countries. There are agreements of technology transfer and commercial negotiations with dozens of countries. The following section will analyze the role of higher education in SCIT.

6.3   The System of Higher Education

The Cuban higher education system[16] has a significant function in the innovation system. It provides the graduate university students needed by country, conducts most of the postgraduate and continuous education,[17] carries out an important part of the national scientific and technological research, is incorporated into the main social programs developed by the country (education, energy) which frequently incorporate the technological innovation, and is responsible for the formation of executives in the country.

As seen before, higher education is not a solitary factor (Arocena and Sutz 2005), at least to the same extent that usually happens in other underdeveloped countries. There are relatively important R&D institutions subordinated to other organizations as, for example, productive Ministries (Agriculture, Transport, Basic Industry, and Public Health), academic institutions (for example, CITMA system), and R&D laboratories linked to enterprises. A significant case is the already mentioned sector of medical–pharmaceutical and biotechnological industry.

The system is made up of 65 higher education institutions (HEIs)[18] and all of them are under public control. The Cuban HEIs offer 98 university courses, which allow the country to take care of a great deal of the formation processes demanded by the development. More than 56,000 full-time professors and about 94,000 part-time professors work in higher education. The Higher Education Ministry (MES) is responsible for the methodological orientation of the whole system (MES 2008).

---

[16] The general information on higher education were offered by the Office of Statistics of the Ministry of Higher Education.

[17] Professional training has an important role in the innovation system. It contributes the graduate university students, develops practically all the important specialties of the country with an efficiency rate of 60% (students who finish their studies in relationship to those who enter). The universities collaborate actively in the determination of necessities of training of the institutions and local governments. At universities, the postgraduate training is developed with the purpose of enhancing teaching and research capacities.

[18] All the HEIs carry out continuous education activities, postgraduate training, and researches, with variable intensity and in accordance with their academic profiles. A dozen of those universities has the fundamental influence in the researches and the doctoral training.

6.3.1   *Training of Professionals and the Innovation System*

An important process comes from training of professionals. Two modalities of studies exist in higher education: exclusive or total dedication studies and partial dedication studies. The first type includes the regular day courses and corresponds to a revenue plan to the higher education approved by the country, according to the demands foreseen in the socioeconomic strategy. This type of studies demands certain terms for its culmination (usually 5 years) and a similar progress rhythm for all the students. When concluding these studies, according to the rank obtained, the State assures the newly graduated professional an appropriate work position. Young bachelors who in most cases take entrance examinations to higher education exceed this course. Full-time studies are characterized by a more permanent presence of students in the classroom and they are usually carried out in the central campus and educational units[19] of the universities. During the academic year 2007–2008, 149,953 students enrolled this type of course. Nearly 60% of the students registered in these studies graduate in the foreseen terms. The composition by specialties is displayed in Table 6.1.

The part-time studies aim to guarantee full access to higher education. These are offered to everybody with middle- or high-level education, without age restriction. They are carried out in after-work schedules. However, the State is not committed to guaranteeing those students an appropriate work position according to their studies profile. These students are often already on the labor market.[20] Each student will

Table 6.1 Enrollment by field of study (full-time study only)

Field of study	Percent
Technology	19.3
Natural sciences and mathematics	2.5
Medical sciences	19.9
Agricultural sciences	1.6
Economics	4.7
Social sciences and humanities	7.4
Pedagogy	36.3
Physical culture	7.8
Plastic arts	0.4

Source: MES. Prontuario Estadístico (2008)

---

[19] The laboring entities that have the right scientific and technical development in the field of such specialty, the necessary quantity of specialists required for students' attention, the general conditions to propitiate the development of lessons, study practice, production practice, term, course and diploma papers, the work of scientific extracurricular research, etc., that they contribute with the development of abilities and professional habits. These units should guarantee the development of systematic or concentrated educational activities, with permanency or not of the students in the educational unit.

[20] It is necessary to take into account that in Cuba the unemployment level is below 2%, what may technically be called "full employment".

advance at his/her own pace, without limits of time to conclude their studies, they have fewer requirements as for the attendance in the classrooms, which are mainly conducted at the municipal campus or other training locations.

After 2001 with the process of "Higher Education Universalization" and the creation of university campuses in all the municipalities of the country, this modality has expanded considerably in several municipalities and other productive and service spaces. This generated a process of modification of the institutional structure in the tertiary schooling that brought about new programs and forms of civic participation in higher education.

This process has originated the creation of university campuses in the 169 municipalities of the country by many HEIs. There are 3,150 university seats,[21] with 609,000 young people studying 47 university specialties in them. This process has allowed 743,000 students to access higher education, which amounts to around 68% of young people between the ages of 18 and 24 years. Sixty-three percent of the students are women and 37% men. Social and humanistic sciences have been predominant in the first stage; the policy aims now at fostering formation processes in specialties needed for local development (farming, agricultural industry processes, industrial engineering, computer science, and maintenance).

Formation processes are characterized by a group of features which allow them to interact with the productive sectors and to influence in the learning and innovation processes; among them are the following:

- Curricula integrate teaching, production, and research activities. During their formation, the students are interned in the productive system and other outstanding spheres of development.
- University formation has become massive, embracing a great deal of young people and workers willing to continue their studies.
- University studies are intimately connected to the socioeconomic strategy of the country. Most students have the guarantee of an appropriate job at the end of their studies.
- HEIs include the whole national territory; this permits closer link of professional formation with the necessities of all the territories of the country.
- The processes of creation of HEIs,[22] specialties, curricula modification, the carrying out of labor practice, realization of student research, creation of training spaces in the enterprises and other organizations, and even the creation of universities are closely connected to the solution of social, economic, cultural, and environmental demands. Thus, knowledge involved in professionals training is closely associated to the country's development.

---

[21] A total of 340 of them are linked to the Ministry of Higher Education, 2,361 to the Public Health Ministry, 209 to the Ministry of Education, and 240 to the National Institute of Physical Education, Sport, and Recreation.

[22] For example, the most recently established HEIs include the University of Informatics Sciences (UCI), with over 10,000 students, reflecting the government's efforts to develop the informatics industry, connect it to the country's development needs, and increase the presence of its products in the country's export portfolio.

6.3.2 The Innovation System and Postgraduate Studies

Postgraduate studies are of great importance for the innovation system. Cuba is among the Latin American and Caribbean countries that have structured a national postgraduate system. That system meets an important part of the formation needs demanded by development. International cooperation supplements the necessities that cannot be satisfied by the national system.

Postgraduate education is conceived as the free opportunity offered to all university graduates for continuing their formation process throughout their working life and still after, and it aims at the upgrading, qualifying, requalifying, and reorientation of graduates in tight association with the job demands (educational, researching, and professional).

In Cuba, the postgraduate education includes what is known in other countries as continuous education (qualification within the enterprises, upgrading of executives) and also masters, doctorates, and specialties suitable to new qualifications. More than 600,000 participants are admitted every year.[23] Formation processes take place not only at universities but also mainly in the enterprises and other scenarios where an effective labor exercise takes place. Thus, postgraduate diplomas contribute to improve qualitatively the job activities of professionals and to the innovation processes.

Master's programs (about 367 with around 2,000 graduating per year) are created fundamentally by initiative of the universities and some research centers, observant to the necessities of economic, social, and cultural development. The specialties (about 169) are conceived as a combined arrangement between the demanding organizations and the universities. In both cases, the interactions are fomented between universities and productive and service sectors, although in the specialties the latter have a leading role, not only contributing to the demand, but also providing the physical space and the resources, and a proportion of professors and program tutors.

Doctoral programs are essentially conceived as processes of investigators' formation at the highest level. Around 300–500 doctors graduate every year (surpassed in Latin America only by Brazil and Mexico). International cooperation holds an outstanding place at this level. The evaluation of doctoral thesis incorporates the opinions of people and institutions that can express rightfully on the quality of results, their practical applicability, and social impact. Thus the idea of peer review is preserved, although it attempts on principles as usefulness, effectiveness, and efficiency, which are not always taken into account by the peer review. It is very common to find among evaluative judgments the consideration of their impacts. About 9,000 doctorates have been formed by the country in the last four decades, with the prevalence of technical, natural, agricultural, and biomedical sciences.

---

[23] All data on postgraduate education have been made available by the Postgraduate Division of the Ministry of Higher Education.

In order to understand the operation of postgraduate education and its articulation to development, it is helpful to explain briefly the settings where it performs.

One of them is that of the ministries, institutions, and enterprises that in accordance to their technical, productive, social, and cultural strategies require the formation of the people that work in them. These institutions usually have mechanisms of human resources in charge of that work. The ministries usually also have "branch schools" in charge of that qualification function.

Universities collaborate actively in providing training and satisfying new needs. This is the stage where new specialties are developed on the basis of priorities. The growth in the number of specialties suggests an improving responsiveness of the organizations to the necessity of developing their human resources.

Another outstanding setting is that of the territories. Each territory has its own economic, social, and cultural strategy, with the necessity of forming its own professionals. The universities and the local governments work together in formulating the research, learning, and innovation necessities of the territories. The universalization of higher education offers new opportunities to knowledge management and innovation for local development on the part of university institutions.

The academic setting deals with the postgraduate activity and takes place basically at universities with the purpose to promote teaching and investigative capacities. The permanent improvement of university professors is part of their contractual obligations. The main efforts aim at the formation of doctors. Among the most prominent universities, doctors represent 40–50% of the educational body, but with only 20% in the other universities. The most encouraging fact is that around 50% of instructors without a doctor's degree are working to obtain that scientific degree.

In all the settings and probably with more importance in the first two, continuous and postgraduate education offer special attention to people who occupy managerial positions in enterprises, local governments, etc., as well as to people who are getting ready to take those responsibilities.[24] Specific formation and qualification strategies incorporate several components: the use of modern management procedures, technical and professional training, economic conditioning, and preparation for the defense of the country and political formation. Those formation processes have the participation of high-level state and government leaders and managers who operate at base levels in organizations and territories. This permits those people who exercise management positions, mostly university graduates, to be qualified for the tasks in their future positions, and improve their job performance. They also frequently participate in other postgraduate formation programs.

The last decade has featured a concept of postgraduate quality management to suit the national necessities, as well as to meet international standards. The quality issue is linked to the problem of innovation. The concept of quality in Cuba

---

[24] They are officially called cadres and reserves, respectively.

includes not only what is usually known as academic excellence, the one that is determined through the peer review of publications, thesis, and other knowledge products, but it also incorporates a central concern for the social relevance of post-graduate programs. The intention is to develop a socially outstanding postgraduate, who will be attentive to the needs of production, services, research, and a valuable academic. That relationship between postgraduate and social demands favors its role as innovation promoter.

6.4 University, Science, Technology, and Innovation

Cuban universities are closely related to society. The university research strategies are formulated in interaction with society. Hence the Cuban model of relationship between university and society has been labeled "interactive model" (Núñez and Castro 2005). The Cuban university assumes that society is much more than market. Knowledge and science can meet commercial demands, but mainly social necessities. Formation and research calendars aim at promoting the widest social appropriation of knowledge and its benefits, in search of equity and social justice. For this purpose, all sources of knowledge are potentially useful: those contributed by science and technology, social and humanistic sciences, and arts.

We consider that the "interactive model" facilitates the participation of the university in the innovation system. Also, that model contributes to the social objective of advancing toward a pattern of social development based on knowledge. The "New University," a model that promotes the universal access of the citizens to university studies and promotes learning spaces all along the country, is an important resource for boosting development. The calendars running scientific and technological research are also guided to produce socially favorable impacts, including innovations with scientific research of excellent academic level, the postgraduate formation, and international collaboration.

The 17 HEIs that are linked directly to the Ministry of Higher Education (MES[25]) stand out for their contribution to the national scientific development. They obtain more than 50% of the annual awards conferred by the Cuban Academy of Sciences (ACC) to the main scientific contributions of the country, more than 50% of the Cuban articles registered in Science Citation Index; form more than 50% of the doctors in sciences; and obtain around 20% of the awards associated with innovation. Cuba has been conferred a total of eight patents by the World Intellectual Property Organization, six of these have been granted to institutions of higher education.

Nearly 5,807 professors, 620 investigators, 254 young graduates mainly dedicated to the research ("scientific reserves"), and other 787 young people ("on the

---

[25] Other HEIs fall under the Ministry of Public Health, Ministry of Education, Ministry of Culture, Ministry of the Armed Forces, etc.

job trainees") carry out several training tasks, including a research component, at the end of which they may join to work in other organizations or continue to do research in those HEIs. More than 21,000 students carry out research activities incorporated into the formation curriculum, almost 13,000 of them in the final years and about 4,000 are considered high yield students whose participation in research is usually important. In general, the organization of research tends to incorporate young graduates and students to the research communities.

The research in HEIs is organized through diverse institutional forms. The most traditional are the teaching departments. Practically, 80% of professors carry out some type of research, sometimes linked to masters, but and mainly to doctoral programs. There is an institutional policy and an incentive mechanism to press in favor of doctoral formation, emphasizing on young people.

Departments frequently also organize scientific work through research groups. The type of research corresponds to the so-called Mode 1 of knowledge production (Gibbons et al. 1994). It takes place in an academic environment, frequently in a disciplinary way; basically generates publications and theses; and is evaluated by the peer review.

There are more than 50 "Entities of Science and Technological Innovation" formed by 20 research centers (the largest can hold a hundred investigators) and around 30 units of scientific and technological development, usually of lesser range and economic autonomy than the research centers. They have frequently evolved into alternative forms of knowledge production similar to those described in "Mode 2" of knowledge production (Gibbons et al. 1994): the "application context" determines the course of the research. This is organized in a multidisciplinary form, and interactions with enterprises and productive organizations take place. It is subjected to a different type of quality control and generates products and technologies that may be commercialized inside and outside the country. More than 90 "Study Centers" developing postgraduate and research activities operate also in HEIs.

The most important research areas are food production; sustainable energy development; health: biotechnology medical–pharmaceutical industry; environment, information technologies, and communications; a group of strategic researches in areas such as nanotechnology, new materials, bioinformatics, and complex systems; and numerous groups of researches in social sciences, humanities, and pedagogy.

The presence of universities in the national scientific activity is revealed in the fact that 43% of the research projects participate directly in the main priorities of the country organized through the National, Branch, and Territorial Programs of Science and Innovation.

The University of Havana, the Higher Polytechnical Institute José Antonio Echeverría, the National Center of Scientific Researches, the Agrarian University of Havana, the National Center of Farming Health, the National Institute of Agricultural Sciences, the Animal Science Institute, the Central University of Las Villas, and the University of Oriente are responsible for most of the research. In a lesser number of specialties and with a more regional scope are the University of Ciego de Ávila, Matanzas, Camagüey, among others.

From the 1980s, in the context of changes in the Scientific and Technological National policy (García Capote 1996), the higher education has made an effort to connect its research more strongly with the productive sector and even to market its results, including exports of products and technologies, preferably to countries of Latin America, Europe, and Asia. To facilitate those purposes, in the late 1990s, the interface institutions called "Research Results Transfer Offices" and also specific financing mechanisms to develop products with the capacity of generating economic revenues were created (Núñez and Alonso 1999).

A recent study about the University of Havana (Núñez and Pérez 2007), the main research university in the country, reveals some issues that derive from the experiences of previous decades:

- The research relevant for development should take into account very carefully the context of its application. It does not reduce the scientific value of the research. The context, the scheme of relationships where scientific practice is inserted, may generate research calendars and techno-scientific trajectories that permit new explorations of the scientific and technological frontier. The research can be outstanding in scientific terms and its application can go beyond the boundaries of the context that originated them. The vaccine against *Haemophilus influenzae* type b (Hib), starting from a synthetic antigen, is an example that shows the benefits of overcoming in the university research dichotomy basic/applied science/technology, academic evaluation/evaluation according to the context, etc. The social pertinence can be placed in the core of our values without hurting the academic quality.
- The outstanding research demands high academic level and claims scientific education of an excellent level, including that of the postgraduate. The learning process is essential.
- Multidisciplinary work, networks, and cooperation are indispensable.
- The systems of evaluation of university science have to surpass the exclusive privilege of the peer review and incorporate diverse approaches, stimulating the work guided to the solution of social problems. Lamentably, we still do not have indicators of the significance and social appropriation of knowledge.
- Society is much more than market. Science takes care of commercial demands, but should also address social necessities. Research calendars also have to be guided by the objective of promoting the widest social appropriation of knowledge and its benefits. Knowledge can be a source of justice and social equity.

6.5 Innovation and Local Development

The already mentioned municipal campuses (SUM), besides constituting a vehicle for widespread university education, are also institutional new actors with enormous potentialities to promote local development based on knowledge and innovation. In fact, these institutions can be pivotal for creation of human and innovative capital of the territory where they act. The universalization of higher education endows the municipalities with institutions of higher education that did not exist before, providing high level training to a significant number of qualified people in each locality, opening the possibility to build networks of lead knowledge and technologies. In this way, they will be able to meet the social needs of the territories in close coordination with the local governments. In other words, SUM collaborate in the identification of local problems that require knowledge for their solution, identify the organizations or people who may contribute to it, and then make the necessary links, networks, and flows of knowledge that allow the assimilation, generation, and use of that knowledge. Those are strategic tasks that SUM begin to carry out.

Recent studies (Núñez et al. 2007) reveal that certain SUM are innovating in hardware (equipment, products), software (computerized systems, management technologies), and orgware (methods of strategic public management). It is clear that a process that just began should meet the challenges imposed by new times. This transformation of the universities will require taking care of the academic level, to recognize interlocutors in the whole society, to study and to perfect the local innovation with its particularities, and to transform traditional systems of evaluation of the university activities.

At the local level, and linked to SUM and the HEIs, a group of networks is operating with a great impact on local development. Among them are the Program of Local Agricultural Innovation led by the National Institute of Agricultural Sciences, with remarkable benefits in feeding and biodiversity; the network of ecomaterials of the Central University of Las Villas that guided the production of building materials for housings; the network of energy efficiency led by the University of Cienfuegos with an important contribution to the energy saving; and the network of dairy farms schools of the Institute of Animal Science with important contributions in the production of milk. Several of these networks have the support of international collaboration.

The combination of the effort of these networks and the role of SUM as agents of knowledge and innovation offer great opportunities to higher education for promoting the innovation for local development.

6.6   Final Considerations

As we have seen, the Cuban universities are closely related to society. The social relevancy is an important value of the Cuban higher education. The formation and university research strategies are built in interaction with society. Hence we have called the Cuban model of relationship between university and society as an "interactive model" (Núñez and Castro 2005).

The formation and research calendars are led by the objective of promoting the widest social appropriation of knowledge and its benefits, seeking for equity and social justice. All the spheres of knowledge are potentially useful: those that contribute to the science and the technology and also the arts, the social and the humanistic sciences.

The "interactive model" enables the participation of the university in the innovation system. Moreover, this model contributes to the social objective of advancing toward a model of social development based on knowledge. The universalization of higher education promotes the universal access of citizens to university studies, and learning spaces in all the localities of the country.

The calendars that guide the scientific and technological research also aim at producing socially favorable impacts, provided by innovations with the scientific research of excellent academic level, postgraduate formation, and international collaboration.

However, the concerns and challenges are multiple. The following are among the most important ones:[26]

1. Presently, there is a coexistence of different university ideals (what Tunnerman 2006 calls "idea of university"). Next to the idea of innovation University with social relevancy (Didriksson 2006), in our opinion coherent with the trajectory of the Cuban university, there is another ideal that comprises the university as a formation space that carries out preferably basic research and another space that conceives the university as a space dedicated to the formation (now universalized). It is obvious that those different ideals have political–institutional consequences that may influence in the forms of participation of higher education in the innovation system.
2. In the productive sector, we find enterprises and institutions that take little advantage of the formation, research, and university innovation. This is influenced by the nonexistence of a widespread system of incentives for the managerial innovation, or a policy to boost the productive sector to support the university, although some good examples exist in this respect.
3. The national Scientific and Technological Policy (PCT) needs to be updated and supported. Since last decade, PCT was guided to the creation of an innovation system strongly supported by science. However, after a decade, it does not seem to be successful enough in the generation of widespread systemic "interactions among the actors of innovation." The use of the research results, in key sectors as the production of food, is still insufficient. This suggests the necessity to check approaches, priorities, management styles, and other instruments that favor, among other things, the integration among institutions of knowledge and other actors.
4. Severe financing and investment problems are observed, with a rapid deterioration of the infrastructure in research institutes and university laboratories. Investments that favor the access to information are also required.

---

[26] Identifying these challenges is the result of the work carried out at the Seminar "University, Innovation and Society" developed by the program on Science, Technology, and Innovation at the University of Havana.

5. Difficulties are observed with the generational relief of professors and high-level researchers due to the decline in the number of science and engineering graduates, and their migration to other better remunerated sectors of the economy.
6. The research guided to the innovation in the university lacks institutional and legally stable and sufficient bases: incentives, financing mechanisms, and channels for the commercialization.
7. The universalization of higher education outlines countless challenges. In the first place are challenges linked to the quality of formation in a context of overcrowding access, and also challenges linked to the management of the institutions of higher education and their capacity to generate benefits to the local development. There exist real possibilities of creating local systems of innovation, with the active participation of SUM. But it will demand very well guided institutional policies that mobilize the consent of numerous actors.

At present, the country is reviewing the structure of the state and government organizations in order to better contribute to its development. This restructuring has impacted both the system of higher education and the system of science and technological innovation in the country.

As a result of this process, modifications have been introduced in the structure of the municipal institutions of higher education, so far known as Municipal University Campuses (SUM). As of the academic year 2009–2010, these campuses are grouped in every municipality to establish the Municipal University Centers (CUM),[27] under the Ministry of Higher Education. The main objective is to ensure that the quality of the graduates is similar to that of the main campuses.

Several aspects of the system of access to higher education have been modified in order to deal with some contradictions arising from the issue of mass access vs. quality. One is the extension of compulsory entrance examinations for all students applying for university programs, including young people from special programs. On the contrary, with a view to achieve a greater social relevance for the CUMs, enrollment quotas for social science programs have been reduced, while there is an increase of enrollment quotas for technical science and agricultural programs.[28] The idea is that, increasingly, CUMs will be able to train professionals taking into account the needs and development plans of each municipality.

While it is too soon to evaluate the new system, these modifications may reduce the percentage of people in the 18–25-year age group enrolling in higher education in the future. While it is true that at some point in time Cuba had a gross enrollment rate in higher education (17%) that was not in line with the principles of social equity and justice of the revolutionary project, the 68% rate achieved in the academic

---

[27] The CUMs are a new university institution that emerges in the wake of the integration of municipalities in the training of professionals in programs under the Ministry of Higher Education (MES), Ministry of Education (MINED), the Ministry of Healthcare (MINSAP) and the Sports Institute (INDER).

[28] This is related with the intention to reverse the trend towards a decline of enrollment in technical science programs.

year 2007–2008 is not very encouraging either, as it always placed us before the challenge of ensuring the quality of university processes.

Generally speaking, it can be held that the imminent impact of the international economic crisis has speeded up the institutional restructuring of HEIs in Cuba. This has long been a political intention but has now become a real transformation.

References

Arocena R, Sutz J (2005). Para un nuevo desarrollo, CECIB, Madrid.

Castro R (2008). Discurso pronunciado por Raúl Castro, Presidente de los Consejos de Estado y de Ministros en las conclusiones de la sesión constitutiva de la VII Legislatura de la Asamblea Nacional del Poder Popular. Periódico Granma. 25 de febrero del 2008.

CITMA (1995). Dirección de Política Científica y Tecnológica: El Sistema de Ciencia e Innovación Tecnológica. Documento Básico. La Habana, diciembre, pp. 3–61.

CITMA (2006). Datos estadísticos. Dirección de Planificación.

Didriksson A (2006). "Universidad, sociedad del conocimiento y nueva economía", Construcción de nuevo conocimiento en el espacio CAB, Convenio Andrés Bello, Fodesep, Bogotá, pp. 70–108.

Fernández C (1994). Contenido tecnológico y competitividad: elementos para la reconversión de la industria cubana. Cuba: crisis y reformas. Boletín ICE Económico. No. 2433, pp. 3027–3034.

Figueras M (1994). Aspectos estructurales de la economía cubana. La Habana (Ed.) Ciencias Sociales, p. 46.

García Capote E (1996). Surgimiento y evolución de la política de ciencia y tecnología en Cuba (1959–1995). En García E, Faloh R (Eds.) Seminario Taller Iberoamericano de Actualización en Gestión Tecnológica, La Habana. GECYT.

Gibbons M, Limoges C, Nowotny H, Schartzman S, Trow M (1994). The new production of knowledge. The dynamics of science and research contemporary societies, Sage, London.

Lage A (2000). Las biotecnologías y la nueva economía: crear y valorizar los bienes intangibles. Biotecnología Aplicada 17: 55–61.

Lage A (2001). Propiedad y expropiación en la economía del conocimiento, Ciencia, Innovación y Desarrollo, Vol. 6, No. 4, CITMA, La Habana.

MES (2008). Prontuario Estadístico. Educación Superior. Enero de 2008. En: http://www.reduniv.ed.cu/estadísticas.

Monreal P (2005). Encapsulating Knowledge: Comments on the innovation function of Cuba's University Networks. Presentación realizada en el Taller Developing Universities – The Evolving Role of Academic Institutions in Economic Growth, Lund University, Sweden, 15–17 June 2005.

Núñez J, Alonso N (1999). "Universidad e innovación tecnológica", en Revista Universidad de La Habana No. 250, primer semestre de 1999, La Habana, pp. 36–56.

Núñez J, Castro F (2005). Universidad, Innovación y Sociedad: Experiencias de la Universidad de la Habana, Revista de Ciencias de la Administración, Vol. 7, No. 13, enero/julio, Florianópolis, Brasil. pp. 9–30.

Núñez J, Pérez I (2007). "La construcción de capacidades de investigación e innovación en las universidades: el caso de la Universidad de La Habana, Revista Educación Superior y Sociedad: Universidad latinoamericana como centros de investigación y creación de conocimientos, Nueva Época, Año 1, Número 12, IESALC, Caracas, Agosto 2007, pp. 146–173.

Núñez J, Benítez F, Pérez MT, Hernández D, Figaredo F (2007). Educación superior y desarrollo social sostenible: nuevas oportunidades y desafíos (en proceso de publicación).

OCCYT (2005). Elementos para una evaluación general del Sistema de Ciencia e Innovación Tecnológica. Resumen ejecutivo. La Habana, Diciembre, 10p.

ONE (2005a). Panorama económico y social. Cuba 2005. Diciembre. 17p.

ONE (2005b). Censo de Población y Viviendas Cuba 2002. Informe Nacional. La Habana, Septiembre 400p.

RICYT (2003). Principales Indicadores de Ciencia y Tecnología Iberoamericanos.

Rodríguez J (2005). Informe sobre los resultados económicos del 2005 y el Plan Económico Social para el 2006, presentado a la Asamblea Nacional del Poder Popular por José Luis Rodríguez, ministro de Economía y Planificación. Periódico Juventud Rebelde. Suplemento Especial. 23 de diciembre del 2005.

Rodríguez J (2007a). Informe sobre los resultados económicos del 2007 y los Lineamientos del Plan Económico y Social para el 2008, presentado a la Asamblea Nacional del Poder Popular por José Luis Rodríguez, ministro de Economía y Planificación. Periódico Juventud Rebelde. Suplemento Especial. 28 de diciembre del 2007.

Rodríguez J (2007b). Panorama actual de la economía cubana. Conferencia Inaugural de Primavera. Universidad de La Habana. 21 de marzo. 28 pp.

Terrero A (2006). Economía del conocimiento: inversión en células grises. Revista Bohemia Digital. 12 de mayo de 2006.

Terrero A (2008). Economía cubana: lecturas de un despegue. Revista Bohemia Digital. 18 de enero de 2008.

Tünnerman C (2006). "Comentarios a la ponencia del Dr. Axel Didriksson" en Conocimiento y Necesidades de las Sociedades latinoamericanas, Vessuri H. (coordinadora), ediciones IVIC, Caracas, pp. 55–70.

Chapter 7
Vietnam: Current Debates on the Transformation of Academic Institutions

Tran Ngoc Ca and Nguyen Vo Hung

7.1 The Vietnamese Context

Vietnam has been experiencing dramatic changes over the past few decades in almost all its political, social, and economic spheres. This has had a strong influence on the evolution of the academic system. Historically, the academic institutions (research institutes and universities) date back to the French regime. The first modern Vietnamese university (specializing mainly in the medical and pharmaceutical fields) was established in Hanoi. In addition, some research institutes operating in the fields of medicine, pharmacology, or biomedicine, such as the Pasteur Institute, were established by the French. Furthermore, during the war, academic institutions were developed both in the North (under the Soviet academic model, e.g., Hanoi Polytechnic) and the South Vietnam (more like the Western style, e.g., Can Tho University). They had a strong imprint on the war-time activities with missions that focused more on training and provision of problem-solving methods to serve military needs.

When Vietnam was reunited after the war in 1976, the economy relied heavily on agriculture and support from abroad. A centrally planned economy was implemented throughout the country. Industrial development focused mainly on heavy industry and was driven by import-substitution policies. Many ministries functioned like big companies, responsible not only for public services, but also for economic activities, which were conducted by state-owned enterprises. The academic sector was organized to support such a structure and was empowered by many enthusiastic young graduates from local universities and former socialist countries. At that time, the universities were responsible for training knowledgeable personnel, and the research institutes were responsible for basic, applied, and engineering research. There was quite a clear division of labor and responsibility

T.N. Ca (✉)
National Council for Science and Technology Policy (NCSTP), Hanoi, Vietnam
e-mail: tranngocca@gmail.com

B. Göransson and C. Brundenius (eds.), *Universities in Transition:*
The Changing Role and Challenges for Academic Institutions,
© International Development Research Centre 2011

among these academic institutions, which reflected their management. Universities and colleges were the responsibility of the Ministry of Higher Education, whereas most academic research institutes came under the aegis of the Vietnamese Scientific Institute or State Commission for Science and Technology, and most engineering research institutes came under their line ministries. Despite the many problems associated with the centrally planned economy, the academic sector functioned quite well with its focus on problem-solving and engineering solutions for the productivity sector.

By the 1980s, the lack of market incentives and the rigidities of central planning practices had dragged the economy into a severe economic crisis and resulted in deteriorating living standards. Forced by the domestic difficulties and encouraged by the changes in China and the former Soviet Union, the Vietnamese government initiated an overall economic reform program known as "Doi Moi" (renovation) in 1986. Since then, the country has gone through a so-called double transition: from a centrally planned economy to a market economy, and from an agricultural to an industrial economy.

After 20 years of radical changes, the country has achieved some significant results. The GDP growth rate has been quite high and stable at around 8% for the last 10 years. The country has increased GDP per capita from US$440 in 2002 to almost US$700 in 2006. More importantly perhaps, Vietnam's standard rate of poverty has been reduced from 30% of total households in 1990 to just 7% in 2005. Most of the economic growth has been generated in the industrial sector, but services have also expanded rapidly. A large part of this growth can be attributed to foreign investment, and more recently, the development of the local private sector. The agricultural sector has been growing at around 4% per annum over the last decade. With liberalization and modernization of the sector, Vietnam has transformed itself from a food-importing nation to one of the top three rice exporters in the world. However, agriculture still accounts for 22% of Vietnam's economic output, and over two-thirds of its employment, primarily on small family farms.

For its economic performance, FDI activity plays a crucial role. Foreign investors have created an imported "private sector" for a country that only had a fledgling private sector of its own at the beginning of the 1990s. With the advantages of short distances and cultural similarities, neighboring countries such as Singapore, South Korea, Taiwan, and Japan established early footholds in Vietnam soon after its open door policy was implemented. By the end of the 1990s, although foreign-invested companies employed less than 1% of the total workforce in Vietnam, they cumulatively accounted for around 27% of the country's (nonoil) exports, 35% of the country's total industrial output, almost 13% of Vietnam's GDP, and contributed around 25% of total tax revenues (Klaus et al. 2006). During 2001–2005, FDI accounted for 16.8% of the total investment, in 2004 the FDI figure was US$4.2 billion, and in 2005 some US$6.3 billion.

Vietnam joined the WTO in 2006 with several important commitments such as trade-related intellectual property rights (TRIPS), trade-related investment measures

(TRIMs), technical barriers to trade (TBT), etc. The state-owned enterprise (SOE) reforms aimed at increasing efficiency have produced significant achievements in reducing the number of state-owned firms from 5,600 in 2005 to 2,600 in 2006. Despite these achievements, there are still some outstanding issues. Although the poverty rate has been reduced, the gap between rich and poor has increased. International integration of the economy has brought benefits but, at the same time, some problems. The process of institutional reform of the legal and banking systems has resulted in demands for a more resolute stance from the leadership.

Nevertheless, economic changes have brought better living conditions for most people and, more importantly, have connected the country to the global economy. The exposure to the global economy has opened up more options for enterprises and they are now freer to look for solutions to their specific problems from international partners. Firms appear to prefer this approach as it can provide quick, tried, and tested solutions for them. Furthermore, in many cases, it helps them to connect with the international production networks, an invaluable asset, which the firms previously did not have. The new generation of productive assets requires new and different skills. All of these factors put pressure on the academic sector and force it to change.

7.2   The Position of Academic Institutions in the Vietnamese National System of Innovation

The present academic organizations of Vietnam can be classified into two groups: (1) general R&D and engineering institutions and (2) higher education institutions. In fact, there are overlaps between these two groups because the former are also involved in some formal training and the latter in doing research. Only a small proportion of Vietnam's R&D is conducted in productive enterprises, which are predominantly small and medium enterprises (SMEs). Data from various surveys on these firms have revealed their perspective on their linkages with R&D institutes and universities and on meeting technology demands of firms (NISTPASS 1999, 2002, 2004). Findings from these studies revealed that in terms of general business services, Vietnamese firms still prefer to perform most services in-house. Firms tend to rely on their internal capacities for engineering, management, and marketing, while relying on outside sources for computer-related services and training. Computer services are considered as the most important to firms, followed by training services. The limited extent of innovation in SMEs is concentrated mainly in process development and quality control.

Many obstacles and disincentives prevent or discourage SMEs from developing their own innovation capabilities. Firms do not have sufficient resources to make long-term investments, including recruitment of highly skilled labor and equipment to innovate, while many technical services are unavailable. They lack information on available technologies. Market barriers are also high, as SMEs are often unfamiliar with product requirements and distribution channels. Finally, SMEs have a hard time obtaining credit from banks.

The views from firms, as reflected in the abovementioned surveys, confirmed that there is demand for technology and training services to be provided by supporting organizations such as R&D institutes and universities. However, this demand has hardly been met. When asked about sources for innovative ideas, only 10% (of 126 respondents) cited R&D institutions and universities as an important source (Nguyen Vo Hung and Nguyen Thanh Ha 2003). The lack of demand for technology services supplied by universities and R&D institutions appears related to what kind of innovation is offered to the firms and perhaps reflects some negative feelings on behalf of firms regarding the supply capability of universities and R&D institutes. Many enterprises do not use technology-related services because they do not believe that providers offer the particular service that they need. This is especially true in the technology consulting field, where the majority of R&D institutes are unable to provide sophisticated services to industry. Findings from the firms' assessment showed that the capability of R&D institutes and universities was below firms' expectations. When it comes to technology innovation, firms tended to do that themselves, or relied on other firms, rather than on domestic institutes and universities. Some of the reasons for this situation are related to the macro-policy environment, monopoly positions, and the capabilities of firms and service providers.

In this context, it appears as if the specific features of the innovation environment in Vietnam have made commercial relationships (including competition) among firms the dominant interaction pattern. As a result, many Vietnamese academic institutions find themselves almost "left out" of the innovation linkages with the firms altogether. They are not effective in providing practical solutions for a range of diverse and specific problems that firms usually encounter in their innovation efforts. They are also not very good at providing integrated solutions, in the form of technological packages, for instance, for firms that are highly influenced by the market.

Aside from this weakness, academic institutions still hold a useful position in the technological advancement of the Vietnamese economy. In many traditional sectors, such as agriculture, forestry, and in some dynamic parts of the country (mainly in the south), academic institutions play a vital role in bringing technical solutions to farmers. For instance, in the Mekong River Delta (the main rice production area in Vietnam), more than 80% of the rice varieties in use have been bred by the Rice Institute of Mekong River Delta (a public research organization). The Institute of Southern Fruit Trees is also very active in identifying quality parent trees for breeding, in developing advanced cultivation methods for different types of fruit trees, and in disseminating technical knowledge to farmers, among others. It can be argued that the academic institutions involved in agriculture and the extension network have played an important role in the success of Vietnam's rice production. Recently, within the framework of the FAO's "South–South cooperation in agriculture," Vietnamese agricultural scientists and technicians have been sent to some African countries where they helped local communities to plant rice and other plants. The results have been highly appreciated by African colleagues and is considered one of the most successful FAO programs in Africa.

Another strong position of academic institutions is with regard to training, which is the principal mandate of universities and some research institutes. Vietnam has quite a well-developed higher education system. The system, to date, has contributed significantly to the provision of educated personnel for virtually all economic sectors in the country. University education has provided students with some basic foundations that have enabled them to continue their learning in the productive sector. However, not all training institutions are capable of training high quality personnel. Vietnam has attained a high literacy rate (94%) through its successful implementation of near-universal primary education. Despite this achievement, access to technical training and higher education institutions has been limited, and the skill level of the general workforce is insufficient for technology development. Enterprises rely on unskilled and semiskilled labor and maintain low productivity levels. Vocational enrollment is low or consists of short-term training, with informal education playing an important role in the acquisition of new skills (UNIDO 1999). Many firms maintain or improve production in export markets by investing in training of their own workforce. But most staff training focuses on short-term needs. Many firms do not train staff to higher technical levels either due to a lack of resources or due to the fear of losing well-trained staff to other firms offering better terms and conditions.

Fast-growing economic activities and the liberalization process have put university training in Vietnam under significant pressure. As outlined earlier, opening up of the economy has allowed productive sectors to acquire capital goods with embedded technology from more advanced countries. This enables firms in developing countries to reap the rewards of R&D conducted elsewhere and utilize them for their own benefit. Having acquired such production facilities, firms need to learn how to operate their production systems more effectively and this often requires direct exposure of engineers and workers to the systems themselves (opportunities that few academic scientists have). Because this process has happened so rapidly, university curriculum can hardly keep up with technological innovations and quickly become out of date. The staff are either overloaded with teaching or incapable of doing research to support teaching. Equally, the financial rewards and incentives are often insufficient to retain good staff in the post. The university graduates lack state-of-the-art engineering knowledge and it might take them several more years to learn on the job before they can work effectively in the productive sector.

With regard to other activities, outside of traditional research and training, Vietnamese academic institutions have begun to offer a variety of technical services to firms, and even free public goods to serve community needs, especially in rural and mountainous areas. However, this "third mission" of academic institutions has faced several hurdles, particularly as the concept of free provision of academic goods is seen as contradicting the market mechanism. There is little argument about the contribution these institutions make to the overall socioeconomic development of the country, but there are still a number of areas to be improved in order to turn them into true knowledge producers and innovation carriers.

7.3 Mapping the Academic System in Vietnam

Following the reform in economic activities, the liberalization of the Science and Technology (S&T) sector was initiated quite early. Having initially been developed following the Soviet-style model, the academic sector has recently undergone several restructuring trials; some of which were quite serious and radical, at least in terms of what was proposed. Among these, Government Decree 35, enacted in 1992, is probably the most acknowledged one. It marked an important change in that the rights of S&T organizations to enter into commercial contracts with economic entities, as well as to establish affiliates (centers) for commercial purposes, were formally recognized. Since then, many centers have been established under this regulation (hence known as "Centre 35s") by public S&T organizations and groups of individuals. However, due to a lack of supporting institutions and commitments, Decree 35 and some other efforts at restructuring the system have failed to deliver the expected outcomes. The S&T sector has lagged behind reforms witnessed in the economic sector and, although there have been some improvements, further critical changes still lie ahead. Recently, by another government Decree No. 115 enacted in 2006, the R&D institutions have been required to become more independent in their management and functions, operating in a firm-like mode. This change would create a significant shift in R&D system.

7.3.1 R&D and Engineering Institutions

7.3.1.1 Public Institutions

The bulk of R&D activities are conducted in research institutes under line ministries, as well as in two national research organizations for natural and engineering sciences and social sciences.[1] More recently, R&D has also been undertaken within some leading universities. Vietnam spent approximately 0.52% of its GDP on S&T activities in 2005 (MOST 2006),[2] with most publicly funded R&D being conducted in government research institutes. The research infrastructure is perceived as being below international standards. Research tends to be theoretical, supply-driven, and only loosely connected to the needs of the productive sector. The national R&D system is "organized, financed and managed in such a way that technology transfer is difficult and expensive" (Bezanson et al. 2000). The total number of R&D organizations is presented in Table 7.1.

While these numbers may seem quite impressive, they do include a number of centers with just one or two staff, which are often set up simply for administrative

---

[1]These are known as Vietnam Academy of Science and Technology (VAST) and Vietnam Academy of Social Sciences (VASS).

[2]Many OECD countries and China spend around 1.5% of their GDP on R&D.

Table 7.1 R&D Organizations in Vietnam by 31 Dec 2005

Type of administration	2002		2003		2004		2005	
	Number	%	Number	%	Number	%	Number	%
State sector	631	56.5	668	55.7	688	56.3	694	52.6
– Line ministries	437	39.1	466	38.9	481	39.4	484	36.7
– Higher education	134	12.0	141	11.7	144	11.8	147	11.1
– SOEs	60	5.4	61	5.1	63	5.1	63	4.8
Collective sector	440	39.5	487	40.6	481	39.4	556	42.1
Private sector	44	4.0	44	3.7	52	4.3	70	5.3
Total	*1,115*	*100*	*1,199*	*100*	*1,221*	*100*	*1,320*	*100*

Source: MOST (2006)

reasons (e.g., they may enjoy more freedom and autonomy in their operations than their parent organizations).

Of all the R&D and engineering organizations in the country, the Vietnam Academy of Science and Technology (VAST) is by far the largest one. It has 18 research institutes and nine regional branches operating in various fields of science and engineering. The academy has established 16 enterprises (start-up); 21 scientific centers (under Decree 35); 16 higher education institutions; 7 administrative bodies; and 11 journals. By the end of 2005, the academy had a staff of 2,404. Another state scientific research institution is the Vietnam Academy of Social Sciences (VASS). By the end of 2005, VASS had 27 research and supporting institutes; 5 administrative bodies; 15 postgraduate institutions; and 30 journals, and employed almost 1,400 people.

Traditionally, these two principal organizations have been privileged to receive funding from central government to carry out the so-called State S&T missions. These missions are usually organized into research programs aimed at providing a scientific foundation for policy formulation and the legislative process (social science), or for creating new S&T outcomes that are significant for economic and social development; for defense and national security; and for human resource development. However, in the absence of an effective mechanism to identify such missions, as well as to distribute their research results, it has been argued that the state S&T programs lack effectiveness. During the last few years, the entire process of identifying, conducting, and evaluating state S&T missions has been reviewed, in an attempt to identify more efficient and effective procedures.

In addition to the above two institutions, there are several scientific organizations which have been set up and managed by line ministries and provinces. These institutions also receive public funding via their ministries/provinces to undertake research which addresses scientific, technical, and/or policy issues directly related to the field of interest of the relevant ministry or province.

Public scientific organizations also include centers belonging to universities and engineering research institutions belonging to state-owned enterprises. With regard to the former, by the end of 2003, 141 centers had been set up and were operated by public universities and colleges. The latter is classified as public R&D

organizations because their parent organizations, the SOEs, are considered as public entities.

7.3.1.2 Nonpublic Scientific Organizations

Nonpublic R&D organizations include (1) R&D organizations of nonstate enterprises; (2) R&D organizations of political, social, and professional organizations; (3) organizations belonging to professional associations; and (4) foreign R&D organizations, including joint-venture R&D organizations. The collective scientific organizations identified in Table 7.1 are also included in this category because most of them fall under subcategory (3) the professional associations.

Given the small scale of domestic private enterprises in Vietnam and the weak links with public R&D organizations, the limited nonpublic R&D activities are mainly conducted inhouse by own staff, who may or may not have any formal education in scientific or engineering fields. R&D as an organized activity is not common in this sector. With regard to the foreign sector, there are relatively few foreign R&D organizations in Vietnam, and the majority of R&D and engineering work for this sector is conducted in the headquarters of parent firms.

There are numerous R&D organizations associated with political, social, and especially professional organizations. However, their interest is mainly in offering consultancy and intermediary services. Few of them have research facilities able to undertake any serious engineering work.

In total, there are 1,320 public and nonpublic R&D organizations, 11% of which come under universities and similar organizations. In terms of human resources, Vietnam has 274 R&D researchers per million people, lower than the average of 384 for developing countries and much lower than the world average of 1,096 (UNDP Human Development Report Statistics 2004a, b[3]). Furthermore, the R&D human resource is aging, suffers from quality control issues, and has skills that are not best suited for the current economic needs of Vietnam. Many of them received their training from learning systems which emphasized the linear relationship between S&T, heavy industry, and state planning and control (Tran Ngoc Ca 2002).

7.3.1.3 Funding and Output of R&D Institutions

With regard to the governance of public scientific organizations, to date, the majority of them report to line ministries and other government bodies, and as a result receive subsidies from the government budget. Table 7.2 shows the number of scientific institutions linked with various government bodies, their affiliates, and how they are funded. The merged column "Number of organizations funded

[3] http://hdr.undp.org/statistics/data

Table 7.2 Funding status of public scientific organizations linked with government bodies

No.	Government bodies	Parent only	Parent & affiliate	Number of organizations funded by government		
				Funded	Semifunded	Not funded
1	Ministry of Agriculture and Rural Development	38	87	1	82	4
2	Ministry of Industry	23	35	1	26	8
3	Ministry of Health	18	20	8	10	2
4	Ministry of Fisheries		7		7	
5	Ministry of Culture and Information		4	3	1	
6	Ministry of Post and Telematics		2	1	1	
7	Ministry of Labor, Invalids, and Social Affairs		5	4	1	
8	Ministry of Construction	15	15	1	12	2
9	Ministry of Resources and Environment	3	9	1	8	
10	Sport & Exercise Committee	1	1	1		
11	Population, Family, and Children Committee	1	1	1		
12	Committee for Ethnic and Highland	1	1	1		
13	State Inspectorate	1	1	1		
14	Labor Union	4	4	1	3	
15	Youth Union	1	1	1		
16	Ministry of Commerce	3	3	2	1	
17	Ministry of Finance	5	5	3	1	1
18	Ministry of Planning and Investment	3	3	3		
19	Ministry of Transportation	10	23	3	19	1
20	Vietnam Academy of Science and Technology	26	44	23	5	16
21	Vietnam Academy of Social Sciences	28	28	26	1	1
22	Ministry of Defense	8	19	19		
23	Ministry of Public Security	10	10	9	1	
24	Ministry of Home Affairs	2	2	2		
25	Vietnam Television	1	1	1		
26	The People's Supreme Court	1	1	1		
27	Ministry of Science and Technology	8	33	1	25	7
28	Ministry of Education and Training	18	155	3	21	131
29	National Steering Committee for Clean Water and Environmental Hygiene	1	1			1
	Total	*230*	*521*	*122*	*225*	*174*

Source: MOST (2006)

by government" shows how many of them are fully funded, partly funded, or not funded by the government. Those that are not receiving funds from the government have to rely partly or wholly on a variety of consultancies with firms or other organizations.

Several interesting features arise from Table 7.2. First, the actual number of public scientific organizations (parent only) is much less than the statistics in Table 7.1, after the "Centre 35s" have been removed. Second, most of them still rely on direct funding from the government. Whether or not this is a negative or a positive indicator is still open to debate. Third, the table does not include public scientific organizations set up by cities and provinces. Although there are still relatively few of them, in recent years, budget-generating cities and provinces have tended to establish research organizations under their own administrations in order to support their administrative works and/or to support their local communities.

Regarding the results of R&D activities, in Vietnam there has been an upward trend in patent applications and registrations in the past decade. The figure for registration of patents for inventions during the period 2001–2005 is given in Table 7.3. It shows the clear dominance of foreign registrations.

The number of patents for inventions[4] is low and mostly applies to foreign ones. In 2001, there were only seven patents for inventions awarded to Vietnamese residents, compared with 47,721 in Taiwan and 121,742 in Japan (Asian Productivity Association 2003). Industrial design patents,[5] on the contrary, are more numerous and mostly obtained by Vietnamese residents, but they usually contain low technological content. The relatively low number of patents may not only partly be due to a lack of capacity to innovate, but also due to unclear and/or

Table 7.3 Registration of invention patents in Vietnam

Years	2001	2002	2003	2004	2005	Total
Registration by Vietnamese applicants	87	136	145	179	362	909
Registration by foreign applicants	1,201	1,206	1,136	1,390	1,800	6,733
Rate of Vietnamese registrations per foreign ones	7%	11%	13%	13%	20%	14%

Source: MOST (2006)

---

[4]An invention is a technical solution that is a world-wide novelty, involves an inventive step, and is applicable to various social and economic fields (Art. 782, the Civil Code). The protection title is valid for 20 years.

[5]An industrial design is a product's shape which is formed by lines, three-dimensional form, and coloes or a combination thereof, and which is a world-wide novelty and is used as the pattern of industrial or handicraft products (Art. 784 the Civil Code). The protection title is valid for 5 years.

unenforceable intellectual property regimes that dissuade inventors from applying, for fear of a loss of intellectual property rights (IPR).

7.3.1.4   Higher Education Institutions

As mentioned above, although higher education institutions are considered an important part of the S&T system, not all of them are registered as S&T organizations in statistics. Table 7.4 shows the number of higher education institutions in academic years from 1995 to 2004.

Almost all universities and colleges fall under the administration of the Ministry of Education and Training (MOET). The ministry is also responsible for primary and secondary education. For the academic year 2004–2005, there were 230 universities and colleges (93 universities and 137 colleges) employing some 47,646 lecturers, of whom 6,223 were doctorates (13%), 14,539 were postgraduates (30.5%), and 26,854 held university degrees (56.4%). There were 446 professors (0.9%) and 1,842 associate professors (3.9%) (MOET 2005).

In Vietnam, the gross enrollment in tertiary education totaled some 8.56% in 2001, up from 1.54% in 1992, and a total of 1.3 million students have attended technical training institutes. However, this still falls far short of Singapore's 45% or Taiwan's 77.12% gross enrollment rates (Asian Productivity Association 2003). In addition, technical, engineering, and management training institutions in Vietnam are of poor quality and do not provide the necessary skills to enable firms to modernize and be more competitive.

Table 7.4   Universities and Colleges in Vietnam

	1995	2000	2001	2002	2003	2004
Universities and colleges		*178*	*191*	*202*	*214*	*230*
Public	109	148	168	179	187	201
Nonpublic		30	23	23	27	29
Teachers (thousands)		*32.4*	*35.9*	*38.7*	*40.0*	*47.6*
Public	22.8	27.9	31.4	33.4	34.9	40.0
Nonpublic		4.5	4.5	5.3	5.1	7.6
Students (thousands)		*899.5*	*974.1*	*1,020.7*	*1,131.0*	*1,319.8*
Public	297.9	795.6	873.0	908.8	993.9	1182.0
Nonpublic		103.9	101.1	111.9	137.1	137.8
In which: full-time training	173.1	552.5	579.2	604.4	653.7	729.4
Public		452.4	480.8	493.8	529.6	601.8
Nonpublic		100.1	98.4	110.6	124.1	127.6
Graduates (thousands)		*162.5*	*168.9*	*166.8*	*165.7*	*195.6*
Public	58.5	149.8	157.5	152.6	152.6	180.8
Nonpublic		12.6	11.4	14.2	13.1	14.8

Source: statistical yearbooks (various issues)

For the last few years, using various sources of funding, the infrastructure and facilities of higher education institutions in Vietnam have been significantly upgraded. Some laboratories have received new equipment, electronic libraries, and electronic communication networks (LAN and websites). The introduction of tuition fees for higher education has also brought about substantial extra resources for the universities. In general, the government has adopted a policy of creating a selective number of strong public universities as a basis for the further development of universities across the country (the establishment of national universities, regional or community and open universities is just a few examples of such changes to the university system). As a result, several national universities such as Hanoi National University, HCMC National University, and the other so-called area universities (serving a group of provinces having common features and conditions) located in Hue, Danang (central region), and Thai Nguyen (north) have been created. This move is aimed at creating "centers of excellence" for university education and research, in an attempt to achieve national recognition.

Another key feature of the university system during the last decade has been the establishment of open universities and the private university system. There are currently two open universities and 15 private universities in operation. Interestingly, these universities rely on teaching staff that still work for public universities (more than 70% of their staff). International cooperation has also been expanded in partnership with many international universities in order to renovate the curriculum and acquire broader experiences. Since 2005, the creation of universities holding an international status has also been explored as a major policy direction, in cooperation with several US and other leading Western universities.

Traditionally, higher education organizations such as universities and colleges did not undertake research, a model similar to the Soviet style, until the mid-1980s. Instead, they concentrated on the provision of a planned labor force. Although training remains the principal mandate of universities, research has become a more routine activity recently, with attempts to turn universities into more research-led organizations. Still, only a limited number of university faculties have adequate resources to carry out significant R&D. Only about 4% of public expenditure for S&T is currently assigned to universities, which accounts for approximately 15.3% of universities' R&D expenditure. The remaining funding for R&D expenditure comes from contracts with other organizations, of which 29.2% is from enterprises, 6.7% is from other organizations, and 48.8% is from international sources (Tran Ngoc Ca 2006). During the period 1991–1996, universities undertook almost 200 pilot production projects relying on their own research results. From 1996 to 2002, universities coming under the MOET, and the two national universities of Hanoi and Ho Chi Minh City, implemented some 3,800 R&D projects and were involved in 90 pilot production projects. Many universities have established their own R&D units. By the end of 2002, within the university sector, there were 167 research divisions and 147 centers dealing with technology development and offering consultancy activities. There has also been some movement toward more entrepreneurial activities within university circles, with teaching staff doing more consulting for firms or local governments on a contractual basis. Nonetheless, it is perhaps too early to say that a strong culture of entrepreneurial universities has emerged in Vietnam.

Research at universities has several drawbacks. In terms of perception and policy, R&D activities within the universities system have not achieved their own recognition until just the last few years. Many universities are far from being considered as R&D "centers of excellence." Universities in Vietnam lack autonomous status. Although their operations have become much more independent than before, they still have to follow many directives and comply with regulations of either the MOET, or in some cases, the line ministries that they belong to. Their staff, especially in public universities, face constraints in terms of salary ceilings, human resource management regulations, financial incentives, etc. In short, they are still deemed as government officials, rather than academics. Despite the move to abolish the separation between teaching and research, there has still been a well-documented lack of research and weak linkages between research and teaching.

The present incentive scheme does not promote a proactive approach among teaching staff in universities. There are few mechanisms to encourage them to interact with other institutions and firms. Cooperation (if any) is usually short term and relies mainly on personal and informal relationships. As such, other than training the new labor force, the contribution of university activities tends to be isolated in nature. In the existing system to date, universities have not seen technology transfer activities as crucial for their own continued survival and any technology innovations are actually not seen as particularly attractive by firms. In many instances, the facilities and practical engineering knowledge of universities lag behind those of firms.

Another issue universities face is that of human resources for teaching and undertaking research. The number of professors and lecturers is relatively small compared with the number of students.[6] Meanwhile, student enrollment is increasing. Between 1995 and 2005, for instance, the student numbers increased by 4.43 times (from 297,900 to 1,319,754 students), while the teaching staff increased by just 2.09 times (from 22,750 to 47,616 lecturers).[7] Due to this overload of teaching, the university staff simply does not have sufficient time left for R&D and/ or other learning activities. Aging staffs is another problem, because the majority of professors and associate professors are over 55 years old, with few replacements in the pipeline. During previous years, many scientific and engineering disciplines failed to attract talented young students and as such, a shortage of human resources in the university system is foreseen. Within the higher education system,

---

[6] One professor has to teach about 30 students, while in other countries this ratio is about 1:15.

[7] Data from Tsinghua University (China) show that it has some 45 academicians, 929 professors, and 1,230 associate professors to serve 30,000 undergraduate students, 5,900 graduates, and 2,600 postgraduate students. As such the ratio is only 1:9.

entrepreneurship is not a tradition. The most entrepreneurial characteristic witnessed to date is reflected in the desire of teachers to do "outside the class" teaching in order to supplement their income. The low basic salary of academic staff is offered as an explanation for this.

In terms of infrastructure and other teaching and R&D facilities, although the system has seen some recent investment for upgrading, this has tended to be only for larger universities. Many universities still use equipment and facilities dating from the mid-1960s or 1970s. Library systems in many universities are small, and outdated in both their quality and the scope of coverage. The bulk of foreign language literature is still in Russian and dates back to the mid-1970s. There has been a lack of electronic links with the national library or investment in centralized information and librarian systems. Moreover, even for universities that have English literature, the rate of use is often low due to the poor English capability of the staff and/or their current teaching workload. As a result, teaching curricula are often old, repetitive, and lack innovative approaches and new knowledge. In terms of international cooperation, the changes of the international setting, causing difficulties in long-term planning and unsuitable choices of the counterparts in cooperation, tend to put the academic system in a disadvantaged situation.

7.4   The Current Vietnamese Debate

As can be seen from the analysis above, the role and contribution of the academic system in the overall socioeconomic development of Vietnam is somewhat unclear and presents a mixed picture. On the one hand, it can be productive and useful for some, and on the other hand, still be of negligible value for others. Regarding the position of the academic system within the innovation community of Vietnam, this has always been an area of serious contention among academics, politicians, entrepreneurs, and the public domain at large.

The first bone of contention relates to the R&D institutions themselves. There are diverse views on the impacts of S&T activities on social and economic development. This has been partly explained by the limited and dispersed resources. Another issue is the struggle between autonomy and command regime as governance principle for R&D institutes and universities. The need to compete for research grants and income-generating activities has also had a strong influence on the process. More recently, the issue of the intellectual ownership of research results has entered the discourse. Many argue that more IPR should be given to the creators of innovation and R&D results, including those working on activities funded by the public purse.[8] In the context of both the drive toward a market economy and the need for poverty reduction among larger communities, the issue of striking a balance between the provision of public goods and services (usually offered for free and intended to serve the needs of the poor

---

[8]As a result, there have been demands for "Bayh-Dole Act" style regulations.

and disadvantaged) and that of private goods and services on a commercial basis has become yet another area for discussion.

As discussed in some of the previous sections, as a result of the specific features of the innovation environment in Vietnam (namely, a passive and underdeveloped innovation system) commercial relationships (including competition) have become the dominant interaction pattern with regard to innovation. Figure 7.1 below illustrates the dynamics of the innovation environment in Vietnam and highlights the dominant role of business interactions over all other interactions, with academic institutions seemingly left out of the picture.

Firms buy capital goods and raw materials from suppliers, and sell their products to, or subcontract to, their customers, who compete with one another. For those local firms which produce components for MNCs and/or large importers, in many cases these innovation activities are determined by their customers. Powerful purchasers might ask their producers to employ capital goods from reliable suppliers in order to guarantee quality. For suppliers, in order to sell their capital goods, they might have to sell on credit, and/or provide access to markets, introducing the firms to customers. The circle surrounding the diamond in Fig. 7.1 indicates that financial institutions, academic institutions, government institutions, and other service providers are not actively involved in the innovation process. The usefulness of these bodies, with regard to their support for innovation in firms, varies from sector to sector (the closer they are to the diamond, the more interaction there is between these institutions and the productive entities).

Recently, there have been a number of critics of the performance of the academic sector in Vietnam (Hoang Tuy 2007; Pham Duy Hien 2006; Pham Duc Chinh 2006), although these critics have paid tribute to the few success stories,

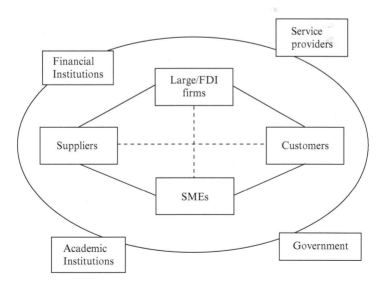

Fig. 7.1 Innovation environment in Vietnam

mainly in the fields of agriculture and public health. With regard to research activities, it has been argued that research undertaken in public R&D organizations and universities is unable to provide what the productive sector really needs. With regard to higher education training, critics have argued that graduates from universities lack practical, engineering, and/or organizational capabilities. The result is that the graduates themselves, or their employers, have to spend significant time and effort retraining on the job, in order to improve their skills set. In general, it is argued that academic institutions fail to support innovations in the productive sector actively.

The second issue being debated is more directly related to universities. The conflicting objectives of these organizations and their staff, i.e., to generate income (via patenting or spin-off activities with commercial value) while simultaneously demonstrating scientific value (e.g., through academic publications), have been noted. The training mandate of universities has been criticized for being too focused on teaching in order to gain degree certificates rather than teaching in order to facilitate actual learning (Vu Duc Nghieu 2005). Teaching is more likely to be driven by theory without necessarily addressing the need for problem-solving skills sought after by the production sector (Vu Cao Dam 2005). In addition, an aging teaching staff with deteriorating and outmoded capabilities has been identified as yet another serious problem. Overall, within academic circles, these debates are viewed as critical and seen as a direct result of the quantitative development of the university system at the expense of any qualitative improvements. Such negative views can be heard being espoused not only from academic staff in national universities, but also from selected policy makers and members of the National Assembly (MPs).

Nevertheless, not everyone agrees with the above arguments. Several national workshops have debated the role of academic institutions without necessarily coming to an agreed consensus (Tran Ngoc Ca and Nguyen Ngoc Anh 2005). Stakeholders in the debate are diverse, coming from a policy-making background, like the National Council for S&T Policy, ministries, universities, and firms. It has been argued that despite all their shortcomings, academic institutions do, in fact, play a useful role in serving the emerging needs of firms, by creating various spin-off companies. Moreover, training, which is after all the key mandate of the universities, is seen to be well delivered, despite its training shortcoming given above. Hence, the quantity versus quality discourse is alive and is being vigorously debated by various key players.

To further explore some of these issues, it is perhaps instructive to begin by understanding the nature of innovation in the context of the country's external innovation environment. The innovation environment in Vietnam, as a transitional and developing country, is quite different from what might usually be found in more advanced economies. Innovations in Vietnamese firms are influenced to a large extent by external factors and also by the fact that institutions offering innovation support simply do not exist in large numbers. Some characteristics of the Vietnamese innovation environment are summarized below:

- First, the majority of firms in Vietnam are small (including FDI and SOEs) and often serve small, underdeveloped, and unstable markets. They compete mainly on their access to cheap labor and the availability of natural resources (including land). Very few firms compete on the grounds of new technology or differentiated products.
- Many firms (especially those in exporting sectors) are making components, or subcontractors, for foreign business and/or MNCs; as a result, their innovations tend to be incremental and determined by their foreign customers.
- The systems of national and sectoral innovation are weak; public resources for R&D and other support for innovation are limited. Central government funding for R&D mainly goes toward projects of large public research institutions, which usually do not have a mandate or the mechanisms to provide services for firms with diversified and specific problems. Local government budgets for S&T activities are also limited and, in many provinces, any budget which exists is used internally, within existing local government bodies.
- A market for technical and innovation services has not yet developed.
- The body of common codified technical knowledge in Vietnamese is poor and not well organized, making it difficult for firms to reference and source.
- Knowledge of engineering is lacking, especially among academic institutions.
- Codifying technical knowledge is not a common practice in firms or academic institutions; as a result, large amounts of potentially valuable knowledge, which could be utilized effectively, are not codified, not generalized, and not appropriated, making it difficult to source.
- The institutional environment lacks transparency, is unpredictable, and is not well communicated to stakeholders. Corruption is present in some public agencies, which inflates the cost of doing formal business. As a result, there are many informal economic activities, which do not favor innovation.
- The financial market is underdeveloped (the stock market is in its infancy and there are a lack of mechanisms for venture capitalists and/or "business angels"), plus the relative informality of business makes it very difficult for investors to put their money safely into innovation projects. As such, many promising innovative projects simply cannot find appropriate funding.
- The lack of a level playing field makes rent-seeking the main priority of many firms, which, in turn, erodes the incentives for innovations.

Next is the issue of the nature of innovation in a different context. Innovations in the Vietnamese economy, as in any typical developing country, differ from innovations in more advanced countries. Having analyzed data from various surveys and case studies, some of the most distinctive features of innovations in Vietnamese firms can be summarized as follows:

- Innovations are either incremental or "new to the firm." Incremental innovations are common when firms try to solve specific technical problems which usually emerge from the operation of imported production systems or when firms try to produce "new" products using their existing production facilities. "New to the firm" innovations are common when firms acquire whole or parts of a production system in order to produce "new" products.

- It is not technological breakthrough, but rather technology diffusion and/or technology learning which is the main mechanism for innovation. Acquisition of embodied technology via capital goods is the critical component of innovation. Partnering international production networks or key international players is important for technology learning.
- Many firms have to take a "second-best" approach in their innovations, which means that they rely on their own in-house teams to solve problems through a lot of "trial and error." Most innovations arose informally, without an appropriate supporting structure such as standards, quality control, metrology, IPR, legal and technical consulting, information services, etc., and without systematically following best practices of technology management. Linkages with business partners, especially foreign ones, play an important role in firms' innovation. Codified technological knowledge is under-utilized.

Another much debated issue is *the mismatch between the production and S&T sectors* with regard to the capacity of academic institutions to carry out technical changes. The central question of "Who can do what best, and for whom?" has been the subject of many workshops and conferences, as well as the media (Tran Ngoc Ca and Nguyen Ngoc Anh 2005). Given the type of innovations described above, the academic sector should be easily able to support firms' innovation effectively. The reason that they have not done so, to date, is because of the limited mandate of the academic institutions and their management bodies. As a result of the clear mismatch between the production and S&T sectors with regard to supporting innovation, it is perhaps not surprising that many firms prefer to do their own research, in cooperation with their business partners.

Since many of the innovations identified in Vietnamese firms are not science based but rather problem solving in nature, firms assume that academic institutions are able to support them solve their problems, through their knowledge capabilities and/or technical services. However, academic institutions are often poorly organized and simply unable to provide effective innovation solutions.

Table 7.5 shows the stark difference between what enterprises wish academic institutions could offer them and what academic institutions think they can, or should, offer enterprises. It is clear that while firms rank *analyzing and testing* as the most desirable service from public research organizations (ranked first), PROs themselves rank this service fourth. Similarly, while firms rank "Installation of new machines and equipment" and "maintenance and fixing production machines" as the second and the third most wanted, these are ranked tenth and ninth, respectively, by academic institutions. Table 7.5 also shows the reverse. While PROs rank "Industrial R&D" as their most capable service (ranked first), it is only ranked sixth by firms. Similarly, "providing technology information" and "advice on buying production machines" are ranked second and third by academic institutions, while firms only rank them seventh and ninth, respectively. It is generally agreed that reform of academic institutions is sorely needed. However, any changes that are to

Table 7.5 Ranking of the most wanted services (by firms) and the most capable activities (for academic institutions) of enterprises and PROs

Type of services	Firms' rank	Academic institutions' rank
Installation of new machines and equipment	2	10
Industrial engineering	5	11
Maintenance and fixing production machines	3	9
Analysing, testing product/material samples	1	4
Technical training	4	5
Modify product design or material specifications	8	7
Modify production machines	11	8
Manufacture production machines or components	10	6
Industrial R&D	6	1
Technology information	7	2
Advice on buying production machines	9	3

Source: Innovation Survey (2002) and PROs Survey (2000). NISTPASS

be made should ensure that they are able to serve better both the needs of economic growth in general and those which have emerged from the innovations of local firms in particular.

According to a survey on firms' innovation activities, the following is a "wish list" of things that firms might wish to see in order to better orientate the academic sector. Given the specific features of innovations in a transitional developing country, firms would wish to see the following:

- A more innovative and friendly business environment where innovation activities were better supported.
- Easy access to detailed information relating to firms' innovation activities. Such information should cover all aspects of these activities, and be widened to include information on markets, materials, etc., and not just technical information.
- Easy access to the pool of common technical knowledge which has already been codified and referenced in appropriate forms and languages, especially Vietnamese.
- Assistance be given in order to create links with production networks, both domestic and international.
- Access to reliable, affordable technologies, preferably in the form of a package of solutions which would usually include capital goods, technological know-how, training, supply of key materials, and access to markets.
- Access to a full range of technical services, at a reasonable cost.
- Better training in technology management.
- Access to appropriate financial resources.

A new dimension has been added to the debate in the context of pro-poor growth and achieving the Millennium Development Goals in Vietnam. In order to contribute to the solution of problems in areas such as the environment, poverty reduction, agricultural and rural development, gender equality, healthcare for all, and education for all, academic institutions are now being asked to do more work on a voluntary basis. To provide free, or virtually free, innovative products to these groups of recipients requires a totally different mindset and mechanism. Not every organization is prepared for this in a market economy. Potential conflicts do exist when they involve the interests of knowledge creators and knowledge users. Non-state stakeholders such as the nongovernmental organizations (NGOs), associations such as the Vietnam Union for S&T Association (VUSTA), Women's Union, or Trade Unions, can and would like to have a stronger voice in shaping the innovation landscape. Interestingly, private sector firms tend to simply stand by and conduct business as usual, with or without the help of academic institutions.

These discussions lead to the debate about the need for an institutional framework for innovation. The *Science and Technology Law*[9] states that it is necessary to combine natural, engineering, and social sciences and humanities; link R&D with training and education; and link R&D with business and production operations, in order to develop a technology market in the country. Another *Law on Education* (in its Article 15) regulates scientific activity (in the education system) and emphasizes that universities and colleges have a responsibility to coordinate their training with research and technology transfer, in order to better serve the needs of social and economic development. Leading Party documents[10] also indicate that academic institutions have to become centers for R&D, technology transfer, and applications in production and economy, in order to ensure closer linkages between research institutes and universities, and to link R&D with productive activities. Recent Laws on IPR (enacted in 2005) and Technology Transfer (enacted in 2006) have contributed a great amount to clarify the issue of intellectual property ownership of research results and their commercialization.

Still, a few continue to argue that the overall policy environment is not always conducive for their interactions. And interestingly, this policy environment could be adjusted and adapted to suit specific geographical locations by their respective governments. This might be explained by the impact of the specific socioeconomic endowment of the relevant provinces and cities on the actions and performance of the academic institutions. But more than that, leadership of institutions is important where they could adopt pro-proactive approach in running activities (Tran Ngoc Ca 2006).

There are a range of policies that need to be improved in order to facilitate improved linkages between academic institutions and firms. There has been a consensus that, overall, the innovation system in the country, in which academic organizations are the key actors, needs to be reshuffled, and research made more market driven, better serving the need of both individual firms and industrial sectors as a whole.

---

[9]Enacted by the National Assembly of Vietnam, regulated in Article 5, subarticle 3 on the Principles of Science and Technology activities.

[10]Resolution of PartyPlenum II on the Direction to develop S&T until 2010. Nhan Dan Newspaper.

7.5   Conclusions

There have been many efforts to restructure the knowledge production system in Vietnam, which has been heavily influenced by the former Soviet-style model. The existing situation relating to the academic system in Vietnam shows that R&D institutions and universities are making significant contributions to the development of the country. Teaching has been the main function of the universities and will continue to be so for more years to come. But there are still problems to rectify: under-qualified lecturers, poor infrastructure and curricula for training, and limited capabilities of graduating students, to name just a few. In addition, innovation seems to be neglected, except for some major universities that have aspirations to become regional centers of excellence in the future.

Therefore, a reorientation of the academic sector is sorely needed and a major overhaul is being planned. However, the roots of the problem lie in inappropriate incentive schemes for the academic system and the lack of a mechanism to diagnose the innovation needs of firms. Academic institutions need to focus more on problem solving, an activity in which they used to excel. More autonomy is being given to academic institutions and with that comes more responsibility. There is also a need for improvement of incentive schemes to make them conducive to supporting such activities.

There are several key policy recommendations that can be made:

- A longer-term vision and a more strategic approach should replace the current short-term objectives of simply earning fees in order to benefit the academic system.
- To overcome the separation of research from teaching in the university system, there should be more autonomy and incentive systems to encourage innovative research.
- Investment should be more focused to avoid wasting resources and fragmentation.
- Modern university and R&D management practices such as peer review, advisory committees, and performance-based evaluations should be thoroughly applied.

Balancing the potentially conflicting interests of offering more commercialized research, teaching, and serving the public need is not an easy task for academic institutions in any economy. The establishment of companies to act as commercial arms or technology transfer offices (TTOs) and technology licensing offices (TLOs) is something which universities could pursue. A model of private universities built as centers of excellence,[11] with social "corporate" responsibilities, might be a sensible option for the country. Internationalization of the academic system (via the introduction of new practices such as more international staff, international

---

[11]Chinese Tsinghua University is seen as a favorite model for Vietnam.

salary levels and modes of management, evaluation criteria and teaching quality, etc.) could create a drive for more competition and improved quality.

With regard to promoting linkages between academic institutions and firms, one should pay attention to both the extent of the linkages and mechanisms which is seen as affecting quantitative linkages, as well as to the mode of linkage that affects the depth of linkages.

Any new mechanisms should be based on the overall principle of moving more toward a market economy, with macro-regulations by the state. This should be seen as a long-term process, requiring determination and flexible solutions depending on the specific circumstances. Development of a technology market is one of the key outcomes of the increasing linkages with the production sector and could be achieved by the following measures:

- Creation and improvement of a legal system for a technology market (including regulations on science and technology contracts).
- Promotion of organizations required for technology management such as arbitration, registration of contracts, management of technology transactions, etc.
- Establishment of organizations dealing with market and technology brokerage, technology agents, and centers for leasing and contracting manpower for science and technology activities.
- Development of new forms of technology transfer, technology services, and other technical issues of technology contracts.

Furthermore, to help solve the problem of inadequate linkages between academic organizations and production activities, several issues should be addressed: capabilities of the human resource; financial packages and incentives; organization of R&D system; IPR issues; and assessment of research results. At the same time, a key issue is to increase innovative capability in order to meet the technological innovation needs of enterprises. In addition to the two traditional domains of teaching and research, a third mission, that of serving the needs of the community, would appear to be appropriate in the current context.

The existing differences in their own capability assessments are one reason for the different approaches and attitudes in developing linkages between research organizations and enterprises. When the universities (similarly to most R&D institutions) continue to under- (or over-) value their own capabilities, they will be seen as ignoring the views of enterprises and creating difficulties for enhancing the link with enterprises. In order to help the research community better understand the needs of production, one option might be to facilitate a dialog between academic organizations and production enterprises to match their innovative need and actions.

Within this overall policy environment, specific policy changes, depending on the actual conditions of each location (cities, provinces), should play a pivotal role in shaping academic behavior into being more business friendly and offering innovative productive patterns through their interactions with firms and the local economy.

This discussion suggests that a more thorough investigation of some of the specific issues that have been raised needs to be undertaken in order to shed light on the academic study system and the balance between teaching, research, and serving the society. This points to the need for case studies of selected universities to examine how this third mission is being carried out in practice.

References

Asian Productivity Association (2003). *Asia-Pacific Productivity Data and Analysis 2003*. Tokyo.

Bezanson K, Tran Ngoc Ca, Oldham G (2000). *A Science, Technology and Industry Strategy for Vietnam*. UNDP/UNIDO, Hanoi.

Hoang Tuy (2007). New year, old stories. Tia Sang. *Journal of the Ministry of Science and Technology*. No. 3–4. February 2007.

Klaus Meyer, et al. (2006). Doing business in Vietnam. Thunderbird International Business Review. Volume 48(2). March–April.

Ministry of Education and Training (MOET) (2005). *Data on Education and Training*. Website: http://www.edu.vn/data/

MOST (2006). *Vietnam's Science and Technology 2001–2005*. S&T Publishing House.

NISTPASS (1999). *Technological Capability of Firms in Economic Sectors*. Final Report of Survey of Six Economic Sectors, Hanoi.

NISTPASS (2000). *Research and Postgraduate Training*. Report of RAPOGE Project, Hanoi.

NISTPASS (2002). *Survey of the Supply Capability of Organizations in the Technology Infrastructure*. Final Report of Survey of R&D and Technical Service Organizations, Hanoi.

NISTPASS (2004). *Reforms of R&D Policy in the Context of the Transition to a Market Economy*. Agriculture Publishing House, Hanoi.

Nguyen Vo Hung, Nguyen Thanh Ha (2003). *Survey on Innovation Activities of Firms with Domestic Investment*. Report of the Project 'Improving the Technological Capability of Vietnamese Industries in the Transition to a Market Economy'. NISTPASS-SIDA/SAREC.

Pham Duy Hien (2006). When would Vietnamese science and education join WTO? Tia Sang. *Journal of the Ministry of Science and Technology*. No. 22. November 2006.

Pham Duc Chinh (2006). To reform more radically. Tia Sang. *Journal of the Ministry of Science and Technology*. No. 24. December 2006.

Science and Technology Law (2000). National Political Publishing House, Hanoi.

Tran Ngoc Ca (2002). *Learning Technological Capability for Vietnam's Industrial Upgrading: the Challenges of Globalization*. The European Institute of Japanese Studies at the Stockholm School of Economics. Working Paper 165.

Tran Ngoc Ca (2006). *Universities as Drivers of the Urban Economies in Asia. The Case of Vietnam*. Policy Research Working Paper. No. 3949. World Bank. Development Research Group. June 2006.

Tran Ngoc Ca, Nguyen Ngoc Anh (2005). *The Role of R&D and Training Institutions in Socio-Economic Development*. Proceedings of the Workshop. National Council for S&T Policy and UniDev Project, Hanoi, December 2005.

UNIDO (1999). *Vietnam Industrial Competitiveness Review*. UNIDO/DSI Ministry of Planning and Investment, Hanoi.

UNDP (2004a). *Millennium Development Goals in Vietnam*, Hanoi.

UNDP (2004b). *Human Development Report Statistics*.

Vietnam Science and Technology (2002). Ministry of Science and Technology, Hanoi.

Vu Cao Dam (2005). *Policy Measures to Enhance Research Capability in Universities*. Paper Presented at the Workshop on Research and Training Policy in the Transitional Period of Vietnam. University of Social Sciences and Humanities, Hanoi. December 2005.

Vu Duc Nghieu (2005). *Policy Reform for University Science and Education in Vietnam*. Paper Presented at the Workshop on Research and Training Policy in the Transitional Period of Vietnam. University of Social Sciences and Humanities, Hanoi. December 2005.

Chapter 8
China: Challenges for Higher Education in a High Growth Economy

Wang Haiyan and Zhou Yuan

8.1 Introduction

A look back at the twentieth century reveals that education provided the momentum for economic growth and social development in both developing and developed countries. The twenty-first century is likely to be dominated by the knowledge-based economy, and the most important sources of economic growth will turn out to be the production, processing, dissemination, and application of knowledge. Therefore, education will play a prominent and basic role both in knowledge creation and dissemination, and human resource development.

China has the largest population in the world. With the reform of the education system, universities have become an important actor in the Chinese National Innovation System (NIS), and play a necessary role in talent training, scientific research, and technology transfer.

This paper examines the roles that universities play in the Chinese NIS and is organized as follows: Sect. 8.2 describes the history of the Chinese NIS and the university system; Sects. 8.3 and 8.4 describe the characteristics of the current Chinese NIS and the university system, respectively; Sect. 8.5 deals with some of the debates concerning the role of universities in Chinese NIS; and Sect. 8.6 draws conclusions.

8.2 Chinese and the University System: A Historical Account

Since the People's Republic of China was founded in 1949, the evolution of China's NIS and its university system has experienced four phases.

W. Haiyan (✉)
Chinese Academy of Science and Technology for Development (CASTED),
Ministry of S&T, Beijing,
Peoples' Republic of China
e-mail: wanghy@casted.org.cn

B. Göransson and C. Brundenius (eds.), *Universities in Transition:*
The Changing Role and Challenges for Academic Institutions,
© International Development Research Centre 2011

8.2.1   Phase I 1950s: The Soviet Pattern

After World War II and the 4-year civil war, the Chinese Communist party established the People's Republic of China in 1949. Following the Soviet pattern, China adopted the planned economy and centralized command system, and the economy began to recover. However, the Chinese NIS was isolated from the Western world.

In this phase, research institutions were the core of the NIS. Influenced by the Soviet Union, the Communist government established a complex system of research institutions, the most important one being the Chinese Academy of Sciences (CAS). The government directly organized and implemented numerous science and technology (S&T) plans and programs, and directly managed research institutions. Much of the research undertaken was military related, and few research results were applied to industrial production. The research institutes, universities, and enterprises were segregated from each other, and researchers had few linkages or interactions with industry.

In this phase, the characteristics of the NIS were as follows (Fig. 8.1):

(a) The government was the only supporter and controller of research.
(b) Research institutions, universities, and enterprises were separated from each other.

During 1949–1952, the Communist government took over the public universities, which were established by the previous government, and gradually transferred the private universities to the public domain. In 1952, the Ministry of Education made an adjustment to the university system and adopted the Soviet model. After the adjustment, Chinese universities were mainly divided into two kinds – comprehensive universities and specialized universities. The task of comprehensive universities was to provide human resources for research institutions or to train teachers for high schools and universities. The task of specialized universities was to provide high-level S&T personnel for enterprises. Consequently, the number of students in engineering and pedagogy was largely increased, while the number of students in humanities and social sciences dropped sharply.

Corresponding to the planned economy, Chinese higher education system was centralized and placed directly under the administration of the central or the local governments. The disadvantages of this system were that, because of government control, universities lacked the flexibility and autonomy to provide education according to the needs of the society.

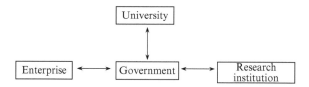

Fig. 8.1 The Chinese NIS in 1950s

Due to the establishment of a large number of research institutes, the research function of the universities weakened. The only mission of Chinese universities in this phase was education.

In this phase, the characteristics of the university system were as follows:

(a) University system was paralleled to research system.
(b) Universities provided skilled human resource for research institutions and enterprises.
(c) Education was the single aim and mission of universities.

8.2.2   Phase II 1966–1978: The Cultural Revolution

The cultural revolution began in 1966 and lasted for 10 years. During this phase, the whole nation was in the grip of political movements, and the development of the economy and S&T system almost came to a halt, which led to even greater isolation from the outside world. The NIS and university system were in a state of chaos and vacuum.

In this phase, the centralized university system established in the 1950s was completely destroyed. Universities became the tool of the despotism of the proletariat and were controlled by soldiers, workers, and students, while many teachers were put in prison or kept under surveillance. Academics did not teach or do research any more, and students did not study but joined political movements. The only mission of universities was to foster people with political ability.

8.2.3   Phase III 1978–1990: The Economic Reforms

In 1978, Deng Xiaoping, the new leader of China, advocated economic reforms that aimed at creating a market-oriented economy. From that time, China began to implement the "reform and opening-up" policy. In 1985, the central government further reformed the S&T system, decentralized fiscal and managerial control, redefined public and private ownership, and encouraged new linkages between research and industry.

In this phase, the Chinese NIS began to change from "government ruling" to "government guiding." State-owned enterprises started adapting to the competition in the marketplace, and private enterprises gradually became more significant. The government reformed the finance system and ceased to finance research institutions and universities, forcing them to find funding elsewhere. Some research institutions began to offer graduate education, and the universities began to undertake research projects, but there was still a lack of interaction between universities and research institutions, and the enterprises were still largely separated from the research system.

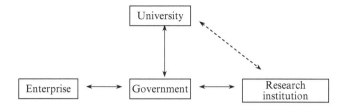

Fig. 8.2 The Chinese NIS in 1978–1990

In this phase, the characteristics of NIS were as follows (Fig. 8.2):

(a) Changing from "government ruling" to "government guiding."
(b) Enterprises were still largely separated from universities and research institutions.

In December 1977, the Chinese government resumed the system of entrance examination for higher education, and ended the recommendation systems for admission into higher education. With the reform of the S&T system since 1985, the transformation of the higher education system was intensified with the aim of extending the rights of self-determination of universities and strengthening their interaction with other actors. The emphasis of education policy shifted from political function to economic function.

The universities were given the twin missions of education and research. In early 1979, the Chinese government decided that some key universities should become research centers, which marked that research formally became a mission of Chinese universities. In the 1980s, the number of research institutions established by universities increased rapidly, and achievements in the R&D field became an important indicator in the evaluation of universities.

In addition, since the 1980s, the universities could cooperate with enterprises without the permission of government. Finally, as government ceased to lend financial support, many universities established self-run enterprises to generate profit.

In this phase, the characteristics of university system were as follows:

(a) Both education and research became the primary missions of universities.
(b) Universities constituted a component of the research system.
(c) University-run enterprises emerged.

8.2.4 Phase IV 1990s: Development of Market-Oriented Economy

In 1992, the Chinese government formally clarified that the aim of economic reform was to develop a market-oriented economy, and the main task was to promote economic development. Many state-owned enterprises gradually changed into joint-stock enterprises, and a large number of private enterprises developed rapidly. In the same year, the Chinese government initiated the project of "enterprise–university–institution

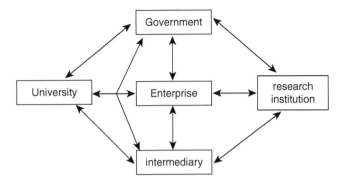

Fig. 8.3 The Chinese NIS in 1990s

cooperation" to encourage cooperation among enterprises, universities, and research institutions. Enterprises played a more active role in technological innovation and were becoming the focus of the NIS.

Corresponding to the economic reform, the S&T system started undergoing rapid reforms. In 1995, the government decided to implement the "Vitalizing the Nation through Science and Education (VNSE) Strategy" in the National Science and Technology Conference. In 1998, the State Council accomplished the internal reform, which accelerated the reform of the research institution and university system. Some research institutions were transformed into enterprises and some were integrated into enterprises to become internal research units of enterprises.

In this phase, the characteristics of NIS were as follows (Fig. 8.3):

(a) S&T System Reform required that research must aim at economic development.
(b) Interaction among enterprises, universities, and research institutions became stronger than before.
(c) The NIS was more open.

In the 1990s, the university system began "the second adjustment" after the first one in the 1950s. Following the US and the European models that emphasize comprehensive universities, many Chinese universities or colleges that had been separated in 1950s began to merge. For example, Hangzhou University, Zhejiang Agriculture University, and Zhejiang Medical University merged to become Zhejiang University, and formed the most comprehensive university in China. In 1998, as a result of the reforms of the State Council, many Chinese universities that were formerly managed by the central government began to be managed by the local government. After the adjustment, the number of universities decreased, but the scale of merged universities enlarged.

Through the second adjustment, China instituted a framework under which the majority of universities are administered by provincial governments and operated jointly by local and central governments. The provincial governments enjoy greater responsibility, authority, and benefits in bringing local higher education under their unified planning. This new system has overcome problems of segmentation and isolation, redundancy, and resource waste; facilitated various relations; activated willingness of the local government and various circles to support higher education development; and tightened links between universities and regional economic and social development, thus having profound and strategic significance for the development of higher education in China (Zhou Ji 2002).

In addition to the system reform, from 1993, the government also carried out a series of steps to further extend the right of universities: universities have the right to enroll self-financing students; to design their own curricula and material; to undertake joint research with enterprises; to appoint and dismiss the vice president of the university; to transfer the educational funds from government; etc. As a result of the reforms, universities could now orient themselves toward the market more actively, and the relationship between the universities and the society has been strengthened.

The mission of universities changed to serve economic development and promote the advancement of S&T. More and more Chinese universities began to set up their own enterprises. On one hand, these university-run enterprises provide necessary financing for universities, and on the other hand, they directly contribute to economic development. More and more people gradually recognized that universities could be the engines for the development of knowledge-based society.

In this phase, the characteristics of the university system were as follows:

(a) VNSE Strategy required that universities must serve economic development.
(b) The cooperation and linkage between universities and research institutions, universities, and enterprises were closer than ever before.
(c) More and more universities set up their own enterprises.

8.3   The Characteristics of Current Chinese NIS

In a knowledge-based society, the generation, diffusion, and appropriation of knowledge are more active than ever before. NIS, as a core conceptual framework for analyzing technological change within a country, is becoming very important. There are many kinds of definitions for NIS, and this paper follows Lundvall's definition: "National Innovation System is constituted by elements and relationships which interact in the production, diffusion and use of new and economically useful knowledge" (Lundvall 1992).

Currently, the Chinese NIS is changing from the former government-dominated pattern to a new market-dominated one. Through a series of reforms, the research system in China has experienced significant changes: the function and position of the former research institutions have been changed; the research capability and the status of the enterprises have been promoted; and the universities have become an important part of the Chinese research system. There are various kinds of interactions among the enterprises, research institutions, and universities. Therefore, a new kind of research system consisting of multitude of actors has formed in China.

The government is still a strong supporter of research. In order to meet the global challenge of new technology revolution and competition, the central government initiated several S&T programs on technologies that small enterprises were not able to undertake, such as the 863 Program, which aims to boost innovation capacity in the high-tech sectors, particularly in IT, biotechnology, advanced materials technology, energy technology, etc.; the Key Technologies R&D Program, which aims to address major S&T issues in national economic construction and social development; and the 973 program, which aims to strengthen basic research in line with national strategic targets (http://www.most.gov.cn).

The government also encourages the development of S&T through restructuring the environment for S&T industries. Many S&T programs have shifted their orientation from project implementation to environment construction, which aims to enhance technical services and exchanges, stimulate development of small and medium-sized S&T enterprises, vigorously develop S&T intermediaries, and create a sound environment for the commercialization and industrialization of S&T findings. Meanwhile, efforts are also being made to promote trade through S&T, provide innovation funding for small technology-based firms, and establish productivity promotion centers, university S&T parks, and agricultural S&T parks.

With the support of the government, the S&T enterprises are playing a more active role in the current Chinese NIS. The R&D input and output of enterprises are increasing significantly. Many enterprises established their own R&D centers and began to cooperate with universities for the development of new products or technologies. The government encouraged greater linkages between universities and enterprises by encouraging university-run enterprises, establishing fiscal and legal services for professorial and student start-ups, strengthening patent laws, and supporting the establishment of university science parks.

The characteristics of current Chinese NIS are as follows:

(a) The government is trying to build up a more effective NIS.
(b) Enterprises are becoming the most important actor, but not yet.
(c) The linkages between actors in NIS are closer than before.

The following part introduces the Chinese NIS by describing the distribution of the R&D expenditure.

R&D activity is an important part of NIS. With the implement of "VNSE Strategy" and the development of economy, the scale of the gross R&D expenditure (GERD) in China has increased rapidly (Table 8.1). From 1998 to 2004, the average

Table 8.1 GERD/GDP in China (2002–2006)

	2002	2003	2004	2005	2006
GERD (100 million)	1,287.6	1,539.6	1,966.3	2,450.0	3,003.1
GDP (100 million)	120,332.7	135,822.8	159,878.3	183,867.9	210,871.0
GERD/GDP (%)	1.07	1.13	1.23	1.33	1.42

Unit: 100 million Yuan. *Source*: China Statistical Yearbook (2007)

rate of increase of the GERD in China was 21.3%, and in 2006, it reached 300.3 billion Yuan. The percentage of GERD/GDP also increased from 0.70% in 1998 to 1.42% in 2006.

Table 8.2 shows the intramural expenditure for R&D by type of research from 2003 to 2007. In 2007, R&D expenditure in fundamental research, applied research, and experimental development were 17.45, 49.29, and 304.27 billion Yuan, having increased by 33.6, 28.6 and 27.0% compared with the previous year, respectively. The percentages of the R&D expenditures in fundamental research, applied research and experimental development were12.04, 0.81, and 29.02%, respectively. Though the expenditure on fundamental research kept increasing year by year, from 8.77 billion Yuan in 2003 to 17.45 billion Yuan in 2007, the percentage of it in the total R&D expenditure was still low, hovering between 5 and 6%. This was partly because of the pursuit of short-term research in R&D activities and the large share of experimental development expenditure in government R&D expenditure, which may exert a negative impact for the development of the long-term research.

In 2007, R&D expenditure incurred by universities was 31.47 billion Yuan, which was an increase of 13.69% over the previous year; R&D expenditure of independent research institutions was 68.79 billion Yuan, an increase of 21.26%; and the R&D expenditure of enterprises was 268.2 billion Yuan, an increase of 25.65% over the previous year. The share of the R&D expenditure performed by universities, research institutions, and enterprises in the gross R&D expenditure was 8.5, 18.5, and 72.3%, respectively. According to the data in Table 8.3, the R&D expenditure performed by enterprises is growing stably, and the enterprises are becoming the core actors of the R&D activities. However, the share of university R&D activities is still much lower.

8.3.1 Public R&D

The sources of R&D funds in China include the government funds, enterprise funds, foreign funds, and other funds. Table 8.4 shows the sources of R&D funds in 2006 and 2007. Enterprise sector has become the major R&D investor in China, and accounted for more than half of the total R&D funds.

The government funding is an important source of R&D funds in China, but its proportion is decreasing. In 2004, the R&D funds from government were 52.36 billion Yuan, or 26.6% of the total funds. Due to its guidance and strategic function, the government funds still play a significant role in the development of S&T.

Table 8.5 shows the distribution of the government R&D funds in 2006 and 2007. More than 95% of the total government R&D fund was distributed to public R&D sector, including research institutions and universities. The share of research institutions was above 64%, while the share of universities was just over 19%. This was mainly because of the traditional Soviet scientific system, which does not attach importance to R&D activities in universities.

Table 8.2 Intramural expenditure for R&D by type of research (2003–2007)

	2003	%	2004	%	2005	%	2006	%	2007	%
Total	1,539.63		1,966.33		2,449.97		3,003.10		3,710.24	
Fundamental research	87.65	5.69	117.18	5.96	131.21	5.36	155.76	5.19	174.52	4.70
Applied research	311.45	20.23	400.49	20.37	433.53	17.70	488.97	16.28	492.94	13.29
Experimental development	1140.52	74.08	1,448.67	73.67	1,885.24	76.95	2,358.37	78.53	3,042.78	82.01

Unit: 100 million Yuan. *Source*: China Statistical Yearbook on Science and Technology (2008)

Table 8.3 Intramural expenditure on R&D by performer (2003–2007)

	2003	%	2004	%	2005	%	2006	%	2007	%
Total	1,539.6		1,966.3		2,450.0		3,003.1		3,710.2	
Independent research institution	399.0	25.9	431.7	22.0	513.1	20.9	567.3	18.9	687.9	18.5
Enterprises (including SOE)	960.2	62.4	1,314.0	66.8	1,673.8	68.3	2,134.5	71.1	2,681.9	72.3
Large and medium-sized										
Higher education institutions	162.3	10.5	200.9	10.2	242.3	9.9	276.8	9.2	314.7	8.5
Others	18.1	1.2	19.7	1.0	20.8	0.9	24.5	0.8	25.7	0.7

Unit: 100 million Yuan. *Source*: China Statistical Yearbook on Science and Technology (2008)

Table 8.4 Intramural expenditure for R&D by source (2006–2007)

	2006		2007	
Total	3,003.1	%	3,710.2	%
Government funds	742.1	24.71	913.5	24.62
Enterprises funds (including SOE)	2,073.7	69.05	2,611.0	70.37
Foreign funds	48.4	1.61	50.0	01.35
Other funds	138.9	4.63	135.8	03.66

Unit: 100 million Yuan. *Source*: China Statistical Yearbook on Science and Technology (2007) and China Statistical Yearbook on Science and Technology (2008)

Table 8.5 Intramural expenditure for R&D from government (2006–2007)

	2006		2007	
Total	742.1	%	913.5	%
Independent research institution	481.2	64.84	592.9	64.90
Enterprises (including SOE)	96.8	13.04	128.7	14.10
Large and medium-sized	60.0		85.7	
Higher education institutions	151.5	20.42	177.7	19.45
Others	12.6	1.70	14.1	1.55

Unit: 100 million Yuan. *Source*: China Statistical Yearbook on Science and Technology (2007 and 2008)

Table 8.6 Industrial structure of GDP in China (%)

	1978	1989	1997	2006
Primary industry	28.2	25.1	18.3	11.7
Secondary industry	47.9	42.8	47.5	48.9
Tertiary industry	23.9	32.1	34.2	39.4

Source: China Statistical Yearbook (2007)

It should be mentioned that SOEs' share of public R&D is not available due to the complicated classification of Chinese enterprises. However, they are the main body of the large and medium-sized enterprises in China, which account for more than half of the total enterprises' R&D expenditure.

8.3.2   Industry R&D

With the implementation of the "reform and opening-up" policy, the industry structure of China has been adjusted continuously. The share of agriculture decreased from 28.21% in 1978 to 11.7% in 2006, while the share of the service industry increased from 23.9 to 39.4%. However, the development of service industry is relatively slower (Table 8.6).

Table 8.7 The R&D intensity of high-tech industries in China (2003)

	R&D intensity
Manufacture of aircraft and spacecraft	15.8%
Manufacture of electronic and telecommunications equipments	5.4%
Manufacture of medical equipments and meter	3%
Manufacture of medical and pharmaceutical products	2.7%
Manufacture of computers and office equipments	2.5%

Source: China Statistics Yearbook on High Technology Industry (2008)

Table 8.8 Percentage of exports of high-tech products, manufactured goods, and primary goods (2003–2007)

	2003	2004	2005	2006	2007
Manufactured goods	92.1	93.2	93.6	94.5	95.0
Of which: high-tech products	25.2	27.9	28.6	29.0	28.6
Primary goods	7.9	6.8	6.4	5.5	5.0
Total	100	100	100	100	100

Source: China Statistical Yearbook on Science and Technology (2008)

In 2003, the average R&D intensity of Chinese manufacturing industries was 2%, much lower than the average level of developed countries. Therefore, the standard used for classification as high-tech industries is also lower in China than the one in developed countries. The high-tech industries in China include manufacture of aircraft and spacecraft, manufacture of electronic and telecommunications equipments, manufacture of medical equipments and meter, manufacture of medical and pharmaceutical products, and manufacture of computers and office equipments. Table 8.7 shows the R&D intensity of these high-tech industries in 2003.

In the past two decades, China has become the sixth largest trading country in the world. Though the share of high-tech products in export is increasing, the main export items are still labor-intensive and low-value-added products, such as textiles, toys, clothing, etc. (Table 8.8).

Table 8.9 shows the share of exports and imports of high-tech products in 2007. The data indicate that Chinese exports and imports of high-tech products are mainly concentrated in three industries: computers, telecommunications, and electronics. The three industries accounted for 93.5% of the total export value and 81.9% of the total import value in 2007.

8.3.3   Universities' R&D

The sources of the R&D funds in Chinese universities are multiplex. External funds, especially from enterprises, are increasing. In 2007, enterprises' funds were 11.03 billion RMB, accounting for 35.05% of total R&D funds in universities, an increase by 9.0% over the previous year (Table 8.10). Compared with research institutions, which depend primarily on government funds, universities are closer to the market, and the relationship between universities and enterprises is much closer.

Table 8.9 Percentage of export and imports of high-tech products (2007)

	Export (%)	Import (%)
Computers and telecommunications	80.4	27.2
Life science	2.6	2.3
Electronics	13.1	54.7
Computer integrated manufacturing	1.4	8.0
Aerospace and aeronautics	0.7	4.5
Optic-electronics	1.0	1.4
Biotechnology	0.1	0.1
Material	0.6	1.8
Others	0.1	0.1
Total	100	100

Source: China Statistical Yearbook on Science and Technology (2008)

Table 8.10 Intramural expenditure for R&D in HEIs by source (2006–2007)

	2006 (100 million Yuan)	%	2007 (100 million Yuan)	%
Total	*276.8*	*100*	*314.7*	*100*
Government funds	151.5	54.73	177.7	56.47
Enterprises funds	101.2	36.56	110.3	35.05
Foreign funds	3.8	01.37	4.8	01.53
Other funds	20.3	07.33	21.9	06.96

Source: China Statistical Yearbook on Science and Technology (2008)

Table 8.11 Comparison of R&D expenditure between research institutions and HEIs

	Research institutions		HEIs	
Basic research	74.7	10.9%	86.8	27.6%
Applied research	227.1	33.0%	161.8	51.4%
Experimental development	386	56.1%	66.1	21.0%

Unit: 100 million Yuan. *Source*: China Science and Technology Indicator (2008)

Comparing R&D expenditure between research institutes and universities, we can see that universities emphasize basic research and applied research, while the research institutions emphasize experimental development (Table 8.11). However, in absolute terms, research institutes still carry our more basic research than universities do.

8.4 The Characteristics of Current Chinese University System

The experience of educational development in China indicates that a high-quality educational system has a particularly strategic role in narrowing the gap between China and developed countries. The Chinese government is vigorously carrying out its educational strategy – Vitalizing the Nation through Science and Education (VESE Strategy) to develop higher education steadily.

Table 8.12 Number of HEIs in China (2006)

	Total	HEIs under central ministries & agencies	HEIs under local authorities	Non-state/ private
Institutions providing graduate programs	(795)	371	424	
Regular HEIs	(479)	98	381	
Research institutes	(316)	273	43	
Regular HEIs	1,908	111	1,502	295
HEIs providing degree-level programs	740	106	604	30
Short-cycle HEIs	1,168	5	898	265
Of which: tertiary vocational	(1,015)	2	754	259
HEIs for adults	413	14	397	2
Nongovernment HEIs	906			1,906

Unit: institutions. Note: Data within brackets do not count number of schools. *Source*: Educational Statistical Yearbook of China (2007)

In light of the changes in socioeconomic development, the Chinese government made an important policy decision to expand enrollment in higher education in 1999. According to official statistics, in 2006 there were 3,543 higher education institutions (HEIs) in China: 1,908 were regular HEIs, of which 740 offered degree courses and 1,015 offered higher vocational courses; 413 HEIs for adults; and 906 nongovernment HEIs (Table 8.12).

According to the International Standard Classification of Education (ISCED), Chinese universities should be referred to as Regular HEIs which provide the 6 level and 5A level education. However, in China, many Regular HEIs also provide 5B level education, and the official statistical data classify the tertiary vocational school into Regular HEIs. Consequently, the figures on Chinese universities in this paper are higher than the ones according to ISCED's criteria.

8.4.1   Number of Students

From 1985 to 2004, the number of Regular HEIs grew from 1,016 to 1,731, and the number of enrollment students increased from 1.7 million to 13.3 million. The total number of students enrolled in the Chinese higher education system in 2005 reached 23 million. This makes the Chinese higher education system the largest higher education system in the world (Wang Libing 2006).

As can be seen in Table 8.13, the number of Regular HEIs fluctuated between 1,000 and 1,100 during the 1990s, but has increased dramatically since 2000. The total number of students has increased continuously.

Table 8.14 shows the number of graduates, entrants, and enrollments of Regular HEIs in 2006. In this year, 7.6 million new students enrolled in the Regular HEIs

Table 8.13 Number of regular HEIs & students enrollment (1987–2006)

	1987	1988	1989	1990	1991	1992	1993	1994	1995	1996
Schools (institutions)	1,063	1,075	1,075	1,075	1,075	1,053	1,065	1,080	1,054	1,032
Students (10,000 persons)	195.9	206.6	208.2	206.3	204.4	218.4	253.6	279.9	290.6	302.1
	1997	1998	1999	2000	2001	2002	2003	2004	2005	2006
Schools (institutions)	1,020	1,022	1,071	1,041	1,225	1,396	1,552	1,731	1,792	1,908
Students (10,000 persons)	317.4	340.9	413.4	556.1	719.1	903.4	1,108.6	1,333.5	1,561.8	1,738.8

Source: China Statistical Yearbook (2007)

Table 8.14 Data on students in regular HEIs in China (2006)

	Graduates	Entrants	Enrollments
Postgraduates	299,614	401,694	1,143,637
Doctor's degree	36,270	51,916	201,129
Master's degree	263,344	349,778	942,508
Undergraduates in regular HEIs	6,242,307	7,570,326	24,090,504
Normal courses	2,670,834	3,641,829	12,470,248
Short-cycle courses	3,571,473	3,928,497	11,620,256

Unit: persons. *Source*: Educational Statistical Yearbook of China (2007)

Table 8.15 Average number of students in regular HEIs per 100 inhabitants (2006)

	2006
Total population (100,00 persons)	131,448
Number of students enrollment (100,00 persons)	2,409.1
Percentage (%)	1.83
Number of graduates (10,000 persons)	624.2
Percentage (%)	0.5

Source: China Statistical Yearbook (2007), Educational Statistical Yearbook of China (2007)

for undergraduate education, resulting in a total enrollment of 24.1 million. The number of postgraduates increased to 1,143,637.

Table 8.15 shows that the average number of students in 2006 in Regular HEIs per 100 inhabitants was 1.83, and the average number of graduates was 0.5.

Table 8.16 shows the number of students in Regular HEIs by academic field. Compared with developed countries, China has a relatively low proportion of students in social science and humanities. However, with many specialized universities changing to comprehensive universities, the number of students in social science and humanities has been growing in recent years, and their respective share in undergraduate and postgraduate was 49.3 and 36.7% in 2007. Administration is an emerging academic field in China, including Management Science and Engineering, Business Administration, Public Administration, Agricultural Economics and Management, and Library and Archive Science. Though administration as a field was introduced to China only a little more than a decade ago, it has been developing fast and has become the largest academic field in social science and humanities. From 2001 to 2007, the number of students granted master's and doctoral degrees in administration accounted for 13.04 and 11.28%, respectively. The number of students granted master's and doctoral degrees in literature is also large, accounting for 6.18 and 8.04% in master and doctor level from 2001 to 2007. According to the academic classification of Chinese universities, literature not only refers to Chinese literature, but also covers foreign language and literatures, journalism and communication, and art. Large numbers of students learning foreign languages contribute to the large share of literature as a discipline.

Table 8.16 Total enrollment in regular HEIs by academic field (2007)

		Postgraduate		Undergraduate	
	Total	1,195,047		18,848,954	
Social science &	Philosophy	14,708	36.7%	7,637	49.3%
humanities	Economics	56,738		971,043	
	Law	80,311		703,132	
	Education	40,980		1,038,604	
	Literature	93,935		2,895,580	
	History	16,389		54,640	
	Military	704		–	
	Administration	135,028		3,614,531	
Natural science	Science	146,146	63.3%	1,105,990	50.7%
	Engineering	436,352		6,720,538	
	Agriculture	45,285		350,970	
	Medicine	128,471		1,386,289	

Unit: persons. *Source*: China Statistical Yearbook on Science and Technology (2008)

Table 8.17 Number of students in nongovernment regular HEIs (2006)

	Graduates	Entrants	Enrollments
Normal courses	30,176	72,555	211,242
Short-cycle courses	337,244	527,097	1,419,419
Total	367,420	599,652	1,630,661

Unit: persons. *Source*: Educational Statistical Yearbook of China (2007)

8.4.2 Nongovernment Regular HEIs

The 1982 Constitution provided a legal foundation for the participation of private HEIs in China, and in 1984, the first nongovernment university – Haidian Day University – was founded in Beijing. However, the development of nongovernment universities was slow in 1980s due to the immature social environment. After the open-minded address of Deng Xiaoping in 1992, the number of nongovernment HEIs increased rapidly, from 450 in 1991 to 1,219 in 1995, and the government had to control the scale of nongovernment higher education in 1997 and 1998 (http://www.cuaa.net).

In 1999, the government formally permitted the foundation of Nongovernment Regular HEIs, and the related supportive law was approved in 2002. During the recent several years, the scale of Nongovernment Regular HEIs in China is expanding. By 2006, there were 906 Nongovernment Regular HEIs and the total number of students was about 1,630,661 (Table 8.17).

The teaching content of Nongovernment Regular HEIs mainly focuses on the so-called hot specialization, such as foreign languages, computer science, economics, management, etc. None of them teach philosophy, history, or military science. Most of them conduct little research.

8.4.3 Tertiary Vocational School

In China, tertiary vocational schools are the main institutions that provide 5B level education. Due to their diversity, there are not exact data to describe the general conditions of the Chinese tertiary vocational schools. According to an article published in Guang Ming Daily Newspaper, from 1998 to 2003, the number of entrants in tertiary vocational schools increased from 0.54 million to 2 million, and the number of enrollments from 1.17 million to 4.8 million, or 52.24 and 43.24% of the total numbers of entrants and enrollments in Regular HEIs, respectively (Wu Qidi 2004). However, as some tertiary vocational schools have not found their suitable orientation and lack adequate teaching competencies, their graduates are not widely recognized by society. The employment rate of the graduates in tertiary vocational schools was only 55% in 2003.

8.4.4 Source of Educational Funds

A comprehensive educational reform changed the old system in which the funding of higher education depended on the governments, and a new system capable of pooling resources from diverse channels with the main responsibilities on government has been gradually established.

Today, there are various channels for Regular HEIs to get funds, including government appropriation for education, funds from social organizations and citizens, donations and fund-raising for running schools, tuition and miscellaneous fees, and other educational funds. Table 8.18 shows different sources of educational funds in Regular HEIs in 2006. Government funds are the most important source for Regular HEIs, accounting for nearly half of the total. The percentage of tuition and miscellaneous fees is growing, and becoming another important fund source.

From 1998, the central government decided that the proportion of education expenditure at the central government level should be increased by 1% each year over 5 years. Under the initiation and encouragement of the central government, local governments and various social sectors have actively increased their financial

Table 8.18 Educational funds in regular HEIs (2006)

Total	25,502,370.8	%
Government appropriation for education	10,908,368.7	43
Funds from organizations and citizens for running schools	1,801,315.4	7
Donations and fund-raising for running schools	210,796.3	1
Tuition and miscellaneous fee	7,919,249.3	31
Other educational funds	4,662,641.1	18

Unit: 10,000 Yuan. *Source*: China Statistical Yearbook (2007)

input to education. In 2001, the education expenditure from the national finance accounted for 3.19% of the total GDP, compared with merely 2.4% in 1997. This has provided a strong support to the nation's educational reform and development (Zhou Ji 2002).

8.5 Some Current Debates on the Roles of Universities in the Chinese NIS

Nowadays, Chinese universities take an active part in the development of the society. Universities are not only education and research centers, but also enterprise incubators and networkers in the NIS. This section describes some current debates on the roles of Chinese universities.

8.5.1 Education: Expansion and Quality Assurance

Education is the most basic role of universities, and universities are the base of talent training in China. Besides regular higher education, Chinese universities also provide continuous higher education through correspondence, sparetime schools, short-cycle courses, etc. (Table 8.19).

However, along with the fast expansion of Chinese universities, since 1999 the quality of higher education has deteriorated. A survey among the undergraduates in Guangdong Province shows that only 2.7% students are satisfied with the educational quality of their university, while 77% are not satisfied. Another survey among 12,398 undergraduates indicates that 79% students believe that they can not acquire useful knowledge in universities, 77% students think that what they learnt is not relevant to the practice, and 80% students are not satisfied with the courses and content (Lin Jian 2001).

Recently, the quality of postgraduate education is becoming the focus of the society. With the expansion of university, the enrollment number of postgraduates has been increasing rapidly, from 65,000 in 2000 to 324,940 in 2005. However, the number of tutors is increasing more slowly. Many tutors need to supervise about 10 postgraduate or doctoral students, and some even have more than 30 students. Many students complain that they do not have the chance to consult their tutor

Table 8.19 The number of students in correspondence divisions, sparetime schools, and short-cycle courses for adults run by regular HEIs

	Graduates	Entrants	Enrollment
Divisions of correspondence and sparetime schools	1,175,243	1,409,868	3,937,877
Short-cycle courses for adults	335,632	267,384	673,012

Source: Educational Statistical Yearbook of China (2007)

frequently and that they must do everything by themselves. Meanwhile, the tutors also complain about the poor quality of postgraduate students. A survey conducted by a project team of Beijing University among more than 1,000 tutors in 97 universities shows that 56.9% tutors of postgraduate and 47.8% tutors of doctoral students think that the quality of students is dropping (Yan Weifang 2006).

Many articles about this issue indicate that the decline of educational quality is due to problems concerning the macrolevel management system, the incomplete legal provisions, the internal management of universities and colleges, the capacity of teachers, and the irregular model of evaluation of teaching and management (Cheng Fangping 2006). Almost all the people admit that the increased concern for the quality of higher education in China might be a natural consequence of the rapid expansion of higher education.

So, how to improve the quality of higher education is still a challenge for Chinese universities. China is establishing a professional accrediting system. In 2002, the Ministry of Education introduced a new quality assurance policy, which would focus mainly on the assessment of undergraduate teaching at HEIs via a four-level gradation scheme for results: they would either be rated excellent, good, fairly good, or failing. According to official statistics, by the end of 2004, 116 HEIs across China had been assessed under the new regime. In August 2004, a semigovernmental national quality assurance agency called the National Higher Education Evaluation Center (NHEEC) was founded to monitor the implementation of higher education assessment in the country (Wang Libing 2006). However, further efforts to ensure the accrediting system are more relevant and effective.

The government's eleventh 5-year plan (2006–2010) on education lists "improving teaching quality" as a goal. In May 2006, the State Council restricted enrollment to control the rapid growth of students, in order to improve their teaching quality. However, college education will continue to expand in line with the national development in a more rational, stable, and sustainable way. The restriction is a mixed blessing to the public. Parents of would-be applicants still believe increased growth in enrollment could provide better chances for their children, while undergraduates are concerned that the expansion would exert more pressure on the employment market.

8.5.2 Research: Teaching and Research, Fundamental Research, and Applied Research

Research is also a basic role of universities. Nowadays, the R&D income and outcome of Chinese universities indicate that they are playing a significant role in R&D activities. Taking full advantages of being a center of knowledge and talent, Chinese universities have improved their research strength and made significant contributions to the economic construction and social development of the country.

Table 8.20 Project funds approved by the National Natural Science Foundation by sector (2007)

	Universities	Research institution	Others	Total
General programs	177,252	46,999	3,207	227,457
Leading programs	40,470	22,190	870	63,530
Major programs	–	–	–	–
Major research plan	13,228	9,210	140	22,578
Programs of joint funds	10,701	4,409	620	15,730
Projects of state sciences foundation for distinguished young scientists	24,060	11,220	–	35,280
Programs of innovation joint research funds	13,515	11,215	–	24,730
President and directors' funds	3,410	1,016	354	4,780
Special funded projects	3,114	1,434	160	4,708
International cooperation and exchange	7,105	4,686	1,436	13,227
Total	361,085	128,077	7,921	497,083

Unit: 10,000 Yuan. *Source*: China Statistical Yearbook on Science and Technology (2008)

Table 8.21 Statistics of R&D projects and achievements in regular HEIs (2006)

	Projects	Awards Total	National
Key HEIs	140,918	2,575	197
Ordinary degree level HEIs	128,695	2,384	68
Short-cycle HEIs	3,455	47	0
Total	273,068	5,006	265

Source: Educational Statistical Yearbook of China (2007)

According to official statistics, during 1996–2000, Chinese universities undertook more than 70% of Natural Science Foundation Projects, more than 30% of the nation's "863 Project," and more than one-third of the National Key Fundamental Research Projects. The National Natural Science Foundation is the most normative and equitable competitive research foundation in China. From Table 8.20, we can see that the universities obtained more than 70% of the total funds in 2007.

Table 8.21 shows statistics for the R&D projects and achievements in Regular HEIs in 2006. The Key HEIs undertook nearly half of the total R&D projects in universities, and they are becoming an important strength in the Chinese NIS.

The debate on the relationship between teaching and research has lasted for more than two decades because research became one of the important missions of universities in 1980s. It has been agreed that teaching and research are interdependent as well as inseparable in higher education, and that research is necessary for updating and verifying knowledge and ensuring the quality of teaching. In fact, however, research in some way exerts negative influence on teaching in some universities. Since the evaluation of a teacher's work highlights research achievements in many universities, more and more teachers devote themselves to research work, at the expense of their teaching, and indirectly cause the deterioration of teaching quality. Moreover, many teachers just do research passively in order to meet the demands of universities, and the research quality and efficiency are not satisfactory. So, how to balance teaching and research, and how to make research more efficient are important challenges facing many Chinese universities.

As a result of the decrease in government funding, universities have to search for extra funds to support their research. Therefore, applied research, which is more likely to yield results quickly, and thus secure future funding, is more attractive than fundamental research which tends to take longer to produce returns. However, fundamental research makes a vital contribution to the development of S&T. Though government support for fundamental research is strengthening year by year, universities still face a difficult choice.

8.5.3   Technology Transfer: University and Industry

In most literature, activities related to technology transfer in universities are called "the third mission." There are many forms of technology transfer in Chinese universities, such as publication, international meetings, co-research, licensing, university-run enterprises, etc. Particularly, Chinese universities have taken an active part in enterprises' initiatives to upgrade technology and in local economic construction, they have worked to transfer R&D results into practical productivity and acted as a vital force in technological innovation of the nation.

8.5.3.1   Publications and International Meetings

Publications and international meetings are common forms of technology transfer for all kinds of universities. However, as the participants are mainly academics, rather than potential technology users, they are not efficient for technology transfer, but good arenas for communication among academics in the same field. Table 8.22 presents data on publications by the Chinese HEIs and Table 8.23 provides data on international collaborative research by the key HEIs.

Table 8.22 The number of publications by regular HEIs (2006)

	Monographs	Papers
Key HEIs	3,375	307,767
Ordinary degree level HEIs	6,051	287,177
Short-cycle HEIs	1,051	15,718
Total	10,477	610,662

Source: Educational Statistical Yearbook of China (2007)

Table 8.23 International communication of key HEIs (2006)

	Send (persons)	Receive (persons)	
International co-research	23,864	27,175	
International academic meeting	Participants (persons)	Paper	Report
	98,888	58,513	8,567

Source: Statistical Data on Science and Technology of Higher Educational Institutions (2007)

Table 8.24 The number of patents granted in universities (2003–2007)

	2003	2004	2005	2006	2007
Invention	7,704	9,683	14,643	17,312	23,001
Utility model	2,375	2,844	3,843	4,376	6,377
Design	173	470	1,435	1,262	3,302
Total	10,252	12,997	19,921	22,950	32,680

Source: China Statistical Yearbook on Science and Technology (2008)

8.5.3.2   Co-research with Enterprises

Due to the traditional S&T system, Chinese enterprises do not have large R&D resources, and their R&D capability is very weak, so they have to seek help from universities for practical technology.

The direct co-research between universities and enterprises in China began in the 1980s. Universities not only provide professional training to employees in enterprises, but also cooperate with enterprises through research projects to resolve the practical problems.

With the implementation of the "enterprise–university–institution cooperation" project from 1992, the cooperation between enterprises and universities was strengthened. Funds provided by the enterprises to the universities for R&D increased from 3.6 billion Yuan in 1998 to 7.45 billion Yuan in 2004. Currently, the enterprise-oriented technology transfer is an important source of R&D funds for universities.

As can be seen in Table 8.11, applied research in universities accounted for 54.2% in 2004.

8.5.3.3   Licensing

Tables 8.24 and 8.25 show the number of patents granted and technical contract deals of Chinese universities from 2003 to 2007. Though the number of patents granted in universities is increasing year by year, the number of contract deals in domestic technical markets with universities as sellers is not increasing as rapidly as the number of patents. This reflects the low commercialization rate of patents in Chinese universities.

Table 8.26 shows the technology transfer data of the key HEIs in China. The technology in key HEIs mainly flows to state-owned enterprises.

Table 8.25 Contract deals in domestic technical markets with universities as sellers (2003–2007)

	2003	2004	2005	2006	2007
Total	267,997	264,638	267,997	205,845	220,868
Universities	37,974	39,289	37,974	18,401	26,963
%	14.2	14.8	14.2	8.94	12.2

Source: China Statistical Yearbook on Science and Technology (2008)

Table 8.26 The data on technology transfer by key HEIs (2006)

	State-owned enterprises	Foreign enterprises	Private enterprises	Others	Total
Contracts	1,757	199	1,240	835	4,031
%	43.59	4.94	30.76	20.71	100
Value (thousand)	664,922	74,136	389,118	207,097	1,355,273
%	49.80	5.55	29.14	15.51	100

Source: Statistical Data on Science and Technology of Higher Educational Institutions (2007)

8.5.3.4 University-Run Enterprises

Before the discussion on Chinese university-run enterprises, we should first understand that they are quite different from spin-off enterprises in USA. A spin-off enterprise by definition is an economic entity of academic origin that becomes an independent entity, while a university-run enterprise is an economic enterprise that remains part of the administrative structure of the university.

The reform of the S&T system in 1985 drastically cut down government funding for universities. Therefore, many Chinese universities decided to run their own enterprises to search for financing support and improve teaching conditions. However, the Chinese university-run enterprises in 1980s were almost all profit-oriented enterprises, such as printing houses, publishing companies, and some service businesses.

In the 1990s, more and more universities directly participated in getting profit from the market through establishing their own enterprises. A major change was that many Chinese universities began to set up S&T enterprises and devoted themselves to S&T development and industrialization. The development of university-run enterprises, especially the university-run S&T enterprises, became an important criterion to evaluate a university. With the support of the government, university-run S&T enterprises are increasingly becoming larger and stronger. Many university-run enterprises have taken a leading role in Chinese high-tech industry, such as Tongfang, Founder, and Dongruan.

On the one hand, the universities certainly obtain quick financial support through these enterprises; on the other hand, these university-run S&T enterprises promote the technology transfer from university to society, and directly make great contributions to the economic development. However, the most important influence might be that more and more people are recognizing the important role of universities in the development of knowledge-based society.

Table 8.27 compares operating data of university-run enterprises in China from 2000 to 2004. In 2004, there were 4,563 university-run enterprises nationwide, and total turnover was 96.9 billion Yuan, an increase of 17.25% over the previous year.

Table 8.28 shows the comparison of operating data of university-run high-tech enterprises in China from 2000 to 2004. In 2004, there were 2,355 university-run high-tech enterprises nationwide, which achieved a turnover of 80.7 billion Yuan, or 82.23% of the total turnover of the university-run enterprises. The total profit of them was nearly 4.1 billion Yuan and generated 2.4 billion Yuan in net profit.

In 2001, the State Council issued the "Circular on the Experiment of Standardizing University-run Enterprises Management at Peking University and Tsinghua University." The government began to restrain university-run enterprises and call for separating them from universities. As a result, the total number of university-run enterprises has decreased since 2001. However, the number of university-run S&T enterprises was not reduced due to their great contribution to the universities and society.

In China, an important medium of technology transfer in some key universities is University S&T Park. In 1991, the first University S&T Park was set up in the Northeast University. Then, Peking University and Tsinghua Universities succes- sively set up their own University S&T Parks. Nowadays, there are 50 National University S&T Parks in China. According to an incomplete statistic of 42 National University S&T Parks, up to the end of 2004, all of them together had 5,037 enter- prises in incubation and 1,256 graduated enterprises. The University S&T Parks

Table 8.27 Comparison of operating data of university-run enterprises in China (2000–2004)

Year	Number of enterprises	Turnover (100 million Yuan)	Total profit (100 million Yuan)	Net profit (100 million Yuan)
2000	5,451	484.55	45.64	36.04
2001	5,039	602.98	48.17	35.32
2002	5,047	720.08	45.93	35.33
2003	4,839	826.67	42.98	27.95
2004	4,563	969.30	49.93	29.53

Source: Center for Science and Technology Development, Ministry of Education of the People's Republic of China, Statistics and Analysis Report on China's University-run Enterprises (2004)

Table 8.28 The comparison of operating data of university-run high-tech enterprises in China (2000–2004)

Year	Number of S&T enterprises	Turnover (100 million Yuan)	Total profit (100 million Yuan)	Net profit (100 million Yuan)
2000	2,097	368.12	35.43	28.03
2001	1,993	447.75	31.54	23.98
2002	2,216	539.08	25.37	18.63
2003	2,447	668.07	27.61	14.73
2004	2,355	806.78	40.98	23.86

Source: Center for Science and Technology Development, Ministry of Education of the People's Republic of China, Statistics and Analysis Report on China's University-run Enterprises (2004)

have been an exchange platform for various innovative resources, and have become important incubators and disseminators of high-tech industry in China.

The fast development of university-run enterprises, in some way, can be attributed to the weak innovation ability of Chinese industry. Most of the Chinese industry operates at a low-tech level in a labor-intensive economy, and they have not become the core actor of Chinese NIS. In this case, Chinese universities take advantages of their S&T resources, and in some way take on innovation tasks to develop new industries and technologies.

Though universities promote technology transfer by establishing their own enterprises, the university–industry gap still cannot be eliminated, due to lacks of linkage between industry and the academia, cultural differences, different systems for cooperation, mission alignment, and different social responsibilities.

Being part of the administrative structure of the university, university-run enterprises have brought confusion in ownership and management, and the debate on university's mission has risen after 2000. Many people complain that the university is becoming an enterprise, and their competition with industry increases the tension between university and industry, which will eventually induce a difficult technology transfer from university to industry. Some people point out that the consultancy activity should be enhanced. In USA, consultancy is an important interaction form between university and industry, while in China only a few key universities do consultancy for industry. Lack of consultancy led to the fact that teaching and research in universities are separated from industrial practice. How to find an effective way to strengthen the cooperation between university and industry is a problem for China to address urgently.

8.6 Conclusions

The role of the university in NIS is not static, and will evolve all the time to adapt itself to the changes in economy, society, and S&T system. The evolution of Chinese NIS and university system reflect that the Chinese NIS is changing from the former government-dominated pattern to a new market-dominated one, and the Chinese universities are not only education and research centers but also have the third mission, which is to make contributions to the development of the society.

A more rational NIS is developing in China, in which universities, research institutions, and enterprises should play different roles. Currently, due to the weak innovation ability of Chinese industry, Chinese universities in some way replace the role of industry as the innovation actor in the NIS. However, with the increasing innovation ability of Chinese industry, the role of university-run enterprises will decline, and cooperation between the university and industry will be closer with the support of the government.

The present global financial crisis has dealt a heavy blow to China's economy. However, the financial system of China is well-functioning and the crisis of China triggered by the global financial crisis is the crisis of overproduction.

Export-oriented small and medium enterprises are the most affected, especially in the southeast of China where a large number of manufacturing enterprises have filed for bankruptcy. Chinese leaders have expressed a high degree of concern with Premier Wen Jiabao proposing to address the crisis by giving full play to the role of scientific researchers, universities, and research institutions and encouraging scientists and researchers to work with the enterprise, to understand business needs, and to help enterprises to tide over their difficulties.

Many local governments have also taken active measures to make scientific and technical personnel better serve the needs of the enterprises. For example, the government of Guangdong Province has implemented a special action. The main component of the action is the collaboration of the Ministry of Science and Technology and the Ministry of Education, Guangdong Provincial Government, in a nation-wide search for outstanding professors of well-known university or research institutes and providing research funds for them to work with enterprises and to provide technical assistance activities for enterprises in Guangdong. The successful introduction of the first group is a total of 157 professors, 155 of them from universities. This approach certainly helps enterprises to address technical aspects of production; so this action implemented by government is welcomed by the enterprises. The scheme will introduce a second group of 2,000 professors. Other provinces have also adopted a similar policy, to facilitate closer university–company cooperation. The action has fundamentally changed the role of universities in the national innovation system of China.

By strengthening cooperation between manufacturing, teaching, and scientific research, the Chinese universities are speeding up the conversion of scientific and technological research results into products. However, the most important mission of university is education and research, followed by technology transfer. How to maintain the teaching quality with the expansion of university system, balance the fundamental research and applied research, and strengthen the linkage between universities and industrial system are the challenges for Chinese universities.

In the future, the role of Chinese universities will evolve continuously. Looking into the future and complying with new opportunities and challenges, Chinese universities bear a more glorious and arduous mission, which will need further effort by the whole society.

References

Center for Science and Technology Development, Ministry of Education of the People's Republic of China: Statistics and Analysis Report on China's University-run Enterprises (2004).
Cheng Fangping: A Comparative Study of the Popularization of Higher Education in China (2006).
China Statistical Yearbook (2007).
China Statistics Yearbook on High Technology Industry (2008).
China Statistical Yearbook on Science and Technology (2008).
CUAA, Evaluation Report of Chinese Non-government Universities (2006), http://www.cuaa.net.

Educational Statistical Yearbook of China (2007).

Lin Jian: The Analysis of Total Quality Management on Talent Training in University, High Education Study (2001).

Lundvall B-A: National Systems of Innovation: Towards a Theory of Innovation and Interactive Learning, Pinter, London (1992).

Wang Libing: Accreditation of Higher Education in China (2006).

Wu Qidi: Developing the Employment-oriented Vocational Education, Guang Ming Daily Newspaper 2004-4-1.

Yan Weifang: The Report of Education and Human Resource in China (2006).

Zhou Ji: The Reform & Development of Chinese Higher Education at The Turn of The Century (2002).

Chapter 9
Tanzania: The Evolving Role of Universities in Economic Development

Burton L.M. Mwamila and Bitrina D. Diyamett

9.1 Introduction

Tanzania is one of the poorest countries in the world, with about 50% of the population living below the poverty line. It is predominantly agrarian, with agriculture contributing about 50% to the gross domestic product (GDP) and engaging over 80% of the total population. Another significant contribution to the GDP comes from the service sector which contributes about 39.3%. The manufacturing sector, which is the most powerful engine of structural change and modernization of the economy, contributes only 7.6% to the GDP and accounts for less than 1% of total exports. The technological base of the sector is very weak, with none of the firms having research and development (R&D) departments, and having very weak linkages with government R&D organizations and universities. A study of 50 randomly selected manufacturing firms in Dar es Salaam indicates that only two of 50 industrial firms have some forms of contacts with universities and R&D institutes (Diyamett 2005). According to Wangwe et al. (2003), the few contacts that exist between industrial firms and the universities and R&D institutes is in the form of consultancies, and largely by large-scale firms (employing more than 100 persons). On the contrary, the agricultural sector which is considered as the back bone of the national economy has been growing by only 3% over the last decade. This growth is considered unsatisfactory because it has failed to improve the livelihood of the rural population, perpetuating the existing pervasive poverty among the farming communities. Despite the large untapped land resource, Tanzania's agriculture has remained subsistence farming with smallholders who cultivate 85% of the arable land working between 0.2 and 2.0 ha, with an average per capita holding of only 0.2 ha per household. The major limitation on the size of land holdings and utilization is the heavy reliance on the hand hoe, which sets obvious limitations on the area that crops can be grown using family labor (Shetto 2005). As indicated above, the Tanzanian economic performance is far from being adequate, even for a moderate

B.L.M. Mwamila (✉)
College of Engineering and Technology, University of Dar es Salaam, Dar es Salaam, Tanzania
e-mail: mwamila@udsm.ac.tz

B. Göransson and C. Brundenius (eds.), *Universities in Transition: The Changing Role and Challenges for Academic Institutions,*
© International Development Research Centre 2011

socioeconomic development. There are indications, however, that there are, or rather there will be, efforts by the government to redress the situation as stipulated in the Tanzanian Development Vision 2025. Quoting one of the major statements of the Vision, "…. by then the economy will have been transformed from a low productivity agricultural economy to a semiindustrialized one, led by modernized and highly productive agricultural activities, integrated and buttressed by supportive industrial and service activities - a solid foundation for a competitive and dynamic economy with high productivity will have been laid" (URT 2000).

The above vision statement on the structural change in the economy can only be brought about by a strong and well-performing national systems of innovation (NSIs), where the university has a unique role to play, not only in contributing knowledge for innovation in the productive sector, but also, and above all, contributing to the knowledge on the dynamics of the NSIs for policy purposes. In Sect. 9.2 that follows, the current NSI in Tanzania is briefly explained with the view to ascertain the role that the universities can play in redressing the situation. Section 9.3 is devoted to the actual role of the university in the NSIs, while Sect. 9.4 presents the specific case studies, illustrating the role of universities in the Tanzanian NSI. Section 9.5 discusses the current debate regarding higher learning institutions. And finally, Sect. 9.6 will draw some concluding remarks. The section also attempts to raise some questions for further work.

9.2   The Tanzanian National Systems of Innovation (NSI)

The state of the NSI in Tanzania is partly reflected by the state of the national economy. The state of affairs in the agricultural and manufacturing sectors, to a large extent, portrays the extent to which the NSI in Tanzania is underdeveloped. In terms of basic infrastructure, however, viz. existence of organizations and blue print policies, the system is appreciably developed, but very weak in terms of linkages that are very crucial characteristics of any innovation system. R&D activities in Tanzania date back to 1892 when the German colonial administration established the first agricultural institute at Amani in the Usambara Mountains. The main objectives of agricultural research at that time was to support the development of the plantations of export crops (sisal, coffee, tobacco, ground nuts, etc.) grown either by foreign companies or individual settler farmers (Liwenga 1988). By the late 1990s, the R&D system had expanded to 62 research institutes and/or centers spread throughout the country and had become more diverse, covering agriculture including livestock and forestry (28), industry (4), medical (11), wildlife and fisheries (4), and 5 universities and/or higher learning institutions where R&D is being undertaken (COSTECH statistics). In terms of funding, the total R&D funding is estimated at 0.1% of GDP, down from around 0.5% in 1984 and very far from the government target of 1% the GDP. More remarkable is the fact that R&D is conducted almost entirely in the public sector (Wangwe et al. 2003). Tables 9.1 and 9.2 show the trends in R&D intensity and share by different sources.

As Table 9.1 indicates, much of the funds flow to the universities. Moreover, much of the R&D activities are being financed from foreign sources, largely the development partners (Table 9.2). As previously pointed out, the major weakness of the Tanzanian innovation system is lack of linkages between the R&D organizations, including the universities and the productive sector. Apart from some few isolated initiatives at the universities and some R&D organizations, the systems in general exist as isolated islands. Notwithstanding the above, however, there is an appreciable difference between sectors and subsectors. A study of three sectors, viz. agriculture, industry, and health, indicates that there are better linkages within the health sector followed by agricultural sector, especially the cash crops subsector sector. Some of the cash crops (coffee and tea) actually do currently run their own private R&D organizations. The situation in the manufacturing sector is the worst: there is virtually very little connection between R&D and the manufacturing industries apart from consultancy projects with a few firms (Wangwe et al. 2003). The large-scale industries are not interested in the products of the R&D – most of them claim that R&D activities are irrelevant to their activities as most of the innovative activities are those of learning-by-doing and using type. However, there are a few, and specifically, multinationals who have some R&D inputs in their activities, but these are linked to R&D conducted by their parent companies abroad (Wangwe and Diyamett 1998). On the contrary, small-scale industries consider R&D organizations as their competitors. This is because with the advent of economic liberalization and government budget cuts, most of the industrial R&D organizations have been left alone in terms of funding for their R&D activities. In order to survive, such R&D organizations have had to somehow turn themselves into small-scale manufacturing firms. Furthermore, the small- and medium-scale enterprises (SMEs) have very little financial means to access products of the R&D institutions (Wangwe and Diyamett 1998). However, as will be discussed in Sect. 9.3, there are currently some initiatives by the University of Dar es Salaam (UDSM) to assist the small-scale industries in terms of technology development.

In the developed world, universities typically collaborate and partner with the industry as part of fulfilling their basic functions. This is not necessarily true in a poor developing country such as Tanzania. For instance, is it correct to talk of equal partnership between the universities and small-scale firms which have turned to the universities for some help, especially if these firms cannot pay for the consultancies? On the contrary, will the scientists at the universities be interested in the work of the firms which employ a very low level of technology? These are very crucial questions to raise as we embark on the long-term and sustainable collaboration between the universities and small-scale industries. According to some anecdotal information, the challenge in the Organization for Economic Cooperation and Development (OECD) countries is more likely to come from the fact that the universities tend to pay less attention to their traditional roles, and concentrate more on the requirement of the industry. This seems to be contrary to the situation in the poor developing countries where universities seem to be more comfortable with their traditional roles than work for the industry, largely because of the dichotomy that exists between science and technology (S&T).

Table 9.1 Trends in total funds flow to public R&D institutions from all sources, by performing sector in current billion TZS

	1995/1996	1996/1997	1997/1998	1998/1999	1999/2000	2000/2001	2001/2002	2002/2003	2003/2004	Total
Higher education	7.25	12.65	13.7	17.36	35.49	40.24	42.4	35.87	39.79	244.75
R&D institutions	15.51	5.85	7	7.88	10.63	14.89	17.88	19.43	24.5	123.57
Total	22.76	18.5	20.7	25.24	46.12	55.13	60.28	55.3	64.29	368.32
Higher education as % of total	31.85	68.38	66.18	68.78	76.95	72.99	70.34	64.86	61.89	66.45

Source: COSTECH (2005) statistics

Table 9.2 Trends of funds to R&D programs in public R&D institutions (in Mill TZS), by source

	1995/1996	1996/1997	1997/1998	1998/1999	1999/2000	2000/2001	2001/2002	2002/2003	2003/2004	Total 1995–2004
Government	614	1,071	933	624	1,175	1,201	1,875	2,024	3,213	12,730
Own generated	319	304	642	396	2,000	5,874	6,906	8,168	4,559	29,168
Other domestic sources	12	116	100	181	192	368	556	1,342	899	3,766
Foreign sources	2,802	3,602	3,749	4,450	5,573	9,051	7,869	4,713	5,447	47,256
Total	3,747	5,093	5,424	5,651	8,940	1,6494	1,7206	1,6247	1,4118	92,920
Govt as % of total	16.39	21.03	17.20	11.04	13.14	7.28	10.90	12.46	22.76	13.70%
Own as % of total	8.51	5.97	11.84	7.01	22.37	35.61	40.14	50.27	32.29	31.39%
Other domestic % of total	0.32	2.28	1.84	3.20	2.15	2.23	3.23	8.26	6.37	4.05%
Foreign % of total	74.78	70.72	69.12	78.75	62.34	54.87	45.73	29.01	38.58	50.86%

Source: COSTECH (2005) statistics

9.3   Mapping the Academic System in Tanzania

An essential prerequisite for a country's technological progress is an early recognition of the necessity of a good education system. At present, the majority of Tanzanians are either without education at all or with only primary school education. Most of these Tanzanians end up being peasants, while a few become vendors or hawkers and others try to become semiskilled operatives or apprentices in family enterprises. Only a very small number of Tanzanians have skills, knowledge, and expertise, and are able to contribute appreciably to national development as artisans, technicians, and professionals.

The Tanzanian Education System is characterized by five distinct levels, namely, primary school education, secondary school education (covering ordinary and advanced levels), vocational education and training, nonuniversity tertiary education and training, and university education. The primary and secondary school education is regulated by the Ministry of Education and Vocational Training (MEVT), while university education is regulated by the Tanzania Commission of Universities (TCU). On the contrary, vocational education and training are regulated by the Vocational Education and Training Authority (VETA), while nonuniversity tertiary education and training are regulated by the National Council for Technical Education (NACTE). Furthermore, whereas TCU and NACTE are autonomous bodies under the Ministry of Higher Education, Science, and Technology (MHEST), VETA is under MEVT. This indicates one very serious problem with the Tanzanian education system, because there is no National Qualification Framework (NQF), the operations of the various regulatory bodies are not coordinated.

The university, whether of S&T or otherwise, is characterized by its ability to advance knowledge and search for new frontiers of knowledge. University training imparts knowledge and understanding of methods, principles, and concepts, and emphasizes research, including basic research and scientific thinking. The university being the collector, distiller, repository, and dispenser of knowledge is an important partner to the government in applying this knowledge to the objective analysis of the national challenges in terms of policies, governance, socioeconomic development, sustainable growth, prioritization, and sequencing of development actions; and providing objective prescriptions and predictions.

The Tanzanian higher education system, with 11 public and 17 private universities as well as technical institutions and institutions under other ministries, enrolled over 55,000 students in the academic year 2005/06 (MoHEST 2006). This represents more than a doubling over the 2001/2002 figure. The UDSM is by far the largest and oldest, with a student population of about 15,000 (as of July 2006). The second largest in terms of number of enrolled students is the Open University of Tanzania (OUT) with 9,232 students. However, the level of graduate throughput at OUT is only less than 50%. The UDSM also offers the largest variety of training programs in the country. Trends in respect of student enrollment and teaching staff are depicted at the end of the chapter. With effect from 2005, all universities in the country, public or private, are governed and regulated by the new Universities Act No. 7 of 2005. Whereas public universities are mainly financed by the government, private universities are owned and financed by private organizations (including religious groups and even individuals) through student fees and other sources.

The government has invited the private sector to contribute to the revitalization of the university education by the following:

- Opening quality universities that offer courses that are relevant to Tanzania's social and economic priorities;
- Financing research and awarding contract consultancies to Tanzanian universities;
- Practicing corporate philanthropy through award of scholarships and funding of professorial chairs;
- Establishing student loan schemes and education endowment funds; and
- Striking a healthy and mutually supportive working partnership with local universities.

In 2004, the Parliament of Tanzania enacted the Higher Education Students Loans Act, which subsequently established a Higher Education Students Loans Board (HESLB) for the purpose of administering loans to higher education students in public and private institutions of higher learning. This facility has been put in place so as to enable the government to operationalize fully the cost sharing of higher education expenses without denying access to students whose parents and/or guardians are unable to provide funds for their children's higher education. The HESLB provides loans to students in both public and private higher education institutions, to varying levels determined on the basis of a means testing exercise carried out by the former for each student wishing to benefit from the facility.

9.3.1 The University of Dar es Salaam

As far as the UDSM is concerned, its Corporate Strategic Plan (CSP) was first conceived as part of the UDSM-2000 Transformation Programme, and operationalized through Five-Year Rolling Strategic Plans. The CSP defined the mission of the University. In 2004/2005, the CSP was reviewed substantially to yield the Corporate Strategic Plan (2004–2013), which is being operationalized through the UDSM Five-Year Rolling Strategic Plan for 2005/2006–2009/2010 (UDSM 2005).

The current vision of UDSM is *To become a reputable world class university that is responsive to national, regional and global development needs through engagement in dynamic knowledge creation and application.* The mission is: *The unrelenting pursuit of scholarly and strategic research, education, training and public service directed at attainment of equitable and sustainable socioeconomic development of Tanzania and the rest of Africa.* During the period 2005/2006–2009/2010, the activities of UDSM have been guided by the theme *Enhancing Quality Outputs in Teaching, Research and Public Service.*

The strategic plan contains the following objectives for the UDSM:

- To preserve, transmit, and enhance knowledge;

- To stimulate and promote intellectual, cultural, and technological developments; and
- To create a sense of public responsibility in the educated and to promote respect for learning and pursuit of truth.

One important characteristic feature of the UDSM's Strategic Plan is that it is rolled forward annually. Internal, but university-wide, implementation review workshops are held twice a year during which the various units report progress made in the implantation of their respective plans for the preceding half year. In addition, consultative workshops involving various stakeholders (viz. government ministries, development partners, the private sector, industry, etc.) are held annually, to review progress and thrash out implementation problems.

The UDSM-2000 Transformation Programme which has been operationalized through five-year rolling strategic plans has enabled turn-around of what was becoming a visionless institution into a vibrant one, by African standards. Among the achievements made through implementation of the UDSM-2000 Transformation Programme are the following:

- Expansion of student enrollment from a mere 3,000 in 1994 to 15,000 in 2005/2006;
- Improvement of the proportion of female students among engineering undergraduates from 3.5% in 1999 to 25% in 2007;
- Diversification of academic programs; e.g., whereas there were only four undergraduate academic degree programs in engineering in 1999/2000, now there are 15 of them;
- Integration of the then Faculty of Engineering and Institute of Production Innovation with subsequent transformation into the current College of Engineering and Technology, as part of the university's policy to cluster academic units accompanied by devolution of powers to the clusters for enhanced management efficiency and effectiveness, and facilitation of optimum utilization of available resources;
- Improvement of the teaching and learning environment, thereby enabling UDSM attain the thirteenth position among all universities in Africa, and the first position among universities north of Limpopo River (Webmetrics International 2005).

9.4 Cases Illustrating the Role of the University in the NSI

9.4.1 The College of Engineering and Technology at the University of Dar es Salaam

9.4.1.1 The Set-Up and Objectives

The set-up of the College of Engineering and Technology (CoET) has been designed to be more responsive to the needs of the Tanzanian society and able to serve it better than before, through its three main pillars, namely (1) the three faculties taken together; (2) the Technology Development and Transfer Centre (TDTC); and (3) the Bureau for Industrial Cooperation (BICO). Both TDTC and BICO are virtual units which depend on manpower from the three faculties and hence the need for close coordination of these three pillars of college. In addition, there is a close linkage between BICO and TDTC in offering some of the community services because both are outreach units.

In line with the CoET set-up, the strategic functions of the three pillars of CoET have been formulated so as to address the following inter-related strategic issues:

- Motivation and retention of CoET staff to ensure sustenance of achievements made to date and further development toward realization of its vision and mission;
- Stimulation and promotion of enhanced innovativeness and competitiveness of firms and farms in the country;
- Stimulation, catalyzation, and promotion of national sustainable growth and poverty reduction;
- Enhanced support of needs of local entrepreneurs for technology management, innovation, and business creation; and
- Provision of think-tanks to direct and spearhead national sustainable development.

In order to realize its vision, it has been necessary for CoET to formulate clear strategic direction to follow. The same has been done in line with the strategic direction of the university and after carefully evaluating the external environment. The strategic direction is characterized by specific strategic objectives in the areas of teaching and learning; research and publications; consultancy and services to the public; organization, management, and culture; optimization of the utilization of human and physical resources; national and international linkages; mobilization and management of financial resources; and marketing and public relations. The basic objectives of CoET are threefold:

- To supply the country with high-level engineering human resources as agents of development and change, thus contributing to the indigenous development of the infrastructure, industry, and trade;
- To perform research and technology development in the interest of suitable exploitation and local processing of natural resources in Tanzania, ultimately leading to the innovation of technical products and production processes in the local industry; and
- To provide expert professional services in the form of learned and knowledge intensive consultancy to industry as well as public and private organizations and institutions, and thereby render new findings applicable to the national development process.

Achievement of these objectives hinges on the synergic interaction of the three pillars of CoET, namely, the three Faculties, TDTC, and BICO (Fig. 9.1).

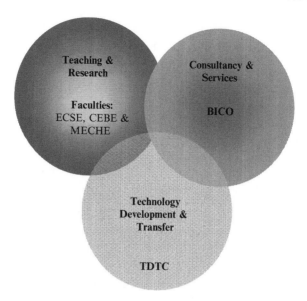

Fig. 9.1 The synergic interaction of the three pillars – the faculties, TDTC, and BICO

9.4.1.2   The Faculties

The three faculties of CoET, viz. Civil Engineering and the Built Environment (CEBE), Electrical and Computer Systems Engineering (ECSE), and Mechanical and Chemical Engineering (MECHE), are responsible for academic training and research through the 12 academic departments. All academic staff members and most technical staff members belong to academic departments. All laboratories and most workshops belong to teaching departments. Thus, the three faculties are the custodians of most of the technoware and humanware available at CoET.

Among the main outputs from the faculties are undergraduate (BSc), postgraduate diploma, masters, and PhD graduates. Thus, the faculties, through their respective academic departments, are solely responsible for the realization of the second basic objective above. The faculties are also solely responsible for research up to when technology development is evident as an outcome of the respective research activity. Otherwise, the most obvious outputs from departmental research are the publications on the activities and the results.

9.4.1.3   The Technology Development and Transfer Centre (TDTC)

Research, in the widest sense, is the basis for the development of any society. It has an important role of advancing and defining knowledge and providing solutions to problems facing the society not only in the local, but also in the wider international context. If a society lacks the indigenous capacity to do research for development or the capacity to manage technological change, it becomes totally dependent on the outside world. Development in S&T is therefore not only an important determinant of a country's level of development, but also enhances its international competitiveness and its position in the world economy.

It has been strongly argued in some international circles that the generation, dissemination, and application of knowledge will have to become a principal function of leading African universities if the continent is to survive and thrive in the knowledge society of the twenty-first century. The economic importance of access to and ability to benefit from modern, research-based technologies in recent years cannot be overemphasized.

Research-based technologies can both be locally developed and brokered from elsewhere. In the former case, research capacity is necessary for the development of the technology, while in the latter case the same is required for the proper selection, adaptation, and further development of technologies acquired from elsewhere.

The CoET recognizes its role toward achieving national socioeconomic advancement through the proper selection, adoption, adaptation, and further development of technological solutions as well as development of appropriate and sustainable technologies. It is thus intended to involve all academic disciplines of the college in prototype development and technology transfer. All technology (prototype) developments by college staff, technology brokerage, and the subsequent transfer to industry are being coordinated by the TDTC.

It is believed that a broker approach to innovation and technology transfer has the potential for significantly increasing the impact on socioeconomic development in the country. Next to developing indigenous technology, it is imperative to ensure efficient absorption and adaptation of imported technology appropriate to national priorities and resources. This entails that the college makes arrangements for technology information exchange with, at least, some leading international technology transfer centers.

TDTC aims primarily to impact on the development of SMEs and on the lives of the general public through the development and dissemination of technologies that have direct relevance to the Tanzanian society.

9.4.1.4 The College BICO

In the 1980s, the then faculty of engineering was faced with serious problems of staff exodus in search of greener pastures, loss of work morale, and gross inefficiencies. In an attempt to redress the situation, an intensive and extensive review exercise was carried out in 1988/1989. The review exercise revealed that to achieve the desired staff retention and motivation, strategies had to be formulated and implemented to ensure that staff members derive adequate satisfaction academically, professionally, and materially. As a result, BICO was established in July 1990 to address the professional and material aspects of the staff retention and motivation mechanism. The following are the specific objectives for which BICO was established and exists to date:

(a) To enhance the capability of CoET to contribute effectively in the industrial development of Tanzania through the provision of consultancy, expert professional services, and professional advancement (or development) of engineers and technologists;
(b) To enable the college to generate funds to subsidize grants from the government and other donors for the college to meet its financial needs;
(c) To enable the staff in the college to supplement their income and thereby enhance staff retention in the college;
(d) To optimize the use of the college expertise and resources to solve societal engineering and technology-related problems;
(e) To provide means for academic and other college staff to gain professional experience that shall be transferred to students and thereby improve quality of outputs;
(f) Make available college training facilities to the general public through short-term and medium-term courses for the purpose of ensuring that engineers keep abreast with the rapidly advancing technology;
(g) To acquire knowledge on new developments and needs in the trade and adjust curriculum accordingly;
(h) To provide expert technical support to existing industrial operations and facilitate developments of new industries;
(i) To facilitate establishment and enhancement of contacts and relations between college staff and industries; and
(j) To provide a platform through which the college staff can transfer their knowledge and skills to industry and to the society.

In a major review carried out in 2003/2004, BICO was observed to have been a great success, with the following key indicators:

• Exodus of staff for mere search of greener pastures has been arrested;
• Staff members' incomes have increased significantly, thereby enabling them to cater for their social obligations;
• Most members of staff participate in professional activities within the country and abroad;
• The industry recognizes BICO as a vital partner in dealing with intricate professional engineering problem; and
• The industry and the public at large recognize BICO as a facility for enabling them keep abreast with advancing technology.

BICO is thus a vital pillar of the CoET.

9.4.1.5   The Innovation Systems and Innovative Clusters Initiative

Innovations in the form of new products, services, and processes or improvements thereof are the basis for sustainable growth and prosperity in a knowledge-based society. The fundamental factors necessary for the development of innovations include skills, exchange of knowledge, and opportunities for mutual learning as part of the interaction between business, research institutions, and political bodies. Research produces new knowledge, but in order to promote growth, it must be translated into innovations, which produce new and/or improved products, services, and processes for which there is a clear demand.

It has been argued that firms that operate close to related firms and supporting institutions are often more innovative and therefore more successful in raising productivity than firms that operate in isolation. The innovative cluster approach is thus an appropriate and established tool for analysis of industrial dynamics and for policy initiatives to foster innovations, growth, and economic development. The challenge embodied in the innovative cluster approach is how best to organize and manage clusters in order to exploit their maximum potentials. Currently, cluster initiatives (CIs) are being launched in nearly all regions of the world. An understanding of the concept and the salient features of innovation systems and innovative clusters, and the critical factors for building and improving them are important prerequisites for Africa to become part of this global initiative.

Arising from consideration of the facts mentioned above, the faculties/college of engineering at three Universities in Eastern Africa, namely, the Faculty of Engineering at Eduardo Mondlane University, the Faculty of Technology at Makerere University, and the CoET at the UDSM, have to date organized two regional conferences on innovation systems and innovative clusters in Africa. The first regional conference was held in February 2004 with a view to creating awareness among African participants about the concepts of innovation systems and innovative clusters, appreciating the state of the art of innovation systems and innovative clusters and their effectiveness in stimulating industrial and socioeconomic development in Africa, and affording participants the opportunity to brainstorm on what could be adopted and adapted to speed up industrial and economic growth in Africa. The second one was held in March 2005 building on the successes of the first conference and confirming the importance of getting Africa to join other regions of the world and adopt the innovative cluster approach.

One of the important outcomes of the first conference was an action plan toward promoting the development of innovation systems and innovative clusters to speed up industrial and economic growth in Africa. The conference also facilitated the creation of more awareness, among the various actors, about issues related to innovation systems and innovative clusters, and management thereof.

After the regional conference, each participating country held a national stakeholders' workshop in which issues pertinent to the particular country were discussed before the second regional conference was held in Uganda in March 2005. One of the key resolutions of the second regional conference was to initiate and spearhead the establishment of an Innovation Systems and Clusters Programme in Eastern Africa (ISCP-EA). CoET was charged with preparing the ISCP-EA proposal and contacting development partners for possible financial support. The program purpose was agreed to be to stimulate and facilitate the development of innovation systems and innovative clusters in Eastern Africa, achievement of which would lead

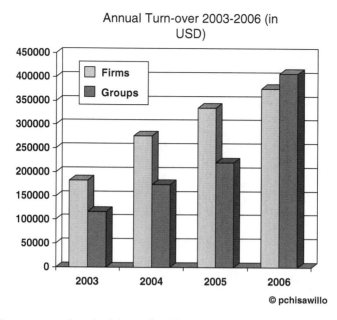

Fig. 9.2 Improvement of productivity attributable to clustering, for the Morogoro Metalworks Cluster Initiative, in Tanzania

to enhanced innovativeness among firms and farms, enhanced competition and cooperation among firms and farms within clusters and sectors, and acquisition of competitive mindset by Eastern Africans in general and the businesses in particular. The Swedish International Development Agency (SIDA), which was the first to respond to the submitted proposal, offered to start by financing a low-budget kick-start implementation of pilot CIs. A week-long training of facilitators of the CIs was conducted in September 2005 for Tanzania and Uganda and June 2006 for Mozambique. Eight and seven CIs were selected and launched in Tanzania and Uganda, respectively, in February 2006. The initial activities of the pilot CIs include the following:

- Mobilization of people and resources within the CI and analysis of the activities of members;
- Preparation of ground for and facilitation of implementation of short-term activities;
- Identification and facilitation of implementation of long-term strategic activities.

ISCP-EA is overseen by the National Steering Committees constituted by members drawn from the academia, other R&D institutions, government, the industry and businesses, nongovernmental organizations (NGOs), and development partners.

In all the three cases, the universities both host and coordinate the national chapters of the program. At the Eastern Africa level, CoET is the coordinator.

Review of the performance of ISCP-EA has revealed that through enhanced trust among cluster firms, and cooperation while competing (coopetition), there has been improvement in the productivity and quality of the products. The Morogoro Metalworks Cluster has reported productivity improvement in excess of 250% for tin-smithery groups, as depicted in Fig. 9.2 (Chisawillo 2006).

9.4.1.6   Collaboration with Tanzania Gatsby Trust

Tanzania Gatsby Trust (TGT) is a nongovernmental organization (NGO), established in 1992, committed to the support of SMEs and alleviation of poverty in Tanzania through credit provision, marketing development training, and technology transfer. TGT receives funding from the Gatsby Charitable Foundation and the Ashden Trust of the United Kingdom. CoET and TGT started collaborating in the field of technology development and transfer (TDT) in 2001. Toward this, a Memorandum of Understanding (MoU) was signed between TGT and CoET in 2001. The specific objectives of the CoET–TGT collaboration include the following:

- To assist SMEs access various technologies developed or brokered by CoET;
- To provide assistance to a select group of CoET students in developing final year "projects" of direct relevance to identified SMEs;
- To facilitate the development of business plans for specific SMEs using members of the university units mentioned above;
- To carry out research and development of new prototypes for SMEs.

To date, the following activities have been undertaken as part of the CoET–TGT collaboration:

(a) *Student projects that have relevance to SMEs.* So far, a total of 55 student projects have been executed, 10 projects in 2002 and 15 each year since 2003. In 2002, all the projects were in the food processing area. From 2003, however, the scope was widened to cover other disciplines while emphasizing stronger SME collaboration.

(b) *Countrywide survey of SMEs' status and needs in Tanzania.* The performance of SMEs in the country have been known to be low with most of the enterprises being in financial difficulties. However, specific problems that these SMEs are facing and what should be done to solve them were not specifically known. Thus it was resolved to conduct an SME survey, which would provide the information needed. CoET with the support of TGT conducted the survey and now there is reasonably sufficient information to design solutions to deal with the observed problems. The survey has also provided information on a sectoral distribution of SMEs in the country which will facilitate the initiation of the establishment of SME clubs and the development of innovative clusters.

(c) *Establishment of a National Technology-based SME Incubator Program.* Technology/business incubation and brokerage are among the most effective strategies for technology transfer and hence the realization of practical applications of research results. The CoET–TGT collaboration program has technology incubation as one of the areas to be addressed. The Carnegie Corporation of New York is also financing part of the project. CoET technology incubator activities are carried out at three localities which have shown good potential, including response by the local actors, namely, Kibaha, Morogoro, and Lushoto. Each of the localities has a local coordinator. Teams have been formed and assigned to each of the localities.

(d) *Establishment of SME clubs (Gatsby Clubs).* One of the ways through which the TGT–CoET project can deliver the services to SMEs is through incubation as described above. However, the number of SMEs, which need services, is quite large and the process to establish incubators is quite lengthy. Furthermore, even when the incubators become operational, only a few of the SMEs will be accommodated. An alternative to this is the establishment of SME clubs through which all kinds of support and services may be channeled. Establishment of the SMEs clubs will also facilitate networking, and the dissemination and acquisition of various technological innovations as will be required by the SMEs.

(e) *Feasibility study on shelter/housing* in Zanzibar, Rukwa, and Mtwara regions and house construction in Zanzibar.

9.4.2 The Faculty of Science at the University of Dar es Salaam

Just like CoET, the Faculty of Science has also been involved in research programs or activities that have direct relevance to and impact on the society around. The case of research in mushrooms, which is increasingly a growing business in Tanzania, is instructive. The faculty, in collaboration with farmers, has been able to identify the types of mushrooms with medicinal value and other uses. However, much of the faculty's research has tended to use a technology push or science push, rather than a demand-pull, approach to produce knowledge that is extremely useful for the Tanzanian Health Sector, but very little has gone outside the doors of their laboratories.

For more than two decades, the Faculty of Science at the UDSM has actively been involved in research on the Tanzanian indigenous plants for natural chemicals that have medicinal potential. A number of scientific discoveries have been made from this research, particularly focusing on biomolecules that have antimalarial properties. Among some of the discoveries are antimalarial and tryponocidal compounds (ability to kill parasites that cause sleeping sickness) (Joseph and Nkunya 2002). Surely these are very relevant research outputs in the context of a country such as Tanzania that is disease stricken. However, very little, if any, has gone outside the doors of the laboratory. Reasons for this are many, but the most obvious is the conspicuous lack of visionary business leaders and entrepreneurs who can turn these into viable pharmaceuticals, i.e., the capabilities for investing into pharmaceuticals are very weak. What a country like Tanzania needs, therefore, is spin-off companies that are led by researchers themselves. This, however, should not be taken as a panacea for the development of new technology-based firms. The experience elsewhere (developed countries for that matter) has shown that there is no short cut to the rules of the game. It is normally a result of a great deal of tenacity, hard work, and courage! In terms of time, the formation of a high-tech industrial venture will take at least some decades, and the requisites are strong research base, smart people (a well-educated labor force), visionary entrepreneurs and a community of high-tech business leaders, and smart capital (ITAC 2002 cited in Diyamett 2004).

9.5   The Current Debate

The current debate about universities in Tanzania largely revolves around the following major issues: financing and affordability, accessibility, gender, quality, and decline of interest in science and engineering courses among students. The first two issues are briefly discussed in the subsections that follow.

9.5.1   Financing and Affordability

The financing and affordability of university education is currently at the top of the agenda for public debate in Tanzania. The problem seems to stem from the fact that education was free in Tanzania before the late 1980s. However, with the increase in population and the number of students completing advanced secondary education, it became a burden for the government to provide free quality education, and hence the introduction of cost sharing. It is evident that the cost cannot be borne by parents, as earlier indicated, as most of the Tanzanians are poor. However, with the emergence of private universities, well-to-do parents are paying for the university education of their children. This is also true for the students in public universities under private sponsorship. However, this has also caused a debate, and complaints from the public started emanating that it is only the children from the richer families that can have access to the university education, which is unfair not only for the children from poor families, but also for the country, as there is a possibility of leaving behind the best brains.

In 2004, the government enacted a law to establish the HESLB to manage a students' loan scheme, primarily to facilitate access to higher education by students whose parents cannot afford to pay for them. Under the scheme, all university students, including those from the private universities, are eligible for the loan. However, given the small size of the loan, it is given to only a small section of the students. The policy is that only those who pass very well in their advanced level examination qualify for the loans. While for girls, it is those who obtain Divisions I and II in the National Form VI Examinations, for boys it is only those who obtain Division I. However, this practice is also being debated with most arguing in favor of all students who qualify for university education to be given loans. But where will the money come from? With regard to this question, there are several proposals. One is the involvement of the private sector. According to Mawenya (2002), given appropriate incentives, the private industry in Tanzania can make significant contribution to the financing of higher education. Mawenya asserts that to make this happen, the higher learning institutions must play their cards well. They must create condition and mechanism that will attract the private sector to do business with them. Given the observation earlier presented, there is a long way to go before this can happen. In short, the issue of financing higher education in Tanzania is not only a big problem, but also a crisis!

9.5.2 *Accessibility*

Accessibility to higher education has been and remains a very serious problem in Tanzania. Only between 1 and 3% of the cohort population has access to tertiary education – of this, access to university education stands at less than 1% of the age cohort. It was for the purpose of enhancing access to secondary education that the government has been implementing the Primary Education Development Programme (PEDP) 2002–2007. It is also for the purpose of enhancing access to higher education that the government is implementing the Secondary Education Development Programme (SEDP) 2004–2009. The outcome of PEDP and SEDP will provide the pool of students required to fill vacancies created by the 27 universities in the country, thereby enhancing access to higher education.

9.6 Conclusions and Future Research

As argued in this chapter, Tanzania remains a poor and nonindustrialized country, heavily relying on agriculture which itself is very underdeveloped. Although there are some isolated good cases, the S&T system as a whole is not optimized to influence innovativeness in firms and farms; above all, there is very weak linkage between R&D organizations and the productive sector, especially the manufacturing sector. Most of the research conducted, especially from the Faculties of Sciences, are not put into practice. For those faculties and colleges with some form of linkages such as CoET in terms of consultancy and SMEs program, most important issue to raise is the balance between their traditional roles and these new and emerging roles in response to the societal needs. This is especially important as there is a big problem of dichotomy between S&T

currently in use in countries such as Tanzania. While science is global, technology is local, and unfortunately at a very low level. In this regard, universities seem to have two options: to do "big" science just for the sake of it, or come down to "small" science that can solve currently existing problems in the productive sector. Or putting it differently, can "big" science solve the problems of "small" technology?

The above raised issues are big issues and can only be adequately addressed through survey of higher education organizations in terms of their changing roles, and how they are addressing issues related to knowledge production and transfer for socioeconomic development. To start with, the survey can include only technical universities such as Sokoine University of Agriculture (SUA), University Colleges such as University College of Lands and Architectural Studies (UCLAS), Muhimbili University College of Health Sciences, and CoET. CoET has already resolved to adopt the model below for enhancing its impact on the society, through the establishment of an Incubator Hub in the vicinity of its premises (Fig. 9.3). The hub is intended to facilitate technology spin-offs as well as business services to start-up SMEs. In addition, the hub is expected to service the incubator stations up country, SME clubs, and the clusters whose establishment is championed by CoET.

Incubator Hub with Linkage to Incubator Stations, Clusters, and SME Clubs

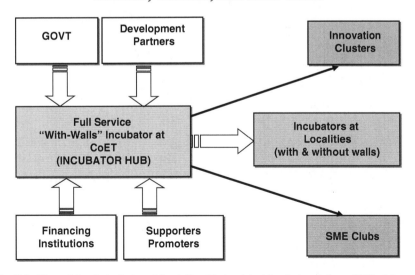

Fig. 9.3 Planned incubator hub and it relationship to virtual incubator stations, SME clubs, and clusters

Apart from inquiring into the university relation with the productive sector, it is also important to look into the relationship between universities and R&D organizations. Currently, there is no clear demarcation line between the role of the university and role of R&D organizations when it comes to research issues. According to some informal information, there are some complaints from R&D organizations, especially agricultural, that universities have currently turned into doing what is supposed to be their domain, i.e., more application-oriented research, instead of more basic research. This tendency seems to have been influenced by donor funding of R&D. Most donors have currently moved into funding research that is more application oriented. However, to establish concrete facts about the role of universities and R&D institutions in research in Tanzania, there is a need to conduct a comprehensive study. Such a study will also look into the perception of the society at large on the role of universities and that of R&D.

References

Chisawillo P (2006). Facilitating Metalworks Cluster, Proceedings of the 3rd Regional Conference on Innovation Systems and Innovative Clusters in Africa, Dar es Salaam, ISBN:9987-9074-4-X, pp. 174–187.

COSTECH (2005) A Report on the Survey of R&D Funds Flow In the Tanzanian Government R&D Institutions. Dar es Salaam.

Diyamett BD (2004). The Concept of Technological Innovation: Theoretical Overview and Some Practical Implication for Africa. In Mwamila BLM, Trojer L, Diyamett B and Temu A (eds) *Innovation Systems and Innovative Clusters in Africa*. Proceedings of a Regional Conference, Bagamoyo, Tanzania.

Diyamett BD (2005). A Mini-study to Test Tools Developed for Innovation Indicators and Surveys for the Tanzanian Manufacturing Sector. UNESCO, Nairobi.

European Commission. Proposed Guidelines for Collecting and Interpreting Technological Data – OSLO MANUAL. Organisation of Economic Cooperation and Development (OECD).

Joseph CC, Nkunya MHH (2002). Natural Products as Potential Environmentally Friendly Pesticides, Proceedings, International Science Symposium on Environment, Faculty of Science, University of Dar es Salaam, September.

Liwenga JM (1988) History of Agricultural Research in Tanzania. In Ter J.M and Mattee A.Z (eds), *Proceedings of a Workshop on Science and Farmers in Tanzania*, Sokoine University of Agriculture (SUA), Morogoro, Tanzania.

Mawenya AS (2002). Private Sector Participation in Financing of Higher Education. In Mwamila BLM, Omari I and Mbuya E (eds). *Financing of Higher Education in Eastern and Southern Africa: Diversifying Revenue and Expanding Accessibility* – Proceedings of A Workshop. Dar es Salaam, Tanzania.

MoHEST (2006). Basic Statistics on Higher Education, Science and Technology, 001/2002-2005/2006, Dar es Salaam University Press.

Shetto RM (2005). Agricultural Mechanization in Tanzania. A paper presented to the 3rd Annual Engineers' Day 2005, Dar es Salaam, Tanzania.

UDSM (2005). Five Year Rolling Strategic Plan 2005/2006–2009/2010, The Institute of Kiswahili Research, Dar es Salaam.

URT (2000). *National Development Vision; Vision 2025.*

Wangwe SM, Diyamett B (1998). Cooperation between R&D Institutions and Enterprises: The case of United Republic of Tanzania. In atas XI-*New Approaches to Science and Technology Cooperation and Capacity Building*. United Nations, NewYork and Geneva.

Wangwe SM, Diyamett BD, Komba A (2003). Trends in R&D Activities in Tanzania: Funding Sources, Institutional Arrangements and Relevance. Research on Knowledge Systems (RoKS), IDRC.

Webmetrics International (2005). http://www.universitymetrics.com

Chapter 10
South Africa: Reforming Higher Education and Transforming the National System of Innovation

Rasigan Maharajh, Enver Motala, and Mario Scerri

10.1 Introduction

The apartheid state in South Africa was recognized throughout the world as a pariah, especially after the United Nations declared its institutional regime a "crime against humanity." Many researchers, commentators, and observers regarded apartheid simply as an irrational state whose dysfunctionality made it both unstable and unsupportable (Alexander 1979). Its ability to survive was based largely on the organized violence and intimidation wrought by its military machinery directed against the majority of the citizenry. This intimidation was perpetrated moreover with the support and complicity of a small domestic minority who were the direct beneficiaries of the system. The apartheid state as a legalized racist formation excluded the majority of South Africans from the general body politic, from real participation in the institutions of state, and limited their ability to access broader economic and social rights. For a substantial portion of its existence, apartheid was overtly and covertly supported by a number of Western countries primarily because of South Africa's strategic position during the ideological confrontation, mainly between the Union of Soviet Socialist Republics and the Western capitalist nations (Cold War). Eventually, however, the condemnation of the apartheid state became almost universal and grew to establish a highly effective international campaign to isolate the South African regime. The collapse of the Soviet Union and the end of the Cold War removed the last overt Western support for the apartheid regime and expedited its eventual demise (Davies 2007).

The apartheid state which evolved from a long period of external colonialism and an intense period of segregation – from the formation of the Union of South Africa in 1910 to the election of the National Party in 1948 – grew into the most powerful location for the production and distribution of goods and services on the continent of Africa (Mamdani 1996). It gave rise to a modernizing economy, with the emergence

R. Maharajh (✉)
Institute for Economic Research on Innovation, Tshwane University of Technology,
City of Tshwane, South Africa
e-mail: maharajhr@tut.ac.za

B. Göransson and C. Brundenius (eds.), *Universities in Transition:*
The Changing Role and Challenges for Academic Institutions,
© International Development Research Centre 2011

and establishment of a proletarian class simultaneously stripping the established peasantry of all access to landed rights (Beinart and Delius 1986). It accelerated urbanization and established sophisticated transport, information and communications technology (ICT) networks, and a globally *competitive* financial sector, all of which are the hallmarks of a modern industrial state. It gave rise to subsystems of production in agriculture, transport, commerce and banking, manufacturing, and mining. Indeed very soon its capabilities in the mining sector were to outstrip most of its global competitors, resulting in South Africa becoming the largest producer of several of the most important minerals and ores required on the world market.

The coercive state which evolved from colonial conquest, through the period of self-government,[1] and to the system of apartheid laid the foundation for the evolution and eventual shape of South African capitalism. South African capitalism assumed a particular form through this period, one characterized principally by its exploitation of cheap black labor, strong controls over the political and other rights of black people in general, and draconian laws restricting various freedoms for the majority of the people of the country. The South African state developed its racially differentiated education and training system which would become a defining characteristic of the national system of innovation (NSI) inherited by the first democratic government. Despite its considerable power, the apartheid state was not unfettered in its designs as its objectives and approaches to development were not easily translated into development strategies and actions. This was, to a large extent, due to the fundamental contradictions within the form which capitalism took under apartheid and the constraints which these contradictions placed on the shift from an essentially resource-based economy to an industrialized, and eventually a postindustrial, system of innovation.

South African capitalism, not only like capitalism everywhere, but also specifically because of its violently racist forms under apartheid, stimulated the emergence of several fronts of countervailing power (Clarke 1977, 1991; Holloway and Picciotto 1978; Mandel 1980). These included trade unions, political organizations, and a variety of other social movements which mobilized civil society to resist the political economy of oppression. Student organizations, women's movements, peasant formations, locally based civics, faith-based associations, and cultural and other popular groups emerged to champion a variety of causes and claims. Not all of these were overtly political, but they were invariably drawn to the politics of the state because of its overpowering racial and antipoor forms of control over civilian life. It was these forms of organization that finally coalesced in their multiplicities, to provide the impetus for the overthrow of the apartheid regime from below (Buhlungu et al. 2007).

---

[1] "Self-government" in the case of South Africa was unique within the British Empire in that it reflected a new status of settler whites* with the continuing disenfranchisement of the large majority of the population. The unique features of this system of dominance and subjugation generated constructs such as "internal colonialism," "colonialism of a special kind," and "racial capitalism." *Note on Racist Nomenclature: In this chapter, the terms "White" and "Black" are used as indicators of race without pejorative meaning. Whites refer to ethnic groups of European descent. Blacks refer to the indigenous ethnic groups together with people originating from parts of South East Asia and those of mixed parentage, also referred to as "colored." A more detailed discussion is contained in Maharajh and Pogue (2009).

The conceptualization of the role of higher education (HE), and science, technology, and innovation (STI) within the liberation movement(s) did not go much beyond ideas about a "democratic" system, untainted by racist, patriarchal, and other unjust practices. Deeper questions about the place of education and science within South Africa's political economy were essentially less fundamental to the debate about defeating apartheid. There was, however, some resonance with these issues in the struggles around "worker education," giving rise to a number of important developments about the relationship of education and science *to* production and workers' control, the recognition of prior and lifelong learning, adult and continuing education, and "political" education. It could be argued that these developments were the direct precursor to the development of the post apartheid "training strategy."

This chapter does not attempt to provide a deeply theorized and "critical" view of HE and system of innovation either historically or at present. What we seek to do is to provide an overview of the evolution of the systemic interrelatedness of HE and the system of innovation as they evolved over the last two centuries. In the first section of this chapter, we outline the historical origins of South Africa's higher education institutions (HEIs) and of the NSI. The second section examines the various strategies evolved toward "reconstruction and development" which have characterized postapartheid South Africa. The third section provides a view of the contemporary features of HE and system of innovation. The concluding section is devoted to exploring some of the emerging and enduring challenges confronting the country's HE and innovation systems.

10.2   Historical Origins of the South African Higher Education Sector and the National System of Innovation

The adoption of the NSI approach to the analysis of dynamic systems brings to the fore the need to understand the specificities of particular systems and to delve into their histories in order to capture these specificities. Historiography is rarely uncontested and its importance arises from the differing analytical points of departure for the contending approaches to the understanding of specific NSIs. In the case of apartheid and the stages preceding it, the two main contending accounts are provided by liberal economic historians on the one hand and Marxist revisionists on the other. The former regarded the "national question" as primarily about the issue of race; they stressed the racist nature of the process of subjugation and the racist forms of control over the lives of the populace and the allocation of public and private resources (Lipton 1986). For this camp, racism was an aberration which impeded the rationality of market-based allocation of resources which would have eschewed any impediments, such as racist laws, on market functioning. Marxist historians, on the other hand, concentrated on the capitalist and exploitative nature of the apartheid system, the process of capital accumulation, and its relationship with the form and function of the state (Davies et al. 1976; Dennis and Fine 1985; Greenberg 1980; Helliker 1987; Kaplan 1977; Legassick 1973, 1974a, 1974b, 1975, 1976; Morris 1977;

Williams 1975; Wolpe 1972, 1974, 1980, 1988). The struggle between capital and labor, the competing claims of different class interests (and of "fractions" within these), the specific form of surplus value extraction, and the "coercive mechanisms" used in regulating labor in general and the subregionally integrated system of migrant labor were particular concerns of this approach (Clark 1986).

In general however, especially toward the 1980s, there were few analysts who did not accept the critically relational nature of these categories ("race" and "class") for analytical purposes. Theory and strategy were implicated in the analysis of the manner in which the state was conceptualized, for instance, in relation to the question of "race," and had direct implications for how the struggle for liberation was conducted. There were, for example, profound differences between the approach adopted by the Black Consciousness Movement, the African National Congress (ANCS associated with the theory of "colonialism of a special type"), within the leadership of the developing labor movement and of other political groupings on the left, largely associated with the tradition of *Trotskyism* in South Africa. Whatever the proclivities of the various participants in the debate, there is no doubt that it provided a much more rigorous, contextually oriented, and coherent view of the "political economy" of the South African state and indeed, it influenced a wide range of disciplinary analyses about the nature of apartheid – in particular, politics, sociology, economics, and history. A gap in the analysis of apartheid and in the formulation of liberation strategy was, however, recognized in relation to issues of gender. This area was not developed to the extent that class and race issues were and, except for a few writings, in-depth analyses were largely absent. As Bozzoli (1983) has shown, our understanding of South African society has been radically revised and deepened over the past decade – but the radical revision of South African history, sociology, and politics has not, by and large, been interwoven with feminist reinterpretations of conventional wisdoms.

The evolution of the HE sector in South Africa from its origins under colonialism until the advent of democracy manifests two enduring characteristics. The first is that it was driven and shaped by the shifting needs of the South African economy and the associated NSI. The second characteristic was its enduring exclusionary nature based strictly on racial grounds. Throughout this period, HEIs were key instruments in servicing the higher-end skills requirements of the NSI. It is worth noting, however, that the "local" South African system of innovation was relatively undeveloped compared with the other subsystems within the British Empire, especially the complex Indian system. As the local production system grew in sophistication and complexity, so did the skills requirements and also the HE sector which provided for them. Until the turn of the twentieth century, the pattern of the growth of the HE sector was to a large extent tied to the development of the primary sectors, especially mining and agriculture. The rapid industrialization during the interwar period, especially combined with overtly interventionist economic policies, provided a strong stimulus for the accelerated development of the HE sector on a wider front. This also provided the stimulus for an expansion of the agencies of the NSI.

From its inception, HE in South Africa was strictly segregated on a racial basis and was based on privileged access for whites until the first democratic elections in

1994 (Kellaway 1984). During the nineteenth century, this was not seriously at odds with practice in the rest of the British Empire but it increasingly became a troublesome contradiction within the rapidly developing industrial economy during the period of South African self-government until 1948. This contradiction was posed by the increasing skills requirements of a modernizing economy and the severe constraints of a racist HE policy which excluded the great majority of the population from participation. With the advent of apartheid and the entrenchment of this particular racially based strategy for the provision of HE, the South African system of innovation evolved in ways that required a greater emphasis on the broader demands for skills. From 1948 until the end of apartheid, the evolution of the HE system helped to shunt the evolution of the NSI on to a trajectory that became, against the postcolonial backdrop, progressively antimodern (Scerri 2009). This was due to the nature of industrial development after the surge in science and technology during the war, a structural change which progressively placed labor skills and the various aspects of human resource development at the core of economic development. The "underdeveloped" countries which assigned a high priority on broad-based education and training became the postwar success stories. The fundamental logic of apartheid through excluding such developmental possibilities relegated the development of the South African economy to a trajectory, which significantly diverged from rest of the rapidly modernizing economies whose acceleration was supported by an increasingly central role of human capability formation in economic development.

The origin of South African university system can be traced to the establishment of the South African College in Cape Town in 1829 as a response to the reliance on overseas study which was costly. The college initially had 115 students and students were prepared for the examinations of the University of London in UK. By the 1870s, a number of other similar colleges were established because of the growing demand for higher levels of education beyond schooling. These included many institutions whose reputations and fame have grown over time, although not all have continued to provide university level education and many have simply concentrated on secondary education. In 1873, the University Incorporation Act was passed by the then Cape Government and the University of the Cape of Good Hope came into existence, modeled on the London University. It conducted examinations in a range of degrees including Law, Arts, Divinity, and Agriculture, and certificates in civil engineering, music, and other courses. There was a great deal of growth in the number of colleges between 1874 and 1916, and various "university colleges" came into being including the South African College, Stellenbosch College, and Rhodes University College.

In 1896, a School of Mines was established in Kimberley but, for reasons that were to become obvious, was transferred to the burgeoning metropolis of Johannesburg in the Witwatersrand in 1903 and became the Transvaal University College. By 1910, it had become the South African School of Mines and Technology while at the same time the Transvaal University College came into being in Pretoria. The Natal University College was set up in 1909. Between 1918 and 1951, six of the seven university colleges originally established became full-fledged universities and a period of rapid growth in university education took place. The University of Cape Town was established as a full-fledged University in April 1918 (Phillips 1993) and the University of Witwatersrand came into being from the South African School of Mines and Technology by 1921. Parliament established the Potchefstroom University College as a part of the University of South Africa (UNISA) which had been established earlier in 1916. The University of Pretoria was established in 1930 and in 1950 the University of Natal came about. Similar developments took place in other provinces of the then Union of South Africa.

In 1916, significantly, the South African Native College was established, growing out of the Lovedale Missionary Institution at the town of Fort Hare in the Eastern Cape region of the Union. It was founded on Christian principles, yet was exclusively meant for black students and later became the University of Fort Hare in 1952. Although limited access was provided to black students at the Universities of Cape Town, Witwatersrand, and Natal, strict segregation was practiced at all institutions with regard to a number of matters such as accommodation, sport, and social function, and indeed at the University of Natal even in relation to academic courses. A medical school was established for "nonwhites" for the first time at the University of Natal in 1950. The establishment of apartheid entrenched in law a comprehensive policy of a racially segregated and exclusionary education. Throughout this period, however, there was considerable resistance to the racist and exclusionary policies of successive preapartheid governments and indeed there were debates even among those in government itself about these policies, especially during the late 1930s and early 1940s (Scerri 2009).

By 1955, the apartheid government began planning toward separate universities for "nonwhites" based on its conceptions of race and ethnic difference following a Select Committee of government's view, which was that *"many educated Africans were not serving their communities because they had been educated along European lines; they were under-developed people who did not yet have the sense of responsibility, the initiative, or the necessary knowledge to found and control their own universities. If the government of the Union of South Africa was in earnest about the full development of the Bantu, then the establishment of their own university colleges was imperative"* (Behr and Macmillan, 1971, pp. 238–239). As a result, the euphemistically called *Extension of University Education Act* was passed in 1959. By this Act, various racially defined institutions were created between 1960 and 1961. These HEIs fell under the control of racially defined Ministries of Education such as the Ministry of Bantu Education. These ministries took control over matters relating to the admission of students to the various types of universities established, especially with a view to preventing access of blacks to white institutions and strictly directing students to institutions defined in particular racial categories as conceived by the government (Beale 1994).[2]

---

[2]For similar policies affecting Technikons (the technical higher education sector under apartheid), see Bot (1988) and Pittendrich (1986).

The total number of students enrolled at these newly established university colleges for blacks was approximately 642 in 1960, rising to 3,774 in 1969. The white students at residential universities, not including UNISA, totaled 49,604 in 1968.[3] There were funding and other disparities affecting these institutions. Also worth noting is the fact that the training and certification of teachers and nurses took place outside these universities in Colleges of Education and Nursing, designed for those purpose and segregated according to apartheid.

10.3   Postapartheid Higher Education and the National System of Innovation

The election of the first democratic government of South Africa was a signal for the radical reform of the education system in the country. The context for its reform of policies and interventions was shaped not only by the legacy it had inherited from apartheid but also by the constitutional imprimatur to transform the social system as a whole in ways that would enhance the possibilities for social justice, human rights, and democracy. And these goals had to be pursued in the context of a rapidly changing global environment in which new regimes of trade, finance, rapidly changing systems of information, and other technologies made incessant and continuous demands for adaptation and accommodation on the part of national states. HE in South Africa was also obliged to deal with the worldwide effects of the commoditization and commercialization of educational services (Burbules and Torres 2000; Delanty 2001; Mittelman and Othman 2001; Muller and Subotzky 2001; Altbach 2001; Hill 2004; Levidow 2002).

A raft of new legislation and policies laid out the agenda of transformation under the presidency of Nelson Mandela. This legislation and the accompanying policies related to all arenas of education from early childhood to adult and from preprimary to HE. HE was specifically dealt with government's White Paper 3 of 1997 (WP3) (Department of Education 1997). The mission of the WP3 to redress the inequalities which had grown to be a systemic and crippling component of the South African system of innovation was explicitly stated. The White Paper outlined the framework for changing the HE system and declared that HE must be planned, governed, and funded as a single national coordinated system. This was necessary to deal with the "... *fragmentation, inequality and inefficiency which are the legacy of the past, and create a learning society which releases the creative and intellectual energies of all our people toward meeting the goals of reconstruction and development*" (WP3, Foreword).

---

[3] Ibid: 240 and 244. Of these white students, almost 15,000 were in the Arts; 7,100 in "pure science"; 8,300 in Commerce and Public Administration; 5,300 in Engineering; and 1,300 in Law.

WP3 placed the goals of HE squarely within the context of social transformation and the government's Reconstruction and Development Programme (RDP):

- To meet the learning needs and aspirations of individuals through the development of their intellectual abilities and aptitudes throughout their lives. HE equips individuals to make the best use of their talents and of the opportunities offered by society for self-fulfillment. It is thus a key allocator of life chances and an important vehicle for achieving equity in the distribution of opportunity and achievement among South African citizens.
- To address the development needs of society and provide the labor market, in a knowledge-driven and knowledge-dependent society, with the ever-changing high-level competencies and expertise necessary for the growth and prosperity of a modern economy.
- To contribute to the socialization of enlightened, responsible, and constructively critical citizens. HE encourages the development of a reflective capacity and a willingness to review and renew prevailing ideas, policies, and practices based on a commitment to the common good.
- To contribute to the creation, sharing, and evaluation of knowledge. HE engages in the pursuit of academic scholarship and intellectual inquiry in all fields of human understanding, through research, learning, and teaching.

The WP3 provided an analysis of the *"challenges," "vision,"* and *"goals"* of the HE system and affirmed its *"purposes"* as part of the broader process of South Africa's transition, including *"political democratisation, economic reconstruction and development, and redistributive social policies aimed at equity."* Furthermore, these challenges were always to be met in a context of global developments and their effects on South Africa. The Higher Education Act of 1997 gave legislative authority to the intentions of the WP3. More importantly, it laid down the provisions that dealt with the establishment, governance, funding, and merger of public HEIs. The Act also established the Council on Higher Education (CHE) and its permanent subcommittee the Higher Education Quality Committee (HEQC).

The shape of the HE sector was still the one inherited from apartheid with its systems of segregation, duplication, stratification, and waste. Although racial segregation had obviously disappeared, it was felt that the structure of the HE sector was still fundamentally flawed by its history. Consequently, in 2000 the CHE constituted a "Size and Shape" Task Team, with members drawn in their individual capacity from labor, business, universities and technikons, the Department of Education, and the CHE to address this issue. Its proposals are documented in the CHE Report of June 2000 – entitled *Toward a New Higher Education Landscape: Meeting the Equity, Quality and Social Imperatives of South Africa in the 21st Century.*

The proposals advanced were occasioned by several weaknesses which referred to the fragmentation and inequalities in the system of HE in South Africa and in recognition of the fact that unless these weaknesses were addressed, the prospects of the HE sector meeting the challenges of the twenty-first century

Table 10.1 SA Public Higher Education Landscape (2009)

Traditional universities	Comprehensive universities	Universities of technology	National institutes
Theoretically oriented university degrees, postgraduate and r esearch capacity	Combined academic and vocationally oriented education	Vocationally oriented qualifications, postgraduate and research capacity	Incubators and coordinating mechanism
1. University of Cape Town	1. University of Johannesburg	1. Cape Peninsula University of Technology	1. Mpumalanga Institute for Higher Education
2. University of Fort Hare	2. Nelson Mandela Metropolitan University	2. Central University of Technology	2. Northern Cape Institute for Higher Education
3. University of the Free State	3. University of South Africa	3. Durban University of Technology	
4. University of KwaZulu-Natal	4. University of Venda for Science and Technology	4. Mangosuthu University of Technology	
5. University of Limpopo	5. Walter Sisulu University for Technology and Science	5. Tshwane University of Technology	
6. North-West University	6. University of Zululand	6. Vaal University of Technology	
7. University of Pretoria			
8. Rhodes University			
9. University of Stellenbosch			
10. University of the Western Cape			
11. University of the Witwatersrand			

would not be realized. The report argued that the country faces a challenge of immense significance in demonstrating the benefits of HE planning that is informed by the requirements of democracy and socioeconomic development. The reconfiguration of HE must be seen as part of the process of constructing a seamless lifelong learning system that embraces schools, further education, HE, workplace-based learning, and nonformal learning. Such a system should provide ever greater levels of access to learning opportunities across a range of programs and entry points in a way that forms the critical basis for social justice and economic revitalization (CHE 2000).

The report also set out the "case for higher education in South Africa," and addressed the "goals, principles, and values" which it regarded as necessary to meet the challenges of the system. It dealt with the fact that all HEIs were products of segregation and apartheid, of the "geopolitical imagination of apartheid planners." It examined questions of "quality" and "standards," "excellence," "efficiency," and "effectiveness" and commented on the "strategies and policy instruments and mechanisms advocated in the White Paper" in relation to the HE system goals. A significant part of the report argued the "case for differentiation and diversity" in the HE landscape in order to meet the wide-ranging challenges facing the system as a whole. The report also provided a set of recommendations on the "shape" and the "size" of the HE system (CHE 2000).

The 2001 National Plan for Higher Education (NPHE) reaffirmed the premises of the White Paper and set out the framework and mechanisms for implementing and realizing the policy goals of the White Paper (Department of Education 2001). This was a critical document as it signalled for the first time the concrete measures to be undertaken by the Ministry of Education toward achieving the goal of reconfiguring the HE system. In the same year, the National Working Group (NWG) was established to advise on the appropriate arrangements for restructuring the provision of HE on a regional basis through the development of new institutional and organizational forms, including institutional mergers and rationalization of program development and delivery. The NWG submitted its report in December 2001.

In summary, the NWG Report provided recommendations on the "appropriate arrangements for consolidating the provision of higher education on a regional basis through establishing new institutional and organizational forms, including reducing the number of higher education institutions" (NWG 2001). It took the NPHE's conception of "fitness for purpose" as its point of departure for its recommendations. After examining the relevant document on this and other issues and after consultations, it came to a number of "guiding principles to frame its work and shape its recommendations and developed an associated set of performance indicators and linked benchmarks" (NWG 2001).

The recommendations were "twofold": The first was related to general issues that cut across all regions. These related to such matters as regional collaboration, the view that universities and technikons should continue to operate as HEIs with distinct programs and mission foci; and "comprehensive" institutions, the college and distance education sector and "satellite" campuses. The second was related to proposals and recommendations for the consolidation of HE provision on a regional basis through establishing new institutional and organizational forms, including a reduction in the number of HEIs from 36 to 21 through mergers and incorporations.

The NWG argued that the implementation of its recommendations would result in the fundamental restructuring of the HE system and transform the apartheid edifice of the HE system to lay the foundation for a HE system that is consistent with the vision, values, and principles of a young democratic order.

In June 2002, based on the advise received from the NWG, the Ministry of Education released a set of proposals for the transformation and restructuring of the HE system. The proposals are contained in the Government Gazette Notice, No. 23549, which is entitled *Transformation and Restructuring: A New Institutional Landscape for Higher Education* (Department of Education 2002). The proposals, which were approved by Cabinet, would result in the consolidation of HEIs from 35 to 23 through mergers of two or more public HEIs into single institutions as well as through the incorporation of subdivisions/campuses of existing HEIs into other HEIs. In total, there were to be ten mergers and ten subdivisions/campuses that were to be incorporated. Of the campuses to be incorporated, five were to be incorporated into institutions that are merging and the remaining five into institutions that were not merging (Table 10.1). Several of these have now taken place as planned, with a few being postponed for reasons of political expediency and capacity constraints.

10.4   Characteristics of the Higher Education Sector and the System of Innovation

According to Table 10.2, the total number of students enrolled in 2005 at public HEIs was 737,472. Of these, the majority (482,595) were contact[4] students, while there were also 252,877 distance students of whom 207,293 were at one institution alone – UNISA. Black students constituted 74 and 76%, respectively, of the contact and distance student population. Female students constituted 53 and 57%, respectively, of these categories, while the distribution of students between science, engineering, and technology (SET),[5] business, and the humanities was 29, 29, and 42%, respectively. Institutional sizes ranged from almost 49,000 contact students at the Tshwane University of Technology to 6,045 at Rhodes University.

Table 10.3 shows that students were distributed as follows in the major fields of study. SET numbers were 211,069 (28.6%), while business and managements had 214,509 (29.1%), education 107,503 (14.6%), and all other humanities and social sciences had 204,391 (27.7%) students enrolled, respectively.

With regard to formal qualifications the 3-year undergraduate qualifications were the preponderant majority of students – 440,680 students. The professional undergraduate degrees constituted 161,392 students. The master and doctoral students constituted 44,533 and 9,434, respectively. The total of all postgraduate degrees including postgraduate below Master's level was 115,589 students. As a proportion

Table 10.2 Overview of South African higher education

	2005	2007
Headcount student enrollments	737,472	761,087
Contact	482,595	474,606
Distance	254,877	286,481
Black students as a proportion of headcount totals (%)		
Contact	74	74
Distance	76	79
Female students as proportion of headcount totals (%)		
Contact	53	53
Distance	57	59
Proportion of contact and distance headcount enrollments in major fields of study		
SET	29	28
Business	29	30
Humanities	42	42

Source: HEMIS Database

---

[4] Those students registered mainly for courses in contact mode.

[5] Majors in science, engineering, and technology. The sciences include health sciences, life sciences, physical sciences, computer sciences, and mathematical sciences.

Table 10.3 Major field of study and qualification headcount

	2005	2007
Major field of study	737,472	760,009
Science, engineering, and technology	211,073	214,341
Business and management	214,510	228,735
Education	107,505	106,330
All other humanities and social sciences	204,391	310,603
Formal qualifications	737,472	761,087
Occasional students	19,271	25,696
Three-year undergraduate degrees and diplomas	440,680	254,789
Professional undergraduate degrees	161,932	370,200
Postgraduate degrees, below master's level	61,622	59,179
Master's degrees	44,533	41,172
Doctoral degrees	9,434	10,204051

Source: HEMIS Database

Table 10.4 Graduates in public higher education by major field of study and qualification

	2005	2007
Major field of study	120,053	126,887
Science, engineering, and technology	33,554	36,637
Business and management	28,127	31,04
Education	29,090	28,332
All other humanities and social sciences	29,292	30,814
Formal qualifications	120,063	127,154
Three-year undergraduate degrees and diplomas	63,702	43,418
Professional undergraduate degrees	23,950	52,388
Postgraduate, below master's level	23,204	22,190
Master's degree	8,018	7,829
Doctoral degrees	1,198	1,329

Source: HEMIS Database

of the total, this constituted about 15.6% of the student population. Some 59.9% were at the 3-year undergraduate level.

Black African students were 60 and 62%, respectively, of the contact and distance students enrolled, while the percentage for white students was 26 and 24%, respectively. The distribution between female and male students between contact and distance students enrolled was 53 and 47% (contact) and 57 and 43% (distance), respectively. In total, 54.5% of students were female, while male students constituted 45.5%.

The number of graduates by major field of study was distributed as follows: SET: 33,561; business and management: 28,126; education: 29,086; and all other humanities and social sciences: 29,290, making a total of 120,053 students. Formal qualifications were concentrated in the 3-year undergraduate degrees and diplomas (63,702), while master and doctoral qualifications numbered 8,018 and 1,189, respectively. There were 23,950 qualifications at professional undergraduate level and 23,204 at postgraduate below master's level (Table 10.4).

Undergraduate degrees and diplomas constituted 15%, masters 18%, and doctorates 13% of the total graduation rates in public HE sector in South Africa. These rates are considerably below the 75% benchmarks set in the NPHE of the completion rates of any cohort of students entering a program. The figures show that only 25% of contact students and 15% of distance students were meeting the benchmark for undergraduate studies, while only 20 and 15%, respectively, were doing so for doctoral-level studies.

Table 10.5 illustrates the high level of employment inequity in the public HE system in 2005. Black staff comprised only 36.8% of the permanently appointed academic staff posts, while the female staff consisted of 41.5% of these staff. Female staff was also preponderant in the administrative functions at 60.2%.

Overall, it can be said that some progress has been achieved in the HE system in South Africa since 1994 (CHE 2004). For instance, the following has been achieved:

- Overall student enrollment (and within all racially specified and gender groups) has increased in both headcount and full-time equivalent (FTE) terms; and student participation rates have increased from 14 to 18%.
- There have been significant proportionate increase in the SET fields of study in accordance with the NPHE targets.
- Small increase has been registered in postgraduate enrollments relative to overall enrollments.
- Student graduate output has improved over time. Notably, in 2002 there was a rise of 24% compared with the figure for 1995.
- The number of international students presently studying in South Africa has increased to a significant number of 53,000 students. These students come to South Africa mostly from the South African Development Community (SADC) Region.

Table 10.5 Public higher education human resources (permanent staff)

	2005	2007
Total permanent staff		
Instruction and research staff	15,315	15,589
Administrative staff	21,375	22,224
Service staff	6,646	5,904
Percentage of black staff in total		
Instruction and research staff	37	39
Administrative staff	56	59
Service staff	97	97
Percentage of female staff in total		
Instruction and research staff	42	43
Administrative staff	60	61
Service staff	39	40

Source: HEMIS Database

Quality assurance is regarded by most observers of the HE system in South Africa as the third of the key levers for the transformation of the system. The Higher Education Act 101 of 1997 also established the Council on Higher Education. Section 7 of the act dealt specifically with the "permanent committee" of the CHE – the HEQC. Its function in terms of Section 7 of the act was to "perform the quality promotion and quality assurance functions of the CHE in terms of this Act." The HEQC was ascribed a wide range of functions, inter alia, relating to the promotion of quality promotion, the audit of the mechanisms for quality of assurance, the accreditation of programs, the dissemination of information, and the performance of other functions which were "conferred" or "delegated" to it.

According to the HEQC, its framework and criteria for quality assurance are based on

- fitness of purpose based on national goals, priorities, and targets;
- fitness of purpose in relation to specified mission within a national framework that encompasses differentiation and diversity;
- value for money judged in relation to the full range of HE purposes set out in the White Paper; and
- transformation in the sense of enhancing the capabilities of individual learners for personal development, as well as the requirements of social development, and economic and employment growth.[6]

The HEQC's mandate has been resolutely advanced since about 2001 when the HEQC was established. It has undertaken a wide range of tasks relating to quality promotion and capacity development, and the implementation of audit and accreditation systems. It has also incorporated developments in quality assurance systems internationally while ensuring that these have contextual relevance and integrity and has done so in ways that allow for meaningful comparability and for the adoption of good practice from other HE systems.

Despite the early scepticism in some quarters about its "evaluative" work, most serious analysts and commentators have regarded the HEQC's work as important for increasing the accountability of public (and private) HE system to society. Its work has raised a wide range of extremely important issues concerning HE.

These issues have led to a considerable broadening of the discussions about how "quality" might be conceptualized in a society in transition from apartheid to democracy, and the relationship between quality and institutional change. More recently, the HEQC has facilitated a discussion about the relationship between quality, social justice, and social transformation. It has raised other issues too. It has been able to reflect self-critically on the purposes and nature of its work, its impact, public credibility, the transparency of its processes and its "independence," the relationship between quality assurance, and the planning and funding of higher education. It has also been able raise debates on more

---

[6] See HEQC Founding Document, January 2001, accessible at http://heqc-online.che.ac.za.

exploratory themes such as questions about how the concept of "public good" might be understood, discussions about the idea of "engagement" between society and HEIs, about "community engagement" as a mandate of HE, the relationship between "accountability" and "academic freedom," the appropriate role for the state in promoting the idea of quality assurance and other such issues (du Toit 2007; Jonathon 2006). Most importantly, the HEQC has also been drawn into providing assistance to institutions outside South Africa (Lange 2003; Singh 2003).[7] At the time of writing, a number of institutional audits and program reviews have been completed and these have received wide public attention and have produced important discussion and debate about the HE system in the context of an integrating SADC.

10.5   The South African Innovation System

South Africa adopted an innovation systems approach to transform the public resources for research, development, science, and technology. This perspective was adopted through the White Paper on Science and Technology in 1996 (Department of Science and Technology 1996). In addition to the 23 public institutions for HE, research and development activities also take place in Public Research Institutions (PRIs) but popularly known as Science Councils domestically. Collectively, they comprise a significant portion of the formal institutional S&T component of the NSI. The White Paper on Science and Technology outlined the South African government's commitment to S&T and signaled a broad set of objectives for the NSI to achieve. These were listed as follows:

- Promoting competitiveness and employment creation
- Enhancing quality of life
- Developing human resources
- Working toward environmental sustainability
- Promoting an information society

Most of the attention of this White Paper was directed at the main performing agencies of the NSI, the Science Councils. It should be noted that only three of these PRIs report directly to the Department of Science and Technology. The others continue to be accountable to their respective sectoral ministries. Table 10.6 provides a snapshot of the current Science Councils.

Subsequent to the establishment of the NSI framework as the key organizing tool for managing the transition, a number of institutional and sectoral interventions were generated including the establishment of a single executive agency for the government of South Africa – the Department of Science and Technology.[8]

---

[7] See various CHE Publications and also Singh and Lange (2007).

[8] www.dst.gov.za.

Table 10.6 Public Research Institutions of South Africa (2009)

Name	Acronym	Core competencies
Agricultural Research Council	ARC	Promoting agriculture and related sectors through research, technology development, and technology transfer
Africa Institute of South Africa	AISA	Africa-focused research organization and think-tank disseminating research, publications, and a massive resource library
Council for Geosciences	CGS	Geological, geophysical, and paleontological research facility supplying geological information to the government and the public
Council for Mineral Technology	Mintek	Enables the minerals industry to operate more effectively, by developing and making available the most appropriate and cost-effective technologies
Human Sciences Research Council	HSRC	Facilitates problem solving and enhances decision making through research excellence in the human and social sciences
Medical Research Council	MRC	Improves the nation's health status and quality of life through relevant and excellent health research aimed at promoting equity and development
National Research Foundation	NRF	Agency for investing in knowledge and innovation across all disciplines of the natural sciences and engineering, as well as social sciences and humanities
Standards South Africa	STANZA	Formerly, the SA Bureau of Standards provides standards that enhance the competitiveness of South Africa, and which provide the basis for consumer protection, health, safety, and environmental issues. It is responsible for the development and publication of standards for products and services.

The vast array of new instruments is manifested through strategies, programs, and projects that collectively seek to improve the quality of life of all South Africans through improving the competitive performance of business enterprises (both public and private). This array includes the National Research and Technology Audit (1997), Review of the Science and Technology Institutions in SA (1998), National Research and Technology Foresight (1999), NACI/ NSTF report: Growth and Innovation (2000), National Biotechnology Strategy (2001), National Research and Technology Development Strategy (2002), Advanced Manufacturing Technology Strategy (2003), Indigenous Knowledge Strategy (2005), R&D Tax Incentives (2006), and the recently released 10-Year Plan: Innovation toward a Knowledge-based Economy (2007) (Department of Science and Technology 2000, 2006, 2007).

The Council for Scientific and Industrial Research (CSIR) is by far the leading public-sector performer of research and development in South Africa. Up until 2005, it existed as an agency of the Department of Trade and Industry and was constituted by an Act of Parliament in 1945[9]. Recent data confirm that it is one of the leading scientific and technological research, development, and implementation organizations in Africa (Kahn and Blankley 2006, p. 270). It was originally conceived of as necessary in responding to the country's problems of "hunger, shelter and health" in the postwar period (Scerri 2009). It is based in Tshwane and is also present in most of the nine provinces of South Africa through regional offices. It undertakes directed and multidisciplinary research, technological innovation, and industrial and scientific development to improve the quality of life of the South Africas' people. It is committed to supporting innovation in South Africa to improve national competitiveness in the global economy. S&T services and solutions are provided in support of various stakeholders, and opportunities are identified where new technologies can be further developed and exploited in the private and public sectors for commercial and social benefit. Its parliamentary grant makes up approximately 40% of its total income, while it also generates income from research contracts, royalties, licences, and dividends to its intellectual property and other commercial operations. Its parliamentary grant is used to generate "precompetitive" research not likely to be privately funded and for the training of young researchers.

The Department of Science and Technology is currently shepherding the country's bid to host the Square Kilometre Array (SKA) Radio Telescope, estimated to cost US$1.5 billion and which would, if successful, become one of the largest such infrastructures in the world. This facility is mainly based in the Northern Cape. Complimenting this is the recently launched Southern African Large Telescope (SALT), which is the single largest Optical Telescope in the southern hemisphere and the largest in Africa. It is colocated with the SKA in the Northern Cape. Other cross-cutting initiatives, such as the Innovation Fund and the Centres of Excellence and Research Chairs programs, have also been initiated. The department acknowledges that "*at the heart of these challenges is educating a new generation of scientists and skilled technical professionals. At the moment, there are too few students entering science and engineering programs in higher education. Moreover, a very low proportion of these undergraduates move into related postgraduate research. … We have to find ways to tap into our existing resources (at universities and science councils) with innovative thinking to make sure we increase the numbers*" (Department of Science and Technology 1996).

In responding to a debate on his State of the Nation address to the opening of Parliament in 2002, the former President Thabo Mbeki thanked members of parliament "*for raising the important issue of science and technology and its relevance*

---

[9] The CSIR's mandate is as stipulated in the Scientific Research Council Act (Act 46 of 1988, as amended by Act 71 of 1990), section 3: Objects of the CSIR: "The objects of the CSIR are, through directed and particularly multi-disciplinary research and technological innovation, to foster, in the national interest and in fields which in its opinion should receive preference, industrial and scientific development, either by itself or in cooperation with principals from the private or public sectors, and thereby to contribute to the improvement of the quality of life of the people of the Republic, and to perform any other functions that may be assigned to the CSIR by or under this Act" (Government of South Africa, 1990).

to the struggle for development and pushing back the frontiers of poverty and underdevelopment" and committed the government to "*undertake a comprehensive review of this important sector to ensure that we correctly position and resource science and technology, research and development as a central driver in the process of the modernization of our country and the creation of a better life for all.*"[10] This reinforced the perception that while the ability of technological progress and innovation to improve the conditions of existence of people was internalized, questions about the institutional capacity to deliver this public good remained to be evidenced. In the next section, we consider some of the trends within the NSI of South Africa.

According to Kahn and Blankley (2007), the main formal R&D institutions within the NSI in South Africa are the research universities (six of these), some government research agencies and museums, the science councils, and some firms. According to them, South Africa's share of world technology exports "appears to relate a dismal tale." For instance, the share of high technology was no more than 0.07 in 2002, while for low technology, it was only 0.30. The top ten manufactured exports, however, show that they are of the medium-technology type and suggest a "story of export-led growth." They also indicate that more important than the rankings in 2002 is the change in rankings indicative of shifts toward: "weapons and ammunition, electronic components, petroleum refineries/synthesizers, engines and turbines, and television and radio receivers"[11] were experiencing the highest increases.

The authors acknowledge the problems of measuring R&D because while R&D measures have been conducted along the lines of the Frascati Manual Series of the OECD (Blankley et al. 2006), they are not adequate for the purposes of capturing the difficulties in measuring innovation activities accurately, particularly because, as they argue, it bears little reference to "the measurement of R&D in the service sector" (Blankley et al. 2006, p. 275).[12] Calculating the Gross Expenditure on Research and Development as a percentage of GDP (GERD), utilizing the Frascati Methodology[13], for the period 1983–2003, generates the result indicating the median level of expenditure on R&D at 0.76% and improving to 0.86% in 2003 (Blankley et al. 2006, p. 278). This means that South Africa had not yet reached the 1% target set by government (Table 10.7).

The sectoral distribution of R&D shows that business and not-for-profit research accounted for 57.4% of the share of R&D expenditure, government and the science councils 22%, and HE 20.6%, respectively, from a total expenditure of 10.081 billion Rand in 2003/2004.[14] By 2003/2004, the major fields of R&D

---

[10]Statement at the Conclusion of the Debate on the State of the Nation Address, National Assembly: 14 February 2002.

[11]Blankley and Kahn (2005, pp. 273–274).

[12] They illustrate this view by reference to particular examples.

[13]'Frascati Methodology' as: OECD, 2002, Frascati Manual: Proposed Standard Practice for Surveys of Research and Experimental Design, Organisation for Economic Cooperation and Development, Paris.

[14]Khan and Blankley, Updated by the Authors.

Table 10.7 Historical trends in R&D expenditure

Year	R&D expenditure (R millions)	R&D as percentage of GDP
1966/1967	37	0.40
1969/1970	59	0.50
1971/1972	75	0.53
1973/1974	94	0.47
1975/1976	142	0.54
1977/1978	225	0.65
1979/1980	310	0.64
1981/1982	497	0.74
1983/1984	769	0.82
1985/1986	1,077	0.84
1987/1988	1,329	0.76
1989/1990	1,775	0.71
1991/1992	2,786	0.84
1993/1994	2,594	0.61
1997/1998	4,103	0.60
2001/2002	7,488	0.73
2003/2004	10,082	0.80
2004/2005	12,010	0.86
2005/2006	14,149	0.92
2006/2007	16,521	0.95

Source: Blankley and Kahn (2005)

investment were the engineering sciences (24.8%), natural sciences (21.9%), medical and health sciences (13.5%), while the social sciences and humanities accounted for 11.8% of the total expenditure in that year. Interestingly, the applied and engineering sciences expenditure has grown by 10% over a decade. Patents of South Africa, granted in USA, have increased from 89 in 1993 to 112 in 2003.[15] These data also suggest that there is a small increase in aggregate numbers of "researcher full time equivalents" between 1992 and 2004, namely, from 9,454 to 10,127. These statistics tend to confirm the perception of South Africa becoming a victim of the combination of its own failure to produce good school leaving candidates for universities and an increase in the mobility of researchers.

The South African expenditure on R&D has been steadily increasing over the last three decades. Revisions were made to the estimation of GDP by the national statistical agency which then caused the GERD figures to be revised downward. According to these statistics, South Africa is yet to meet its declared commitment to investing 1% of GDP on R&D (Table 10.7). These aggregates however mask intranational discrepancies. With the majority of science councils, major corporate offices, and nearly six universities based in the Province of Gauteng, this region has well exceeded the target at the cost of the rest of the country.

---

[15] Ibid: 280.

Concentration in the sector, as is the case more generally in South Africa, is heavily path dependent, contingent on postapartheid transformation, and most especially, influenced by historical accumulation. It is therefore unsurprising that five universities (Cape Town, Natal, Pretoria, Stellenbosch, and the Witwatersrand) accounted for 61% of the 1991–1992 R&D expenditure in HE. By 2001–2002, these five, while still dominant, had lost 4% to now command only 57% of the total.[16]

10.6 Conclusions: Enduring Challenges for SA HE and the NSI

There is a rich history of analysis and debate about the apartheid state. This litera-ture is instructive for thinking about the contemporary postapartheid state and their differences. Indeed, the very nature of state analysis under apartheid would suggest how contemporary analysis might be different, what its key elements should be, and how the differing objectives of the state then and now (and its similarities) might inform analysis.

Developments today need to be understood both contextually and historically, to the extent that societies are always in the grip of history and of its stubborn continuities – such as in relation to questions of how power is socially distributed – in the aftermath of apartheid and the effects of the Bill of Rights contained in the postapartheid constitution. Contestation continues to be the case in the postapart-heid period even though the forms of that contestation are very different from those that existed during apartheid. Interest in the democratizing state arises from its considerable power to organize and use the potential resources at its disposal in ways which facilitate particular approaches to social, economic, political, and cultural development. Hence social actors and classes will continue to maintain a critical perspective on the role of the state and on how it shapes its regulatory mechanisms, laws, and policies.

An example of this contestation at this time is a simmering contest between capital and labor over questions about the "flexibility" of the labor market (and unemployment levels), differences about social policy such as the contests over medicine pricing and the treatment of disease, school fees, housing and social ser-vices delivery, the role of the Sector Education and Training Authorities, inflation targeting and monetary policy, the role of the central bank, "decentralization" of decision making, the renaming of cities and towns, Black Economic Empowerment, etc. Concepts such as "transformation," "innovation," "development," "empower-ment," "the state," "markets," and others are very much a part of that contestation.

Most of this contestation in the postapartheid period owes its origin to the approach to macroeconomic planning formally adopted in 1996, at the time of the publication of the *White Paper on Science and Technology*. The original draft

---

[16]Ibid: 155.

macroeconomic planning framework which was later superseded was Keynesian and its scope is succinctly summarized in Maharajh (2005a, b): *With respect to economic policy, the formation of the Macroeconomic Research Group (MERG) by the African National Congress in 1991 was critical in gathering those sympathetic to the growth through redistribution thesis. The MERG report published in 1993 argued for a radical restructuring of the economy mainly through labour market interventions in education and training and skills development while simultaneously raising wages. Its report outlined a coherent program of state intervention with high levels of regulation, taxation and competitiveness oversight. The MERG report also argued for the creation of tripartite supervisory boards for large companies.*

Eventually, however, this view was supplanted by a neoliberal approach encapsulated in the 1996 *Growth, Employment and Redistribution* (GEAR) program. This program gained ascendancy for two reasons. The first was the concern about the state of the public fiscal resources which had been seriously compromised by the extreme profligacy of the last years of the apartheid regime. In this respect, there was a concern that a Keynesian program would place even more pressure on public expenditure. The second concern arose from the need to follow the lead provided by the World Bank and the International Monetary Fund in its approach to fiscal and other policies intent on establishing the global hegemony of neoliberal ideologies (Hill 2004). The effect of the adoption of this approach on STI planning was the paradigmatic divergence between the *White Paper on Science and Technology* and the macroeconomic plan within it was set. This divergence placed severe constraints on the implementation of an integrated policy to address the recognized shortcomings of the NSI. However, the increasing disillusionment with the macroeconomic performance of the GEAR program, in particular, and with the neoliberal ideology, in general, has substantially altered the location of innovation policy within the overall policy framework.

Contests over the ideological framework informing state policies in the postapartheid period have remain unresolved. While the struggles between "capital" and "labor" which were so fundamental to an analysis of the apartheid period might not be as prominent now, the contradictions between the interests represented by them remain – even if they are not expressed in the forms of legislative control and the strong limitations on organization that existed under apartheid. Moreover, these contradictions remain pervasive in so far as the phenomena of social inequality and unemployment, ill-health, and lack of good quality education for the poor remain pervasive.

In this period, these contradictions are compounded by the way in which the democratic state interprets its role in regard to the power of the "market." It could be argued that now, more than in the past, the powerful hand of the "market" was an important factor in the evolution of the postapartheid state and that this must be understood much more fully. Given the global crisis of capitalism today, it is hardly possible to evaluate the behavior of the state outside such a relationship because markets impose a particular "will" (even if not unfettered) on the behavior of the state, on its regulatory mechanisms, and on the limits it imposes on what is possible for the state in its mediatory role. This is most evident in public policies relating to finance, growth, and industrial strategies, macroeconomic and financing strategies, welfare, health and education policies, and the like and on the approaches it brings to a host of governmental activities through its financing, planning, and administration activities. And as Dreze and Sen argue, participation is important to economic and social opportunity because those who are solicitous of the idea that opportunities of market transaction should be open rather than restricted have good reason to consider not only the liberty of the rich to participate in market activities, but also the opportunity of the poor to join in what the market can offer (Dreze and Sen 2002).

Critically, Dreze and Sen link questions of the market to the importance of "participation" as it relates to institutions such as the market, the judiciary, public services, and political parties. They remind us of the connectedness between state, markets, and the public and how this needs to be viewed in the context of a larger framework and not as "simple formulae used by different sides in the contemporary debates." As Sen had argued earlier, it is hard to think that any process of substantial development can do without very extensive use of markets, but that does not preclude the role of social support, public regulation, or statecraft when they can enrich – rather than impoverish – human lives (Sen 1999). The approach used here provides a broader and more inclusive perspective on markets than is frequently invoked in either defending or chastising market mechanisms.

Indeed, the General Secretary of the Congress of South African Trade Unions (COSATU), in his political report to the tenth national conference, offered the following assessment of the general transition into a postapartheid dispensation: *"The blind belief in market forces, for that matter the apartheid market, has not only entrenched the inequalities of the past but has further widened them. A black elite has emerged and together with its white counterpart has reaped most of the benefits of democracy. However, the fundamental national, class and gender contradictions remain firmly entrenched in postapartheid South Africa. White men still monopolize positions of power and influence especially in the private sector. The endurance of the systemic inequalities makes a compelling case for a working-class led national democratic revolution. The working class must unite the broadest section of the South African society to move beyond the neo-colony to a truly democratic, nonsexist and nonracial society"* (COSATU 2009).

Policy analysis can hardly ignore the impact of global policy regimes and the conditionalitie they impose on seemingly sovereign states. In developing countries, moreover, the extraordinary grip of iniquitous trade, debt, and even "aid" makes any idea of sovereignty (and the sovereign state) tenuous given the relative powerlessness of these states in the face of militant markets and unaccountable and even submissive regimes of comprador elites. Any serious analysis of the state's social policies must, therefore, have some view of the effects of such global regimes on the possibilities for national development. These contested limitations are sharply contrasted in South Africa as the country seems to have affected an internal transfer of power.

While a former national liberation movement, the ANC has successively ruled the postapartheid South Africa and was again returned by a significant electoral majority in 2009; a range of progressive resolutions taken at its 52nd conference held in Polokwane in 2007 seem to suggest a break from the earlier 15 years. The ascendency of the ruling party's alliance partners in the South African Communist Party (SACP) and COSATU offers interesting times ahead. The Ministers of both Higher Education and Training and Science and Technology are now from the ANC. The former is also the current General Secretary of the SACP. These new deployments will, besides enjoining these cadres in realizing the core aspirations of the ANC, also offer new openings for advancing more radical options. These changes will also inform and influence the agendas of further reforming the HE sector and thereby furthering the transformation of South Africa's NSI. The results of this coevolution within a conjuncture of radicalization offer new possibilities of advances and retreats in seeking the improvement of the quality of life for all South Africans through a return to a more participative engagement with stakeholders and role players.

References

Alexander, N. [No Sizwe] (1979). *One Azania, One Nation*, Zed Press, London.

Altbach, P. G. (2001). Why Higher Education is not a Global Commodity, *Chronicle of Higher Education*, May 11.

Beale, M. A. (1994). *Apartheid and University Education, 1948–1959*, Dissertation Submitted to the University of Witwatersrand for the Degree of Masters of Arts, Johannesburg.

Behr, A. L. and Macmillan, R. G. (1971). *Education in South Africa*, van Schaik, Tshwane.

Beinart, W. and Delius, P. (1986). *Putting a Plough to the Ground: Accumulation and Dispossession in Rural South Africa 1850–1930*, Ravan Press, Johannesburg.

Blankley, W. and Kahn, M. (2005). The History of Research and Experimental Development Measurement in South Africa: Some Current Perspectives, *South African Journal of Science*, 101, March/April, 151–156.

Blankley, W., Scerri, M., Molotja, N., and Saloojee I. (2006). *Measuring Innovation in OECD and NON-OECD Countries: Selected Seminar Papers*, HSRC Press, Tshwane.

Bot, M. (1988). *Training on Separate Tracks*, South African Institute for Race Relations, Johannesburg.

Bozzoli, B. (1983). Marxism, Feminism and South African Studies, *Journal of Southern African Studies*, 9, April, 139–171.

Buhlungu, S., Daniel, J., Southall, R., and Lutchman J. (2007). *State of the Nation, South Africa 2005–2006*, HSRC Press, Tshwane.

Burbules, N. and Torres, C. A. (2000). *Globalisation and Education: Critical Perspectives*, Routledge, New York.

CHE (2000). *Toward a New Higher Education Landscape: Meeting the Equity, Quality and Social Development Imperatives of South Africa in the Twenty-first Century*, Council for Higher Education Policy Report, Tshwane.

CHE (2004). *Higher Education in the First Decade of Democracy*, Council for Higher Education, Tshwane.

CHE (2005). *Toward a Framework for Quality Promotion and Capacity Development in South African Higher Education*, Research Report for the QPCD Framework, Council for Higher Education Discussion Document, Tshwane, December.

Clarke, S. (1977). Marxism, Sociology and Poulantzas' Theory of the State, *Capital and Class*, 1 (2), 1–31.

Clarke, S. (1978). Capital, Fractions of Capital and the State: 'Neo-Marxist Analysis of the South African State, *Capital and Class*, 5, 32–77.

Clarke, S. (1991). *The State Debate*, Macmillan, London.

COSATU (2009). *Political Report to the Tenth COSATU National Congress: Consolidating Working Class Power in Defence of Decent Work and for Socialism*, Congress of South African Trade Unions, Midrand.

Davies, J. E. (2007). *Constructive Engagement? Chester Crocker and American Policy in South Africa, Namibia and Angola 1981–8*, Ohio University Press, Athens.

Davies, R., Kaplan, D., Morris, M., and O'Meara, D. (1976). Class Struggle and the Periodisation of the State in South Africa, *Review of African Political Economy*, 3 (7), 4–30.

Delanty, G. (2001). *Challenging Knowledge: The University in the Knowledge Society*, SRHE and Open University Press, Buckingham.

Dennis, D. and Fine, R. (1985). Political Strategies and the State, Some Historical Observations, *Journal of Southern Studies*, 12 (1), October, 25–48.

Department of Education (1997). *A Programme for the Transformation of Higher Education, Education White Paper 3*, Government Gazette No. 18207, Government Printers, Tshwane.

Department of Education (2001). *National Plan for Higher Education*, Government Printers, Tshwane.

Department of Education (2002). Transformation and Restructuring: A New Institutional Landscape for Higher Education, *Government Gazette No. 23549*, Government Printers, Tshwane.

Department of Science and Technology (1996). *White Paper on Science and Technology: Preparing for the 21st Century*, Government Printers, Tshwane.

Department of Science and Technology (2000). *National Research and Development Strategy*, Government Printers, Tshwane.

Department of Science and Technology (2006). *Annual Report of the Department of Science and Technology*, Public Finance Management Act, Government Printers, Tshwane.

Department of Science and Technology (2007). *Innovation Toward a Knowledge-Based Economy: Ten-Year Plan for South Africa (2008–2018)*, Government Printers, Tshwane.

Dreze, J. and Sen, A. (2002). *India: Development and Participation*, Oxford University Press, New Delhi.

du Toit, A. (2007). *Autonomy as a Social Compact*, Research Report, HEIAAF, No 4, February, Tshwane.

Government of South Africa (1990). *Scientific Research Council Act, Act 46 of 1988, as Amended by Act 71 of 1990*, Government Printers, Tshwane.

Greenberg, S. (1980). *Race and State in Capitalist Development*, Ravan Press, Johannesburg.

Helliker, K. D. (1987). *South African Marxist State Theory – A Critical Overview*, Paper delivered to the 18th Annual Congress of ASISA, University of Western Cape, June.

Hill, D. (2004). Educational Perversion and Global Neo-Liberalism: A Marxist Critique, *Cultural Logic: An Electronic Journal of Marxist Theory and Practice*, http://clogic.eserver.org/2004/hill.html.

Holloway, J. and Picciotto, S. (1978). *State and Capital, a Marxist Debate*, Edward Arnold, London.

Jonathan, R. (2006). *Academic Freedom, Institutional Autonomy and Public Accountability: A Framework for Analysis of the 'State Sector' in a Democratic South Africa*, Research Report, HEIAAF Series No 1, November, Tshwane.

Kahn, M. and Blankley, W. (2007). The State of Research and Experimental Development: Moving to a Higher Gear, in S. Buhlungu et al. (Editors). *State of the Nation, South Africa 2005–2006*, HSRC Press, Tshwane.

Kaplan, D. (1977). Capitalist Development in South Africa: Class Conflict and the State, in T. Adler (Editor) *Perspectives on South Africa: A Collection of Working Papers*, African Studies Institute, University of Witwatersrand, Johannesburg.

Kellaway, P. (1984). *Apartheid and Education: The Education of Black South Africans*, Ravan Press, Johannesburg.

Lange, L. (2003). *Critical Reflections on the Notion of Engagement*, Council on Higher Education, Tshwane.

Legassick, M. (1973). *The Making of South African "Native Policy" 1903–1923: The Origins of Segregation*, Institute of Commonwealth Studies, London, Mimeo.

Legassick, M. (1974a). Capital Accumulation and Violence, *Economy and Society*, 2 (3), 253–291.

Legassick, M. (1974b). Legislation, Ideology and Economy in Post-1948 South Africa, *Journal of Southern African Studies*, 1 (1), 5–35.

Legassick, M. (1975). South Africa; Forced Labour, Industrialisation and Racial Differentiation, in R. Harris (Editor) *The Political Economy of Africa*, Schenkman, Boston.

Legassick, M. (1976). Race, Industrialisation and Social Change in South Africa: The Case of R.F.A. Hoernle, *African Affairs*, 75, 224–239.

Levidow, L. (2002). Marketising Higher Education: Neoliberal Strategies and Counter-Strategies, *The Commoner*, 3, January accessed at http://www.commoner.org.uk/03levidow.pdf.

Lipton, M. (1986). *Capitalism and Apartheid: South Africa, 1910–1986*, Rowman and Allanheld, New Jersey.

Maharajh, R. (2005a). *In My View: South Africa needs to move forward on the basis of Broad National Dialogue*, in Innovations, a supplement of the *Financial Mail*, Johannesburg.

Maharajh, R. (2005b). *Science, Technology and Innovation Policy in South Africa: 1994–2004*, Unpublished Working Paper, IERI, Tshwane.

Maharajh, R. and Pogue, T. (2009). *Transforming South Africa's National System of Innovation for Accelerated and Shared Growth and Development*, BRICS Project Report, International Development Research Centre.

Mamdani, M. (1996). *Citizen and Subject: Contemporary Africa and the Legacy of Late Colonialism*, Princeton University Press, Princeton.

Mandel, E. (1980). *The Marxist Theory of the State*, Pathfinder Press, New York.

Mittelman, J. H. and Othman, N. (2001). *Capturing Globalisation*, Routledge, New York.

Morris, M. (1977). Capitalism and Apartheid: a Critique of Some Current Conceptions of Cheap Labour Power, in T. Adler (Editor) *Perspectives on South Africa*, African Studies Institute, Wits, University Press, Johannesburg.

Muller, J. and Subotzky, G. (2001). What Knowledge is needed in the New Millennium, *Organisation*, 8 (2), 163–182.

NWG (2001). *The Restructuring of the Higher Education System in South Africa: Report of the National Working Group to the Minister of Education*, Government Gazette No. 23549, Government Printers, Tshwane.

OECD (2007). *Review of South Africa's Innovation Policy*, Directorate for Science, Technology and Industry, Committee for Scientific and Technological Policy, DSTI/STP (2007)12, Organisation for Economic Co-operation and Development, Paris.

Phillips, H. (1993). *The University of Cape Town: The Formative Years: 1918–1948*, UCT Press, Cape Town.

Pittendrich, A. (1986). *The Technikons in South Africa*, Thesis Submitted for the Degree of Doctor of Philosophy, Department of Education, University of Natal, Durban.

Scerri, M. (2009). *The Evolution of the South African System of Innovation Since 1916*, Cambridge Scholars Publishing, UK.

Sen, A. (1999). *Development as Freedom*, Oxford University Press, Oxford.

Singh, M. (2003). *Universities and Society: Whose Terms of Engagement?* Council on Higher Education, Tshwane.

Singh, M. and Lange, L. (2007). Exploring the Surfaces and Depths of Quality Assurance, *Perspectives in Education*, 25 (3), September, 197–206.

Wolpe, H. (1972). Capitalism and Cheap Labour Power in South Africa: From Segregation to Apartheid, *Economy and Society*, 1 (4), 425–456.

Wolpe, H. (1980). Toward an Analysis of the South African State, *International Journal of the Sociology of Law*, 8 (4), November 399–421.

Wolpe, H. (1988). *Race, Class and the Apartheid State*, James Currey, London.

Wolpe, H. (1974), The Theory of Internal Colonialism: The South African Case, *Institute of Commonwealth Studies Seminar Papers*, 5, London.

Primary Data-Source

Department of Education (2009). Higher Education Management and Information System Database, http://www.education.gov.za/dynamic/dynamic.aspx?pageid=326&dirid=14

Chapter 11
Latvia: Repositioning of Academic Institutions in a Catching-Up Country

Anda Adamsone-Fiskovica, Janis Kristapsons, Erika Tjunina, and Inga Ulnicane-Ozolina

11.1 Introduction to the Latvian Context

Latvia is a small country with 2.3 million inhabitants located in the North-East Europe at the Eastern coast of the Baltic Sea. It is a catching-up economy, which in the 1990s underwent political and economic transformation from an authoritarian communist party rule and centrally planned socialist economy to a democratic multiparty government and liberal market economy. In 1991, Latvia regained its political independence from the Union of Soviet Socialist Republics (USSR), which also largely implied breaking the economic ties with the ex-Soviet economic structures in which the Latvian economy had been deeply integrated during the previous 50 years.

Similar to other postcommunist countries in Central and Eastern Europe (CEE), Latvia initially followed a neoliberal economic policy, which emphasized privatization, deregulation, and liberalization (JIRD 2002). After the breakdown of the socialist planned economy, the active role of the state in the economic development was discredited and a strong belief that the liberalization of the market forces will lead to economic prosperity prevailed. This attitude started to change as it became obvious that market forces alone do not lead to the development of a knowledge-based economy. Moreover, in recent years, integration into the European Union (EU)[1] has also pushed toward a more active role of the state as the allocation of the EU prestructural and structural funds[2] is based on the rationale that the state can

---

[1] Latvia became a Member State of the EU on 1 May 2004.

[2] Prestructural funds (for candidate countries) and structural funds (for member states) are funds allocated by the European Union allowing national governments to grant financial assistance to resolve structural economic and social problems.

A. Adamsone-Fiskovica (✉)
Centre for Science and Technology Studies, Latvian Academy of Sciences,
Riga, LV, 1524, Latvia
e-mail: anda@lza.lv

B. Göransson and C. Brundenius (eds.), *Universities in Transition:*
The Changing Role and Challenges for Academic Institutions,
© International Development Research Centre 2011

play a proactive role in economic development through developing infrastructure and human resources as well as supporting entrepreneurial activities including research, technological development, and innovation (RTDI).

The economic performance of Latvia recovered after the deep economic recession during the first years of transition. Since the second half of the 1990s, the Latvian economy has experienced a steady growth. In 2005–2007, GDP grew annually by 11% on average (Ministry of Economics 2008, p. 9). Economic growth took place in all sectors of the economy but in particular in construction, trade, hotels and restaurants, manufacturing, and transport and communications. Although Latvia is catching-up, at the moment it is still one of the poorest countries among the EU Member States (MSs). While, according to Eurostat, in 1997, its GDP per capita in Purchasing Power Standards (PPS) was only 35% of the average of all current EU member states (EU-27), in 2007 it was already 58% of the EU-27 average. Similarly, labor productivity per person employed has grown from 36% of EU-27 in 1997 to 54% in 2007. The unemployment rate has continuously decreased from 14.3% in 1998 to 6% in 2007, which was below the EU-27 average (7%). In recent years, Latvia has experienced one of the highest inflation rates in the EU (10% in 2007).

The national economy is dominated by service sectors, with services accounting for 74.7% of GDP (by value added) in 2007 (Ministry of Economics 2008, p. 23). The main service sectors are commercial services (27.8% of GDP by value added), trade, hotels and restaurants (22.2%), public services (13.8%), and transport and communications (10.8%). The industrial sector is relatively small and decreasing. In 2007, the share of manufacturing in GDP structure by value added was 11%, down from 14% in 2000. Primary sectors (agriculture and fisheries) contributed 3.6% of GDP by value added.

The structure of the economy in terms of employment is very different from the structure by added value due to a great difference between the productivity levels in various sectors of the economy. Measured according to the number of employees, the main sectors in 2007 were trade, hotels and restaurants (19.8% of total employment), public services (18.6%), and manufacturing (14.9%). On the whole, the economic activity of the population (participation in the labor market) in Latvia is close to the EU average, while the economic activity of women has already exceeded the average indicators of the EU.

The structure of Latvian exports is dominated by low- and medium-tech sectors. In 2007, 22.5% of commodity exports were wood and wood products, 14.6% metals and metal products; 14.4% agricultural and food products; 11% machinery; and 10.4% products of chemical industry and plastics. In 2006, only 4% of manufactured exports were high-technology exports, which is well below EU-27 average of 17%. In 2007, 40% of exports went to EU-15 (Western Europe), 30% to Lithuania and Estonia, 15% to the Commonwealth of Independent States (CIS), and 15% to other countries. Although both exports and imports have been growing, the external trade balance is negative.

As in other CEE countries, Foreign Direct Investment (FDI) has an important role in the Latvian economy. In 2006, the range of the goods and services produced by companies by using foreign capital amounted to 54.4% of GDP, constituted

55.4% of the volume of Latvian exports, and employed 12.5% of the total number of employed persons (Ministry of Economics 2008, p. 55). With Latvia's accession to the EU, the intensity of FDI has increased considerably and the investment mainly comes from the EU MSs, the biggest investor countries being Sweden, Estonia, Germany, and Denmark. Sectors with the biggest FDI stock are commercial and financial services, while the most attractive manufacturing sectors for foreign investors have been food industry and wood processing.

The Latvian economy is dominated by small- and medium-sized enterprises (SMEs). In 2007, more than 99% of economically active enterprises fell in the category of SME. According to the European Innovation Scoreboard 2008 (EC 2009), Latvia is lagging behind in terms of innovativeness. The EIS 2008 ranked Latvia 26th of the EU-27 MSs (followed only by Bulgaria). Relative strengths of Latvia, compared with its average performance, are in human resource endowment, while relative weaknesses are in patents, trademarks, medium- and high-tech manufacturing, and exports (Table 11.1).

One of the main obstacles for development of research and innovation in Latvia is the low level of R&D expenditure. According to Eurostat, in 2007, total gross domestic expenditure on R&D (GERD) in Latvia was 0.59% of GDP, while for the EU-27 average, it was approximately three times higher – 1.85% of GDP. Although since 2005 GERD, which previously stagnated around 0.4%, has increased compared to other EU MSs, it is still quite low, in particular with regard to business R&D expenditures (Table 11.1).

Table 11.1   European innovation scoreboard 2008 – selected indicators

Indicator	EU 27	Latvia
New S&E and SSH graduates per 1,000 population age 20–29 years	40.3	56.4
Population with tertiary education per 100 population age 25–64 years	23.5	22.6
Participation in life-long learning per 100 population age 25–64 years	9.7	7.1
Youth education attainment level (% of population age 20–24 years having completed at least upper secondary education)	78.1	80.2
Public R&D expenditures (% of GDP)	0.65	0.42
Business R&D expenditures (% of GDP)	1.17	0.21
IT expenditures (% of GDP)	2.7	2.3
Employment in knowledge-intensive services (% of total workforce)	14.51	10.57
Medium- and high-tech manufacturing exports (% of total exports)	48.1	23.8
Employment in medium-/high-tech manufacturing (% of total workforce)	6.69	1.88
EPO patents per million population	105.7	5.7
Community trademarks per million population	124.6	23.7
Community designs per million population	121.8	21.0

Source: European Communities (2009) *European Innovation Scoreboard 2008* (based on data for 2005–2007)

11.2   The Position of Academic Institutions in the National Innovation System of Latvia

11.2.1   Evolution of the National Innovation System in Latvia

The national innovation system (NIS) in Latvia is still under formation, having experienced a certain upsurge since the late 1990s. From the socialist period, Latvia inherited a Science and Technology system (S&TS), which had many similarities with other communist countries and especially with other republics of the Soviet Union (e.g., Meske 2004; Hirschhausen and Bitzer 2000; Etzkowitz 2000; Radosevic 1999; Meske et al. 1998; Balazs et al. 1995).

The socialist S&TS evolved as a hierarchically structured and politically governed system based on the linear model of innovation reflecting the institutional separation of R&D, whereby innovation was separated from production and the market. Under socialism, R&D activities were organized into three distinct and sharply separated sectors, namely, academies, universities, and industrial sectors, based on the general principles of central planning, namely, specialization, rationalization, and centralization. Universities were primarily training bodies, while basic research was carried out in the academies of science, with applied research and product development being the prime task of industry institutes and special design offices. Production was separated from research and education and it was solely undertaken by industry, which in turn had no relation to research with nonexistent inhouse R&D activities in enterprises. There was no feedback from end-users and strong administrative barriers between the individual industrial branches hindered technology diffusion and transfer. Networking under the socialist regime was mainly managed on a formal level by the state authorities, and links between domestic users and producers as well as between foreign and domestic sellers were weak. This division was transformed following the breakdown of the socialist system. However, lack of interaction between these units and their former fragmentation continues to form one of the basic problems for establishing a well-operating interactive innovation model. Though formally channeled contacts were supplemented by informal links, many of the latter were ruptured or vanished in the reform process.

The abrupt change experienced by postsocialist countries is seen as a technology trajectory change or a paradigm shift in the science and technology (S&T) field, due to the marked differences in both the perception of innovation per se and the actor interplay and role division – a change from top-down to bottom-up approaches. While the former socialist S&TS was characterized by an overarching role of the state, fully secured government funding, and decision making on merely political rather than monetary bases, the emerging postsocialist innovation system implies private initiative, market mechanism operation, and monetary constraints. Naturally, this major change and current shift to the knowledge-based economy could not be realized on the spot, because the preconditions existing in the developed democracies were not present in postsocialist countries. Although legacies from the socialist period in Latvia left strong capacities in some areas of basic science, they also presented major challenges for building up a new NIS, e.g., reorientation of military R&D capacities to civilian sectors, considerable cuts in the government R&D expenditures, which have to be replaced by private funding, and integration of universities and research institutes.

Altogether after restoration of its independence, Latvia took a rather radical and revolutionary approach to its R&D system reform (Kristapsons et al. 2003, pp. 39–40). In 1989–1990, a new system of funding and management of science was established in Latvia whereby direct funding of scientific institutions (institutional funding) was replaced by competitive project-based funding. The state budget of Latvia allotted a specific amount for fundamental research projects, market-oriented research, and research commissioned by ministries. The Council of Science distributed funding earmarked for projects among the sectoral commissions of different science fields. According to the new system, research institutes, as organizations, received no funding from the state budget in Latvia. The necessary resources for the general maintenance of institutes were obtained as overhead costs (by way of deducting a certain percentage from each grant). Yet, the system has been readjusted in 2005 with institutional funding again reintroduced along with the competitive project-based funding.

As to bridging the former divide between universities and research establishments, in 1997–1998, the bulk of the former academy institutes in Latvia was integrated into the universities, while the remaining institutes became public or state institutes or transformed into independent scientific centers (Kristapsons et al. 2003). The reorganization of state research institutes was completed in 2006. Altogether 20 research institutes had been incorporated into universities with the primary aim of modernizing and strengthening the research capacity of these universities and the quality of study programs (Ministry of Education and Science [hereinafter MoES] 2005, pp. 21–22). This integration and incorporation of research institutes included participation of institutes at all levels of higher education (HE), participation of scientists from institutes in competition for academic positions at universities, organizational restructuring, and reassessment of accreditation criteria for study programs.

11.2.2 Characteristics and Assessment of the Newly Emerging System

In the context of system transformation and in the development of an efficient innovation system, the role of the government and state policy both in regard to science and more generally to innovation is of particular importance in Latvia. Two major governmental bodies involved in the NIS are the Ministry of Education and Science (Department of Science, Technologies, and Innovations since 2006) and the Ministry of Economics (Innovation division since 2003). Recently, the Ministry of Regional Development and Local Government are also taking a more proactive role. Yet, the mutual coordination of governing bodies is still assessed as rather limited and fragmented with no single high-level body being in charge of R&D issues (Adamsone-Fiskovica et al. 2008, pp. 9–10).

The business sector is mainly represented by SMEs, with a comparatively small share of large companies. The relatively new enterprise sector, which largely emerged during transition in the 1990s, has so far embodied one of the major weaknesses of the NIS as a result of its low innovative capacities, especially in the case of SMEs (Watkins and Agapitova 2004). According to the results of the Community Innovation Survey, in 2004–2006, only 16.2% of enterprises in Latvia had conducted innovative activities featuring even a drop from 18.6% in 2001–2003 and 17.5 in 2002–2004 (Central Statistical Bureau [hereinafter CSB] 2008, p. 7). At 84%, Latvia has the highest share of noninnovative firms in the EU where on average 45% of companies are classified as innovative. In 2006, two-thirds (76%) of the total innovation expenditure by Latvian companies was spent on machinery and equipment acquisition and only about 5.5% of the total innovation expenditure was spent on R&D. According to the RIS study on the strategies for the promotion of knowledge-based business in Latvia carried out in 2004, the low innovation capacity of companies has been explained by the lack of such elements as a basic management competence, an insight on internal barriers to growth, knowledge of the innovation-supporting resources available, and collaborative relations with external partners (RIS Latvia 2004, pp. 9–15). Innovative companies, in their turn, mention too high innovation costs, lack of resources within ones enterprise or group as well as financial resources from sources outside ones company, market dominated by established enterprises, and lack of qualified personnel as the main factors (mentioned by more than 20%) hampering innovation (CSB 2008, pp. 19–20).

Innovation and business support organizations form an expanding element of the NIS of Latvia with an increasing number of industrial parks, technology centers, risk capital funds, consulting companies, and various other intermediaries. Many of these represent a rather novel phenomena in Latvia that are expected to strengthen the enterprise sector by assisting established companies and encouraging the formation of start-ups and new technology-based companies. Nevertheless, innovation-service suppliers have been generally reactive rather than proactive, lacking specialization and innovativeness and unable to deliver holistic service due to the sector's isolation within innovation support (RIS Latvia 2004, p. 13). According to the RIS study, many SMEs in 2004 were also not aware of the available financial support schemes and even fewer used them (RIS Latvia 2004, p. 14). The study also pointed to the lack of appropriate financial instruments to support an innovation-based growth as well as a lack of competence among financiers and underdeveloped venture capital market. Since then, rather notable developments have taken place in this domain, especially in the light of the support measures launched under the EU SFs that became available since 2004–2005 and their advertising. As a result, several new technology transfer offices and risk capital companies have emerged; yet, a challenge still remains to make them fully operational and efficient in serving the exact needs of their clientele.

Last but not least, the academic institutions represented by higher education institutions (HEIs) and research institutes make up an essential element, particularly through their provision of human capital and knowledge. Their role in NIS is becoming even more pronounced with an expanding focus on the need to shift from a purely educational function of HEIs to that of research as well as entrepreneurship, thus bridging the gap and making the necessary link with the other elements of the system, especially industry (Adamsone-Fiskovica et al. 2009b). The challenges faced by the HE system of Latvia over the last decade have been related to the relevance of HE for the national development, the quality of teaching, the institutional organization of HE, the capacity to produce and disseminate innovations, the need to establish funding mechanisms, and improve governance and coordination (Brunner 2003). Accordingly, the HE system of Latvia has been experiencing rapid and profound changes with significant progress achieved in reforming and modernizing HE, yet the low needs orientation of applied research, low transfer competence of R&D institutions, and lack of incentives and entrepreneurial culture (Watkins and Agapitova 2004; RIS Latvia 2004, pp. 11–12) that became topical with an expansion of the mission of HEIs are still high on the agenda. Difficulties in building the linkages between R&D organizations and enterprise sector arise also due to asymmetrical relationships between the sometimes highly sophisticated R&D skills in the science sector, on the one hand, and the weak enterprise sector with underdeveloped innovative capacities, on the other hand. Similarly to other countries at a medium level of economic development, where the majority of enterprises work in the field of less complex products and services and R&D absorptive capacities of firms are missing, major link between HE and business sectors is the provision of highly qualified graduates (Göransson et al. 2009, p. 159).

11.2.3 Policy Developments

After major changes in the political and economic system in the early 1990s, a new basis for research policy was founded by the adoption of the law *On Research Activity* in 1992, which defined anew the status of a scientist and the structure for funding and governance of science in Latvia. In its turn, in 1995, the *Law on Higher Education Institutions* regulating the status, rights, and responsibilities of HEIs, students, and the Council of Higher Education was adopted. Subsequently, the scientific community and administrators of research policy developed several drafts for strategic policy documents regarding R&D issues, yet none of those gained political support. For instance, the *Guidelines for the development of higher education, science and technology for 2002–2010* – a document setting out a strategic aim to improve HE, science, and technologies as the basis for the long-term development of civil society, economy, and culture – was only taken into consideration but not adopted by the Cabinet of Ministers. One of the main tasks envisaged by the guidelines was related to the strengthening of the leading role of universities in the development of HE and science by establishing universities as the main science centers in Latvia uniting high-level research activities with high-quality academic and professional studies in a wide range of thematic fields.

The negligence of research and innovation issues during the 1990s can also be traced in the declarations of the Latvian governments, which define the main goals and intended activities of the Cabinet of Ministers. In the declarations of the time with regard to RTDI mainly two issues are mentioned: first, the need to integrate science in HE and, second, the need to set clear priority areas for science. From time to time, other science- and innovation-related issues have also fragmentarily appeared on the political agenda, e.g., with regard to the need of developing science-based industry, stopping of brain drain or increasing R&D funding. However, practically no measures were taken to address these issues at that time.

A certain shift occurred only after the turn of the century with a more commercial-oriented *innovation policy* being developed in Latvia. The process started with a small innovation policy community that came together to develop the first policy documents on innovation. The Cabinet of Ministers approved the *National Concept Paper on Innovation Policy* in 2001 and the *National Programme on Innovation for 2003–2006* (NPI) in 2003. The NPI was the basic innovation policy document at that time with annual action plans elaborated for its implementation. Alongside the long- and medium-term goals, the short-term objectives of the program were related to the coordination and improvement of the innovation system, promoting the interest of society in the practical use of knowledge in business, as well as a successful development of education, science, research, and innovations. Among other initial policy documents addressing R&D and innovation issues, one should mention the *Long-term Economic Strategy of Latvia* adopted in 2001, which outlines the model of developing a knowledge-based economy in Latvia. The necessary shift from a labor-intensive to knowledge-intensive economy was also stressed by the *Single Economic Strategy of Latvia* adopted in 2004.

The most recent years (2005–2007) have been marked by an even further intensification of the strategic policy orientation with a more pronounced prioritization of S&T-related issues in the declarations of the Cabinets of Ministers and the release of additional four core documents covering R&D: the *National Lisbon Programme of Latvia for 2005–2008* (2005), the *National Development Plan of Latvia for 2007–2013* (2006), the *Programme for Promotion of Business Competitiveness and Innovation for 2007–2013* (2007), and the *National Strategic Reference Framework of Latvia for 2007–2013* (2007), with its accompanying operational programs "Human resources and employment" and "Entrepreneurship and Innovation." It can be argued that most of these documents came as a result of the accession of Latvia to the EU that resulted in its commitment to the common EU goals (e.g., the Lisbon strategy[3]) and clearly defined strategic orientation required for mastering the EU SFs.

---

[3] The Lisbon Strategy, also known as the Lisbon Agenda or Lisbon Process, is an action and development plan for the European Union. It was set out by the European Council in Lisbon on March 2000. According to this strategy, the EU set itself a new strategic goal for the next decade to become the most competitive and dynamic knowledge-based economy in the world, capable of sustainable economic growth with more and better jobs, and greater social cohesion by 2010. It was relaunched as the "Community Lisbon program" in 2005 with the new focus on growth and employment. Subsequently, each Member State had to elaborate its national reform plan in meeting the set goals.

These documents emphasize the main economic policy directions aimed at stimulation of knowledge and innovation as well as improving education and skills. The more concrete measures address the renewal and development of intellectual potential in science, modernization of scientific infrastructure, and promotion of transfer of knowledge and technologies in production, achieving correspondence between the supply of the education system and the labor market needs, raising the quality, cost-efficiency, and accessibility of education at all levels, etc. Many of the documents also stress the importance of strengthening the leading role of HEIs in the development of science and research. Likewise, the documents set out an aim to foster business development, increase the capacity and efficiency of the NIS, and increase competitiveness and productivity of the national industry by producing products with high value added. This is to be achieved through a facilitated cooperation between education and research sectors, knowledge transfer, and commercialization. This period also witnessed changes in respect to knowledge demand with the definition of research priorities and elaboration of respective state research programs in the identified fields of science, which are fully funded from the state budget.

The same period was also marked by a new legal basis for research policy, which was provided by the new law *On Research Activity* (2005) replacing the one from 1992. Among other things, this law includes an article on research activity at the HEIs, defines the unity of science and HE, rights, responsibility, independence and academic freedom, professional and social guarantees of scientists, competency, and obligations of public institutions in the provision of research activity. One of the key features of this law is the envisaged substantial increase in state funding for research and the introduction of institutional funding for university research. Furthermore, in the second half of 2005, the Ministry of Education and Science elaborated a new draft *Law on Higher Education* with its main emphasis on the regulation of the processes, procedures, and outcomes rather than the organizational structure of HEIs. Yet, this law has been undergoing the process of public consultation for almost 4 years. Another example of a protracted discussion is represented by the continuously postponed adoption of the *Guidelines for Development of Science and Technology for 2009–2013*, initial drafts of which also date back to 2005. Against the backdrop of otherwise seemingly progressive turns in terms of policy design, these two cases demonstrate the still present and newly emerging stumbling blocks on the way of agreeing upon and putting in place the new framework and consistently following the set course.

11.3 Mapping the Academic System in Latvia

11.3.1 Historical Insight

The development and traditions of the academic system in Latvia have been largely conditioned by the complicated history of the nation in various periods being under German, Polish, Swedish, and Russian rule. Schools providing Latvian-language education began to develop in the wake of the Reformation, in the mid- to late sixteenth century when Western European S&T also began to be introduced in present-day Latvia (Stradins 1982). Systematic research began at the end of the eighteenth century and education saw rapid development in the nineteenth century and particularly in the years of the Latvian National Awakening in the second half of the century, when a stratum of Latvian intellectuals emerged and established itself. From 18 November 1918, with the foundation of an independent Latvian state, the titular nation gained the guaranteed right to obtain all forms of education in Latvian. Modernization trends in Eastern Europe and the Russian Empire provided the stimulus for establishing the Riga Polytechnic in 1862. This HEI was the first polytechnic university in the Russian Empire. The attainment of independence made it possible, in 1919, to establish the University of Latvia – the first broad-ranging university in the new state. Along with engineering, agriculture, and chemistry, the University of Latvia also conducted research in the humanities, natural sciences, medicine, and social sciences. In 1939, another HEI was established in Jelgava – the Academy of Agriculture, and the first attempts were made to establish a Latvian Academy of Sciences.

World War II, occupation, and annexation to the USSR, along with the deportations, was a crushing blow for Latvia's flourishing scientific activity (Stradins 1998). Of the prewar scientists, 60% emigrated to the West, where many continued their research work. After World War II, science in Latvia developed within the USSR as a more or less anonymous constituent of "Soviet science." Research at universities and colleges declined, but an Academy of Sciences of the Latvian SSR was founded in 1946. The Academy of Sciences, with its 15 major institutes, conducted important research in physics (magnetohydrodynamics and solid state physics), astronomy, mechanics of composite materials, information science, chemistry (medical chemistry, chemistry of heterocyclic compounds, wood chemistry, low temperature plasma chemistry, and electrochemistry), hydrobiology, virology, and molecular biology.

In the Soviet R&D system, research in the academy institutes was separated from research carried out in the universities by departmental barriers and, until 1946, universities contributed the core of research in the Baltic States (Kristapsons et al. 2003, pp. 52–55). Formation of the Soviet-type academies of science destroyed the historically formed research system, whereby research came to be centered in the research institutes, and education was the focus for the universities. In 1990, there were 33 specialized research institutes in Latvia, which worked in isolation from institutions of HE (MoES 2005, p. 21). This isolation did not augur well for the development of strong links between research and HE. At that time, 30,000 people were employed in science (including 12,000 researchers, more than half at doctoral level). Although international acclaim was won in several fields of the exact and natural sciences, and although young and capable scientists emerged, this development was one sided and geared to the needs of a great power, and not those of a small country (Stradins 2000). Additionally, isolation from the West was felt acutely.

Starting in the early 1990s, the Latvian Academy of Sciences was transformed into a corporation of individual members on the Western European model, electing many new members from among scientists at home and abroad. The former research institutes have generally been incorporated into the University of Latvia, where they continue their work under the new conditions. When Latvia regained its independence in 1991, the directions and scope of science changed, as did research priorities (Stradins 2000). With the establishment of the Latvian Council of Science, the evaluation of research was based on internal competition – the standard of research and the productivity of researchers. In 1992, the Danish Research Councils performed an international assessment (Danish Research councils 1992) of the Latvian science, giving a positive evaluation of the level attained and formulating proposals for restructuring research. In 1997, a study of the management structure of Latvian R&D commissioned by the European Commission found that the downscaling of R&D in Latvia, as in other CEEs, had decreased the practical capacity for scientific research. Nevertheless, science in Latvia seems to have survived and repositioned itself following the turbulent period of system transformation, with rather notable results being demonstrated at least in selected fields of research.

11.3.2 Current System of Education and Research

Although there has been a move away from the strict separation of education and research, the following sections are formally divided into these two components because their integration is still in process.

11.3.2.1 System and Characteristics of Higher Education in Latvia

In 2007, there were 34 accredited HEIs in Latvia, most of which belong to the state (5 public universities and 14 public specialized universities and university colleges), the rest having been founded by other legal entities or private individuals (MoES 2008b, pp. 8–9). Additionally, there are 23 colleges (18 public and 8 private). While the number of public HEIs in 1990–2007 has increased from 10 to 19, the accompanying growth of private HEIs has been an even more substantial one from 2 to 15. Latvia accordingly stands out among other European countries both in terms of the number of HEIs per million inhabitants and the number of students per 10,000 inhabitants (552 in 2007 compared with the EU27 average of 379 in 2006).

Since 1991, the number of students in Latvia has increased at least threefold by 2007/2008 (Fig. 11.1). Yet, they are very unevenly distributed among both public and private HEIs. The two biggest public HEIs, the University of Latvia and the Riga Technical University, in 2007/2008 accounted for 23,801 (20.7%) and 16,879 (14.7%) students, respectively, while approximately half of all HEIs (14 in total) had less than 1,000 students (MoES 2008b, pp. 59–60). Thereby also resources and research are mainly concentrated in the biggest HEIs, while the others are highly specialized or perform mainly teaching.

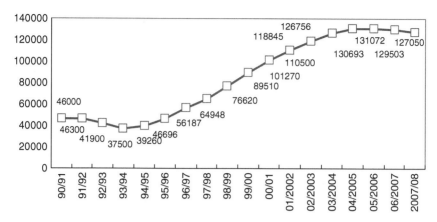

Fig. 11.1 Number of students in HEIs and colleges in Latvia (1990/1991–2007/2008)
Source: Ministry of Education and Science (2008b, p. 57)

Auers et al. (2007, pp. 478–479) mention three main reasons for rapid expansion of HE sector (both in terms of number of institutions and number of students) after 1991. First, demand for new qualifications, knowledge, and skills necessary for political and economic transformation increased. Study programs in new disciplines were opened, master studies were introduced, and people educated in the socialist system enrolled into HEIs to obtain new qualifications. Second, reforms in the HE system allowed for the creation of private tertiary institutions to compete with the state sector. Third, the Law on Higher Education Institutions (1995) only allowed teaching in the Latvian language in state financed HEIs, thereby private HEIs attracted many Russian speakers by providing education in Russian.[4]

At the same time, it should be noted that HEIs are to a certain degree forced to take more students than it would be optimal for retaining the quality of teaching and for developing research activities due to the large dependence on the budget income mainly generated by student fees (Muiznieks 2005, pp. 114–115). This is largely due to the fact that HE in Latvia is only partially state-subsidized because government-funded student places covering tuition fees and monthly stipends are made available on a merit basis to only one-fourth (25.0% in 2007/2008) of all students at public HEIs and colleges. For rest of the students with lower grades at public HEIs and for all students at private HEIs, each institution sets a tuition fee. Since the Education Law of 1991 introduced tuition, the share of tuition-paying students has rapidly grown from 32% in 1995 to 57% in 1998 (Kasa 2008, pp. 89–90).[5]

---

[4]The ethnic composition of Latvian population is as follows: Latvians – 59.2%, Russians – 28%, Byelorussians – 3.6%, Ukrainians – 2.5%, Poles – 2.3%, Lithuanians – 1.3%, Jews – 0.4%, and other nationalities –2.7%.

[5]In 2007/2008, the share of students in HEIs funded by public resources made up only 25%, compared with 75% funded by private ones (CSB 2009, p. 7).

A financial assistance system was subsequently introduced in the form of loans covering student living costs launched in 1997 and loans covering tuition available since 1999 (Kasa 2008, p. 90). In 2001, the student loan system was reformed [6] and the new requirement for student borrowers was introduced to provide individual loan guarantees in the form of a wage-earning cosignatory, real estate, or securities (Kasa 2008, pp. 90–91).[7] In order to ensure that low-income students have an access to HE, the local municipalities have a responsibility to assist those students (Kasa 2008), while a large number of students support themselves by combining employment with full-time studies (Auers et al. 2007).[8]

As to the division of students by fields of studies, only a small proportion of students is undertaking studies in engineering, mathematics, and natural sciences with every second student studying social sciences (Fig. 11.2). This thematic division has not changed substantially during the last decade – according to Eurostat, the number of S&T graduates (per 1,000 of population age 20–29 years) has only slightly increased from 6.1 in 1998 to 9.2 in 2007 (in comparison to the EU-27 average of 13.4), despite the rather substantial allocation of additional state-financed study places in the respective study programs since approximately 2005.

In terms of gender, there is a comparatively larger proportion of female students (63% in 2008/2009) in HEIs and colleges in Latvia as well as among the graduates (71.6%) (CSB 2009, p. 2). In terms of thematic groups of HE, female students are predominant in the study programs of health care and social welfare (86%), teacher training (85%), followed by humanities and arts (78%), and social sciences, business, and law (68%), while being underrepresented in the field of engineering, manufacturing, and construction (20%) and natural sciences, mathematics, and information technologies (32%). In terms of academic staff at HEIs, the share of females in 2007/2008 made up 54%, yet the ratio gradually decreases at the top level, with 46% of associate professor positions being occupied by women and only 29% of full professorships (MoES 2008b:123). Nevertheless, compared with other countries, the representation of women in science in Latvia is still among the highest in Europe (see also Adamsone-Fiskovica et al. 2009a, pp. 37–38).

---

[6]Reforms included involvement of commercial banks in actual lending to students, while the government continued to provide a subsidized loan interest rate, grace period, loan forgiveness, and assumed its role as a second guarantor for 90% of loan amount to students (Kasa 2008, pp. 90–91).

[7]Reforms included involvement of commercial banks in actual lending to students, while the government continued to provide a subsidized loan interest rate, grace period, loan forgiveness, and assumed its role as a second guarantor for 90% of loan amount to students (Kasa 2008, pp. 90–91).

[8]It is difficult to obtain reliable data on exact share of working students. In their sample of under-graduate social science students, Auers et al. (2007, pp. 482–483) found that 44% of respondents are working. But as their survey was carried out before or after compulsory classes, they admit a risk that working students may be under-represented as they are less likely to attend classes. Auers et al. (2007, p. 481) cite results of the survey carried out by the Latvian Student's Association, indicating that 54% of students were employed. Among graduate students, almost all are working.

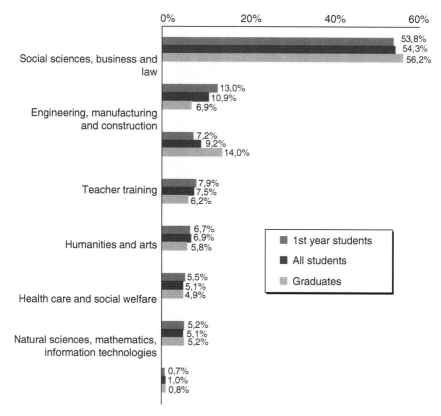

Fig. 11.2 Distribution of students by thematic groups of education in 2007/2008
Source: Ministry of Education and Science (2008b, p. 108)

Two of five public universities are located outside the capital city, with several other major HEIs present in the regional centers of Latvia. Majority of students undertaking studies in these HEIs come from the respective region of Latvia – the possibility to obtain qualification in the region of one's residence is the main benefit of the increasing number of regional HEIs, thus reducing the drain of the rising generation to the capital and the overall regional disparities. With a smaller tuition fee and a rather broad spectrum of study programs offered, regional HEIs are increasingly gaining their niche in the educational market.

11.3.2.2 Research Performance

While there is a rather high share of R&D institutions in the business enterprise sector (R&D units in companies), *research* in Latvia nowadays is mainly performed at the scientific institutes and HEIs (including R&D institutions under surveillance of HEIs) with the majority of R&D personnel employed in the HE

(71%) and government (18%) sector and only 11% in the business enterprise sector (Table 11.2). The University of Latvia, which is the oldest and largest university in Latvia, hosts most of the scientific institutes (including nine agencies, seven research institutes, and four faculty institutes). Aside from the University of Latvia, there are over 15 university research institutes at other universities (both public and private HEIs) and 12 independent state research institutes, which are under the surveillance of the Minister of Education and Science or corresponding branch ministers.

Research performance of academic institutions can be to some extent assessed through such output indicators as international publications and patents. Yet for the time being, Latvia in these terms is still a catching-up country. While universities and research institutes generate the major share of SCI publications in Latvia (Kristapsons et al. 2004), the overall output level is very low compared with other European and non-European countries. In the case of the Baltic countries, a mutual benchmarking between the three is being frequently used. While, based on the data of the Web of Science, in 1990 all the three Baltic countries were rather equal in terms of their quantitative performance (250 SCI publications per country a year), in 2007 Lithuania produced 1,000, Estonia 800, and Latvia only 350 publications. The respective annual output figure for Latvia of 150 publications per million population (with the EU average being 650) has remained largely unchanged since 2001, while it has been gradually increasing for both Estonia and Lithuania. According to the alternative data from the SCImago database, there has not been any major improvement in the number of publications of Latvian scientists over a decade from 1997 to 2007, yet there has been a slight increase in terms of international collaboration (Table 11.3). For the time being, the number of patents is also

Table 11.2 R&D institutions and staff in Latvia (2000, 2007)

	Number of institutions		Number of R&D personnel (FTE)	
	2000	2007	2000	2007
Higher education sector	49	47	2,156	3,016
Government sector	31	22	662	744
Business enterprise sector[a]	193	403	996	463
Total	273	472	3,814	4,223

Source: Central Statistical Bureau of Latvia (2006, pp. 27–28) and Central Statistical Bureau of Latvia (2008, p. 34)
[a]Including private nonprofit sector

Table 11.3 Publications of Latvian scientists included in the Scopus database

	1997	2003	2004	2005	2006	2007
Number of publications	400	347	381	442	407	457
Percentage of publications coauthored by peers abroad	49	59	62	63	61	54

Source: SCImago (2007)

rather negligible for Latvia: 6 EPO patents a year per million population compared with the EU27 average of 125 patents (EIS 2008).

In terms of human resources, in 2007 there were 3.8 researchers pet 1,000 employed in Latvia (5.4 on average in EU25). There was a total of 3,603 PhD holders, of which 19% were aged 65–69 years and 35% aged 55–64 years (CSB). The small and aging number of researchers thereby poses a challenge to maintain a critical mass of R&D base. Their number has substantially decreased after 1990, with an increased aging of academic staff and a lack of young researchers, especially in the fields of natural sciences and engineering. While the number of R&D personnel (full-time equivalent) has increased by 10% in 2000–2007 (mainly in academic institutions), this is still an insufficient number for ensuring long-term and accelerated development of research capacity of the country.

The number of newly awarded PhDs in 2005–2007 made up only 121 persons on average per year (Table 11.4), while the target set by the Ministry of Education and Science to be reached by 2013 is 425 new PhD holders a year (MoES 2009) in order to ensure the necessary critical mass. While generally there are relatively a large number of students all levels taken together, in 2007/2008 PhD students made up only 1.6% of the total number of students. Those having graduated from master and doctoral programs in 2007 made up only 11 and 0.6% of all graduates, respectively (MoES 2008b, p. 5).

According to the NORBAL study on the awarded doctoral degrees in the Nordic and Baltic countries, about two-fifths of the total number of doctoral degrees in the region in 2005 were awarded in Sweden, one-fifth in Finland, and one-eighths in Norway, while the share of the Baltic countries combined amounted to only about one-tenth. Besides, in 1997–2005, the number of doctoral degrees awarded as a percentage of the population size had increased in all countries except Latvia. In 2007, the number of doctoral degrees per million capita in Latvia was the lowest among the eight countries (Gunnes 2009), though the new incentives and additional funding being allocated for PhD studies from the EU SFs are expected to raise the number of newly awarded doctoral degrees in the years to come. While the average age at the time of dissertation or award is relatively high in all these countries, there has been a slight decrease in Latvia over a decade in comparison to that in mid-1990s. Additionally, it should be noted that in the Baltic countries (including Latvia), the female percentage has remained high throughout this period, with a more marked increase from lower levels for the Nordic countries.

With independence and its integration into the EU, Latvia has been increasingly entering the international arena, not least in terms of education and research. Latvia has signed a range of international conventions (Lisbon – 1997; Salamanca – 2001) and declarations (Sorbon – 1998; Bologna – 1999), as well as a range of intergovernmental agreements on cooperation in education and R&D with countries both within and outside Europe. The Latvian scientific community is actively participating in various international projects, including those in the EU Framework programs. Researchers from the large universities and their affiliated institutes have been most active in drawing up project applications for the fifth FP, with a success rate of around 25–30% (Bundule and Jansons 2005). Altogether 1,027 RTD project applications involving

Table 11.4 Doctoral degrees awarded in Latvia (1995–2007)

	1995	1996	1997	1998	1999	2000	2001	2002	2003	2004	2005	2006	2007
Awarded doctoral degree													
Total	67	93	118	174	122	21	48	52	80	79	112	93	158
Of which females	25	38	46	73	53	11	28	33	46	49	63	48	95
Average age of degree holders at the time of conferment													
Total	41	42	40	39	38	35	35	38	36	36.5	37.4	36.5	37.3
Of which females	39	39	40	39	37	38	37	37	36	37.6	38	37.8	39.5

Source: NORBAL
[a]The considerable fall in the number of awarded doctoral degrees after 1999 was initially due to organizational and managerial changes and the resulting readjustments, and later on due to stricter requirements for the candidates introduced with the transition from two-stage to one-stage system

participants from Latvia were submitted under the FP6, with 21% of those being granted funding by the European Commission (MoES 2008a). These results have placed Latvia among the most successful countries among the new EU MSs, though still featuring a lag behind the performance level of the old MSs. Another indicator of internationalization is the high percentage of publications of Latvian scientists coauthored by their peers from other countries. Over a 7-year period (1997–2003), Latvian scientists had had collaborative publications with scientists from almost 60 countries with the majority of those coming from Germany, Sweden, Russia, and USA.

11.4   The Current Debate

Recent debates in the Parliament, various corporate forums and the academic community have focused on the discussion of the following key problem areas in relation to the scientific and technological development of the country that have an important influence on the further fate and activities of the academic institutions in Latvia:

- Allocation and distribution of state funding for R&D;
- Promotion of private sector investments and involvement in R&D activities;
- Identification of priority research areas;
- Protection of intellectual property and commercialization of research results;
- Integration of universities and research institutes.

Although specific problems are discussed mainly among the R&D community, recently R&D issues have also attracted attention of mass media and the broader public. Popular debates concentrate more generally on the challenge to develop a knowledge-based economy, in which research, education, and innovation are among the main determinants of competitiveness.

11.4.1   Securing Government R&D Funding

During the last 15 years, a persistently problematic domain for the Latvian academic institutions has been related to the provision of funding. Until 2005, practically no changes had taken place in this respect with comparatively negligible allocations for research activities being made from the state budget. A certain turn was marked by the adoption of the new *Law on Research Activity* in 2005 envisaging that "the Cabinet of Ministers, when submitting to the Parliament the annual law on state budget, allocates an annual increase of funding for research activity not lower than 0.15% of GDP until the government funding for research activity reaches at least one percent of gross domestic product."[9] The Parliament adopted

---

[9]Following the example of Finland in the 1980s, the scientific community of Latvia advocated 0.1% increase for several years, while the current provision is based on more recent calculations of the Minister of Education and Science in order to reach 1% by 2010.

the Law unanimously presenting one of a few cases of agreement among the government and opposition parties in the Latvian Parliament.

These developments can be explained largely by the broader processes of integration into the EU that raised awareness of national policy makers on a range of issues along with the general commitment to the goals of the union not least in the field of R&D. This determination was highlighted when the State President formed a Commission of Strategic Analysis to elaborate potential scenarios for the national development. A similar unit (subcommission on the Future development) has been formed in the Parliament. The Minister of Science and Education at the time played an important role actively promoting the interests of science (in comparison with some former Ministers of Education and Science who saw their primary task in the solution of education problems). Likewise, unlike the former Cabinets of Ministers, the government of that time was rather determined to fulfill its promises despite the concerns voiced in respect to the capability of the Latvian education and research system, dealing with a range of problems, to absorb such an amount of money. Therefore, it was subsequently perceived to be largely up to the research community to provide specific tangible results aside from an increased number of students and new equipment for justifying this commitment and investments (Ekmanis 2005).

The year 2006 for Latvia's science was the year when the new Law on Research Activity started its full operation and the Cabinet of Ministers adopted several new regulations, rules, and directions in accordance with the given law. Accordingly, the funding from the state budget grew by the envisaged 0.15% of the GDP, including an increased funding of science for HEIs and state research programs along with a partial reintroduction of institutional funding. While previously the major concern was related to the lack of money, the new inflow of financial resources has trigged debate on a new kind of issue dealing with the best and most efficient ways of spending this funding and gain maximum return (Ekmanis 2007). However, in the end of 2007 under the slogan of fight against the high inflation, the annual envisaged increase of public R&D funding fixed in the Law was already endangered by the governing bodies with an excuse of budgetary restrictions. Accompanied by the frequently changing governments, this, in turn, casts strong doubts on the capacity of the governing bodies to ensure a succession and fulfillment of existing commitments made in previous years (Ekmanis 2007).

11.4.2 Promotion of Business R&D Funding

Despite the policy developments since 2005 and commitment of the Latvian government to reach the Lisbon target for public expenditure on R&D (i.e., 1% of GDP by 2010), the annual increase in the government funding, even if implemented, would not solve problems of the overall R&D funding (the Lisbon strategy envisages that by 2010 business R&D funding should reach 2% of GDP). Though, as noted in a study commissioned by the Ministry of Economics in 2005, the low level of public R&D funding and the existing system of research funding do not act as a catalyzer for attracting private sector investment in R&D (Bilinskis et al. 2005). In order to facilitate private sector investment in R&D, the government has envisaged not only support for state research institutes but also incentives for academic institutions and scientists to cooperate with private sector in developing technologies.

In 2005, the Confederation of Industrialists deemed that there are two main reasons for the so far weak cooperation among scientists and entrepreneurs. On the one hand, many entrepreneurs have not expressed interest in innovations and have not made timely investments in innovative activities. On the other hand, due to the lack of resources, the technical sciences were not able to provide an adequate supply of new technology. The Task force on Education, Science, Technological Development, and Innovation at the Commission of Strategic Analysis has pointed out that in the first few years, it would not be possible to provide two-thirds of increase of R&D funding from the private sector given the problems persisting with respect to the cooperation of Latvian scientists with local enterprises, the low innovative activity, interest, and financial capacity of enterprises (Grens 2005). Some economists (Gulans 2005) have doubted whether at the moment there are any enterprises in Latvia, which would demand knowledge and expertise of Latvian scientists due to the large share of foreign-owned companies. These enterprises currently view Latvia mainly as a site for production rather than one for a strategic technological development and are thus unlikely to provide any R&D funding to the Latvian industry.

On the basis of these debates, some initiatives have started to emerge. In the state budget for 2006, three million lats[10] had been allocated for the Ministry of Economics to implement competitiveness and innovation programs. In order to facilitate application of research results in the business sector, the Ministry decided to allocate these funds for the creation and operation of liaison offices of technology transfer; for joint projects of entrepreneurs and scientists to conduct applied research; and for an innovation incubator program. Suggestions to review the tax policy and to include business cofunding for participation in the state programs and projects in justified business expenses (Grens 2007) as well as to review tax allowances for high-technology export products and unification of income tax for all types of business activities have been voiced. It has been argued that the problem of the involvement of local private business in research – both applied and technological – should be carried out in collaboration with the Ministry of Economy, Ministry of Education and Science, and researchers (Ekmanis 2007). While the problem with involvement of the private sector has not yet been solved, the evolving discussion has initiated an assessment of these issues, realization of their topicality, and the much-needed change in the mindsets of the involved parties.

---

[10] 1 LVL = 1.423 EUR = 1.721 USD (rate on 31 January 2006).

11.4.3 Identification of Priority Research Areas

Another much debated issue affecting the developments in the academic community concerns the selection of priority research areas in Latvia. The government decree from 1997 defines the priority research areas as receiving additional funding through state research programs, though no actual funding was made available for this purpose until almost a decade later.[11] Justification of these priority areas has been based on the scarce resources at the disposal of the Latvian government, inhibiting the development of extensive scientific projects and applied research in all research areas and implying the necessity to select a limited number of basic technologies for receiving state support in education, scientific research, and innovation (Grens 2005).

Traditionally, the Ministry of Education and Science together with a small working group of scientists prepared a draft decree on the priority research areas, which was not openly discussed in the scientific community. But since 2005, a wider debate on these priority areas, which was intensified by the additional government funding allocated for academic institutions, has taken place. The main discussion has revolved around the potential shift in the proportions of funding distributed among the different research branches, which were decided back in 1990–1991 and which have not been significantly changed ever since. While it has been noted that this change should happen in a balanced manner with the provision of opportunities to develop new subfields, on the contrary, others have been insisting on the need for a balanced development of research fields only with established traditions and scientists. Radical opinions altogether denying the necessity of priority areas have also been expressed. This position has been based on the assumption that Latvia will never be able to produce world-class knowledge even in priority areas, as the risk that other countries will surpass is very high. Nevertheless, the existing priorities have been based on the historical heritage and arguments on the need and prospects of undertaking research in the respective fields of science (see also Kristapsons et al. 2009, pp. 22–25). The definition of the current nine priorities has also largely come as a result of interest expressed by the sectoral ministries to develop research in their respective areas.

The issue of priority areas has also been linked to the development of science in the regions. Since currently scientific activities are highly concentrated in the capital city, a strong necessity to elaborate regional development policy of Latvia that would promote the development of science in the regions is being stressed. A certain solution to this problem is seen in the introduction of regional coefficients in the distribution of research funding, providing an opportunity to develop the prerequisite infrastructure, increase the level of salaries, and correspondingly the attractiveness of work in the regional centers of science.

---

[11] On 30 May 2006, the Cabinet of Ministers approved nine thematic priorities for funding basic and applied research for 2006–2009: agrobiotechnology, biomedicine and pharmacy, energy, information technologies, Latvian studies, material science, forestry, health, and environmental science.

11.4.4   Protection and Commercialization of Intellectual Property

A fundamental problem is the protection of intellectual property and the related commercialization of research results. While in the late 1980s under the conditions of a soviet socialist economy up to 1,000 inventions were annually registered in Latvia, indicating the country's notable innovative potential, nowadays the scene has changed drastically with only 100–150 patent applications a year (Kristapsons et al. 2004). Currently, not all inventions are being processed as patent applications by Latvian scientists. Instead they are often sold to foreign partners simply as know-how. In many cases, an interested foreign company turns up, undertakes all the patenting issues, and subsequently gains the ownership over the particular invention. As acknowledged by the draft *Guidelines for Strategy of Science, Technological Development and Innovation*, the insufficient experience and resources possessed by Latvian scientists necessary for the legal protection of their intellectual property in Europe and worldwide poses a serious threat to the anticipated economic output of R&D investments (Grens 2005). Besides, in many instances, Latvian scientists and inventors cannot afford patenting due to mere financial reasons, thus leading to the situation that several substantial inventions are not being patented even in Latvia. The insufficiently active and inefficient commercialization of research undertaken is also being related to the inadequate remuneration of the staff for the intellectual values created (University of Latvia 2004).

According to the views voiced by scientists, the solutions should focus on financial support from the state for patenting abroad along with efforts to motivate scientists to develop patentable solutions. However, opinions on this matter differ. For example, the development strategy of the University of Latvia envisages the creation and implementation of intellectual property as one of the tasks of its academic staff, in case of success ensuring their eligibility to a certain share of income generated by the exploitation of this property. It seems that such a formulation is useful in the case of well-developed and elaborated practices of patenting and commercialization but not of those in a very initial stage of development. On other occasions, it has been noted that an inventor should receive at least 50% of the given income from the exploitation of his/her intellectual property. Several scientists have argued that it is important to demonstrate the growth potential in applied science – in case money is earned, it can be added to one's project without any excessive bureaucratic procedures.

A government initiative in this area has been related to the provision of state aid for the establishment of liaison offices of technology transfer at academic institutions – both universities and research institutes – launched at the end of 2005. This initiative addressed longstanding problems related to the provision of scientific services to entrepreneurs as well as the training of engineering specialists and served as an incentive for promoting the commercialization (and protection) of research results. In addition, the government has established the Intellectual Property Board affiliated to the Patent Office of the Republic of Latvia and charged with the task of coordinating and promoting the protection of intellectual property rights in the country.

11.4.5   Definition of the Status and Role of Research Institutes

Discussions in the scientific and academic community during the last years have focused on the status and role of research institutes in Latvia's R&D system with many meetings held between the directors of the institutes, representatives of the Ministry of Education and Science, the Academy of Sciences, university senates and special commissions, the Union of Scientists and trade unions, etc. These debates have been largely conditioned by the following conflicting motives:

- The universities' intention to integrate the formerly legally independent institutes, thus acquiring an additional strong research potential, and to turn prospectively into a research-type university (following the pattern abroad);
- The institutes' intention to keep their legal independence thus keeping the flexibility in choosing their research subjects and managing the financial resources;
- The subjective considerations on behalf of the institute directors and the leading scientists having to do with the unwillingness to lose their existing administrative status.

There are rather different conceptual approaches taken by universities and research institutes to these organizational issues because the concept of the separation of science and university characteristic of the last century is still very alive in the minds of people and also the press. Although this separation was not as typical in Latvia as in many other places in the former Soviet Union, the university is still considered to be aimed at teaching exclusively, while scientific research is performed at the institutes of the Academy of Sciences (Kristapsons et al. 2003). The Development strategy of the University of Latvia (2004) recognizes that the university still features the division between the structural units of studies and those of research – a trend atypical of the European universities. This strategy envisages an encouragement of both the existence of institutes alongside faculties and the incorporation of institutes as structural units within the faculties. According to this conception, research institutes, not being the basic structural units of the university, cooperate with the university and take advantage of its name on a contractual basis. In its turn, the draft Development Strategy of the Latvian science (Grens 2005) includes a statement envisaging an integration of research institutes corresponding to the activities of universities into the structure thereof, in line with the new Law on Research Activity simultaneously ensuring the position, the organizational structure, and the autonomy of institutes in the university constitution.

The built-in conflicts in the relations between universities and institutes have not been solved in over 15 years following the reforms of the funding and management system of science in 1990. Since the science funding was distributed by the Council of Science, according to the level of research performance (on the whole being higher in the institutes), the universities received a relatively small share of these financial resources. At present, the largest share of the increased state funding for science is allocated for the development of science at the universities, thus bypassing the expertise system of the Council of Science. This, in turn, implies an expanding influence of universities in the field of science and a simultaneously diminishing role of the Council of Science elected by the scientists themselves, which is often seen as an example of a pronounced democracy in the field of science management among the East European countries.

Change in the distribution mechanism of science funding has one unique peculiarity. While formerly all the state funding for science was distributed via a competition of submitted project applications with practically no involvement of institutes and universities in the assignation procedure, under the new system the major part of the state funding goes directly through the academic institutions, with a certain share of funding allocated to applied research projects.

11.5   Conclusions

On the whole, Latvia has undergone considerable change in the role and the functions of academic institutions in the transition from the soviet-type S&TS to the NIS, although many related issues still remain to be addressed. The currently forming NIS in Latvia has to evolve and academic institutions have to operate within the context of being a new EU Member State, which aims at catching up with the developed countries. Despite high economic growth rates demonstrated in 2005–2007, the prospects of long-term economic development face many challenges, including a weak enterprise sector, regional disparities, a negative trade balance, a weak industry dominated by low- and medium-tech sectors, etc. Nevertheless, recent policies characterized by an increasing value attached to education and science rather than cheap labor as the basis of the country's competitiveness point to a turning point in the overall development of Latvia. The chosen model of knowledge-based development sets education, science, technological development, and innovation as preconditions for a successful and sustainable development of the country.

The principal challenges in regard to the overall knowledge-production system in Latvia are related to the level of R&D expenditures and especially the respective share coming from the private sector. Although substantial progress has been made by the adoption of the new legislative norm providing an annual increase in GOVERD as well as additional allocations from the state budget and EU structural funds through various state aid programs, complementary funding from the enterprise sector is still severely lacking. This has largely to do with the weak business involvement in the innovative activities and the underdeveloped collaboration models with potential partners both from the industry and the academic circles. Although policy documents increasingly stress the stimulation of cooperation between the academic research and the private sector in the field of new technology development, additional efficient measures have to be sought. Underdeveloped linkages and cooperation can also be observed between other stakeholders of the NIS as well, including various governmental and nongovernmental bodies.

More specifically, the main challenges for the academic institutions in Latvia are related to the integration of scientific and entrepreneurial activities with respect to the development of an overall entrepreneurial culture within the research community and building competence in transferring and commercializing the knowledge produced. A further problem lies in the unsatisfactory integration of teaching and research, which is largely embodied in the still problematic relations between HEIs and research institutes, though a trend toward the development of research universities is becoming evident in Latvia. Finally, there is also a need of further integration into the European Research Area and the international academic community in general. In addition, the future development is currently threatened by the limited inflow of a younger generation to replace the drastically aging academic staff and by the recurrent brain drain of talented researchers.

On the whole, the science of Latvia seems to have entered a new phase of development in 2005–2007 marked by the adoption of the new Law on Research Activity, the increase in science funding, and a targeted shifting of these resources toward new priorities, new conditions, and new directions in the science organization in Latvia. The university system has been receiving the major share of additional funding allocations motivated by the necessity of uniting education and research activities. The independent state research institutes, in their turn, have access to additional funding allocations through the system of state research programs that are more targeted at generally boosting the competitiveness of the national science in Latvia and thereby contributing to the overall competitiveness of the national economy and advancement of society.

References

Adamsone-Fiskovica, A., Kristapsons, J., Ulnicane-Ozolina, I. (2008). *INNO-policy trendchart – policy trends and appraisal report: Latvia*. European Commission, Enterprise Directorate-General.

Adamsone-Fiskovica, A., Kristapsons, J., Lulle, A. (2009a). *Erawatch analytical country report 2009: Latvia. analysis of policy mixes to foster R&D investment and to contribute to the ERA*. European Commission, Directorate-General for Research.

Adamsone-Fiskovica, A., Kristapsons, J., Tjunina, E., Ulnicane-Ozolina, I. (2009b). "Moving beyond teaching and research: economic and social tasks of universities in Latvia." *Science and Public Policy*, Vol. 36, No 2, March, pp. 133–137.

Auers, D., Rostoks, T., Smith, K. (2007). "Flipping burgers or flipping pages? Student employment and academic attainment in post-Soviet Latvia." *Communist and Post-Communist Studies*, Vol. 40, pp. 477–491.

Balazs, K., Faulkner, W., Schimank, U. (eds.). (1995). "The research system in post-communist Central and Eastern Europe." *Social Studies of Science*, Vol. 25, No 4, EASST Special Issue.

Bilinskis, I., Ekmanis, J., Jansons, J., Borzovs, J., Cvetkova, I., Aispurs, V., Elerts, M., Avotins, V., Tju ina, E. (2005). *Recommendations for funding research activity through the attraction of private sector investments* (in Latvian). Riga: Ministry of Economics.

Brunner, J. J. (2003). *Latvia higher education: changing conditions, problems, challenges and policy options*. The World Bank Europe and Central Asia Human Development.

Bundule, M., Jansons, J. (2005). "International scientific cooperation." In: *Building knowledge society*, Elmars Grens (ed.). Strategic Analysis Commission. Riga: Zinatne, pp. 70–92 (in Latvian).

Central Statistical Bureau of Latvia (2006). *Research and development, and innovation statistics*. Riga: Statistical Data Collection.

Central Statistical Bureau of Latvia (2008). *Research and development, and innovation statistics*. Riga: Statistical Data Collection.

Central Statistical Bureau of Latvia (2009). *Educational institutions in Latvia in the beginning of the academic year 2008/2009*. Bulletin, Riga (in Latvian).

Danish Research Councils (1992). *Latvian research: an international evaluation*. Copenhagen: Danish Research Councils.

Göransson, B., Naharajh, R., Schmoch, U. (2009). "New activities of universities in transfer and extension: multiple requirements and manifold solutions." *Science and Public Policy*, Vol. 36, No 2, pp. 157–164.

Ekmanis, J. (2005). "Current trends of science development in Latvia. Toward building a knowledge-based society." *Proceedings of the Strategic Analysis Commission*, Vol. 2, No 3, pp. 30–39. Riga: Zinatne Publishers (in Latvian).

Ekmanis, J. (2007). Opening speech of the president of the academy of sciences at the general meeting of the academy on 22 November, 2007. In: Yearbook 2006/2007 of the Latvian Academy of Sciences, pp. 177–179. Riga: Zinatne Publishers.

Etzkowitz, H. (2000). "Technology transfer and the East European transition." *Science and Public Policy*, Vol. 27, No 4, pp. 230–234.

European Communities (2009). *European innovation scoreboard 2008. Comparative analysis of innovation performance*. PRO INNO Europe paper N°10. Belgium: European Commission, DG Enterprise and Industry.

Grens, E. (2005). "Building a knowledge society." *Proceedings of the Strategic Analysis Commission*, Vol. 2, No 3, pp. 7–11. Riga: Zinatne Publishers (in Latvian).

Grens, E. (2007). "Science, research and innovation: advancing Latvia's development." *Proceedings of the Strategic Analysis Commission*, Vol. 3, No (14), pp. 7–9. Riga: Zinatne Publishers (in Latvian).

Gulans, P. (2005). Speech at the general meeting of the academy of sciences, April 14, 2005. *Zinatnes Vestnesis*, April (in Latvian).

Gunnes, H. (2009). *NORBAL – statistics on awarded doctoral degrees and doctoral students in the Nordic and Baltic Countries: main findings – 2007*. NIFU STEP.

Hirschhausen, C. von, Bitzer, J. (eds.) (2000). *The globalisation of industry and innovation in Eastern Europe: from post-socialist restructuring to international competitiveness*. Great Britain: Edward Elgar.

JIRD (Journal of International Relations and Development) (2002). Special issue *In Search of growth strategies: innovation policy in EU accession countries*, Vol. 5, No 4.

Kasa, R. (2008). "Aspects of fiscal federalism in higher education cost sharing in Latvia." *Peabody Journal of Education*, Vol. 83, No 1, pp. 86–100.

Kristapsons, J., Martinson, H., Dagyte, I. (2003). *Baltic R&D systems in transition: experiences and future prospects*. Riga: Zinatne.

Kristapsons, J., Tjunina, E., Adamsone-Fiskovica, A. (2004). *Latvian scientific publications, citation indices, patenting activity*. Riga: Centre for Science and Technology Studies of the Latvian Academy of Sciences (in Latvian).

Kristapsons, J., Adamsone-Fiskovica, A., Ulnicane-Ozolina, I. (2009). *ERAWATCH country report 2008 – an assessment of research system and policies: Latvia*. JRC Scientific and Technical Reports, European Commission, Directorate-General for Research.

Meske, W. (ed.) (2004). *From system transformation to European integration: science and technology in central and Eastern Europe at the beginning of the 21st century*: Münster LIT Verlag.

Meske, W., Mosoni-Fried, J., Etzkowitz, H., Nesvetailov, G. (eds.) (1998). *Transforming science and technology systems – the endless transition?* NATO Science Series 4: Science and Technology Policy, Vol. 23, Amsterdam: IOS Press.

Ministry of Economics (2008). *Economic development in Latvia*. December, Riga.

MoES (2005). *R&D in Latvia*, 3rd revised edition. Riga Ministry of Education and Science.

MoES (2008a). *Latvia in EC 6th framework programme 2002–2006*. Riga Ministry of Education and Science.

MoES (2008b). *Report on higher education in Latvia in 2007 (figures, facts, trends)*. Riga: Department of Higher Education (in Latvian). Ministry of Education and Science.

MoES (2009). *Draft guidelines for development of science and technology for 2009–2013*. Riga. Ministry of Education and Science.

Muiznieks, I. (2005). "The future of universities and scientific activities." In: *Building knowledge society*, Elmars Grens (ed.). Strategic Analysis Commission. Riga: Zinatne, pp. 93–120. (in Latvian).

Radosevic, S. (1999). "Transformation of science and technology systems into systems of innovation in Central and Eastern Europe: the emerging patterns and determinants." *Structural Change and Economic Dynamics*, Vol. 10, pp. 277–320.

RIS Latvia (2004). *The Latvian innovation system: strategy and action plan 2005–2010*. Available at: http://www.innovation.lv/ris/Latv/Dokum/RIS_Strategy_Latvia.pdf.

SCImago (2007). SJR – SCImago journal & country rank. Available at: http://www.scimagojr.com (Retrieved on 19 August 2009).

Stradins, J. (1982). *Sketches on the history of Latvian science*. Riga: Zinatne (in Latvian).

Stradins, J. (1998). *Latvian academy of sciences – origin, history, transformation*. Riga: Zinatne (in Latvian).

Stradins, J. (2000). "Science in Latvia – trends, topics, traditions". In: Yearbook 1999, P. Kauranen (ed.). Helsinki: Finnish Academy of Science and Letters, pp. 63–73.

University of Latvia (2004). *Development strategy of the university of Latvia*. Riga. Available at: http://www.lu.lv/dokumenti/resursi/attistibas-strategija.doc (in Latvian).

Watkins, A., Agapitova, N. (2004). *Creating a 21st century national innovation system for a 21st century Latvian economy*. Policy Research Working Paper WPS3457. World Bank: Washington D.C.

Chapter 12
Russia: Universities in the Context of Reforming the National Innovation System

Leonid Gokhberg, Tatiana Kuznetsova, and Stanislav Zaichenko

12.1 Introduction to the Russian Context

The concept of National Innovation Systems (NIS) initially developed by Freeman (1987, 1995), Lundvall (1992), and Nelson (1993) has proved to be a useful tool for the analysis at national, regional, and sectoral levels as well as for the design of policies to promote science and technology (S&T). Its considerable contribution reveals the role of the national institutional context as the main factor of economic growth based on innovation and learning.

The foundation for high-quality standards of R&D in Russia was laid as far back as the Tsarist era (Gokhberg et al. 1997). During that period, research activities were carried not only at the Academy of Sciences, but also at the leading universities and the military laboratories. Later, after the communist 1917 revolution, the "Soviet" institutional model of S&T was established. This model reallocated research capacities between different sectors on the basis of their main activity: research efforts were concentrated primarily in the Academy of Sciences and the sectoral R&D organizations, while the higher education institutions (HEIs) focused on the implementation of large-scale education and training programs.

The post-Soviet S&T system was confronted with new challenges: a necessity of getting adapted to newly established market relations, a substantial reduction of public budget allocations, and a decreasing demand for R&D by government ministries and enterprises. All these resulted in drastic changes in the R&D sector. At the same time, the S&T system has retained many features of the Soviet past. Thus, the research institutes independent of universities and industrial enterprises still dominate the national R&D efforts.

Contribution of the universities to innovation and economic growth is an important focus of the NIS studies (Bartzokas 2000). Analyses indicate strong systemic linkages between the academic impact of HEIs and technological innovation activity (Patel

L. Gokhberg (✉)
Higher School of Economics, Moscow, Russian Federation
e-mail: lgokhberg@hse.ru

B. Göransson and C. Brundenius (eds.), *Universities in Transition:*
The Changing Role and Challenges for Academic Institutions,
© International Development Research Centre 2011

1998). In Europe and USA, universities have been traditionally regarded as key institutions for knowledge generation, competence building, R&D, and innovation excellence. Today, the Russian scholars seem to fall into the same pattern (Gokhberg et al. 2008; Yudkevich 2007).

Russian HEIs traditionally occupy a marginal part in the national R&D landscape vis-à-vis the mature market economies. Their central function is still considered in a linear mode to provide education and training while research is given a lower priority, with the exemptions for a few elite universities.

This paper refers to a contemporary discussion of S&T and innovation activities in Russian universities and the respective national policies in the context of transforming the NIS.

12.2   The Position of the Academic Institutions in the Russian System of Innovation

One of the key features of the Russian NIS is its primary focus mainly on research rather than innovation (Gokhberg 2003a, b). To a great deal, it reflects a peculiar institutional structure biased toward legally independent research institutes separated from both education and industry (Fig. 12.1).

Together with the specialized design organizations, the independent research institutes account for 64% of the total R&D-performing units (Table 12.1) and they contribute with 78 and 64% of R&D personnel and expenditures, respectively.

The shares of HEIs and industrial enterprises among other R&D institutions are as low as 14 and 6%, respectively. It is explained by an increasing number of research institutes (until 2002), which resulted from the disintegration of large institutions belonging to former industrial ministries and the Academy of Sciences into smaller ones in the 1990s. Newly established units preserved the status of State Entities. The isolation of Russian universities from the science sector was also related to the shortage of research funds, while multiple private HEIs have been organized to meet the growing demand from the students for university degrees without any research orientation. Only 44% of HEIs are currently engaged in R&D (Table 12.2).

Another important factor affecting the Russian NIS is the still existing broad research front inherited from the former USSR. It was established under the conditions of long-term political and economic autarky. For nearly 70 years, the national S&T community had to meet only the domestic demand of strengthening defense, increasing economic growth, and social welfare. Following this strategy, the Soviet S&T sector incorporated practically all research orientations. For the development of new scientific areas, the government used to multiply the number of R&D units. However, this system emphasized the areas that met primarily the requirements of the military and considerations of political prestige as well as needs of heavy industry. They included physics, chemistry, earth and space sciences, and engineering.

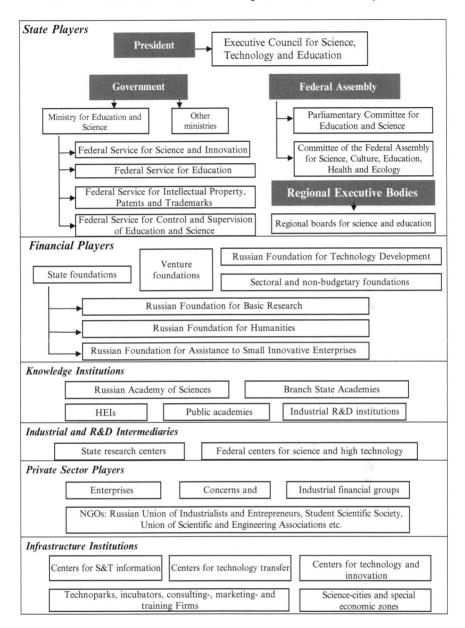

Fig. 12.1 Institutional structure of the Russian S&T

Figure 12.2 shows main R&D funding flows in Russia. Though its total amounts have increased twofold in real terms during 1995–2008, but as a percentage of GDP it is still low at 1.03% (1.05% in 2000). At the same time, the output indicators continue to decline. For the number of scientific articles published in SCI journals, Russia moved to the eleventh place (2.4% of the world total) from the seventh position in

Table 12.1 R&D institutions in Russia by type

	1990	1995	2000	2001	2002	2003	2004	2005	2006	2007	2008
Total	4,646	4,059	4,099	4,037	3,906	3,797	3,656	3,566	3,622	3,957	3,666
Research institutes	1,762	2,284	2,686	2,676	2,630	2,564	2,464	2,115	2,049	2,036	1,926
Design organizations	937	548	318	289	257	228	194	489	482	497	418
Construction project and exploration organizations	593	207	85	81	76	68	63	61	58	49	42
Experimental enterprises	28	23	33	31	34	28	31	30	49	60	58
Higher education institutions	453	395	390	388	390	393	402	406	417	500	503
Industrial enterprises	449	325	284	288	255	248	244	231	255	265	239
Others	424	277	303	284	264	268	258	234	312	550	480

Sources: Gokhberg (2003b), Science Indicators (2009), Science. Innovation. Information Society (2009)

Table 12.2 Higher education institutions

	1990	1995	2000	2001	2002	2003	2004	2005	2006	2007	2008
Total	514	762	965	1,088	1,039	1,046	1,071	1,068	1,090	1,108	1,134
HEIs providing R&D	453	395	390	388	390	393	402	406	417	500	503
HEIs providing R&D, %	88.1	51.8	40.4	35.7	37.5	37.6	37.5	38.0	38.3	45.1	44.4

Sources: Education in the Russian Federation (2007), Science Indicators (2009), Science. Innovation. Information Society (2009)

1995 and the third place occupied by the USSR in 1980. Exports of technology amounted to 833.2 million USD in 2008, compared, for example, with 1.6 billion USD for Hungary and much greater for larger Organisation for Economic Cooperation and Development (OECD) economies.

Institutional linkages are unlikely to be efficient and remain a weak point of the Russian NIS. They retain mostly "vertical orientation" as in the former centrally planned system and reflect a paternalistic practice of government directed R&D. The government remains the main partner for NIS institutions and the main sponsor for R&D. It provides 65% of the total R&D expenditure, which resembles a rather centralized R&D system. This trend does not follow the tendencies of major market economies where governments contribute with much smaller percentages of R&D funding: 28.4% in Germany, 32.8% in the UK, 23.0% in Korea, and 16.8% in Japan (Science Indicators 2009).

Such a situation creates little incentives for horizontal cooperation between the NIS institutions in Russia. In HEIs, 62.4% of R&D expenditure comes from the government and only 28.6% from the private sector. For the Russian Academy of Sciences, these shares are 83.6 and 12.1%, respectively. Innovative industrial clusters are concentrating around three sectors: civil engineering, chemicals, and food. These include 70% of all innovative enterprises, and their average innovation activity

Sources of funding

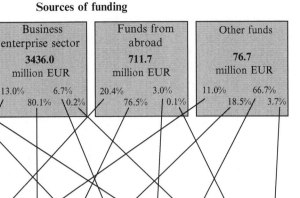

Government
7749.8
million EUR
38.8%   6.5%
54.5%   0.3%

Business
enterprise sector
3436.0
million EUR
13.0%   6.7%
80.1%   0.2%

Funds from
abroad
711.7
million EUR
20.4%   3.0%
76.5%   0.1%

Other funds
76.7
million EUR
11.0%   66.7%
18.5%   3.7%

Government
sector
3607.5
million EUR

Business
enterprise sector
7533.5
million EUR

Higher education
sector
801.9
million EUR

Private non-
profit sector
31.3
million EUR

Sectors of performance

Fig. 12.2 R&D funding flows, 2008. *Source*: Science. Innovation. Information Society (2009)

level is twice as high as the average in industry (Innovation Indicators 2009). But the innovative firms' behavior remains inert. Between 1992 and 2008, the level of innovation activity decreased from 16.3 to 9.6%. At the same time in the EU member states, this indicator varies from 27% (Greece) to 75% (Ireland).

The Russian NIS suffers a lot from the shocks following the political, social, and economic transition of the 1990s. Therefore, it is necessary to overcome a number of interdependent barriers in order to introduce and develop efficient and competitive NIS elements and mechanisms, including R&D activities at universities. For the topic discussed here, it is important to consider the main specific barriers: inflexible legislation and regulations, weakening scientific human resources in HEIs, and decreasing attractiveness of academic careers.

The legislation barriers for university R&D became crucial by the end of the 1990s. Considerable restrictions emerged from the budgetary, tax, and property legislation. First of all, legal forms available for the research organizations became too limited in scope for the market economy. Universities, as well as research institutes, in reality were regarded to be budgetary-funded entities with very strict funding procedures. There are very few legal ways for them to get funding from other sources in addition to the budgetary provisions. In many cases, reallocation of budgetary funds between different cost items is restricted. Consequently, a research institute is not allowed to reallocate budgetary funds for educational activities and, on the contrary, HEIs cannot use their education-intended budgetary funding for R&D purposes. The same problem concerns the use of premises. Furthermore, the existing legislation does not determine any legal forms for the integration of education and R&D (though it does not prohibit creation of any forms of integration). Second, one should mention a strict legal restriction on the educational activities of noneducational institutions, making it rather difficult to launch educational units inside an R&D institution or vice versa.

S&T human resources were also affected by transition shocks. Today 1.27% of employed population in Russia is involved in R&D (about half of them, 0.66%, are researchers). In comparison with other countries, this proportion is rather high: in France and Japan, it is similarly close to 1.4%, in Germany 1.2%, in Canada 1.1%, etc. (Science Indicators 2009). Against the background of the overall decline of R&D personnel by 58% after 1990, at the Academy of Sciences it decreased by less than a quarter (24%). The higher education sector is notable for the largest decline of R&D employment compared with other sectors of performance – by 71% (R&D in the Higher Education Sector 2005; Science Indicators 2009). Nowadays the latter is represented by 5.4% of total R&D staff.

In total, 26.9% of the employed population in Russia has obtained university degrees (in Canada 23.3%, the UK 20.8%, Finland 18.1%, and Germany 14.8%) (Education Indicators 2008). These figures show a profound potential of human resources. However, financial resources invested in knowledge activities are not adequate to the scale of the latter: for example, R&D expenditure-to-personnel ratio in Russia is considerably low – just USD 21,000 (2005). For the higher education sector, this amount accounts for about USD 14,000 (Science Indicators 2009). It is far below the level achieved by other nations: in Canada these figures reach USD 122,900 and USD 173,800, respectively, in Korea USD 146,900 and USD 114,600, and in Spain USD 76,000 and USD 70,200 (Science Indicators 2009).[1]

The HSE Institute for Statistical Studies and Economics of Knowledge provides regular surveys on public awareness of science, technology, and innovation (Gokhberg and Shuvalova 2004). The results show decreasing prestige of a university as an R&D institution. Currently, only 7% of respondents think that a scientific career is a promising perspective, and 10% believe that this job is prestigious. One-third of respondents have reported that scientific knowledge is not important in their day-to-day life. To compare, in USA and China, this opinion was shared only by 15 and 17% of respondents, respectively (Eurobarometer 224 2005; National Science Board 2006).

The trends mentioned above reflect obstacles on the way to integrate research and education activities. The described legal barriers impede reallocation of budgetary funding and property between education and R&D activities, combining education and R&D functions into a single budgetary-funded entity and obtaining supplementary nonbudgetary funds for it. This is crucial for the Russian innovation system because of the dominant role of budgetary-funded institutions, including

---

[1] Calculated using GDP purchasing-power parities.

HEIs and R&D institutes. These barriers to a great extent contribute to underfeeding or inefficient funding of R&D as well as combined R&D and education activities. Therefore despite a high human resource potential in S&T, the R&D funding per employee declines, and researchers leave HEIs for other more profitable occupations. The scientific career becomes less attractive, and in the long run both the quantity and quality of R&D personnel can decrease dramatically. The situation can be seen even in a more alarming mode taking into account other external interdependent barriers growing from other institutional areas beyond S&T and education, namely; "oil-based" economy strategies and subsequent low demand for innovation, IPR shortcomings, and so on.

12.3   Mapping the Academic System in Russia

The higher education sector in Russia is represented not only by HEIs (including universities), but also by some R&D centers, construction project and exploration organizations, experimental enterprises, and others. But compared with the whole R&D system (Table 12.1), the HEIs are dominant here (83.4%). During the period of 1995–2008, HEIs number rose from 762 to 1,134 (mostly private ones: from 193 to 474). At the same time, there was a little shift in number of HEIs performing R&D (Table 12.3).

In comparison with the OECD economies, Higher Education R&D (HERD) is rather low in Russia (Fig. 12.3). However, relative HERD per researcher tripled during last 10 years (the R&D staff in Russian HEIs decreased by 16%). Low HERD-to-GDP ratio is explained mostly by its little weight in gross expenditure on research and development (GERD) (see below).

Even though the situation for the university R&D in Russia is not problem free, there are reasons to believe that its development can still be ensured. Thus, as statistics show, the Russian higher education sector has maintained a considerable potential for R&D and innovation. Currently, HEIs provide one-fifth of principally new technologies created in this country, although R&D expenditure in this sector does not reach 6% of the national

Table 12.3 R&D performing organizations in the higher education sector

	1995	2000	2001	2002	2003	2004	2005	2006	2007	2008
Total	511	526	529	531	526	533	539	540	616	603
HEIs and other universities	395	390	388	390	393	402	406	417	500	503
R&D centers	88	107	111	113	108	106	109	106	95	80
Construction project and exploration organizations	18	19	19	17	17	17	17	14	12	11
Exploration enterprises	1	2	1	2	–	1	–	–	1	1
Others	9	8	10	9	8	7	7	3	8	8

Source: Science Indicators (2009); Science. Innovation. Information Society (2009)

HE expenditure on R&D (thousand current PPP $), per
one HE researcher (FTE),
1995-2008

HE expenditure on R&D as a percentage of GDP (%),
1995-2008

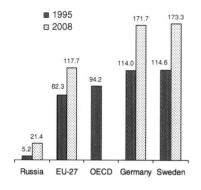

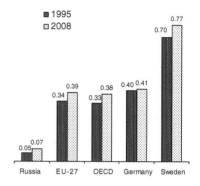

Fig. 12.3 Higher education sector expenditure on R&D indicators. *Sources*: OECD 2008; HSE
Institute for Statistical Studies and Economics of Knowledge

Table 12.4 R&D performance of the Russian Academy of Sciences and Universities: 2008

	R&D funding, %	Nonbudgetary R&D funding per 1 Ruble of the budgetary R&D funding	New technologies created, %
Total	100	0.55	100
Higher education institutions	5.9	0.57	18.7
Russian Academy of Sciences	13.0	0.14	4.0

Source: HSE Institute for Statistical Studies and Economics of Knowledge

total (Table 12.4). Furthermore, 28.6% of this funding comes to HEIs from the private
sector. During 2002–2005, patenting activity of HEIs has increased 1.4-fold (up to 20%
of resident patent applications). These facts reflect the evidence of a still remaining
comparatively strong innovation base at the universities in Russia.

Today certain leading Russian universities perform R&D and educational activities
at equal scales. Therefore, they have already achieved a balance between efforts for
R&D and education (Fig. 12.4). It is also noticeable that the average ratio between R&D
and education relative to annual expenditure is 37:27 thousand Russian Rubles (RUR).
This means that in general the scale of R&D activities exceeds that of the teaching.

The new Federal law on the integration of science and education (Federal Law
2007) was adopted at the end of 2007 to boost S&T and innovation activities at
universities and establish closer linkages between HEIs and research institutions.
The new law legalizes existing models of such integration and provides a scope for
efficient forms including a subset of necessary regulations. These regulations
should help to avoid serious institutional barriers described earlier. Unfortunately,
the discussion around the law lasted for 4 years. The main problem for all this
period of time was to achieve a compromise between the government, the university

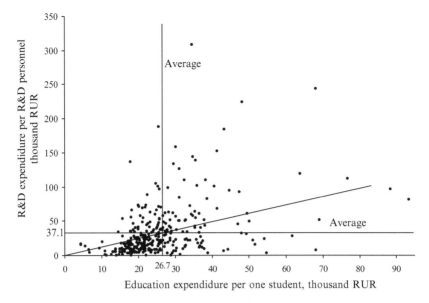

Fig. 12.4 Distribution of R&D and education expenditure at HEIs: 2005. *Source*: HSE Institute for Statistical Studies and Economics of Knowledge

community, and the research institutions sector. As a result, the final version of the law does not satisfy any of these sides. It allows solving just some evident problems of the integration. But further amendments are required to make the integration between science and education not only possible, but also efficient.

Another important dimension of the integration policy is the support extended to the best "innovative HEIs" or "research universities." The Priority National Project "Education" involves specific policy actions in this direction. An important component of this project, entitled "Support Measures for Higher Education Institutions Implementing Innovative Education Programmes" is devoted to the distribution of competitive grants for the innovation development of universities, including human resource development, unique R&D and innovation projects, improvement of innovation infrastructure, acquisition of research equipment, etc. (Government Statement 2006). There were 57 winners in the 2006 competition. Each of them received funding in the range of 200 million–1 billion RUR depending on the scale of projects. The average annual R&D expenditure of the grant winners was 123.3 thousand RUR per one member of R&D and teaching staff, but the difference between minimum and maximum amounts (1.1 and 586.6 thousand RUR, respectively) was very high. It means that only a part of the winning universities really could develop a large-scale innovation activity. However, it was a first government experiment toward the earmarked support of research universities as "centers of excellence." The main challenge today is to continue this practice on the regular basis. If so, it could be a powerful driver like university block grants in the UK or Japan.

There is also a promising program for developing R&D and innovation human resources in HEIs that deserves to be mentioned. The Federal Program, entitled "Science and Education Human Resources for Innovational Russia" was designed for the period 2009–2013 (President Commissions 2006). The aim of the program is to provide institutional support for efficient human resource development in the S&T and innovation sphere. In order to achieve this goal, it is proposed to attract and involve young talents and highly skilled professionals in S&T and innovation projects and to consolidate efficient and competitive scholars in the best universities and R&D institutes. In this regard, the program includes a number of actions and instruments: centers of excellence for science and education, a system of grants for young promising scientists and teachers, special schemes to attract young promising scientists and teachers from abroad, grants for the innovation infrastructure development, etc.

Nowadays, it is rather difficult to develop innovative university programs and to provide integration of science and education in the framework of an outdated "budgetary-funded institution" legal form which is typical for public universities. A new more flexible model is known as "autonomous institution" (AI) (Federal Law 03.11.2006). In contrast to the existing budgetary-funded institutions, the new structures will not be funded through fixed budgetary institutional grants; rather, they will receive funding from various sources (including the government). This would increase their responsibility for the expected results. At the same time, they will remain government-owned entities. AIs will have certain autonomy and independence in attracting (and spending) funds from nongovernment sources, including credits and investments. It will give them new development opportunities that are not available to the "traditional" budgetary-funded institutions.

Prospects for transition of the government-owned R&D organizations into the new form are outlined in strategy of science and innovations (Interdepartmental commission on R&D and innovation policy, 15.02.2006). At least 250 R&D institutions and HEIs should turn into the new status in a rather short period of time. Taking into account the planned period for the institutional transformation, this task looks quite complicated. The discussion around it lasts for more than 2 years, but there still exist many questions and uncertainties. First AIs transferred from the budgetary-funded ones should be in operation by the end of 2008. By 2009, the AIs were expected to amount to about 12% of all government sector R&D institutions, and by 2010, this proportion should reach almost 22%. Unfortunately, by the end of 2009, no S&T AIs were created. It is the effect of severe faults of the contemporary AI regulation.

12.4 The Current Russian Debate

The decreasing competitiveness of higher education in Russia has been a "hot issue" since the mid-1990s. According to the PISA survey, Russia occupies 28th position by the quality of the primary education – between Turkey and Uruguay (OECD 2007), while for the higher education competitiveness index

(World Economic Forum), Russia is in the 45th position. During 1996–2006, the share of teachers engaged in R&D at universities declined from 38 to 16%. Today the total share of university training programs based on original inhouse R&D does not exceed 20%. In 2006, teaching as a career was regarded as prestigious only by 8% of the adult population (Shuvalova 2007). For a scientific occupation, this figure amounts to 10%.

Unified State Examinations (USEs). Since 2001, this form of final examinations is one of the most discussed topics concerning the higher education sphere. Initially, it was proposed as an experiment (Government Statement 16.02.2001) to provide more clear and efficient mechanism for school graduation and HEI enrollment at the same time. In 2005 USEs were adopted as a compulsory form. Its main idea is to guarantee equal opportunities for students irrespective of their residence or type of school graduated. However, this form is considered to be too formalized and too unified to reflect all necessary competences adequately and to meet enrollment requirements of different HEIs. Therefore, USEs practice is revised and adjusted on a regular basis.

Funding of higher education. During the period 1991–2006, the number of students increased more than 2.5-fold. At the same time, the budget for higher education (in real prices) has not exceeded 1.5-fold in value from 1991. The lack of funding has resulted in decrease not only in terms of funding per student, but also in teachers' salaries and HEIs' real assets. During the 2006 public opinion polls, 79% of respondents said that the state support of universities should be considerably increased (Shuvalova 2007).

The gap between the university graduation structure and employers' demand. Despite considerable changes in professional structure of grades during last 10–15 years, it does not meet the labor-market demand. About 26% of employed population in Russia has higher school degrees, but only 20–50% of HEI graduates succeed in finding a job within their specialization (depending on the HEI profile) (Education in the Russian Federation 2007).

Innovative university (IU) programs. This issue, already mentioned earlier, is closely connected to the previous point. A solution lies in the new institutional model to be established in the Russian higher education sector. This model will be built around research universities notable for innovative state-of-the-art education programs. The important function of these universities will be the integration of science and education. In 2008 two IUs were created. In 2009 more new IUs appeared, including the State University – Higher School of Economics.

Integration of science and education. According to expert forecasts (Kuzminov and Frumin 2008), the budgetary funding for R&D in HEIs should increase up to 25% of the budgetary funding for education by 2015 and up to 35% by 2020. After the first results of the Education Program, it is planned to select and develop research universities on a regular basis (there should be at least 12 such HEIs by 2010 and more than 20 by 2020). In addition to surplus funding for R&D and education activities (especially for PhD programs), these institutions will be provided with wider autonomy in their management activities and reallocation of funds.

AIs. This new form mentioned above also came up for a heated discussion during the last years. Critics of the new law often point to the difficulties with evaluation of AIs' assets and possible risks related with their splitting. This criticism is based on the negative experience of privatization in the science sector (in the beginning of the 1990s' Russian reforms). The key point with AIs is the intention to increase productivity in the government R&D sector, and to meet the state's and society's demand for more efficient R&D products. But there are still some limitations on their activity, unsuitable for creditors and investors. The government refuses to pay off AIs' debts and restricts considerably operations using their assets. Besides, there exist new challenges for ministries and agencies: to define clearly the objectives, functions, assets, and financial resources of the new structures.

12.5   Conclusions

The analysis presented here showed a picture of an underdeveloped and inefficient NIS in Russia. It is rather predictable taking into consideration the deep transition crisis of the 1990s. Many other countries moving from planning system toward market economy faced similar problems. But it is rather difficult to imagine that such a transitional stage lasts for 17 years, without any radical improvements in terms of efficiency despite the steadily increasing financial support. The Russian NIS has substantial potential for development, but nowadays the national economy is oriented toward natural resources, instead of innovation. Lack of demand for innovation will keep the NIS frozen until the drop of world prices on natural resources or until the NIS looses its potential irreversibly. But there exist mechanisms powerful enough to give a strong impulse to the innovation system. As already mentioned, integration of science and education is one of them.

This brief review shows that the innovation activity of Russian universities is far from optimal, as there exists a system of interdependent factors hampering this activity. Some of them arise directly as a consequence of the barriers against integration of science and education activities, some others are related to the drawbacks of the entire Russian NIS. Certain factors originate from deep structural breaches that are far beyond the reach of S&T and education. Some facts and figures provide evidence of a high innovation potential of the Russian higher education sector, and it is time to maintain and build on this opportunity. A number of corresponding government initiatives have started recently or are going to be launched in the next few years. All the actions mentioned above should boost significantly the R&D and innovation in the Russian HEIs sector and have a considerable impact on the Russian NIS and economic growth. It is also important that various policy actions concerning the NIS be coordinated in close correspondence with each other. Otherwise it may undermine S&T and innovation activities in HEIs against the background of rather low industry demand for R&D.

References

Bartzokas, A. (2000). The Policy Relevance of the National Systems of Innovation Approach, UNU/INTECH Discussion Paper 2003.

Education Indicators (2008). Data Book. Moscow: State University–Higher School of Economics (in Russian).

Education in the Russian Federation (2007). Data Book. – Moscow: State University–Higher School of Economics (in Russian).

Eurobarometer 224 (2005). Europeans, Science and Technology. Luxembourg: Office for Official Publications of the European Communities.

Federal Law (03.11.2006). "On Autonomous Institutions", No. 174-FZ

Federal Law (01.12.2007). "On Changes to the Selected Legal Statements of the Russian Federation Concerning the Integration of Education and Science", No. 308-F

Freeman, C. (1987). Technology Policy and Economic Performance: Lessons from Japan. London: Francis Pinter.

Freeman, C. (1995). The National System of Innovation in Historical Perspective. Cambridge Journal of Economics, Vol. 19, No. 1. February, Special Issue on Technology and Innovation, pp. 5–25.

Gokhberg, L. (2003a). Russia: A New Innovation System for the New Economy. A background material for a presentation at the First Globelics Conference "Innovation Systems and Development Strategies for the Third Millennium", Rio de Janeiro, November 2–6, 2003.

Gokhberg, L. (2003b). Statistics of Science. Moscow: TEIS (in Russian).

Gokhberg, L., Shuvalova, O. (2004). Russian Public Opinion of the Knowledge Economy: Science, Innovation, Information Technology and Education as Drivers of Economic Growth and Quality of Life. The British Council.

Gokhberg, L., Peck, M., and Gács, J. (eds) (1997). Russian Applied Research and Development: Its Problems and its Promise. Austria: International Institute for Applied Systems Analysis, Luxembuorg.

Gokhberg, L., Kitova, G., Kuznetsova, T. (2008). Strategy of Integration Processes in Science and Education, Issues of Economics, No. 6.

Government Statement (16.02.2001). "On Organisation of Experimental Introduction of the Unified State Examinations". No. 119.

Government Statement (14.02.2006). "On the Government Support Measures for the Education Institutions Implementing Innovation Education Programmes", No. 89.

Innovation Indicators (2009). Data Book. Moscow: State University–Higher School of Economics (in Russian).

Interdepartmental Commission on S&T and Innovation Policy (15.02.2006). R&D and Innovation Development Strategy in the Russian Federation until 2015.

Kuzminov, Y., Frumin, I. (2008). Education in Russia – 2020: A Model of the Education System for the Knowledge-Based Economy. Report for the IX International Conference "Modernisation of the Economy and Globalisation" – Moscow, SU-HSE: 1–3 April 2008 (in Russian).

Lundvall, B.-A. (Ed) (1992). National Systems of Innovation. Towards a Theory of Innovation and Interactive Learning. Printer: London.

National Science Board (2006). Science and Engineering Indicators. Washington: US Government Printing Office.

Nelson, R.R. (Ed). (1993). National Innovation Systems. A Comparative Analysis. Oxford University Pres, New York.

OECD (2007). PISA 2006. Science Competencies for Tomorrow's World. – Paris.

OECD (2008). Main Science and Technology Indicators. Volume 2008/1. – Paris.

Patel, P. (1998). Indicators for Systems of Innovation and System Interactions TSER-IDEA project, No. 11.

President Commissions to the Government of the Russian Federation (04.08.2006), No. Pr-1321.

R&D in the Higher Education Sector (2005). Data Book. Moscow: State University–Higher School of Economics (in Russian).

Science Indicators 2009 (2009). Data Book. Moscow: State University–Higher School of Economics (in Russian).

Science. Innovation. Information Society (2009). Data Book. Moscow: State University–Higher School of Economics (in Russian).

Shuvalova, O. (2007). The Image of Science: Public Opinion on the Scientific Activities Results, Foresight, 2007, No. 2 (2), pp. 50–59 (in Russian).

Yudkevich, M. (2007). Activity of Universities and Scientists: Economic Grounds and Academic Explanations // Economy of a University: Institutes and Organisations. Moscow: State University–Higher School of Economics, pp. 48–77 (in Russian).

Chapter 13
Germany: The Role of Universities in the Learning Economy

Ulrich Schmoch

13.1   Introduction to the German Context

Germany as a nation has its roots in the eight century; originally the term "German" only referred to the language in the eastern part of the realm of Franconia. Since that time, Germany existed in various configurations, partly as a kingdom, partly as an empire. In all of these political structures, Germany consisted of a variety of smaller states with a high level of autonomy, which is the basis for the strong federal system shaping the present political situation. The state of Prussia developed into a dominant central power in the eighteenth century and established a stable German realm (Deutsches Reich) in the period of 1871–1918. The strong position of Prussia had a high impact on the political and cultural orientation of Germany in general.

The nineteenth century was also a period of considerable industrial and economic growth, in parallel triggering the considerable strengthening of the education and science system.[1] This extremely prosperous period was terminated by the First World War in 1914. In 1918, the German Reich was followed by the so-called Republic of Weimar, which was characterized by enormous political instability. The major reason for this unstable situation was the permanent economic crisis, which favored the empowerment of Hitler and the establishment of National Socialism. This chapter is not appropriate to discuss all the disastrous problems linked to this regime; but in the context of the development of science in Germany, the expulsion of intellectuals and leading scientists has to be explicitly mentioned.

The Second World War initiated by Hitler led to the severe destruction of many industrial enterprises, causing enormous economic problems. A further consequence was the separation of Germany into the Federal Republic of Germany (West Germany), under the auspices of the Western allied countries France, the UK, and

---

[1] For a detailed description of this period, see Keck (1993).

U. Schmoch (✉)
Fraunhofer Institute for Systems and Innovation Research, Karlsruhe, Germany
e-mail: ulrich.schmoch@isi.fraunhofer.de

B. Göransson and C. Brundenius (eds.), *Universities in Transition:*
The Changing Role and Challenges for Academic Institutions,
© International Development Research Centre 2011

USA, and the German Democratic Republic (East Germany), under the auspices of the Soviet Union. West Germany was integrated into the Western alliance by an association to the NATO in 1963 and more importantly, with the European Economic Association in 1957, later on the European Economic Community and the European Union.

In West Germany, the 1960s were characterized by enormous economic growth, the so-called economic miracle, which turned Germany into the most important economic power in Europe. The most relevant political event after the Second World War was the reunification of Germany in 1990. This enlargement of German territory and population additionally strengthened Germany economic and political weight. In 1991, West Germany including West Berlin had a population of 64.5 million inhabitants and East Germany including East Berlin 15.8 million inhabitants; thus the share of the East German population was 19.7%. At the same time, the costs for the economic and social integration of East Germany proved to be enormous, and even today the financial flows from West to East Germany are considerable; the social and economic balance between East and West Germany has not been achieved yet and will need a further decade at least.

However, German unification is only one reason for the economic problems in Germany; first signs of stagnation already became visible in the 1980s. These problems may be documented by a variety of economic indicators, but they are well illustrated by the growth of unemployment. In long time series, since the beginning of the 1950s, the number of unemployed people after the Second World War had a level of about two million and steadily decreased until the very low level of 150,000 by the middle of the 1960s. By the end of the 1980s, the number went back to about two million unemployed. After the unification, unemployment increased up to a level of 4.5 million in 2004 and in recent years, it even increased up to five million. Besides all methodological insufficiencies in the interpretation of unemployment data, the general economic problems of Germany became visible in recent years. The major reasons for this development are

- German unification in 1990;
- the challenges of globalization, in particular the movement of low-tech industries toward countries with lower wages;
- the insufficient move of German industry toward leading-edge technology;
- the inflexibility of the German labor market; and
- the crisis of the social security system.

German industry has a traditional focus on mechanical engineering and basic materials chemistry, and both may qualify as high-level technology. In contrast, German industry has no special focus on microelectronics, information technology, fine chemistry, or biotechnology, which may be qualified as leading-edge technology.[2] The comparison with other industrialized countries shows that countries with a

---

[2] As to the definitions of high-level technology and leading-edge technology, see Legler et al. (2006: 7).

stronger focus on leading-edge technology are more successful in the world market. Therefore, Germany must move toward other industrial sectors in order to maintain competitiveness. At present, the most important sector with a high R&D level is the automotive industry with an increasing focus on leading-edge technology, for instance, in the context of automotive electronics or advanced materials.

In principle, the German economy may be qualified as capitalistic, but in the prosperous period of the 1960s, the concept of social market economy was introduced. It is characterized by a high level of social security with regard to unemployment, health risks, and retirement pensions. This concept implied a high level of social welfare and security,[3] and it is maintained until today, although the financial basis is being eroded by the increasing number of unemployed and retired persons and a decreasing number of employed people financing the social security system. As the crisis of the social security system is largely linked to the general economic problems, it seems to be foremost a consequence than a reason of the economic crisis. However, a further cause of the crisis of the social security system is the low birth rate and linked to that the increasing imbalance between young and old people.

Beside these obvious economic problems, it has to be stated that the economic power of Germany is still considerable. In 2002, Germany had 82.5 million inhabitants and a gross domestic product of $1,984 billion; therefore Germany is, in economic terms, the most important country in the European Union and also the largest in terms of population. To summarize, in the last two decades, Germany's economy was less dynamic than that of other countries, a development which is documented in the moderate average growth rate of the gross domestic product of 1.6% between 1990 and 2002 (Albrecht et al. 2004). Therefore, the relative position with reference to other industrialized countries became weaker, but Germany is still one of the largest economies worldwide and ranks in fifth position behind USA, the Peoples' Republic of China, Japan, and India.[4] The rank of India and China before Germany is not only a new phenomenon and means an important challenge, but also a big opportunity for the German economy, which has a distinct focus on exports.

13.2 The Position of Academic Institutions in the German National System of Innovation

As described in Sect. 13.1, the situation in Germany has been characterized by economic growth since the 1960s, and in parallel, a tremendous increase in the R&D budgets of enterprises, universities, and other research institutes can be observed as well (Fig. 13.1). As the depiction in Fig. 13.1 is dominated by the enterprises, the situation for universities is separately illustrated in Fig. 13.2, which

---

[3] Linked to that, the level of criminality is quite low.

[4] Calculated in purchasing power parities (http://de.wikipedia.org).

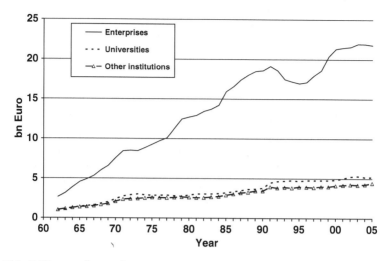

Fig. 13.1 R&D expenditures of major organizational sectors in Germany (in real terms). *Source*: BMBF (2000, 2004, 2006, 2008), BMFT (1993), own computation

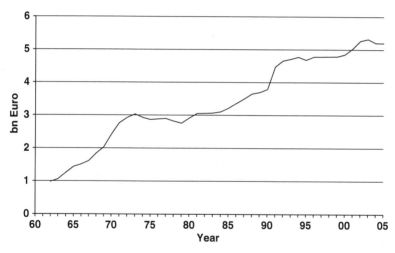

Fig. 13.2 R&D expenditure of German universities (in real terms). *Sources*: BMBF (2000, 2004, 2006, 2008), BMFT (1993), own computation

documents their steadily increasing R&D budget.[5] The sharp increase between 1991 and 1992 is striking; it is linked to the fact that until 1991, only the universities of West Germany were considered, and after the German unification, the universities of East Germany have been included since 1992.

---

[5] Only in the last documented year, a slight decrease appears due to decline of external funding from industry.

The impact of German unification on universities is less important than often assumed. The share of the East German population at the beginning of the 1990s was about 20%, and the number of East German students was only at a level of about 10% (IW 2006). In 1991, the share of East German scientific publications was about 12%, which declined to 9% in 1993 and increased to 18% in 2001 (Legler et al. 2004). So the level of university activity in terms of education and research in the new Eastern States was moderate at the time of unification and has considerably improved since then. As to scientific quality, German unification implied a distinct drop in the German citation rates (Schmoch 2005). This is partly linked to a limited scientific impact of East German papers, but primarily due to their insufficient orientation toward Western journals. Meanwhile, the citation rates of 1990 have been attained again. All in all, the efforts to integrate East German universities were considerable, but the process of increasing the number of students and of reaching a high level of scientific output in terms of quantity and quality has been success-fully accomplished. The general aim to equal the structures in East and West Germany has been largely attained in the field of science.

As to the contribution of universities to the German economy, the main contribution is the provision of a competent labor force. So in the 1960s and 1970s, teaching was far more important than research with regard to economic growth. With the rise of the knowledge-intensive economy, illustrated in the growing relevance of R&D, the con-tribution of university research to economic performance becomes more relevant, but teaching still remains the most important element, in particular in the disciplines of engineering and natural sciences (Salter and Martin 2001). The German university system is multifacetted and consists of different types of high-level education institu-tions. One important type is the (full) universities with a broad spectrum of disciplines, all in all 100 universities where 35 operate their own clinics (Table 13.1). However, people generally do not consider the offer of clinical facilities as the most important contribution of universities to society, as many other public and private institutions run clinics as well. So the major contribution of universities in the medical sector is the development and application of advanced medical treatments.

Table 13.1 Number of different types of high-level education institutions in Germany

Institution	Number
Universities thereof	100
with clinics	35
with engineering dpts.	17
Pedagogical schools	6
Theological schools	16
Art schools	52
Polytechnical schools	168
Administration schools	29
Total	*371*

Source: Hochschulrektorenkonferenz (HRK)

Seventeen universities run engineering departments. These universities, sometimes called technical universities, originally were pure engineering high-level schools, but increasingly integrated other disciplines and achieved the status of university. But in most cases, the engineering departments are still dominant. Already in 1899, the technical universities obtained the right to assign doctorates in engineering, and thus were acknowledged as academic institutions (Manegold 1978).

Of the 100 universities, 13 are organized by private agencies, but these universities still play a minor role, as they teach only about 0.54% of all students at all universities and they are not engaged in research. In most cases, the private universities are focused on few disciplines, primarily in economics. The low level of private universities is linked to the public policy to provide university education at a high level of quality without tuition fees. With the increasing scarcity of public money, many federal states are going to introduce tuition fees, but still at a moderate level in comparison with private universities.

In addition to universities, 6 pedagogical schools, 16 theological schools with parochial agencies, 52 art schools, and 29 administrative schools can be counted among the high-level education institutions in Germany. With regard to their contribution to the economic needs of society, the 168 polytechnical schools, sometimes called polytechnics, polytechnical, or universities of applied science,[6] have to be mentioned as relevant actors. Compared with full universities, their courses are less theoretical and more oriented toward application. The average length of the course of studies at polytechnical schools is about 3 years, compared with 5–6 years at universities. With reference to public agencies, the number of students in polytechnical schools represents about one-third of those in full universities. The polytechnical schools are strongly oriented to teaching; their contribution to research is negligible.

For an improved understanding of the size of the German higher education system, it is useful to look in to further detail at the number of students. In 2004, 1.9 million students were registered at German high-level institutions, thereof 1.4 million at universities. So with reference to the population, 23.8 students per 1,000 inhabitants were registered, thereof 16.6 at universities and 7.2 at other institutions. This means that on average, a university has about 13,700 students, and other institutions about 2,200.

Since the beginning of the 1970s, enormous efforts were undertaken to increase the number of students. At universities, 410,000 students were registered in 1970, 1,188,000 in 1990.[7] Therefore, within 20 years, the number of students has increased by a factor of 2.9. In 2000, the number of students was a little bit higher, at 1,311,000, but this difference is primarily due to the inclusion of East Germany. In 2004, about 220,000 students successfully passed their final examinations; thereof about 98,000 achieved university diploma or master's degrees and 23,000 doctoral degrees.

The present structure of research at (full) universities is characterized by large shares of disciplines relevant for technological application, in particular natural sciences, engineering, medicine, and to a lesser extent, agriculture (Fig. 13.3).

---

[6] In German: Fachhochschulen.

[7] With reference to West Germany (IW 2006).

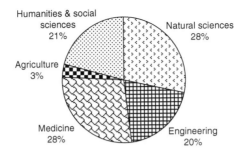

Fig. 13.3 Research expenditure at German universities by disciplinary field, 2006. *Source*: StaBu Fachserie 11 Reihe 4 3 2 (2009)

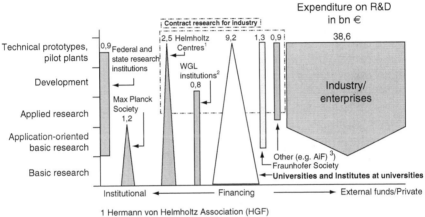

1 Hermann von Helmholtz Association (HGF)
2 Science Association Gottfried Wilhelm Leibniz (WGL)
3 Federation of Industrial Research Associations 'Otto von Guericke' e.V.

Fig. 13.4 Depiction of the German research landscape, 2005. *Source*: Fraunhofer ISI, BMBF (2008)

However, the share of about 20% of the humanities and social sciences is quite high by comparison to other industrialized countries.

In the German research landscape, the universities are only one among a broad variety of public research organizations and private industrial enterprises. The tremendous increase in the R&D budgets of the universities since the 1960s also applies to other research institutions (Fig. 13.1), in particular the enormous growth of the R&D activities of firms is striking, but a high share of their activities refers to experimental development. Nevertheless, firms represent the largest organizational sector in research. With the growing relevance of knowledge-based technologies, German firms substantially engaged in knowledge production and developed a considerable absorptive capacity and thus became appropriate partners for universities.

Among the research institutions with public agencies, the universities are only one of a broad variety of other research organizations. Among them, the most important ones are the Helmholtz Centers, the Max Planck Society, and the Fraunhofer Society (Fig. 13.4). All public nonuniversity organizations taken together represent about 80% of the university research. Thus, there is also an explicit competition within the public research sector between universities and nonuniversity institutions (Heinze and Kuhlmann 2006). The high share of nonuniversity institutions is again based on the division of labor between central government and the federal states. On the one hand, the federal states are responsible for the basic funding of universities; the central government strives to get a high relevance in research by supporting nonuniversity institutions. In consequence, the nonuniversity institutions are primarily financed by the central government.

As to their general orientation, the Max Planck institutes are engaged in excellent basic research and primarily rely on institutional funding.[8] The main areas of Max Planck institutes are physics, biology, and chemistry, but there is also a relevant share of the humanities and social sciences. In general, the mission of Max Planck institutes is to conduct forefront research in important or strategic fields of science with an adequate concentration of personnel and equipment; to enter newly emerging fields quickly, especially those outside the mainstream, or fields that cannot be covered sufficiently at the universities; and to conduct research that requires special or large equipment or research that is so costly that it cannot be undertaken at universities. Some of the leading researchers of Max Planck also teach part-time at universities, but the general focus of Max Planck institutes is on research. Due to this general orientation, the Max Planck institutes are able to perform better than universities, for instance, in terms of publications per researcher. An indicator for the excellent performance of Max Planck institutes is that most German Nobel Prize winners are from Max Planck institutes.

Although the Max Planck institutes are focused on basic research, their activities increasingly provide results that are useful for industrial application, for instance in the fields of chemistry or biotechnology. Therefore, the Max Planck Society has established a specific office to apply for patents related to inventions of their researchers and in particular to look for appropriate license partners. This patent and license institution called Garching Innovation was established in 1970. In Germany, it is acknowledged as the most professional institution for the transfer of public research results to private partners. In the last years, Garching Innovation has also been engaged in supporting the establishment of start-up companies in addition to their patent and licensing activities.

The Fraunhofer Society has a distinct orientation toward applied research and is primarily financed by external funds, in particular from industrial enterprises. The Fraunhofer Societys mission is the distinct counterpart of that of the Max Planck Society. The Fraunhofer Society was founded in 1949, but it was not until 1973 that it obtained its present role. The decision to strengthen the Fraunhofer Society has to be seen in the context of the intense discussions that were taking place at that time about the technological gap between Europe and USA, and the more active technology policy being implemented by the German federal government (Schimank 1990).

---

[8] The following description of German nonuniversity institutions is largely based on Encarnação and Schmoch (1997: 302 ff).

Nearly all of the 58 Fraunhofer institutes have a specific technical focus covering the areas of information and communication technology, life sciences, microelectronics, surface technology and photonics, production, and materials. The major transfer mechanism of Fraunhofer research results to industry is contract research, which represents about 40% of the Fraunhofer activities. However, the Fraunhofer model could not exist in an isolated way; the research activities are closely related to those of other research institutions, in particular universities. The main element of such relationships is the joint appointment of a full professor as director of a Fraunhofer institute and to a university chair. At the university, the Fraunhofer director can carry out basic research funded by institutional funds of the university, and he is in close contact with other academic researchers. At the same time, the university gets acquainted with the needs of applied research, as the Fraunhofer director is a member of the faculty and can directly influence its research policy. A further important element of this close relationship to universities is the direct access of Fraunhofer institutes to qualified students.

In relation to its number of researchers, the rate of Fraunhofer publications is low compared with that of Max Planck researchers, whereas the number of patent applications is high. Again, this structure reflects the opposite missions of Fraunhofer and Max Planck. In recent years, the support of start-ups of former Fraunhofer researchers is becoming a more relevant mechanism of technology transfer, as well as the licensing of Fraunhofer's patent applications and know-how related to software.

The first Helmholtz centers were founded in the late 1950s, when the allied forces gave Germany permission to perform nuclear research; at that time, they were called large research centers (Grossforschungseinrichtungen). Following the pattern of US and British national laboratories, all Helmholtz centers initially worked in various areas of civil nuclear research. Since the late 1960s, other areas of research have been added, such as aeronautics, computer science, and biotechnology. It is not possible to describe the research orientation of Helmholtz in terms of simple categories such as basic or applied. Their activities include

- basic research requiring large research facilities;
- large projects and programs of public interest, requiring extraordinary financial, technical, and interdisciplinary scientific resources and management capacities; and
- long-term technology development, including preindustrial fabrication.

In the 1980s, the focus on civilian nuclear research was abandoned, so that in present times, only a limited share of the Helmholtz activities are still linked to that field. Therefore, the mission of the Helmholtz Association is less clear than that of the Max Planck Society and the Fraunhofer Society. In recent years, a move toward a stronger focus on basic research can be observed, but the debate on the role of the Helmholtz centers within the German research landscape is not terminated.

Against this institutional background, the universities have to define their specific role within this differentiated research landscape. Their major mission is still the education of highly qualified students and the conduct of basic research, but in recent years technology transfer was added as third mission into the university law (Hochschulrahmengesetz).

13.3   Mapping the Academic System in Germany

The historic roots of the present university system in Germany trace back to the founding of the Berlin University in 1809/1810 which was located in Prussia. Due to the prominent role of Prussia in the foundation of Germany, as described in Sect. 13.1, the concept of the Berlin University became the paradigm for the universities in Germany in general. The model of the Berlin University was conceived by German idealist philosophers, in particular Wilhelm von Humboldt, and is therefore often called Humboldt University (Keck 1993: 108). The "classic order of knowledge" according to Humboldt's ideal can be described by four elements of the "constitution of science," which may be characterized as institutional decoupling of science by four major separations:

- "Separation of cognition and property
- Separation of ideas and interest
- Separation of theory and practice and
- Separation of science and state" (Spinner 1994: 87ff).[9]

These separations were introduced to permit independent research activities by universities without the government or private enterprises exerting influence. This concept induced a distinct orientation of universities toward the generation of pure knowledge and thus toward basic research. Humboldt's concept was revolutionary in the context of that time which was characterized by a strong central government which tried to control nearly everything. This general orientation of universities in Germany persisted until the 1960s and then partly eroded, due to the growing relevance of knowledge-based technologies. This change is visible in the position of the universities in the depiction of the German research landscape according to Fig. 13.4 where they are positioned in the middle of the diagram; this means that their activities are no longer based exclusively on institutional funding.[10] Furthermore, the orientation of university research is still focused on pure basic research and application-oriented basic research, but there are also relevant activities in applied research and even development. A decade ago, the universities were still located more on the left side of the diagram with a stronger focus on basic research.

In the funding system of public research in Germany, the federal states (Länder) provide base funds for the universities and these are used both for teaching and research without a clear budgetary separation. Up to now, most universities have not established an accounting system that would allow for a clear distinction of the activities on which these base funds are spent. As a consequence, all available statistics on university research are based on estimates.[11] Despite these restrictions, some statements about the structures of German universities are possible. The total

---

[9] Translation by the author.

[10] The new funding structure is explained further below.

[11] As a further problem, the statistics from universities are not available for recent years and stem from different, not completely consistent sources.

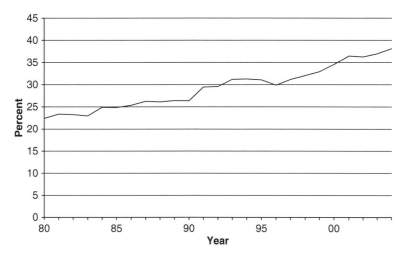

Fig. 13.5 Share of external funds within the R&D budget of universities (data for 2004 projected). *Sources*: BMBF (2006), BMFT (1993), HRK (1996), WR (1993, 2000b, 2002), Encarnação/Schmoch

expenditures of the higher education institutions for education and research are estimated at about € 20.2 bn for 2002; about 44% of these expenditures, thus about € 9.0 bn, were spent for research and development. Within the university budget, external funds play an important role; they are primarily used for R&D activities. The share of external funds tremendously increased since the beginning of the 1980s and in particular during the 1990s. The absolute level of base funds decreased in real terms in the last decade, in particular since about 1997; in the "old" western states, the stagnation of base funds began even in 1996. Against this background, the increase of the total R&D budget, depicted in Fig. 13.2, is due to the growing relevance of external funds. The share of external funds within the total R&D budget rose from 22% in 1980 to 38% in 2004 (Fig. 13.5), and it can be assumed that this share is presently more than 40%. This figure is an average value for all disciplines, so that in some disciplines in the natural and engineering sciences, it is even distinctly above 50% (Haug and Hetmeier 2003: 56 ff). In consequence, the R&D activities of many disciplines heavily rely on external funding.

According to statistics on the sources of external funds (third-party funds), the largest share is provided by the German Research Association (Deutsche Forschungsgemeinschaft, DFG) (Fig. 13.6). The German Research Association is a government agency which is primarily oriented to supporting research at universities with a focus on basic research. But in recent years, an increasing share of DFG-funded research projects is linked to application. At the third position of external funding of universities is the federal government, in most cases represented by the Ministry for Education and Research (Bundesministerium für Bildung und Forschung, BMBF). Whereas the topics of DFG-financed projects can be suggested by the professors themselves, projects of the BMBF are generally linked to specific

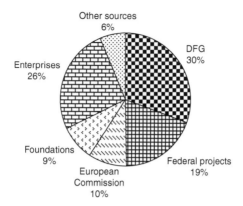

Fig. 13.6 Sources of external funds of German universities, 2006. *Source*: StaBu (2009)

programs, and most projects are linked to collaborative research with industrial enterprises (Verbundforschung), an activity which was introduced in 1984. The projects of BMBF are generally quite application oriented, but they also sometimes support basic research projects.

The contribution of enterprises to the external funding of university research is at the second position and is almost equivalent to that of DFG. The share of funding of the European Commission with reference to the total research budget is still modest, but for some fields such as microelectronics, biotechnology, or materials sciences, its significance is very high. As a general trend, the share of funding by enterprises and by the European Commission is steadily growing. The external funding by foundations primarily comes from the *Volkswagenstiftung*, which mostly promotes basic research similar to the orientation of the German Research Association (DFG).

The increasing importance of external funding at universities implies an organization of research in the form of projects with a definite length and deliverables. In the case of projects on behalf of BMBF, enterprises, or the European Commission, the orientation toward application purposes gets more importance, and the universities are no longer free in the choice of their research topics. They have only the alternative to participate or not to participate in such projects, but in view of decreasing basic funds, they must engage in these projects to a certain extent. This implies that Humboldt's ideal of the clear separation of ideas and interests, of theory and practice, and of science and state is only partly maintained. The growing dependence on external funds implies that the competition between universities for external funds is a major characteristic of the situation in recent years.

The performance of universities is increasingly assessed by their contribution to technology, a requirement that is directly reflected in the steady growth in the number of patents generated by universities (Fig. 13.7). The substantial decrease of patent applications in 2001 is linked to the crisis of the New Economy at that time, in particular in high-technology sectors, and the decrease in 2002 to a new organizational

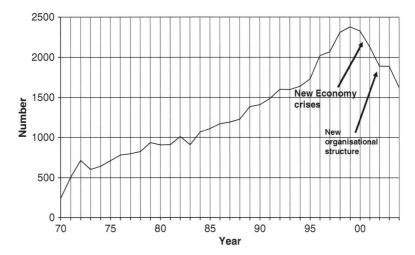

Fig. 13.7 Patent applications of German universities at the German Patent and Trademark Office (Deutsches Patent- und Markenamt, DPMA). *Source*: Database PATDPA (STN), computation by Fraunhofer ISI

structure of the transfer units at universities. Although a further decrease in 2004 can be observed, there are clear indications that patent applications by universities will rise again in the next years after a modification to the new organizational structure.

The change in the organization of intellectual property issues at universities is linked to a change in the law. Since the end of the 1950s, professors had the privilege to exploit inventions generated in the context of their university research for their private benefit. In contrast, inventors in private enterprises have to notify their inventions to their enterprise, and then the enterprise decides whether it intends to exploit the invention and apply for a patent for it. The special regulation for university professors was introduced with the assumption that the number of university-based inventions was negligible, so it was not necessary to introduce a special organizational structure for this purpose. Meanwhile, the number of patent applications of university origin rose to a level of more than 2,000 applications per year, and the need for a new legal regulation became obvious. Therefore, the so-called professors' privilege was abolished at the beginning of 2002, and now the professors have to notify the universities of their inventions, similar to the situation in private enterprises. However, the application of patents, the identification of potential license partners, and the negotiation of appropriate license agreements require substantial expertise and therefore each federal state established at least one transfer unit (Patentverwertungsagentur, PVA), and these units are partly supported by the federal government. The introduction of PVAs was a necessary step to take the financial risk of patent applications and to identify appropriate license partners, so that the professors can be relieved of these time-consuming activities and can focus on their main duties in education and research. However, the establishment of the transfer units is still in a transition period.

The direct contribution of universities to technology as reflected in patent activities does not cover all technology areas, but it is focused on knowledge-intensive ones. Most of the patent applications have a disciplinary background in chemistry and mechanical engineering. The institutional basis of this focus is a specific strength of German industry in these sectors. In addition, universities provide patent applications in electrical engineering and in medicine at medium level, and in physics at a low level. On an average, the contribution of universities to the German domestic patent applications is at a level of about 4.5% (Schmoch 2004). This share is not very high, but in relation to the primary orientation of universities to basic research, it is substantial. When the focus is directed to specific knowledge-intensive technologies such as biotechnology, semiconductors, organic chemistry, materials, control, surface technology, medical technology, or polymers, the share is substantially higher, with a level between 10 and 30%, whereas in low-tech fields, the contribution of universities is negligible. So universities fulfill their primary mission to engage in complex research.

The application-oriented research activities of universities have to be assessed within the broader framework of industrial activities in Germany. As described in Sect. 13.1, German industry is focused on high-level technology and in the next years, it will have to effect a change in the direction of leading-edge technology. Therefore, the German government strives to increase industrial activities in leading-edge products and thus supports R&D activities. In this context, universities are expected to play a substantial role.

The increasing societal expectations that universities should actively engage in knowledge and technology transfer lead to corresponding political expectations. Therefore, a clear trend in favor of short-term results is visible, whereas long-term research is increasingly neglected. Many political actors have an insufficient understanding of the university focus on complex areas and, hence, are not aware that this contribution of universities to low and medium technology will be and should be moderate. Furthermore, the user needs are often insufficiently differentiated. Many small and medium-sized enterprises need technology solutions at a low and medium level; for these purposes, universities are not the appropriate partners (Meyer-Krahmer 2000). With regard to the more applied needs of small and medium-sized enterprises, Fraunhofer institutes are often the more appropriate partners compared with universities. Furthermore, the polytechnical schools with their distinct focus on applied topics should play a more important role, but still the infrastructure in terms of staff and technical equipment is insufficient for these purposes. However, some federal states have started initiatives to strengthen the role of polytechnical schools in technology transfer to small and medium-sized enterprises (Kulicke et al. 2004).[12]

---

[12] The state Baden-Württemberg, the so-called Steinbeis Foundation, has established an effective network with institutes of polytechnical school to support technology transfer.

13.4 The Current German Debate

The current German debate on universities is decisively influenced by the increasing scarcity of public funds in general and in particular public funds for research. Therefore, Humboldt's ideal of complete freedom of research is no longer maintained in strict terms, but the question of an effective use of public money for research gets more attention where the term "effective" is often linked to "economically useful and profitable."[13] In this context, a relevant arena for debate is a criticism, in recent years, of the performance and flexibility of research at universities (Schimank 2001; Krucken 2001; Wissenschaftsrat 2000a; Krull 2005). In particular, universities are blamed for distributing their funds in an egalitarian way and not on the basis of performance criteria, and hence, cannot build up clear profiles. In the previous decades, it was an explicit target of education policy that all universities should provide high-level education in all disciplines, so that the quality level in all universities was largely similar. This basic orientation of the German university system is the direct opposite of the US model, which is characterized by some outstanding universities and a large number of low-level universities, often without own research activities.

In the context of demand for an improved performance and flexibility of the universities, "new public management" (NPM) has become a key word since the 1980s (Schimank 2005). NPM is characterized by the call for more market orientation, less regulation, and strong leadership. "The 'traditional' German university was once described … as a combination of political regulation by the state and professional self-control by an 'academic oligarchy'" (Schimank 2005: 363). So the traditional organization of German universities is largely the opposite of the NPM model. As a consequence of this debate, Germany is going to introduce assessment activities similar to the research assessment exercise (RAE) in the UK. For instance, the German Research Association has established an Institute for Research Information and Quality Assurance (Institut für Forschungsinformation und Qualitätssicherung, IFQ), which is supposed to assess all German public research institutions in about 5 years. In parallel, the German Research Council (Wissenschaftsrat) is starting a rating activity referring to disciplines with the aim to cover all relevant disciplines within the next 5 years. Many states and universities collect performance indicators with the aim to link the level of base funds to performance (Leszczensky and Orr 2004). However, the impact of these measures on the base funds is still limited, so that from the perspective of the universities, the acquisition of external funds is more relevant.

As a recent trend, the universities are achieving increasing autonomy in the use of their financial resources, staff recruitment – including professors, and their organizational structures. This transfer of responsibilities from the federal states to the presidents of the universities is still an ongoing process, which has been accomplished to varying degrees in different states. It implies a new distribution of power

---

[13] Archibugi (2006) characterizes this trend as "neoliberal revolution."

within the universities, with higher clout for the president and his or her central administration to the disadvantage of the committees of professors. On the one hand, a stronger central administration means stronger units can be strengthened and weaker units can be straightened out or even shut down to achieve a clearer profile; on the other hand, the central administration needs improved access to reliable information on the performance of the multiple units of the university. This is one reason for the growing relevance of the various assessment exercises mentioned above. It is obvious that there is an internal opposition to these new structures, and it will take several years until a new appropriate balance of power is achieved.[14]

As to the situation at full universities, the requirement of an effective knowledge transfer increasingly comes into conflict with the legacy of organizational structures of a public institution, characterized by low flexibility and long response times to external demands. As a reaction, many technology transfer activities are not organized directly in the university, but in its close environment, for instance in private firms of professors or as public associations or foundations (Bierhals and Schmoch 2000; Schmoch 2003). One relevant form of these external activities is the so-called An-Institute which is a research center located near the university, but which is legally independent of the university. Based on cooperation agreements with the university, the director of an An-Institute is in parallel a part-time professor at the university. The An-Institutes generally get base funds from the federal states where they are located, but they have to acquire the majority of their funds from external sources, similar to Fraunhofer institutes. As a rough estimate, the activities of An-Institutes in technology-related areas have a volume of about one-third of all Fraunhofer institutes combined, but it is impossible to enumerate the technology transfer activities in the environment of the universities in a more precise way, due to the broad variety of organizational types and transfer mechanisms (Bierhals and Schmoch 2000). As a reaction to this trend, the universities try to build up new internal organization structures in order to achieve a higher visibility in transfer. This change toward more effective and flexible organization units will have an impact on the university system in general.

In the context of the economic problems, public awareness for supporting innovation is increasing. Against this background, many activities at the central government and in particular at the state level are being undertaken to support technology transfer from universities to industry. In this context, science parks are established or initiatives have started to create competence clusters with networks of universities and enterprises in specific technology areas.

A further relevant novelty is an agreement between the central government and the federal states to provide additional research funds to excellent universities (Elite-Universitäten) selected in a specific competition. One effect of the ongoing selection procedure seems to be that the participating universities introduce new

---

[14] In the context of this debate, a research group examining the governance of research recently published a set of theses on the "framework of capable publicly financed research" in Germany (Forschergruppe 2007).

organizational structures, implying the establishment of clearer profiles and more flexible organizational units. So the deep-rooted resistance to reforms for many decades (Schimank 1995) may be broken up due to the prospect of gaining substantial additional funds.

To summarize, there is a trend toward assessing universities too one-sidedly, only by their success in technology transfer. In the long run, the specific role of universities in basic research has to be adequately acknowledged. With regard to economic roles, a reform of teaching seems to be more relevant, as it has to be taken into account that a large share of the graduates will not work in scientific organizations, but in enterprises. With this in mind, teaching in many disciplines can be improved considerably. Recent studies show that in about 10 years, economic development in Germany may be substantially hampered by a scarcity of skilled staff, in particular of university graduates in the natural sciences and engineering (BMBF 2005, 2006). From this perspective, higher quality of teaching, implying a higher success rate of students, may be more crucial than more effective technology transfer. Furthermore, it will be necessary to attract a higher share of female students in the natural and engineering sciences. However, the debate on the scarcity of skilled staff is still only beginning.

Finally, the universities have to take care of the reputation of the nontechnical disciplines and show their relevance to society. If they are not successful in this regard, the share of these disciplines will steadily decrease.

A very topical debate concerns the shortage of highly skilled labor force, in particular engineers. Although the focus of the German industry is still on high-level technology (see Sect. 13.1 above), a steady increase of the academics in all sectors of the economy can be observed, linked to the increasing complexity of technologies and services (EFI 2008: 98 f; Leszczensky et al. 2008). At the same time, the share of people with a university degree in Germany is quite low compared with that in other industrialized countries (OECD 2007), and the number of students is decreasing due to low birth rates and an aging society. Already in the present situation, various enterprises have to limit their production due to a shortage of engineers, in particular in mechanical engineering. Against this background, a recent study forecasts a cumulated shortage of 95,000 engineers and 397,000 other academics by the year 2014, assuming an average annual growth of the economy of 2.5% (BMBF 2007). Due to this shortage of highly skilled labor force, many enterprises may decide to move toward other countries with better human resources. This debate increasingly draws the attention to the first mission of the universities, i.e., teaching, and thus the provision of well-educated academics. In detail, the following measures are suggested to cope with this problem:

- Improvement of school education with the aim to increase the share of pupils with an option for university education;
- Reduction of the social divide to improve the access to higher education for children of less wealthy;
- Improvement of the conditions for women to achieve academic degrees in engineering and work in enterprises; and

- Improvement of the attractiveness for highly skilled people from foreign countries to work in Germany (EFI 2008: 36 ff).

The last point may be qualified as a new type of imperialism. In any case, it clearly shows that the availability of highly skilled labor force will be increasingly relevant and that there will be a growing-related competition between countries at all stages of economic development.

13.5   Conclusions

From a more general perspective, the present situation in Germany can be termed as a period of transition. This refers to a transition from abundance to scarcity, a situation that is not accepted by the society. Individuals notice that, for instance, the purchasing power of private households has steadily been reducing during the last decade, but they still try to keep the old standards in all areas of life. This implies that necessary reforms for adapting to the new structures in the context of globalization and the aging society will be introduced, but quite slowly. Many experts see a faster downward spiral, as the necessary reforms are introduced too late. On the contrary, the strengths of Germany are still considerable, so that a restabilization is probable, but perhaps at a lower level. Among these strengths, the high quality and competences of the labor force, the high level of industrial innovation, as, for instance, reflected in patent activities, and the excellent infrastructure have to be mentioned. Although large parts of the German economy are still focused on high-level technology, an increasing number of firms are successful in leading-edge technology as well.

With regard to universities, the consequences of this transition are reflected in different aspects that are sometimes contradictory. The first consequence is the reduced availability of funding for scientific research, and the universities try to maintain the previous level of funding through an increasing acquisition of external funds. Although not all possibilities for external funding have been totally exploited yet, there will be an upper limit, so that the universities have to cope with restricted resources even more than the present situation.

At the same time, policy makers and scientific organizations try to enhance the efficiency of scientific research through organizational reforms, the introduction of new incentive structures, and regular assessments of institutions and research groups. In this regard, Germany is still at an early stage compared with other countries such as the UK, the Netherlands, or Australia, and it is likely that the German universities have a long way to go until a new structure is established. Presently, the strong focus of the evaluation exercises on scientific excellence in basic research does not adequately consider the broad spectrum of activities in the context of research and the division of labor between different research groups and research institutions.

A second aspect of the transition period is the increased call for knowledge and technology transfer activities. In principle, universities have to play a relevant role in the restructuring of the German economy toward leading-edge technologies and knowledge-intensive services. Although the mechanisms and structures for knowledge and technology transfer from universities can be improved in various aspects, the contribution of universities to technology is already quite high presently (Schmoch 2000). A key problem in this context is the potential conflict between the requirement for excellent basic research and increased technology transfer. In any case, there is an ongoing debate whether basic science and transfer activities are contradictory or not (cf. Van Looy et al. 2004). Whatsoever, we know some cases where professors actively engaged in technology transfer have to fulfill many different duties, encompassing the negotiations with companies, research, teaching, supervision of junior and senior researchers, etc., so that their regular duties in teaching are compromised. So the rating institutions have to think about improved evaluation models, where transfer activities are considered as equivalent to scientific excellence.

The orientation toward application implies a strong pressure on the universities to focus on the medical, natural, and engineering sciences and to reduce the social sciences and humanities in exchange. This erosion of the social sciences and humanities reflects the present public discourse with a focus on the economic prospects of Germany in the context of globalization. Other possible contributions of universities to society, for instance, with regard to ethics in life sciences or the orientation of human beings in a world with a high level of technology, or changing social structures in a context of increasing unemployment or higher relevance of non-German inhabitants, are relegated to the fringe.

A further relevant trend for universities is the progressing European unification that already has a high impact on standards of university teaching. At present, first activities in establishing common standards for assessing and comparing research performance can be observed. This change will enforce the trend toward regular assessment already described above.

The scarcity of public funds will lead to a broad introduction of tuition fees, but these fees will still be moderate compared with the fees at private universities. So there is no indication that private universities will achieve a substantial share in the German university system. They will be limited to few disciplines, and even there, they have to show their higher quality compared with that of the public universities.

Beyond all discussions about research and the third mission activities of universities, their crucial role in the education of highly skilled personnel will become more relevant.[15] At present, the responsible policy makers try to displace this topic, but in about 10 years the availability of highly skilled personnel will be visible as a crucial factor for the competitiveness of the German economy. In this context, universities have to think about a better didactic training of their personnel and an improved relation between students and teaching staff in order to raise the success rate of students. In addition, it will be necessary to attract more female students to

---

[15] In a similar way, Archibugi (2006) argues that in recent years, the emphasis of the knowledge transmission from universities to enterprises has been emphasized too extensively.

the fields of natural sciences and engineering, and finally, the attractiveness for foreign students has to be improved as well.

A recent relevant event for universities is the clearer division of labor between the central government and the federal states (Länder), wherein the *Länder* get the full responsibility for the universities. The consequences of these new structures are not clear yet. Some experts see a general improvement of teaching and research linked to the strengthened competition between the *Länder*; other experts complain about the increasing structural differences between the *Länder* with respect to the standards of teaching and research and see a reduced mobility of students and a growing gap between universities in poor and rich *Länder*. The supposable consequence may be that poor *Länder* reduce their teaching in engineering, as many of their graduates get jobs in large enterprises in rich *Länder*. Thus it will be necessary to find appropriate compensation mechanisms to ensure a sufficient provision of graduates in these disciplines.

A further consequence of the ongoing restructuring of the German university system will be the greater specialization of the universities in specific fields with an aim to get a clearer profile. The present ambition that all universities cover nearly all disciplines at a similar quality level cannot be maintained in the long run. Already now, some universities have already achieved a distinctly higher quality level of teaching and research (Friedmann et al. 2004; Wegner et al. 2004) and this development will move on. As to the structures in about 15 years, an extreme scenario may be the American university structure with a limited number of excellent universities and a high number of universities with a low teaching level and no research at all. Probably, this situation will not occur in Germany, but a more distinct differentiation will be established in any case.

Despite all turbulences in the present situation of restructuring, the role of universities will become more relevant already in a midterm perspective, as their adequate contribution to knowledge-based industries and services is crucial for the competitiveness of the German economy. In particular, in the context of the debate on the scarcity of highly skilled labor force, the first mission of the universities, i.e., teaching, will get a new impetus.

References

Albrecht, B. et al. (2004). Der Fischer Weltalmanach 2004. Zahlen, Daten, Fakten. Frankfurt a. M.: Fischer Taschenbuch Verlag.

Archibugi, D. (2006). In defense of public science. Contribution to the "Going Global Conference. The Challenges for Knowledge-based Economies" in Helsinki, Finland, September 21–22, 2006.

Bierhals, R., Schmoch, U. (2000). Wissens- und Technologietransfer an Universitäten, in: Schmoch, U., Licht, G., Reihard, M. (eds.), Wissens- und Technologietransfer in Deutschland. Stuttgart: Fraunhofer IRB Verlag, pp. 74–114.

Bundesministerium für Bildung und Forschung (BMBF) (2000). Bundesbericht Forschung 2000. Bonn: BMBF.

Bundesministerium für Bildung und Forschung (BMBF) (2004). Bundesbericht Forschung 2004. Berlin/Bonn: BMBF.

Bundesministerium für Bildung und Forschung (BMBF) (2005): Zur technologischen Leistungsfähigkeit Deutschlands 2005. Berlin/Bonn: BMBF.

Bundesministerium für Bildung und Forschung (BMBF) (2006). Forschung und Innovation in Deutschland. Berlin/Bonn: BMBF.

Bundesministerium für Bildung und Forschung (BMBF) (2007). Bericht zur technologischen Leistungsfähigkeit Deutschlands 2007. Berlin/Bonn: BMBF.

Bundesministerium für Bildung und Forschung (BMBF) (2008). Bundesbericht Forschung und Innovation 2008. Berlin/Bonn: BMBF.

Bundesministerium für Forschung und Technologie (BMFT) (1993). Bundesbericht Forschung 1993. Bonn: BMFT.

Encarnação, J., Schmoch, U. et al. (1997). Technology Transfer in Germany, in: Abramson, H.N., Encarnação, J. et al. (eds.), Technology Transfer Systems in the United States and Germany. Lessons and Perspectives. Washington, DC: National Academy Press, pp. 241–348.

Expertenkommission Forschung und Innovation (EFI) (2008). Gutachten zu Forschung, Innovation und technologischer Leistungsfähigkeit 2008. Berlin: EFI (accessible through www.e-fi.de).

Forschergruppe "Governance der Forschung" (2007). Forschungspolitische Thesen zu "Rahmenbedingungen für eine leistungsfähige öffentlich finanzierte Forschung", Berlin: FÖV.

Friedmann, J. et al. (2004). Die Elite von morgen, in: Spiegel, Vol. 48, pp. 178–200.

Haug, H.-F., Hetmeier, H.-W. (2003). Bericht zur finanziellen Lage der Hochschulen. Wiebaden: Statistisches Bundesamt.

Heinze, T., Kuhlmann, S. (2006). Analysis of heterogeneous collaboration in the German research system with a focus on nanotechnology, in: Jansen, D. (ed.), New Forms of Governance in Research Organizations. From Disciplinary Theories towards Interfaces and Integration, Heidelberg: Springer, forthcoming.

Hochschulrektorenkonferenz (HRK) (Hrsg.) (1996). Zur Finanzierung der Hochschulen. Dokumente zur Hochschulreform 110/1996. Bonn: Hochschulrektorenkonferenz.

Institut der deutschen Wirtschaft (IW) (ed.) (2006). Deutschland in Zahlen. Köln: Deutscher Instituts-Verlag.

Keck, O. (1993). The National System of Technical Innovation in Germany, in: Nelson, R.R. (ed.), National Innovation Systems. A Comparative Analysis. New York/Oxford: Oxford University Press, pp. 115–157.

Krücken, G. (2001). Wissenschaft im Wandel? Gegenwart und Zukunft der Forschung an deutschen Hochschulen. In: Stölting, E., Schimank, U. (eds.), Die Krise der Universitäten. Leviathan Sonderheft 20. Wiesbaden: Westdeutscher Verlag, pp. 326–345.

Krull, W. (2005). Eckpunkte eines zukunftsfähigen deutschen Wissenschaftssystems. Zwölf Empfehlungen. Hannover.

Kulicke, M., Stahlecker, T., Hemer, J., Wolf, B., Malcherek, A., Wranik, A., Hercher, A. (2004). Forschungslandkarte Fachhochschulen. Potenzialstudie. Berlin: BMBF.

Leszczcensky, M.; Robert Helmrich, R.; Frietsch, R. (2008). Bildung und Qualifikation als Grundlage der technologischen Leistungsfähigkeit Deutschlands. Studien zum deutschen Innovationssystem. Nr. 8-2008. Berlin: EFI (accessible through www.e-fi.de).

Legler, H., Gehrke, B., Schasse, U., Rammer, C., Schmoch, U. (2004). Innovationsindikatoren zur technologischen Leistungsfähigkeit der östlichen Bundesländer. Studien zum deutschen Innovationssystem Nr. 20-2004: Berlin: BMBF.

Legler, H., Rammer, C., Schmoch, U. (2006). Technological Performance – Concept and Practice, in: Schmoch, U., Rammer, C., Legler, H. (eds.), National Systems of Innovation in Comparison. Structure and Performance Indicators for Knowledge Societies. Dordrecht: Springer, pp. 3–14.

Leszczcensky, M., Orr, D. (2004). Staatliche Hochschulfinanzierung durch indikatorengestützte Mittelverteilung. Dokumentation und Analyse der Verfahren in 11 Bundesländern. Kurzinformation Hochschul-Informations-System A2/2004. Hannover.

Manegold, K.-H. (1978). Technology Academised. Education and Trainig of the Engineer in the Nineteenth Century, in: Krohn, W., Layton, E.T., Weingart, P. (eds.), The Dynamics of Science and Technlogy. Social Values, Technical Norms and Scientific Criteria in the Development of Knowledge. Dordrecht/Boston: R. Reidel Publishing Company, pp. 137–158.

Meyer-Krahmer, F. (2000). Vernetzung zwischen Wissenschaft und Wirtschaft – ihre Bedeutung für Wachstum und Beschäftigung, in: Stiftung Brandenburger Tor (ed.), Wissens- und Technologietransfer. Berlin: H&P Druck, pp. 18–27.

Salter, A.J., Martin, B.R. (2001). The economic benefits of publicly funded basic research: A critical review, in: Research Policy, Vol. 30 (3), pp. 509–532.

Schimank, U. (1995). Hochschulforschung im Schatten der Lehre. Frankfurt a. M.: Campus Verlag.

Schimank, U. (2001). Festgefahrene Gemischtwarenläden – Die deutschen Hochschulen als erfolgreich scheiternde Organisationen, in: Stölting, E., Schimank, U. (eds.), Die Krise der Universitäten. Leviathan Sonderheft 20. Wiesbaden: Westdeutscher Verlag, pp. 232–242.

Schimank, U. (2005). 'New public management' and the academic profession: Reflections on the German situation, in: Minerva, Vol. 43, pp. 361–376.

Schimank, U. (1990). Technology policy and technology transfer from state-financed research institutions to the economy: some German experiences, in: Science and Public Policy, pp. 219–228.

Schmoch, U. (2000). Abschließende Betrachtungen. in: Schmoch, U., Licht, G., Reihard, M. (eds.), Wissens- und Technologietransfer in Deutschland. Stuttgart: Fraunhofer IRB Verlag, pp. 423–429.

Schmoch, U. (2003). Hochschulforschung und Industrieforschung. Perspektiven der Interaktion. Frankfurt/M.: Campus Verlag.

Schmoch, U. (2004). The technological output of scientific institutions, in: Glänzel, W., Moed, H., Schmoch, U. (eds.), Handbook of Quantitative Science and Technology Research. The Use of Publication and Patent Statistics in Studies on R&D Systems. Dordrecht/Norwell/New York/London: Kluwer Academic Publishers, pp. 717–731.

Schmoch, U. (2005). Leistungsfähigkeit und Strukturen der Wissenschaft im internationalen Vergleich 2004. Studien zum deutschen Innovationssystem, Nr. 6-2005. Berlin: BMBF.

Spinner, H.F. (1994). Die Wissensordnung. Ein Leitkonzept für die dritte Grundordnung des Informationszeitalters. Opladen: Leske + Budrich.

Statistisches Bundesamt (StaBu) (2009). Various tables (Fachserien). Wiesbaden: Statistisches Bundesamt.

OECD (2007). Education at a Glance 2007. Paris: OECD.

Van Looy, B., Ranga, M., Callaert, J., Debackere, K., Zimmermann, E. (2004). Combining entrepreneurial and scientific performance in academia: Towards a compounded and reciprocal Matthew-effect?, in: Research Policy, Vol. 33 (3), pp. 425–441.

Wegner, J., Müller, B., Siefer, W., Weber, C. (2004). Die besten Universitäten, in: Focus, Vol. 39, pp. 110–120.

Wissenschaftsrat (WR) (1993). Drittmittel der Hochschulen 1970 bis 1990. Köln: WR.

Wissenschaftsrat (WR) (2000a). Thesen zur künftigen Entwicklung des Wissenschaftssystems in Deutschland. Köln: WR.

Wissenschaftsrat (WR) (2000b). Drittmittel und Grundmittel der Hochschulen 1993 bis 1998. Köln: WR.

Wissenschaftsrat (WR) (2002). Eckdaten und Kennzahlen zur Lage der Hochschulen von 1980 bis 2000. Köln: WR.

Chapter 14
Developing Universities: The Evolving Role of Academic Institutions in Denmark

Birgitte Gregersen and Jørgen Gulddahl Rasmussen

14.1 Introduction to the Danish Context

From a traditional economic point of view, it may seem as a paradox that a small country (5.5 million inhabitants) with high wages, high taxes, a large public sector, a relatively low level of R&D activity, and a relatively low proportion of people with a higher education in science and technology has been able to stay relatively competitive and rich for decades. Especially two interrelated explanations have been put forward in recent studies of the Danish National System of Innovation (Lundvall 2002b; Christensen et al. 2008).

14.1.1 Social Cohesion and the Danish Welfare State Model

The first explanatory factor is related to the Danish welfare state model with its long tradition for emphasizing social cohesion. A crucial ingredient in the social cohesion model has been a relatively equal income distribution obtained by comprehensive redistribution mechanisms.[1] Another is the long tradition of equal access – meaning in principle, independent of income and social status – to a relatively high level of public-financed welfare state services such as education, health care, social services, environment, and infrastructure. The importance for creating and maintaining social cohesion by, for instance, bringing the majority of children from all social groups together in a common public school system should not be underestimated, neither should the principle of "free" and equal access to health care services.

---

[1] Gini index for Denmark: 23.2 (2005, rank 1), HDI: 0.949 (2005, rank 14) and GDP per capita (PPP US$ 2005): 33,973 [source: OECD 2008 and UNDP 2007].

B. Gregersen (✉)
Department of Business Studies, Aalborg University, Denmark
e-mail: bg@business.aau.dk

B. Göransson and C. Brundenius (eds.), *Universities in Transition:*
The Changing Role and Challenges for Academic Institutions,
© International Development Research Centre 2011

Since the beginning of the twentieth century, Denmark has had strong trade unions and center-left wing political groups with the welfare state and social cohesion as their main political agenda. A central societal institution in formulating and implementing the welfare state model has been the corporatist system of interaction between the state, the trade unions, and the employers' organizations. This cooperation has created the so-called Danish flexicurity-model combining a high flexibility for employers to hire and fire with relatively high degree of income security for the employees. Related to the social cohesion model is the relatively high labor market participation rate for women in combination with an extended public supported childcare scheme since the 1960s.

However, the social cohesion model has during some years been exposed to increasing political pressure from neoliberal tendencies. This is reflected in increasing income inequalities, reductions in the social benefits, changes in the social insurance system toward a higher proportion of private insurance and pensions, more private hospitals, and more parents sending their children to private schools. Although the average unemployment rate during the last couple of years has been reduced to around 3%, still groups with low formal qualification have difficulties in getting and keeping steady jobs – a tendency that has been fortified by the current financial crisis. This is especially the case for many immigrants from outside Europe and USA. The Danish society has not been efficient in integrating these groups into the labor market.

14.1.2 Low R&D Intensity but Continuous Incremental Innovations

A second hypothesis why Denmark has been able to maintain its high-income status has to do with continuous product, process, and market innovations carried out by the majority of small and medium-sized firms. However, this dominating sector of small and medium scale enterprises (SMEs) invests very little in R&D and has only modest direct interaction with universities. One exception from this general picture of the Danish business structure dominated by SMEs is the traditional scale-intensive agroindustrial sector. This sector is today characterized by a high degree of standardization of products and processes, heavy EU subsidies to the primary production, an efficient processing industry, and a few dominating distribution channels. Another exception is the fast-growing science-based pharmaceutical industry with a high level of patent activity.

Many small countries have a business structure with specialization based on low- and medium-tech goods, but according to Maskell (2004), the Danish case has some specific features contributing to the competitiveness. Especially informal institutions such as the negotiated economy, the egalitarian culture, and the smoothening of exchange of information resulting from established trust relations seem to be significant elements (Lundvall 2002b; Maskell 2004). The combination of such structures with stable macroeconomic conditions is an important key to understand how Danish industry has sustained relatively competitive without substantial inputs of formal R&D (Christensen et al. 2008).

Despite a relatively high specialization in low-tech sectors, Danish total R&D spending relative to GDP has more than doubled since the beginning of the 1980s (from around 1% in 1980 to approximately 2.5% of GDP in 2007). However, among the Nordic countries, Finland and Sweden clearly outstrip Denmark with higher figures throughout the same period. Both these countries' R&D spending is now above 3% of GDP.

As can be seen in Table 14.1, the public R&D spending has not increased to the same extent as the private. However, recently the Danish Government has announced substantial increase in the public R&D budget in 2009 and 2010 in order to fulfill the 1% Barcelona target in 2010.

In the last two decades, the sectors of Danish industry with the greatest research requirements and activities have been the pharmaceutical industry and the ICT/tele-communication sectors. The private research departments in these sectors cooperate closely with Danish and foreign universities, but there is an increasing tendency for Danish business to establish laboratories outside Denmark (The Danish Institute for Studies in Research and Research Policy 2003/2009). For instance, the pharmaceutical firm Novo Nordisk spends around one billion Euro per year on R&D and employs globally around 4,600 people in R&D (2008 figures). Of Novo Nordisk's total of 27,000 employees, 52% are based outside Denmark.

Even if the averages are above the European Union (EU) and the Organisation for Economic Cooperation and Development (OECD) averages, the distribution of R&D expenditures is skewed. Generally, 1.5% of the firms conduct 47% of the total R&D in Denmark in 2006 (The Danish Institute for Studies in Research and Research Policy 2008a), even though since the mid-1990s the small firms have increased their R&D effort.

As Table 14.2 shows, expenditure on total education (primary, secondary, and tertiary) measured as a percentage of GDP has gradually increased since the mid-1990s and exceeds the OECD average as a consequence of an increasing political focus on human resources as driving force for innovation and growth.

Table 14.1 Denmark's R&D spending as a proportion of GDP 1995–2007 (%)

Sector	1995	2000	2001	2002	2003	2004	2005	2006	2007
Private	1.05	1.50	1.64	1.73	1.78	1.69	1.67	1.65	1.65
Public	0.78	0.75	0.75	0.76	0.78	0.78	0.76	0.80	0.88
Total	1.83	2.25	2.39	2.49	2.56	2.47	2.43	2.45	2.53

Source: The Danish Institute for Studies in Research and Research Policy (2003a, 2003b, 2005, 2008a, 2008b;) Eurostat

Table 14.2 Expenditure (all sources) on educational institutions as a percentage of GDP (1995, 2000, 2005)

	Denmark			OECD average		
	1995	2000	2005	1995	2000	2005
Total education	6.2	6.6	7.4	...	...	5.8
Tertiary education	1.6	1.6	1.7	...	...	1.5

Source: OECD 2008, Education at a Glance 2008, Table B2.1

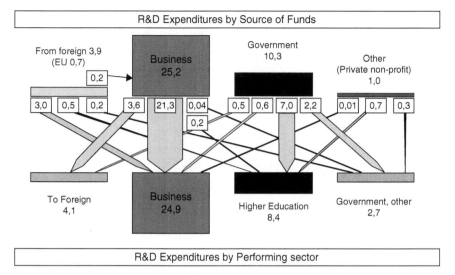

Fig. 14.1 R&D in Denmark by financing and performing sector 2003 (bn DKK). Source: The Danish Centre for Studies in Research and Research Policy (2005)

Taking a closer look at the distribution of R&D expenditure by funding sources (Fig. 14.1), the private sector make up for nearly 60% and the public sector for nearly 30%. The private sector share is relatively high – above EU(27) level but below, for instance, Sweden and Finland. It is also worth noting that the relative share of funding from foreign sources has nearly doubled from 5% in the 1990s, reflecting a general tendency of globalization of knowledge production. Turning to the distribution on performing sectors, the private sector accounts for more than two-third of the R&D activities, higher education (primarily universities), and other government research institutes for nearly the rest. Over time the university share has increased – as indicated above.

14.1.3 Enrollment in HE, PhD, and Lifelong learning

For the last two centuries, all children have attended at least 7 years of primary school. Several decades ago, this was changed into a minimum of 9 years and the large majority today spends at least 12 years in the educational system (including secondary school), ending either with a vocational education or as graduates from high school – general, technical, or commerce. On top of this, an increasing share of young people attends tertiary education. In the early 1980s, around 15% of young people in the age group of 25–64 years had a tertiary (short, medium, long) education. In 2006 this share was increased to 35% (OECD 2008). The increase in the enrollment rate has been especially high for female students, and today young women outnumber men enrolled in tertiary education, but with a wide variation between the different fields, see Table 14.3.

Table 14.3 Tertiary education enrollment distributed by field of education, Denmark, selected years, %

	2000		2005		2007	
	Total	F share	Total	F share	Total	F share
Education	11	69	11	71	11	71
Arts & humanities	17	65	15	63	15	62
Social sciences, business and law	23	47	30	50	29	51
Science	10	33	8	32	9	35
Engineering	10	28	10	33	10	33
Agriculture	2	52	1	52	1	54
Health & welfare	24	80	22	81	22	80
Services	2	27	2	22	2	22
Total	100	57	100	57	100	58
Total enrollment	189,162	107,644	232,255	133,376	232,194	133,684

F share: Share of females enrolled within each field of education
Source: UNESCO Institute for Statistics 2009

The Danish Industry Association and the Danish Government have for many years initiated campaigns to increase the interest for science and engineering among the youth, referring to a potential future lack of engineers in the Danish society, but the overall distribution of enrollment seems difficult to change.

For many years, all Danish students have had the right to study and have their study supported by a state grant of about US$900 a month (2008) plus loans for the standardized duration for a bachelor and master study – in total 5–6 years. This means that all young people will be able to finance their higher education nearly without economic support from their parents or other sources. In addition to this, an increasing number of bachelor and master programs have been expanded in capacity, and only a few of the programs have limitations in their intake. Both the grant system and the liberal admission to higher education are now and then discussed among politicians, but restrictions have up to now only been introduced for the admission for non-European students who from 2006 will have to pay a tuition fee. For European students, no tuition fee has to be paid for normal daytime bachelor and master students, only for MBA and other part-time master studies.

Also the number of PhD students (and degrees) has increased especially during the last 10 years, reflecting an international trend toward more formal research training.[2] However, compared with Sweden and Finland, Denmark is still lagging behind, although the government has recently increased the PhD budget in an attempt to catch-up to the Finish level.

During the last 5–10 years, there has been a steady increase in the number of master's level courses offered within a wide range of disciplines as continuing education based on work experience of the participants. Currently, all Danish universities offer such master programs together with a wide palette of other activities under the heading of Open Education programs.

---

[2] The entrance of doctorate students has increased from 1,168 in 1998 to 2,072 in 2008. The female share has increased from 39% to 47% in the same period (Statistics Denmark, 2009).

Denmark has a long tradition of adult education and training – including vocational training. According to various EU surveys, the Danish work force is among the most active when it comes to participating in continuing education and lifelong learning activities, and the public sector has hitherto spent a higher share of GDP on life-long learning activities than most other countries (Christensen et al. 2008).

14.2 The Position of Academic Institutions in the National System of Innovation

The Danish innovation system includes (2008) a wide grid of academic institutions: eight universities, four governmental research institutions for specific sectors and areas, four university hospitals, nine GTS Institutes,[3] several centers of tertiary education (in Danish CVU) and Business academics, seven science parks, and approximately seven "innovation milieus."[4]

Most of these institutions are public or semipublic. The large, but decreasing share of funding for the activities of these institutions comes from the yearly state budget.[5] A smaller but increasing share of the institutional budgets are funding for strategic purposes, programs, and projects, both from public and private sources. The vast majority of the public R&D investment is allocated to universities (higher education).

In the following, the main focus is put on universities and to a lesser extent on the governmental research institutes and the university hospital – the three groups that together take out the lion's share of the resources.

14.2.1 Linkages and collaboration

In what areas and with whom to cooperate are to a large extent within the decision power of the single institution or its subsections – which in fact can be the individual research group or researcher – as long as it can be financed by the institution itself or financed through the linkages. Therefore, the history of the institution, its traditions, and the mutual benefit from linkages play an important role in how relationships are exploited.

In the Danish context, the existing business structure and the knowledge-intensive public sector activities play an important role in forming the linkages. The

---

[3] GTS–Danish acronym for Approved Technical Service Institutions.

[4] After 2007, the Danish map of academic institutions has changed due to a new merger process. A few of the existing 12 universities merged into eight, and the majority of the existing 21 governmental research institutions were at the same time merged or integrated with the universities.

[5] The public-financed share fell from 97.5% in 2000 to 96.7% in 2006.

agricultural sector, the pharmaceutical sector, the energy sector, and not the least the public hospital sector are central partners in collaboration on research and knowledge production. These sectors are dominated by large companies and in that sense relatively few companies account for a substantial part of the linkages with specific research groups within universities and governmental sector research institutions.

Besides these kinds of linkages, the innovation system also includes a number of science parks typically related to a university. The above-mentioned linkages also include spin-offs from larger companies or from universities, which are part of the science parks and "innovation milieus." Such parks and milieus can also have sectoral research institutions and GTS institutes as tenants – and even regular university research can take place on such locations.

In a small economy, such as the Danish, the products produced through this knowledge are sold internationally. This is today not only the case for those activities that is going on between large companies and the research institutions, but also for young and small spin-off companies. The demand for their products and the R&D partners are very internationally oriented.

The firms that mainly produce for the home market or produce rather low-tech products are less involved in research and innovation linkages with the universities than the more research-intensive firms operating in foreign and domestic markets. The GTS institutes have as a part of their mission to increase the creation of linkages between such firms and the more advanced parts of the innovation system, but up to now this has not resulted in any dramatic change in the interaction pattern. It seems as if it is a clear advantage to have employees with an academic degree situated in such firms before the actual linkage-building activities start (Christensen et al. 1999; Vinding 2002). On the contrary the part of Danish business that is only concentrating on the domestic market is gradually decreasing, which means that an increasing part of business is gradually becoming more research intensive.

Weak linkages to the research system have not up to now been directly reflected in a general orientation toward the local market, but with a larger part of business facing a more intensive competition from foreign companies, knowledge becomes an increasingly important competitive factor. Therefore, they have to become more involved in R&D activities. The success of this seems to be dependent on how fast university graduates can find employment in these firms and what their competence can offer to such firms. This implies that university and college education is offering qualifications suited for this.

14.3 Mapping the Academic System in Denmark

In order to map the academic system, this section will present a short history of the higher education institutions, a history of the governance system, and a description of main linkages between academic institutions and other partners in society.

14.3.1   A Brief History of Higher Education

The University of Copenhagen was established in 1479 as a seminary for catholic priests recognized by the pope, but with programs in law, philosophy, and medicine (Ministry of Science, Technology and Innovation 2003:3). This university was during several centuries the only institution for higher education in Denmark. This changed at the end of the eighteenth century when a number of teachers' colleges were gradually established in connection with the introduction of the general primary school, an activity that increased the demand for teacher education.

In the first half of the nineteenth century, the College of Advanced Technology, now the Technical University of Denmark, was established (1829) and later in that century the Royal Veterinary and Agricultural University (1856) and the Danish University of Pharmaceutical Science (1892) were established. This was followed in the first half of the twentieth century with two business schools and the University of Aarhus (1928). Finally, in the second half of this century, the universities of Odense (1966), Roskilde (1972), and Aalborg (1974), and the Danish University of Education were founded in 2000 by merging a number of smaller institutions. Both Roskilde University Center and Aalborg University introduced from the very beginning a Problem Based Learning model (PBL) as their overall pedagogical teaching model.

The teachers' colleges were in the twentieth century followed by a number of colleges for the education of different kinds of professionals within the area of pedagogy and preschool teachers, and a gradual transformation of the training of health personnel from inhouse vocational to institutionalized education. Including the teachers' colleges, this group of institutions counted more than one hundred before a series of mergers began. In addition to this, a number of engineering colleges existed and a number of high schools within business and technology started to offer short-term higher education of 1–2 years within their specific fields.

This increase in the number of academic institutions has within the university sector up to now been followed by only a small number of mergers: One between the University of Odense and a small business school in the southern part of Jutland to the University of Southern Denmark (1998) and another concerned the earlier mentioned University of Education (2000). Within the college sector, the Ministry of Education has through the last 10 years urged the institutions concerned with professional fields to merge, and a series of mergers have diminished the number of these types of institutions rather dramatically. In 2007 the Minister of Science, Technology, and Innovation launched the idea of further mergers within the university sector. The outcome of these negotiations became a kind of "moderate" solution with a total of eight universities.

A large number of relationships at the individual level exist between specific groups of researchers and teachers related to similar programs. The number of linkages at the institutional level is considerably lower and is normally used to secure institutions with small research resources with the support of institutions with larger research resources and thereby enhance the quality of education in the former institution.

14.3.2 The Development of University Governance System

14.3.2.1 From a Collegial Governance System…

Since the Reformation in 1536, universities in Denmark have been state institutions, but with some degree of autonomy. This means that a collegial governance system based on the professors through a senate has governed the university. Starting 1968, the students demanded more influence on decision making within the universities, and in the beginning of the 1970s, the governance structure that functioned during the next couple of decades was passed by the parliament. In this act, the university senate consisted of a share of 50% professors, 25% students, and 25% technical administrative staff. Their constituencies within the university elected their members of the senate, and the same constituencies in the same proportions elected the rector. During the first half of the 1970s, the faculties, each including a number of departments with faculty councils, were constituted in all the universities. These councils had the same constellation as the senate and had the decisive power on budgets, plans, and academic matters, and they elected a dean for the faculty. In the departments, the entire staff of researchers, teachers, technical administrative staff, and a number of elected students governed the department and elected the head of the department.

For all master's level programs, a Study Board consisting of equal representation of teachers and students was elected and these boards decided upon curricula, course programs, and other matters concerning teaching and education. This was done under an ordinance for each master program made by the Ministry of Education that at the national level defined the general goals of the specific master education. In this way, the governance of study programs to some extent was divided between the Ministry and the Study Board. At the same time, it is important to notice that neither boards nor universities were – and still not are – allowed to start new master's or bachelor's programs without the permission from the ministry, and the ministry has always had the power to assess the quality of existing programs.

During the 1980s and 1990s, the ways of allocating resources to university education changed in a number of steps. For many years, the resources were allocated according to a formula that took into account the number of students and the salaries for the number of permanent research and teaching positions. In the changed allocation system, money to the universities was distributed according to the number of bachelors and masters who graduated. In this way, the mechanism for allocation of means for education changed from input criteria to output criteria. This change was part of the new general principles of allocation of state funds to its institutions, and the change for the universities was to some extent part of the national government's experiments with these new principles.

On a number of occasions, individual professors, some political parties, and different societal organizations did complain, especially about the influence of students and technical administrative staff on research and administrative decisions in universities, and in 1992 the Parliament passed the center-right government's new act on university governance. In this act, the most important change was that rector, deans, heads of departments, and heads of study formed a more traditional hierarchy and got a more specific leadership mandate. But the election system was continued, and the most important change in governance was the abolishment of a number of committees and the handing over of operative management to the individual leader.

14.3.2.2 To a Hierarchical Top-Down System

This system was also criticized from different angles. The most often heard critique was that this democratic system was too slow in its decision-making processes. Even if this was never proven, the government anyhow, in 2003, put a new and different act on university governance in operation. In this act, the senate and the faculty boards were abolished and instead a number of advisory academic councils were established. A university board with a majority of external members from business, cultural institutions, and foreign universities formally got most of the power that hitherto had been located in the senate. Furthermore, the rector, the deans, and the heads of departments are appointed, not elected. The rector is appointed by the board, deans by the rector, and heads of departments by the dean. The academic council decides only on strictly academic matters. The individual managers on the different levels decide on all other areas. The only governance structure that has not been changed concerns the Study Boards.

The governance structure as it looks today is formally more autonomous than the former structures. The universities are not any longer formally an integrated part of the state administration, but are defined as kind of firms with a governing board, where the external majority appoints the new members of the board, and the economic and financial responsibility is placed entirely on the board. On the contrary, the universities are still mainly financed by public means, and the government and the minister still have a number of mechanisms to control specific fields and the power to start evaluations into specific universities on subjects of interest. At the same time, the system for allocation of resources for education has during the years been more detailed. The allocation of resources for research has in the same period slowly transformed from a lump sum based partly on traditions and partly on the mechanisms for allocation of educational funding toward a system based on strategic and political priorities.

Along with the new governance structure came a new "resource allocation device" in the form of a formal "development contract" between the ministry and the individual university. The contract normally runs for a period of 4 years and it specifies a number of goals concerning external resources; research publications; international, national, and regional cooperation; number of graduates; PhD production; and a number of improvements of more administrative and organizational kind. Combined with this, most universities have started to develop and announce their strategies, connecting the more specific goals in the contract to more long-term goals and missions of the university (Rasmussen 2006).

These developments are part of a kind of new public management development in the entire State governance. This brings, according to the proponents of such systems, the universities and their management capacity more in line not only with their dynamic environment in general, but also with a national government that demands more flexibility of its institutions and a research funding system that is increasingly geared toward strategic research programs allocated from the ministry's chair. This is also reflected in the structural development of the national research funding system, where the traditionally discipline directed national research councils have been merged and changed in the direction of more broad areas and programs and away from disciplines and projects.

To complete the description of the national governance system, two additional elements should be mentioned: One is the Standing Committee on Research in the Parliament that debates most legislation on higher education and matters concerning research. The other element is the current structure of the national government where two ministries are responsible for education. The Ministry of Science, Technology, and Innovation is responsible for the universities, and the Ministry of Education is responsible for primary and secondary education and for the part of tertiary education that is outside the purview of the existing eight universities.

14.3.3 Linkages Between Academic Institutions and Other Partners in Society

14.3.3.1 Linkages Within the Educational System

As mentioned above, the main body of the educational system from primary education to PhD is public, under the overall responsibility of the Ministry of Education, and in the case of universities, the Ministry of Science, Technology, and Innovation. This is the case even when, as in primary and lower secondary schools, 15% of the children attend private schools. The rules and regulation for private schools and public schools are identical. Within the education sector, the formal linkages between the State and each of the subsectors seem to be more frequent and dominating than linkages between the different sectors (for instance, between the primary and the secondary school sector, or the upper secondary school and the universities). This is also the case for the linkages between the state-owned institutions for vocational training and the other parts of the educational system. But increasingly, additional agreements are made directly between individual institutions on different levels and sectors within the Danish educational system. Most clearly, this is seen between the university colleges and the universities in relation to how shorter and longer higher education can be combined for students who start in the university colleges but want to pursue higher-level postgraduate university programs.

14.3.3.2 Linkages Between Higher Education and Business and Public Administration

The increase in number of university graduates with jobs in business and public administration has in itself created important linkages between higher education and these sectors in society. What can be noticed is a much more even relationship between higher education and society. Higher education and academia are not any longer to the same extent seen as institutions with an unbridgeable distance to society, and the knowledge base present within the research-intensive business sector is increasingly comparable with the universities. At least this seems to be the fact with respect to the large knowledge-based firms and the knowledge-based part of public institutions. So even if this is only a small part of the business sector and the public administration, it results in both an increasing understanding between those sectors and in an increasing critique from business and the public sector, when they find that things are not conducted well enough within the university. At the same time, it has dramatically increased the involvement of firms and institutions as providers of cases, projects, and traineeships for university students.

14.3.3.3 Lifelong Learning

Another kind of linkages between higher education institutions, private firms, and public institutions has evolved during the last 10–15 years, where an increasing number of employees have participated in part-time further education, mainly at the master's level (MBA and similar). Some students finance these education activities by themselves, but do often get reduction in their working hours. Other students get part of their tuition fee paid by their employer and others are encouraged strongly by their employer to take part in such kinds of education. As a linkage, this development is not only increasing the competences of experienced employees, but also giving the higher education institutions a closer connection to the everyday life in business and public administration. In time it might also increase the role of alumni organizations that up to now has been nearly completely absent in Denmark when compared with many other countries.

14.3.3.4 Linkages in Research

Linkages in research have been established many decades ago. Establishing the first monofaculty universities in the middle of the nineteenth century could be seen as a result of the needs expressed by agriculture and industry. Not least, agriculture has, from the very start of the cooperative movement to until recently, been among the most impressive builder of linkages to research. On the one hand, the relative weight of these traditionally strong research linkages related to agriculture seems to decrease in the Danish case concurrent with the increasing outsourcing of processing of agricultural products and the decreasing numbers of farmers. On the other hand, the increasing focus on organic farming, genetically modified organisms (GMOs), functional foods, animal cloning, pesticides, pharmaceuticals and animal diseases has in a sense revitalized the traditional research area and strengthened the relations to especially the chemical industry and the pharmaceutical industry. The research linkages that have increased the most during the last decades are between large research-intensive firms and university research. Especially the growing pharmaceutical and ICT industries have developed strong research linkages to the universities, and other industries are gradually following the same track.

The linkage between SMEs and university research activities is currently not very strong. Recently, several initiatives have been taken by the government, the industry itself, and the universities to try to strengthen the collaboration between the universities and the SMEs, but there still seems to be a long way ahead. Instead, knowledge diffusion to the SMEs has primarily been the responsibility of a variety of technological service institutes, including the earlier mentioned GTS institutes. These institutions direct their activities toward all sectors within the economy and have to a large degree functioned as intermediates for new knowledge produced in Danish universities and the SMEs for implementation of these technologies. They have also, to some extent, functioned as knowledge-diffusing institutions to different types of public (municipal) institutions. Most of these institutions were established by the State and partly financed by public support for basic activities. During the last decade, these institutions have received reduced basic funding from the government and have had to earn more money in the market. Consequently, a number of structural changes within the sector have followed.

14.3.3.5   Technology Transfer Institutions Within the Universities

Over the years, the role of the universities in knowledge and technology transfer has increased. From being institutions engaged in teaching and research – eventually in cooperation with other research institutions – the so-called third mission of knowledge diffusion and transfer has become an important target. This development has slowly and rather organically obtained increasing importance within the individual universities and especially with an emphasis on the technical knowledge. From the start, this was not any joint or state-supported development, but it emerged through different research groups and milieus in specific departments. This has led to a situation now where all the Danish universities have established technology transfer offices, patent offices, network centers, incubators, knowledge ambassadors, etc., all different kinds of organizational structures and institutions that service knowledge diffusion and technology transfer activities. Today these activities are explicitly included in the University Act and the activity contracts that universities have to make with the Ministry.

14.4   The Danish Debate on the Role and Development of Academic Institutions

During the last 5 years, the academic institutions in Denmark have been a subject of debate both among the political parties in parliament and among several societal institutions such as employers' associations, trade unions, and professional associations, and among people directly involved in university activities and in creating linkages between universities and other partners in society. The reasons for this have both been the global developments and internal changes in the national innovation system. Such debates flare up for different reasons and have been initiated by different organizations. Debates on different topics within this field, to some extent, circle around efficiency, quality and dynamics within individual institutions, groups of institutions, types of linkages, and the entire knowledge producing and diffusion system. The debates, because of their interlinkages, can be divided into several sets of clusters. In this chapter, the following division will be used: financial aspects, types of knowledge production and diffusion, the future academic workforce, and the way universities are governed, and how the future set up of the tertiary education system should look like.

14.4.1 Money Makes the World Go Round

One of the arguments within the discussion about the future competitiveness of the Danish society in a globalizing world takes its starting point in how firms in the future will be able to develop new and innovative products and sell these. This debate has a national perspective that relates to the specific Danish industrial structure with many small and medium-sized firms and a large part of the entire production system being relatively low tech. Furthermore, it has an international perspective that relates to the EU and its goals on global competitiveness.

The present government has committed itself to the Bologna Agreement, meaning that the total national R&D spending should amount to at least 3% of GDP by 2010. This is a goal that has a broad support among political parties, societal organizations, and universities. It is at the same time a policy in accordance with the EU ambitions and is in that respect often seen as a kind of national contribution to the European competitiveness.

A debate on this subject has started because it has been a little difficult for many observers to see how the government will live up to its own ambition of 1% public R&D spending. Several university rectors have complained that when they look into the yearly national budget proposed by the government and into the basic state funding of their own institutions, the only thing they see is relative budget cuts due to built-in productivity increase and reallocation to specific research areas. So instead of a yearly increase in the state-funded research, a decrease or at least stagnating allocations during the last couple of years seem to them to be a more accurate picture of the situation. Confronted with this, the Minister of Science promised that the following year an increase would be seen, and the financing goal would be met in 2010.

Regardless, critics express their skepticism. The reason for this is that the government for the last 8 years successfully has followed a policy of no tax increases of any kind. At the same time, the expenditures on health and other social areas are increasing. In addition to this, the coalition that forms the political majority in parliament is kept together on policies that to some extent point in another direction than increasing state funding of research. This is one of the bases for the skepticism within the universities. Another worry expressed by those who fear about the future development is that the way to fulfill the financial ambition on research could be done through even more severe cuts in the funding of university education than what has already been seen during the past several years. The minister promises that this will not be the case, but this debate hardly stops until the targeted percentage for research spending is met through additional funding.

Summarizing, the debates on the funding of research, teaching, and service concern (1) how the total national budget within these fields develops; (2) how the allocation of resources between different scientific fields such as natural science, humanities, and social science evolves; and (3) how the mechanisms that create public funding for areas, programs, and projects change. Concerning mechanisms, one of the most important changes seems to be an increased use of cofinancing where public funding follows funding from private sources.

14.4.2   Research and Research Linkages

Both in the internal university debates, at the national political level, and among societal organizations with interest in research, a debate is running on which areas to allocate the scarce means directed toward research. This debate can at the same time be seen as related to a global, national, and regional dimension as well as to different disciplines, areas, and objectives. One way to explain why this debate has been going on for several years now is that the national resources used for research – including what the private sector is using – with a population of only five million, are seen as very limited in a global perspective. This brings about an argument that a small nation has to concentrate its research activities to specific fields in order to become excellent in knowledge production.

This debate on concentration runs in a different direction. One concerns the contradiction between being on a world-class level within specific areas of basic research, and the counter argument that raises the question if this in reality will support national business, social, and cultural needs. This can be seen as a debate in a certain perspective of mode 1 versus mode 2 research (Gibbons et al. 1994). In that perspective, this debate relates to another debate where the government seems to be in favor of universities and other research institutions directing their activities more directly toward producing results that can be useful specifically for the national and local business. To make things even more complicated, this debate also includes two other contradicting views. One is that more emphasis should be put on hard sciences to make it possible to compete at the global level. The other is that soft sciences are not only more needed for the further development of the Danish welfare state, but are also one of the factors behind the country's successful competitiveness, through its specific social organization. The perspectives of these debates on the future national business structure with its weight on service and creative industries and the increased outsourcing of traditional industrial and technical areas seem at present to gain in importance.

As mentioned, this debate has been ongoing in different versions for a number of years, and no formalized policy – neither at the national level nor at the level of the individual institutions – has been decided upon. This can perhaps be explained through the fact that no stable and strong coalition has up to now been formed on a united strategy pointing at one specific type of concentration. In all political coalitions, there seems to be proponents for several different kinds of concentration. Furthermore, a look into the more "unstructured" development within the research funding landscape during the last decade might show a slow but steady move away from the humanities and the social sciences and toward the natural sciences and technology. This is a movement that has been possible because of the gradual decoupling of the funding streams for research and education. But a more explicit policy on how much and what kind of concentration seems not to be on the agenda in the short run and is not much echoed in national debates on the development of research.

This means that the linkages that are being established with global research centers, global companies, national research centers, domestic firms, and public institutions and regional partners to a large extent have been a result of a natural development of local research interests and results. National and international institutions, such as the EU institutions, can be supportive in these processes, and so can the universities themselves, but the important players are the research groups themselves and in some cases, firms and other kinds of organizations raising demands and offering support. Concentration in the form of research relations has in this way been part of a rather organic development.

14.4.3   Debates on Higher Education

The number of programs that offer free admission has increased, and only a few studies such as medicine are strongly restricted. Despite this, the share of university students (long tertiary education) measured as share of the entire population is at the same level as in most other comparable high-income countries, and the government is constantly complaining that the young people are starting their university studies too late. According to the government, this harms the national economy.

The rather free admission of individuals of other European nationalities has several times fueled a debate on the possibility of restrictions. This has been the case because, for instance, medical studies receive a large share of Swedish and Norwegian students who are able to follow programs where Danish is the language of instruction. This has got some politicians to demand that they should not be allowed to study in Denmark without paying, but the government has rejected such ideas as violating rules and regulations within the EU. But these politicians have had more success in restricting the admission of non-European students. From 2006, they must pay a tuition fee to be allowed into a Danish higher education facility.

A debate, which to some extent is pulling in another, on a more global direction, centers around how it should be possible, through a focused use of extra resources, to have a small proportion of students who in the future as graduates will be able to compete and participate in the knowledge production at the highest level. This debate between elite and mass education has recently gained momentum. The debate includes positions that can be seen as rather similar to some of the research policy positions. One is for free and broad admission as has been a Danish tradition, and the other is for reallocating resources in order to concentrate on a small number of programs that have shown great strength in an international perspective and can be seen as vital to the national competitiveness. Several arguments have been presented in this debate – from master-level programs that clearly see themselves as candidates for such an honor to rectors who claim that if the government does not continuously cut the budgets for university education, then excellence in education would on a broader scale be a goal that is within reach in the present structure.

In another perspective, a debate flourishes concerning the direction of university education. This is a debate that can be seen as trying to raise and fulfill goals in quite an opposite direction. The question raised here is how much weight should be given to university bachelor's, master's, and PhD's competence in innovation and entrepreneurship. One of the arguments for this is that it might create more successful start-ups of new firms by university graduates and at the same time make bachelors and masters more useful for small and medium-sized firms. Many universities are experimenting in this field, and the debate is more concentrated on how this could be done than on whether it should be done.

14.4.4   Internal Governance Structures and External Linkages' Structures

As explained earlier in this chapter, both the internal structures in university governance and the overall set up of the higher education system have been through several processes of change in the most recent decades. This has not happened without debates between different partners in society and among politicians. At the moment, these debates have calmed down, but they tend to flair up now and then. One is the debate about the conditions for internal governance in universities, especially when the ministry interferes into what the universities see as their internal affairs. Another debate is of a more inter-institutional nature and concentrates on mergers and new linkages between university colleges and between universities and university colleges.

The basic fuel for the debate on university governance is the contradiction between what in the government's language could be called institutional autonomy, and the many direct and indirect governance mechanisms that still and perhaps increasingly are in the hand of the Ministry of Science, Technology, and Innovation. Even when the universities are not any longer seen as traditional state institutions, a detailed state control still prevails. From the period of genuine collegial governance, the framework that has been set up by the government has always been rather narrow. At the same time, all universities have national teams of external second examiners who participate in most examinations in the university and are appointed by the ministry. Such possibilities for inspection have not been changed as a result of the formal autonomous status conferred on the universities.

Years ago such control methods did not create much debate. The universities were rather unaffected by the external state control. The daily operations and decision making took place in an organic way that was normal when it concerns the development and planning of teaching and research, and the funding for the larger part was a lump sum. These activities were not affected in everyday life by the State regulation. If any real problems were recognized, this was often negotiated on a national scale between the Ministry and representatives from the study boards, deans, or in institutional matters by the Danish Conference of Rectors. This could now and then lead to public debates, but they mostly concern the specific problem more than the matter of governance structures.

One explanation on why the debate has turned more toward governance structures and has become more intense could be categorized into three factors: One is that the dynamic relates both to an increase in the number of new demands that confront universities, and at the same time a situation where systematic budget cuts make state governance more visible inside the universities. Second, the discrepancy between the formal autonomy and the actual governance makes it increasingly difficult for the universities to live up to internal and external expectations. And third, the new autonomy is followed by a demand for the universities to show more systematic management. This means that these leaders are not only appointed by their boss, but are also expected at each level to use managerial methods that often internally are felt as rather mechanistic in a type of organization that has been used to a more organic way of handling things (Rasmussen 2002). Therefore, the debate that takes place on an everyday basis in all universities now and then is reflected in the media and results in discussions on principles and how they are implemented in practice.

The reason why the debate within and between the nonuniversity higher education institutions is different from the university discussion is connected to two other factors. One is the formalization of the educational structure within these institutions in order to increase the level of education to professional bachelor degrees. The other is the need for critical mass, which forces a large number of small institutions to merge and to form university colleges. One difficulty in this process is the rather loose framework the Ministry of Education has set for this process, something that seems to be new for these type of institutions. At the same time, it is a precondition that the education in university colleges is in some ways connected to research, although not research based as in universities, but the university colleges are not provided with state funds to do research. Therefore, some kind of linkage to universities is seen as a way to solve this ambition of a research connection.

The debate within this field has for a large part been related to a question about who should merge with whom and what kind of governance structure should be set up in such a new university. The process started with more than one hundred institutions, and according to the Ministry of Education, it should end with less than ten large institutions. This has resulted in a number of different structures and with different kinds of linkages to universities. Some have formed rather loose mergers containing institutions with very different areas of education (nursing, teachers' education, and business education), while others have either formed more homogeneous or more centralized institutions. Some mergers include linkages to a university while others do not. At the same time, the first alterations of such new constellations have already been seen.

14.5 Concluding Remarks

The increasing interaction between universities and other actors in the innovation system [small and large firms, high-tech and low-tech firms, technological service institutes, hospitals, consultancy and other knowledge-intensive business services (KIBS), public agencies, other educational institutes, etc.] involves a variety of forms ranging from joint labs, spin-offs, licensing, research contracts, mobility of researchers, copublications, conferences, exhibitions and specialized media, and informal contracts with professional network, to flow of graduates. Most countries, including Denmark, have implemented multifaceted strategies to stimulate collaboration between universities and other actors in the innovation system (Mowery and Sampat 2005). However, it is not an easy task to design and implement mutually beneficial collaboration between actors with different missions, cultures, resources, power structures, and knowledge bases (Arocena et al. 2004). There are massive variations among technological fields and sectors in their capabilities and opportunities to create and maintain linkages with universities and other research institutions. For less research-intensive firms and institutions, it might not even be relevant to engage in such direct collaboration. Seen from the perspective of the universities and other academic institutions, they face a complex mix of challenges in order to fill out their "new and bigger shoes" in the modern learning economy (Lundvall 2002a). In this concluding section, we only list a few of these interrelated challenges.

14.5.1 Globalization and Restructuring of the Production System

Historically, a substantial part of the national academic institutions has been linked directly to the national production system. Most clearly, this is reflected not only in the monofaculty universities (for instance, agriculture and pharmaceutical) and in the set up of sector-specific governmental research institutes, but of course also in many other areas as law, business, and engineering. The ongoing globalization and restructuring of manufacturing and services are one of the most important (and difficult) challenges for the contemporary national academic institutions. For instance, if the future software industry is to be relocated to India or China, is it then relevant to continue educating Danish IT specialists? Or if most of the manufacturing is outsourced, where should the production engineers go? Or if the internationalization and mergers within KIBS continue, will they all end up in London or Beijing? Multinationals set up and close down R&D departments according to contemporary national strengths. Multinationals have for instance during the last 10 years established R&D departments within mobile communication and pharmaceuticals in Denmark, but recently some of the mobile research units have been closed or reduced. At the same time, Danish research-intensive firms establish R&D units outside Denmark and to an increasing degree collaborate with foreign universities and research institutes. How can or should the academic institutions react to this?

One small-country strategy could be a specialization strategy, where a substantial part of the scarce resources is allocated to a few specific areas. To identify these and not least to agree on the selection is a challenge in itself. Nonetheless, it seems as if many countries, including Denmark, try to implement such a specialization strategy and it also seems as if there is a common understanding that areas within ICT, nanotechnology, biotech, and pharmaceuticals should be among the selected, based on expectations about future key technologies and related growth industries.

In the Danish case, another specialization (or maybe diversification) strategy could be to further strengthen the linkages between the academic institutions and public administration, the health care sector, the alternative energy sector, and the environmental industry – areas where the Danish Innovation System still has some internationally competitive strengths.

14.5.2 Increased Internationalization of Knowledge Production and Knowledge Diffusion

Concurrent with the increasing globalization and restructuring of manufacturing and services is an increasing internationalization of knowledge production and diffusion. One important part of this has to do – as mentioned above – with the MNCs' restructuring of R&D activities and the outsourcing of high-skilled jobs. However, it also affects the academic institutions more directly in the form of increased focus on international research collaboration, more international staff and student mobility, and a growing focus on international publishing. In that way, universities and research institutions have to balance between increasing demands toward international engagements on the one hand, and commitments to collaborate with domestic firms and other actors in the national innovation system on the other. In countries where the domestic production structure is dominated by SMEs within low-tech industries that do not invest much in R&D and have no or very little tradition to collaborate with universities and other research institutions, this dilemma is more manifest (Arocena et al. 2004).

Furthermore, the increasing internationalization of the knowledge production system is forcefully stimulated by national and international R&D and innovation policies. In the Danish context, various EU policies – for instance, the different generations of framework programs – have had substantial influence on the national policies and the academic institutions' responses to these new funding possibilities. The increasing demand for forming Networks of Excellence spurs in the same direction.

14.5.3 Increased Marketization of Public Sector Activities

Since the 1980s, there has been a general shift in the public service philosophy toward more and more marketization (Peters and Olssen 2005). This tendency has also made its entry into the academic institutions and its relations to other actors in the innovation system. It is echoed in several ways. First, it is reflected in the increased policy focus on the production of so-called useful knowledge primarily defined as knowledge with a direct economic benefit for the private sector. This is valid both for the ongoing "modernization" and fine tuning of study programs and for allocation of public research funds. Second, the marketization philosophy also prevails in the increasing dependency on external funding. On the one hand, this may stimulate research collaboration between the academic institutions and external partners. On the other hand, there is a risk that an increasing dependency may favor short-term research within a few selected areas at the expense of more long-term research within a broader range of disciplines and thus maybe emptying the key source for collaboration in the long run. Third, the earlier mentioned shift in the allocation mechanism from input criteria to output criteria drives in the same direction.

14.5.4 Increased Commodification of Knowledge

The enhanced possibilities for universities and research institutions to take out patents have revitalized the classical dilemma between, on the one hand, a broad and easy access to public financed research and, on the other, private appropriation as one of the basic incentives to innovate. But more importantly, the increasing tendency to treat information and knowledge as commodities introduces a basic contradiction in the learning economy. On the one hand, firms and now also universities try to capture knowledge economies through intellectual property rights. On the other hand, knowledge is socially produced in groups and networks, which may be destroyed or damaged when knowledge is treated as a commodity. Furthermore, the commodification of knowledge is accompanied by increasing costs for developing and maintaining an adequate knowledge infrastructure including various transaction costs following the commodification process and protection of property rights.

Most European countries have recently implemented equivalents to the American Bayh-Dole Act, hoping for future revenues from patents taken out by universities. In the Danish case, a new patent act was implemented in 2000 (L347), aiming to increase the commercialization of public research. The new act has given the public research institutions the possibility to take over the rights to an invention done by a public researcher by paying a "fair" compensation. Furthermore, L347 gave the public research institutions an obligation to work actively for putting the research to commercial use. It is of course too early to evaluate the long-term effects, but commercialization surveys confirm that setting up the necessary institutional infrastructure related to intellectual property rights (IPR) is both a costly, risky, and lengthy learning process (Danish Agency for Science, Technology and Innovation 2007).

It is an important question if the changing IPR regime in public research will influence the internal and external collaboration patterns in the long run. Will the university management allocate more resources to areas with higher probability to patent? Will the demand for secrecy influence the interaction between colleagues, students, and external partners?

References

Arocena, R., Gregersen, B. and Sutz, J. (2004). "Universities in Transition – Challenges and Opportunities in Small Latin American and Scandinavian Countries", Paper presented at The Second Globelics Conference, *Innovation Systems and Development: Emerging Opportunities and Challenges*, Beijing, October 16–20, 2004.

Christensen, J.L., Gregersen, B., Johnson, B., Lundvall, B.Å., and Tomlinson, M., (2008). "An NSI in transition? Denmark", in Edquist, C. and Hommen, L. (Eds.) *Small Country Innovation Systems – Globalization, Change and Policy in Asia and Europe*. Cheltenham, UK: Edward Elgar.

Christensen, J.L., Gregersen, B., and Rogaczewska, A.P. (1999). *Vidensinstitutioner og innovation, DISKO report no. 8.* Copenhagen: Industry and Trade Development Council.

Danish Agency for Science, Technology and Innovation (2007). *Public Research Commercialisation Survey 2006*, Copenhagen.

Gibbons, M., Limoges, C., Nowotny, H., Schartzman, S., and Trow, M. (1994). *The New Production of Knowledge. The Dynamics of Science and Research in Contemporary Societies.* London: Sage.

Lundvall, B.A. (2002a). "The University in the Learning Economy", *DRUID Working Paper* No. 02-06, Aalborg.

Lundvall, B.-Å. (2002b). *Innovation, Growth and Social Cohesion: The Danish Model.* Cheltenham: Edward Elgar.

Maskell, P. (2004). "Learning in the village economy of Denmark. The role of institutions and policy in sustaining competitiveness", in Cooke, P., Heidenreich, M., and Braczy, K.H.J., (Eds.) *Regional Innovation Systems. 2nd edition.* pp. 154–185. London: Routledge.

Ministry of Science, Technology and Innovation (2003). *Danish universities in transition – Background report to the OECD examiners panel*, Copenhagen.

Mowery, D.C. and Sampat, B.N. (2005). "Universities in National Innovation Systems", in Fagerberg, J., Mowery, D.C., and Nelson, R.D. (2005). *The Oxford Handbook of Innovation.* Oxford, UK: Oxford University Press.

OECD (2008). *Education at a Glance 2008, OECD Indicators.* Paris: OECD, ISBN 978-92-64-04628-3.

Peters, M.A. and Olssen, M. (2005). "'Useful Knowledge': Redefining Research and Teaching in the Learning Economy", in Barnett, R. (Ed.). *Reshaping the University – New Relationships Between Research, Scholarship and Teaching*, The Society for Research into Higher Education.

Statistics Denmark (2009) http://www.dst.dk

Rasmussen, J.G. (2006). "Steering processes in and around Danish universities. Mechanic governance in organic institutions?", III SEMINAR ON STRATEGIC CHANGE IN HIGHER EDUCATION, the Generalitat Valenciana and the International Management Higher Education (IMHE) Programme, OECD, Valencia, April 27–28, 2006.

Rasmussen, J.G. (2002). "Management between the Shop Floor and the Corporate Level", *European Journal of Education*, Vol. 37, No. 1, 43–56.

The Danish Centre for Studies in Research and Research Policy (2003a). *Innovation in the Danish private sector 2000* [in Danish].

The Danish Centre for Studies in Research and Research Policy (2003b). *Private sector R&D. R&D statistics 2001* [in Danish].

The Danish Centre for Studies in Research and Research Policy (2003/2009). *Research Management Processes under Rapid Change*.

The Danish Centre for Studies in Research and Research Policy (2005). *Danish research- and innovation indicators 2005* [in Danish].

The Danish Centre for Studies in Research and Research Policy (2008a). *Public Sector R&D, R&D statistics 2006*, [in Danish].

The Danish Centre for Studies in Research and Research Policy (2008b). *Private Sector R&D, R&D statistics 2006*, [in Danish].

Vinding, A.L. (2002). *Interorganizational Diffusion and Transformation of Knowledge in the Process of Product Innovation*, PhD thesis, Department of Business Studies, Aalborg University.

UNDP (2007). *Human Development Report 2007/2008 – Fighting Climate Change: Human Solidarity in a Divided World*. New York: UNDP.

UNESCO Institute for Statistics (2009). *Global Education Digest 2009, Comparing Education Statistics across the World*. Montreal, Canada: UIS, ISBN: 978-92-9189-070-5.

Chapter 15
The Role of Academic Institutions in the National System of Innovation and the Debate in Sweden

Claes Brundenius, Bo Göransson, and Jan Ågren

15.1 Introduction to the Swedish Context

The Swedish Welfare Model, or for that matter the Nordic Welfare Model, has often been referred to as an example of systemic success. The 1930s have been regarded as the beginning of this model, which was subsequently developed and maintained throughout the post-World War II period, and it has been characterized by equitable and long-term sustained economic growth.

The Great Depression hit Sweden severely in the early 1930s, causing widespread despair, with high unemployment rates and the collapse of financial institutions. It was under these circumstances that the Social Democratic Party came to power in 1932, and the party has been in power since then, except for short periods, when the center-right opposition had reigned. But even with the opposition in power, there has practically been no questioning of the principle of a welfare model.

The vision of the Social Democratic party was the creation of *Folkhemmet* (People's Home), transforming Sweden into a safe haven for all Swedes. The fight against unemployment was originally the top priority on the agenda, and the economic policy, for a long period of time, had been based on the idea, influenced by Keynes, of finding ways and means to increase aggregate demand and stimulate the expansion of public utilities. The welfare model had several different features (based on Andersson and Gunnarsson 2006):

1. A first aspect is the principle that the welfare insurance system should be publicly funded via extensive income transfers. It is basically a system for ex-post redistribution, i.e., redistribution of the fruits of growth. However, in the Swedish context, income transfers had a special meaning, namely, to push up domestic demand, which via accelerator effects would stimulate investments and growth. Therefore, initially, there was strong growth-enhancing mechanism built into the redistributive system.

C. Brundenius (✉)
Research Policy Institute, Lund University, Lund, Sweden
e-mail: Claes.Brundenius@fpi.lu.se

B. Göransson and C. Brundenius (eds.), *Universities in Transition: The Changing Role and Challenges for Academic Institutions*, © International Development Research Centre 2011

2. A second aspect is the public sector involvement in terms of provision of free education, health care, social security to all, and other services provided by the state. An intrinsic concept was to provide equal opportunities to all citizens.
3. A third aspect was that the model focused on the labor market regulations, first through a centralized wage negotiation system between employers and trade unions, and second through the so-called solidaric wage policy that was implemented from the beginning of the 1950s.

However, the so-called golden period of growth (that lasted from 1950 to more or less the mid-1970s) is over, and it is quite clear that Swedish model is not unique any more. A number of countries have reached, and surpassed, Sweden's per capita income, and Sweden's welfare system today contains only a few features, which cannot be found in many other countries. The original Swedish Welfare Model is generally regarded to have come to an end.

On the contrary, in spite of several years of economic drawback, especially in the 1990s, Sweden is still one of the richest countries in the world, and has kept high standards as per the United Nations Development Programme (UNDP's) Human Development Index (HDI), which uses indicators such as GDP per capita (PPP), life expectancy, adult literacy, and infant mortality. However, it becomes apparent that other countries are catching up, and Sweden's position has come down on the global HDI ranking. In 2005, Sweden held the sixth position in UNDP's Human Development Report (2005), compared with the fourth in 1995 (UNDP 1995).

15.1.1 The Decline of the Original Model

The start of the decline of the Swedish Model can be traced to the early 1970s. Then the Swedish state started intervening in a new manner at the labor market, introducing a series of laws affecting fundamental aspects of the labor–capital relationship. Later, the Swedish Trade Union Confederation (LO) challenged the Saltsjöbaden Agreement,[1] claiming control over investments of Swedish firms. This challenge was to break a 30-year long understanding between the LO and SAF, thus weakening the alliance between labor and capital, which was so central to the Swedish Model. Finally, in 1976, a center-right wing coalition took over the control of the government. For the first time in 34 years, the Social Democratic rule was set aside by a different political ideology, a fact that has been pointed out as the end of the Swedish Model.

---

[1] An agreement reached in 1938 between the Swedish Trade Union Confederation (LO) and Swedish Employers' Confederation (SAF), significantly lowering the need for state intervention on the labor market.

15.2   The Role of the Academic Institutions in the Swedish System of Innovation

15.2.1   An Introduction to the Swedish System of Innovation

Research and development (R&D) in Sweden has received a high priority for the last several decades. Sweden is actually at the top of Organisation for Economic Cooperation and Development (OECD) countries in the terms of R&D expenditures per capita. In 2005, Swedish R&D amounted to 3.88% of GDP, slightly down from 4.3% in the peak year 2001. It should be stressed that the business sector accounts for the bulk of this percentage (or 74% of the total in 2005). However, it is likely that this share will decline as a result of the trend of outsourcing of corporate R&D activities to new and emerging economies. But even so, it is quite clear that Sweden has been, and continues to be, at the top in R&D spending on a global scale. Research at the universities and other higher education institutions accounted for 21% of the total in 2005, while the remaining 5% of research expenditure was accounted for by government agencies, including research foundations and the private nonprofit sector (Table 15.1).

The state has traditionally played an important role in Swedish education and research. The Uppsala University was created as early as in 1477 and is the oldest university in the Nordic countries, and the Lund University, in Skåne (South Sweden), was founded in 1666 (just after Skåne region became Swedish after the Danish rule). The Royal Academy of Sciences was created in 1739 with the objective of "using science in the service of society." In 1811, the Royal Academy of Agriculture and Forestry followed suit and in the nineteenth century, research began taking an important position at the Swedish universities. In the twentieth century, the expansion of universities intensified, especially toward the end of century, and today Sweden has 13 state-owned universities and 23 other state-owned academic institutions (university colleges and professional schools).

State resources have traditionally gone directly to the universities as part of the government appropriation bill. In addition, however, a system of research councils, along the US and the British models, has been put in place gradually since the

Table 15.1   R&D expenditure per sector 1995–2007 (current million SEK)

Year	Total	Private sector (%)	Universities/ colleges (%)	Government agencies (%)	Nonprofit organizations (%)
1995	59,297	74.25	21.93	3.66	0.16
1997	67,007	74.84	21.54	3.54	0.08
1999	75,813	75.12	21.40	3.36	0.11
2001	97,276	77.24	19.84	2.83	0.09
2003	97,101	74.10	22.03	3.48	0.39
2005	103,814	74.12	20.86	4.72[a]	0.29
2007	110,451	73.74	21.29	4.80[a]	0.16

Source: Adapted from SCB (2007b) and SCB (2009)

[a] Includes municipalities

1940s. From the 1960s forward, resources for research have grown impressively, as a result of a rapid expansion of the higher education system and big investments in sectoral research. In the 1970s, the awareness rose about the need for national research policy where the state was to take an active rector role. In the 1960s and 1970s, the OECD countries had become increasingly aware of the imperative of states to have a policy on science and technology (OECD 1969). In 1979, the Swedish Government presented its first research policy bill. The Parliament not only approved the bill but it also decided that this kind of bill should be submitted to it during each term in office, serve as "instruments for long-range planning and coordination of public sector R&D investments."

As mentioned earlier, the state directly (through the budget) accounts for the funding of most of the research activities in the higher education sector. In 2001, this funding amounted to 47% of the R&D revenues of this sector. The rest was accounted for by external financing (most of which were national research councils, central government agencies, and research foundations). External financing is particularly high in engineering sciences (two-thirds of the total), while the share in humanities and law is only one-third. In social sciences, medicine, and natural sciences, the share is about 50%.

Medical sciences absorbed 27% of total R&D resources in 2001, while 23% went to engineering sciences, 19% to natural sciences, 11% to social sciences, 6% humanities, and 5% to agricultural and forestry sciences.

15.2.2 The Swedish Knowledge Economy Confronting the Challenges of Globalization

During the beginning of the 2000s, the Social Democratic Government produced a series of reports aimed at coming to grips with the challenges of globalization, and the opportunities (and threats) that the increased global competition implies for the Swedish knowledge and learning economy. In a recent report from the government (the Ministry of Industry, Employment and Education 2005), it is stated that "(T) he role of the state is to create the conditions that will enable Sweden to provide the best research and education in the world and to maintain a stable economy, a first-class business climate and efficient innovation systems."

The report stresses that in order to ensure "high-level growth and increased productivity, and thus our future welfare, we must develop conditions that are conducive to innovation and we must enhance the innovation climate." The challenge is to maintain the competitiveness of the Swedish industry (in a broad sense) in an increasing competitive climate. In this endeavor, the knowledge intensity in industry (products, processes, and services) is vital. Hence, not only is an attractive investment climate important for industries to grow, traditional and new industries alike, but it is also as important to create the conditions for an attractive knowledge and learning economy at large. However, large companies are as a rule international and they base their operations in whichever countries best suitable for their business.

In June 2004, the government launched a new innovation strategy, Innovative Sweden: A Strategy for Growth Through Renewal – a platform that would pursue the "vision of Sweden as the most competitive KBE (knowledge-based economy) in the world." This strategic plan was the result of discussions involving various ministries (most importantly, the Ministry for Industry and Trade and Ministry of Education and Science) and representatives of academia, the business sector, public authorities, and labor organizations. In connection with the launching of this new strategy, the government also appointed an ad hoc Innovation Policy Council. These initiatives are in line with the Lisbon Strategy (of the European Union), which has a pronounced goal of making Europe the most dynamic and competitive economy in the world by 2010. The Lisbon Strategy calls for innovation strategy initiatives that strive to the promotion of business investment in R&D, commercialization of research results, creation of new dynamic (SME) firms, injection of venture and seed capital, and the providing a fertile environment for regional cluster development. Sweden also takes an active part in the European Union (EU) Framework Programs for Research, Technological Development, and Demonstration.

As part of the innovation strategy, the government is developing programs for maintaining and strengthening Sweden's leading position in some key sectors: the metallurgy industry; the forest and wood industry; the vehicle industry, the pharmaceuticals and biotech industry; the IT and telecom industry, and finally, but not least, the aerospace industry.

Sweden is very much dependent on and sensitive to the world economy, as are most other countries in the present trend of globalization. In the case of Sweden, there is a special type of dependency, although not unique, resulting from the dominant position that large multinational corporations (such as Ericsson, Volvo, Saab, ABB, and AstraZeneca) have in the Swedish NSI. The industries listed in the sector program above account for 80% of Swedish business investment in R&D; they generate about US$70 billion in exports and provide almost 600,000 jobs in Sweden.

15.2.3 Cluster Policies and the Role of Vinnova

Due to the benefits associated with a range of so-called agglomeration economies, the concepts of Innovation Systems and Clusters have attracted the interest of the research community and policy makers wanting to facilitate innovation and competitiveness in industrial growth sectors such as biotechnology and telecommunications, as well as to support local economic development in disadvantaged localities and regions.

Proponents of clusters tend to be more prone to emphasize spontaneous interactions and concrete efforts by firms, whereas proponents of innovation systems are likely to place relatively greater weight on the role of public institutions and framework conditions. Such differences may, or may not, show up or have practical implications in the specific case. Furthermore, both approaches can be useful in enhancing each other and setting up of proper policies.

The stakeholders, institutions, and infrastructure that are the nucleus of a regional innovation system existed prior to these new efforts, such as targeted FDI promotion, incubators, science parks, applied research and engineering, IPR reforms, and university/industry collaboration. What are new from these last years are approaches that try to systemize the relationships between the components and how to improve the system.

The Innovation System and Cluster thinking has been present in Sweden for a number of years both at the national level and at the regional levels. The topic of clusters has mainly been promoted by the Ministry of Industry, not only from a growth perspective, but also from the Ministry of Education due to the links between universities and industry, and also by the Foreign Ministry as a way to promote FDI, mainly through the Invest in Sweden Agency (ISA).

Sweden has in a pioneering way developed a specific governmental organization focused on supporting the development of innovation systems, Vinnova (an acronym for the Swedish Agency for Innovation Systems). Vinnova's mission is to promote sustainable growth by financing R&D and developing effective innovation systems; it does so by integrating research and development in technology, transport, and working life.

Vinnova has launched a cluster program as a means to push for new ways of approaching the regional policy more broadly. Through the so-called Vinnväxt program, Vinnova is attempting to inspire both enhanced competition and cooperation, and experimentation through a contest over which regions are able to advance the most competitive clustering alliance in a particular field. Different regions are encouraged to build broad-based alliances of actors, from universities, private, and public sectors. These alliances should interact in particular fields in order to enhance the regional innovation system and make them globally competitive and also secure resources in order to match the Vinnova funding. If a project is chosen, Vinnova provides SEK 200 million for 10 years for projects.

All regional business development agencies have been asked to incorporate cluster and regional innovation systems thinking in their regional development programs (RUP) and in their regional growth programs (RTP). The national business promotion agency (Nutek) is assigned to coordinate this work, by analyzing the needs of different actors, possible collaborative efforts, and the promotion of best practices.

Vinnova, Nutek, and ISA (Invest in Sweden Agency) have jointly launched *the Visanu program*, which is an effort to strengthen clusters and innovation systems as policy tools. It consists of three main components: (1) process support, which is given to regional innovation systems and clusters that have been chosen by regional government as suitable for increasing international competitiveness. In total, around 30 regional initiatives have been given support; (2) knowledge development with the aim of supporting the development of dynamic clusters and innovation systems; and (3) international promotion, in order to attract foreign investments and international competencies. Visanu has also created a network for regional process leaders and is involved in the creation of the Dahmén Institute, a nonprofit organization aiming to link researchers and practitioners in the development of innovation systems and clusters.

Vinnova's program, Forska&Väx, was introduced in 2005 with the purpose of contributing to the R&D efforts in small and medium enterprises (SMEs). Both policymakers and company representatives have declared the program to be a success. The traditional Swedish strength – some very large and successful, but mobile multinational companies (MNCs), contributing with about two-thirds of Swedish R&D – has increasingly been challenged by various manifestations of globalization. This has in turn meant that innovative SMEs now much more than before are at the policy focal point. A comprehensive policy effort, *Innovative SMEs – The Future of Sweden*, has recently been launched by Vinnova in order to suggest policies on a whole range of areas for these companies.

15.2.3.1   In Search of a New Model

Sweden provides an intermediate case between USA and Japan, with a mix of bottom-up and top-down initiatives. A relatively weak "top-down" introduction of a "third mission" for universities to be more involved in society has been variously interpreted. It can mean anything from educational outreach to better inform the public about academic activities to the establishment of a range of technology transfer mechanisms. Intellectual property emanating from academic research, irrespective of the funding source, is owned by academics and its disposition is up to them. It can be transferred to an existing firm, handed over to a university organization, or used as the basis for firm formation, as academics see fit. Given a tradition of industrial interaction primarily with large firms, most intellectual property flows to companies through informal relationships, as in Japan.

15.3   Mapping the Academic and Innovation Systems in Sweden

15.3.1   Expansion of Higher Education

Compared with several other European countries, Sweden has a relatively small research institute sector. Instead, the Swedish academic system is dominated by universities and university colleges. In the Fall of 2006, there were 41 universities and university colleges, of which 36 were state-owned and five state-supported foundations.

The size of these academic institutions differs considerably, ranging from under a hundred employees for the smallest colleges to close to 6,000 full-time employees

Table 15.2 Registered students at universities/university colleges 1979/1980–2004/2005

Year	1979/1980	1984/1985	1989/1990	1994/1995	1999/2000	2004/2005	2006/2007
Students	184,095	187,773	193,175	269,632	319,036	394,393	380,147

Source: SCB (2007c)

and over 34,000 registered students at the largest university, in Lund, during the academic year 2006–2007. Together, the ten largest universities employed 71% of the total number of personnel in 2006, measured in person-years (SCB 2007a). In terms of R&D person-years, this dominance is further accentuated with 52% of total person-years carried out at the five universities in Lund, Uppsala, Gothenburg, and Stockholm in addition to Karolinska Institutet (SCB 2007a). Research in the academic system is, thus, fairly concentrated in the large universities.

The size and the number of academic institutions have increased considerably in the post-World War II period to accommodate a large-scale expansion of higher education. In the early 1960s, higher education was a matter for a small and select group. From a few thousand students, higher education has grown to today's mass university system with close to 400,000 students engaged in studies at the university system. As can be seen from Table 15.2, the number of students enrolled at the universities more than doubled over the 27-year period 1980–2007.

15.3.2   Research Performers

Public research is performed mainly, about 64% of it, by the universities and the university colleges. The financial resources for public research are distributed by way of direct block funding to these institutions and by the research councils to individual researchers or research groups. Research at these institutions is also financed by funds from the EU, the Swedish industry, and research foundations. On an average, the fixed funding constitutes slightly less than 50% of the total funding of research in Swedish universities and university colleges. However, there is a considerable variation between different research subjects in this respect. Research within the technical sciences is to a high degree (2/3) externally financed and research within the humanities is the least externally financed area (1/3) (Government bill 2004, p. 18).

15.3.3   Research Funding

There are three public research councils in Sweden. The Swedish Research Council (Vetenskapsrådet) is the largest, with SEK 2,523 million at its disposal in 2005 for basic research in all areas of research (Government bill 2004, p. 17). It is a government agency under the Ministry of Education, Research, and Culture, and it has three main areas of responsibility: research funding, research policy, and science communication. Furthermore, it includes three scientific councils: for humanities and social sciences, for medicine, and for natural and engineering sciences. Two other public councils are targeting specific research areas: Swedish Council for Working Life and Social Research (FAS), with access to SEK 291 million, and The Swedish Research Council for Environment, Agricultural Sciences, and Spatial Planning (FORMAS), with SEK 531 million for distribution in 2005. Representatives from the research community are in the majority in these bodies, and international experts are frequently consulted to evaluate their policies and activities.

As discussed earlier, Vinnova is another important actor in research financing. In addition to developing effective innovation systems, it has the mission to finance Swedish R&D. For that latter purpose, it had SEK 1,122 million at its disposal in 2005. Several other governmental agencies are funding research within their specific areas of competence.

The public funds for research and development also comprise research financed with funds from research foundations, established in 1993–1994 with capital from employee funds. These entities receive no capital from the State, though the government appoints their boards of trustees. At the time of founding of these foundations, The Bank of Sweden Tercentenary Foundation got a share from the dissolved employee funds and is now the largest financiers of research in social science and the humanities. Together these foundations, in 2004, distributed about SEK 1,500 million. Some foundations of private origin are also of significant importance. The Knut and Alice Wallenberg Foundation donated about SEK 950 million in 2004. Within the field of medicine, there are several important actors financing research, e.g., funds for cancer, heart and lung diseases, and diabetes. Together, these private or nongovernmental organizations (NGOs) financed research, mainly within the universities and university colleges, to the extent of SEK 2,200 million in 2001 (Government bill 2004, p. 17). Figure 15.1 provides an overview of the flows of funding in 2005 between the financing sectors and the research-performing sectors.

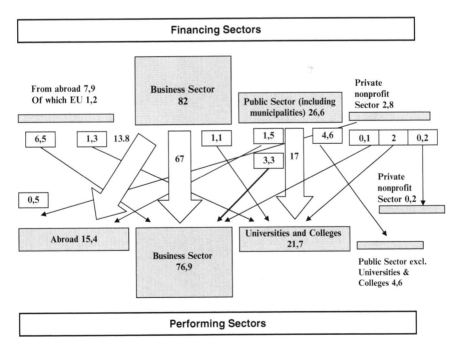

Fig. 15.1 R&D in Sweden by financing and performing sector 2005 (SEK bn).
Source: Adapted from SCB 2009

15.3.4   Informal Relations

Traditionally, for many Swedish academics, the interaction with firms takes place through their regular academic role. The usual relations have involved transferring different inquiries to people who are suited for answering them and dealing with matters concerning students. The traditional form for commercial involvement has, therefore, been as consultants. Restrictions on their professorial role have largely limited their involvement with professorial firms to part-time, one-person consulting operations. The type of involvement is, therefore, relatively limited in terms of time and financial support, and it seldom develops into long-term interaction with customers. Thus, there is a clear separation between consulting activities and academic work.

15.3.5   The Third Mission

Even though the educational system is the main vehicle for academic entrepreneurialism as in most European countries, there is also a movement toward more direct involvement of university professors in commercial activities. In 1997, Swedish universities were given a third mission in the Higher Education Act, besides education and research, to support economic and social development and play a greater role in explaining academia to the broader public. In contrast to Japan, this rather strong legal framework has, however, not been supplemented by similarly strong implementation mechanisms. The type of entrepreneurship that has emerged is, therefore, mainly an indirect kind, where other firms or students act as carriers of commercial ideas.

15.3.6   The Bologna Process

Historically, Sweden has scored low on "export of students," i.e., for studies abroad. For Swedish students, new opportunities for university studies in Europe arose with the Swedish adherence to the EU in the mid-1990s, e.g., within the Erasmus program that makes possible for students to study for part of their degree in other European countries. The current debate has to a large extent evolved around the so-called Bologna process, which perhaps should be seen against the background of the Lisbon Strategy, which includes measures in areas such as economic reform, R&D, and social coherence. The overreaching target of the Bologna process is to create a single European area for higher education. The European Higher Education Area (EHEA) comprises in practice more than EU member states (40 states had adhered after a meeting in Berlin 2003). One operative target is to harmonize the academic credit system and the cycles of higher education (Kim 2005). Sweden has participated in a somewhat more defensive manner in this process than its neighbors Norway, Finland, and Denmark. Sweden has emphasized the importance of some domestic, distinctive features such as a 4-year doctoral education (Kim 2005).

15.3.7   University Holding Companies

The Swedish Parliament gave in 1994 the right to universities and university colleges to establish holding companies to procure, hold in trust, and sell shares in project and service companies engaged in R&D. Later they were also given a right to have companies with the purpose of arranging commissioned education. Such holding companies have so far been established at 14 universities and university colleges. These companies have evolved in somewhat different ways in accordance with differences in specialization, size, and the structure of the local business environment. According to Vinnova (Vinnforsk VP2003:1), the Swedish research institutions have already sufficient funds to support and strengthen the incentives for the commercialization of research results. The primary weakness in the system is rather insufficient financial resources in the holding companies. Vinnova consulted also on this issue a number of actors and stakeholders. Most of them agreed with the findings and conclusions of Vinnova on a general level, but some of them pointed at the lack of resources and competence, and the negative attitudes toward commercialization of research results as highly potent obstacles for the institutions.

Uppsala University, Göteborg University, the Faculty of Engineering at Lund University, and The Royal Institute of Technology argued that the role of research institutions must be strengthened. Others pointed to the fact that these institutions are part of a larger system with many different types of actors and that a suitable delimitation of their functions must be elaborated (e.g., Linköping University, Blekinge Institute of Technology, and the Swedish Energy Agency). Teknikbrostiftelsen in Linköping held that universities are unsuitable to "godfathering" innovation systems, and that they are a very natural actor in the first part of the process but that they do not have enough knowledge or position for such a task. Furthermore, they pointed out that the problem is not the lack of financial resources, but a lack of clarity on what the holding companies shall accomplish.

The Confederation of Swedish Enterprises and other organizations representing the private companies have underlined the importance of an increased cooperation between the universities and the private sector. Several participants, such as Uppsala University, Göteborg University, The Royal Institute of Technology, the airplane and car manufacturer SAAB, and The Swedish Trade Union Confederation wrote that the holding companies could be made more useful in developing the innovation systems of the learning institutions and for the first steps of commercialization, e.g., through legal and business consultancy services.

The Knowledge Foundation (KK-stiftelsen) is working to enhance Swedish competitiveness by supporting, e.g., new universities and university colleges and competence development in industry. They stressed that every institution should have the right to establish holding companies, but that this should not be mandatory. To be effective, these companies demand a high degree of experience concerning commercialization, business development, patenting, etc., and that it would be difficult for many to sustain such competence. It should be explored if one could find ways for cooperative structures between such companies at different learning institutions (Government Bill 2004, pp. 168–169).

15.4   The Current Swedish Debate

It is generally acknowledged that the debates on editorial pages of the most influential daily newspapers are an increasingly preferred method used in order to influence policymakers and other important stakeholders in Sweden. In fact, politicians and other policymakers themselves see these articles as an effective and expedient way to get their message through. Ample space is available for each article, but the writers are carefully selected by the editor, seemingly much in accordance with the "news' value" of the topic and the position of the writer in Swedish society. The higher education and research policy issues have increasingly been highlighted in this context.

A few years ago, Ulf Sandström (2002), research leader at the Swedish Institute for Studies in Education and Research (SISTER), presented some empirical findings from their research on the Swedish debate on research policy and its "long waves" from 1980 to 2001. During the 1980s, the debate on these issues in the daily newspapers was quite sparse and more descriptive than normative. When a center-right government took office in the early 1990s, at the beginning of a deep economic crisis, significant critique began to appear. Professors from the humanities protested against diminishing funding, the question of industrial relevance of university research became a hot topic, and the position of women in the Swedish research system. When the social democrats came back to power and appointed a new Minister for Higher Education, Carl Tham, the position of female researchers came at the center of the debate (Sandström 2002, pp 53–54). The new minister also came under increasing pressure from well-organized groups of researchers concerning diminishing research funding (Benner 2002). The confidence between researchers and politicians was indeed low, and this was indicated by an increasing amount of debates in the media (Sandström 2002).

The next Minister of Higher Education, Thomas Östros, also a social democrat, presented in 2000 an official report, with the laconic title "Research" ("Forskning"). It was considered rather friendly toward the aspirations of the research community but instead a renewed critique regarding relevance of Swedish research, for industry and society at large, began to appear. During Minister Östros' term of office, the amount of media debates on research policy and associated issues increased, stabilizing at a high level (Sandström 2002).

The current Swedish debate can best be categorized under three general headings, though the particular issues often are overlapping, interacting, or clashing:

(1) A general debate regarding higher education and research, such as organization, funding, the quality of university education and research, academic freedom, and internationalization.
(2) A debate concerning rights and promotion of, e.g., women, ethnic minorities, social class, and regions considered as underprivileged in the present Swedish education and research system.
(3) A debate concerning the economic and industrial relevance of Swedish research. In this category, economic growth is an explicit or implicit policy goal.

Some issues will be discussed under each of these headings, but emphasis will be put on the third.

15.4.1   The Third Mission: Doubts About Its Relevance

Since the late 1990s, the Swedish system for higher education has been given a so-called Third Mission, meaning that in addition to the two traditional tasks, education and research, the universities and other academic institutions are also obliged to interact with surrounding society and economic life. The legislation was closely connected with worries regarding economic growth and increased unemployment rates. The new task highlights a classical discussion on "academic freedom" within independent universities and "the university in service of society." In a report made shortly after the introduction the third mission amendment, two researchers from the Centre for Regional Science in Umeå asked representatives from seven Swedish universities and university colleges on their views of different aspects of the third mission. Heads of departments, directors of studies, and administrative personnel from selected departments (Computer Science, Physics, and Biology) were interviewed. The institutions for higher education consulted in the report were Umeå University, The Technical University of Linköping, Örebro University College, The Royal School of Technology, Karolinska Institutet, Lund University, and Karlskrona/Ronneby University (Asplund and Nordman 1999). Based on the survey, the authors concluded the following inter alia:

- Attitudes toward the third mission differed considerably between universities and also between departments within universities. For example, of the six universities with a department of computer science, half of them were positive toward the third mission and half were negative.
- The third mission is of greater importance to the small university colleges as the smaller universities, to a higher degree, need to build alliances with the local community in order to raise external funds to complement funds from the government.
- Time–pressure and massive burden of work on researchers are felt to be major obstacles for the researchers. The research community creates new ideas with a potential for economic growth, but often lacks time to develop them.
- The third mission is regarded by many to exert an extra administrative burden and an annoying source of paperwork, i.e., "more talk and less action" (Asplund and Nordman, 1999, pp. 30–31).

15.4.2   The Question of Affirmative Action in Recruitment

According to Laila Abdallah, a cultural anthropologist and gender issue specialist, women applying for research funding are not directly discriminated against in the Swedish system (Abdallah 2002, p.177). It is, however, a fact that so far women are underrepresented at the higher levels of the research hierarchy, and one reason may be the existence of barriers of an informal character, such as lack of access to informal networks (Abdallah 2002, pp. 186–188). The gender issue is a much debated topic in Sweden throughout the society as a whole. Moreover, "socially biased recruitment" is a longstanding issue, given the persistent low enrollment level of students from homes without academic traditions.

15.4.3   Are There Myths in the Debates on STI Policies in Sweden?

The Swedish paradox is a frequently discussed topic. How is it that Sweden, which statistically spends more on R&D and other factors of growth than perhaps any other OECD member, gets so little in return in the form of innovation and long-term growth? Anders Granberg, RPI at Lund University, and Staffan Jacobsson, Chalmers University of Technology (Granberg and Jacobsson 2006), have scrutinized some dominant and persistent beliefs in the Swedish science policy debate that might shed light on this question. They conclude that the map based on these beliefs is "misleading because it depicts Sweden as a nation;

1. Which has an outstanding volume of academic research, whereas (they) suggest that Sweden is but one of many OECD countries in that respect, given the peculiarities of the Swedish R&D system and the multiple functions assigned to the academic sector. Indeed, the use of time expenditure is an alternative indicator that opens up for the possibility that Sweden may even have a lower volume of academic research than some other OECD countries.
2. Where "curiosity-driven" research dominates, whereas (they) suggest that the direction of knowledge and competence development is largely in the hands of external funding of "needs-driven," or "strategic" research. In addition, at least at technical universities, block funding allows for virtually no "curiosity-driven" research, i.e., exploratory research.
3. Where "curiosity-driven" research is a threat to innovation and economic growth, whereas (they) argue that not only is the dichotomy between such research and "needs-driven" research misleading but also that these forms of research are complementary.
4. Where there is a distance or a substantial gap between academia and industry, whereas (they) argue that there is much evidence that suggests the opposite, although (they) agree that more can and should be done to exploit the "complementarities" (Granberg and Jacobsson 2006, p. 334).

Deploring that the imperfect map has resulted in a "simple-minded focus on the 'commercialization' issues" they point to three policy challenges. First, they suggest "that academic research may not have the volume required to provide an attractive location for industrial R&D efforts but that there are still opportunities to pursue an offensive cluster-focused policy. Such a policy needs, however, to go much beyond simply increasing the volume of 'needs-driven' R&D." Second, "the depletion of block funding has gone so far that it is likely to be harming the ability of the Universities (at least the technical universities) to fulfill their mandate and to be effective in implementing a cluster-focused science policy. The balance between external funding and block funding needs to be redressed." Third, they point out that "the ability of the Universities to play a role that is truly complementary to that of industry is threatened and has to be safeguarded. If that ability is reduced, universities may fail to live up to perhaps the most important part of their mandate, namely to be 'responsive' to scientific and technological opportunities and generate capabilities before industry articulates a demand for a 'needs-driven' science policy" (Granberg and Jacobsson 2006).

The Swedish Association of Graduate Engineers, represents an important group in the Swedish system of innovation, and from another perspective than Granberg and Jacobsson, they reject the often discussed dichotomy between "curiosity-driven" basic research and "needs-driven" research. Pointing at MIT and its outward orientation that commenced some 100 years ago, they maintain that "needs-driven" research often leads to basic research, and that this creates new openings between different research areas (Civilingenjörsförbundet 2003, p. 15).

15.4.4   The Entrepreneurial University

Sweden is a staunch defender of intellectual property rights (IPRs) in international forums, notably concerning patents. In the Swedish University System, "researchers have long had ownership rights for the intellectual property resulting from their work, and the debate has centred on the feasibility and advisability on shifting these ownerships from the individual to the institution" (Mowery and Sampat 2005, p. 232). Several official reports have analyzed the issue whether the ownership now granted to teachers and researchers at the universities ("professor's, or university teacher's exception," i.e., an exception from Swedish legislation indicating the employer's right to the inventions of his employees) should be maintained. This was most recently done by Vinnova in the report Vinnforsk, concluding that the individual researcher should have a right to report patentable inventions and computer programs to the university or the university college, where he or she is employed. Secrecy, at the full disposal of the researcher, should be connected to this, and the researcher should be recognized as the inventor (patent) or author (computer program). It should furthermore be considered if the university should have a right to a reasonable refunding from the net revenue from, e.g., patentable inventions. In preparation of the report, Vinnova consulted a number of important actors in the Swedish innovation system. Some of their conclusions are presented below:

In a comment, Lund University wrote that the report had treated the question superficially, and advocated unequivocally, that "the teacher's exception" should be abolished. It was inter alia maintained that much research is conducted in research groups, where individual researchers often are not participating for the whole duration of a research project, and it is then a difficult task to judge the contribution from these individual researchers. The principal objection, however, was that making research results useful, closely connected with the academic institution as they are, should not be a private matter.

The Royal Institute of Technology and the Chalmers University of Technology were both of the opinion that "teacher's exception" should be maintained in the short run, but saw the need for changes in the longer run. The Göteborg University held that an effective innovation system in the longer run would lead to the abolishment of the exception, and that it is not sustainable to view the rights of research results as solely a matter for the individual researcher.

Teknikbrostiftelserna (seven regional foundations designated to develop linkages between academia and industry, now integrated with *Innovationsbron* AB) argued, with one exception, for status quo, and so did Företagarna, the national organization for SMEs. The Confederation of Swedish Industries (larger companies), on the contrary, advocated for an abrogation.

The Swedish Trade Union Confederation pointed out that, in the light of ongoing attempts to strengthen efforts to make use of research results, it is natural to give research institutions ownership to these results. SACO (The Swedish Confederation of Professional Associations) and SULF (Swedish Association of University Teachers) both wanted the exception to remain. So did TCO (The Confederation of Professional Employees), but wrote that future efforts should be directed at changing the Swedish science system so that the teacher's exception can be abolished.

15.4.5   The Need for Venture Capital

Joseph Schumpeter underlined the importance of financial capital for the entrepreneur to carry out new combinations (Schumpeter 1934). As already indicated, financial actors are important elements in the STI approach, and individual entrepreneurs often regard access to capital, particularly in the early stages of the innovative process as their main problem. For this reason, there has been a continuing demand to improve the system for access to such capital. The problem was accentuated with a dip in the business cycle beginning in 2001, and new companies in ICT and biotech were hit particularly hard, which in turn led to a sharply decreased access to venture capital. The Royal Swedish Academy of Engineering Sciences (IVA) has argued that it is important that the State has clear responsibility in the field of seed financing. IVA has initiated a project, CONNECT, which brings together risk capitalists, various experts, and innovators to stimulate the development of growth companies and convey competence and capital (IVA 2003, p. 13). In an article in the daily newspaper Dagens Nyheter in January 2005, the Minister for Higher Education, Thomas Östros, presented to the public a government plan to use SEK 2,000 million to strengthen the ability of Swedish companies to commercialize their research results. The program was implemented shortly thereafter and intends to secure access to capital for companies, as well as to strengthen competence building and to develop networks. A holding company, *Innovationsbron Ltd.* (Innovation Bridge), has been created with seven regional affiliates in close collaboration with the universities in Uppsala, Lund, Göteborg, Stockholm, Luleå, Umeå, and Linköping. Vinnova works closely with the new company and has been given the task to establish new incubators (DN Debatt, February 18, 2005 and http://www. innovationsbron.se).

15.4.6 Regional Development

The systems of innovation, clusters, and business networks are to some extent related concepts and perhaps in some cases in the real world not easy to distinguish from one another. Academia, industry, and policymakers are the three critical types of actors for networking and interaction in the Triple Helix concept, and for clusters and systems of innovation, relevant actors must be extended with at least two additional types: financial actors and intermediary organizations. Asheim and Gertler (2005) point at the regional level as important for successful innovation. As important parts of knowledge are tacit and "sticky," and as "learning through interaction" often is crucial for innovation, geography matters in spite of the communications revolution (Asheim and Gertler 2005, p. 293).

The public debate on regional issues has largely been confined to two controversies. First, there has been a debate of a more general political character on whether the regions should have additional political power. Sweden has no federal tradition, but pressure from the regions have increased since the Swedish adherence to the EU. Second, there has been a debate on whether it is at all desirable to have active policies on innovation systems and clusters. The combatants have mostly been economists. At one extreme, the ultra liberals have maintained that there should be no such policies, because the market is always more economically effective. On the other extreme, some interventionists and protectionists have claimed that, e.g., clusters can be created from practically nothing, and that self-contained clusters can protect from outside competition. Mostly however, the debate has been carried out between these extremes.

15.5 Concluding Remarks

It would seem clear from the presentation that the Swedish Academic System has been successfully expanded, maintained, and adjusted according to policy targets in the post-World War II period. Indicators on research input such as size of funding, as well as output such as number of patents and citation scores, point to the fact that the academic system produces research results of high international standards.

Although there is a discussion as to the reliability of the indicators, most observers would agree that the Swedish universities hold their own against their counterparts in most other countries.

What is also clear, however, is that when the discussion centers on how the role and performance of academic institutions could be further enhanced to meet the challenges ahead, there is a great deal of confusion particularly on how universities can operate in tandem with the surrounding society and function as an engine of growth through providing innovations and entrepreneurship. One conclusion from a study on the attitudes toward the third mission of Swedish universities was that the smaller university colleges by necessity are more integrated into the local community and regional development (Asplund and Nordman 1999, p. 30). Under favorable circumstances, such integration could ideally result in a symbiotic relationship between the private sector and the academic system in knowledge production and, possibly, the emergence or enhancement of local clusters. It would be interesting to follow this line of thought by examining and comparing the potential role of universities in a context of a local rather than national knowledge system.

References

Abdallah, L. (2002). 'Kvinnor, forskning och karriärhinder' in Sandström, U. (ed.) Detnya forskningslandskapet, Stockholm: SISTER.

Andersson, M. and Gunnarsson, G. (2006). 'Egalitarianism in the Process of Modern Economic Growth: The Case of Sweden', Background paper for World development Report 2006, Washington, D.C.: The World Bank

Asheim, B.T. and Gertler, M.S. (2005). 'The Geography of Innovation: Regional Innovation Systems' in Fagerberg et al. (eds.) The Oxford Handbook on Innovation, London and New York: Oxford University Press.

Asplund, P. and Nordman, N. (1999). 'Attitudes Toward the Third Mission. A Selection of Interviews from Seven Universities in Sweden', SNS and CERUM Working Paper no. 15:1999. Umeå: Centre for Regional Science.

Benner, M. (2002). 'Ställningskrig: Reflektioner kring debatten 2001' in Sandström, U. (ed.) Det nya forskningslandskapet, Stockholm: SISTER.

Civilingenjörsförbundet (2003). 'Ökad tillväxt eller stillad nyfikenhet? En analys avsvensk forsknings drivkrafter'. http://www.cf.se.cf_tycker_naringspolitik.htm

Government bill (forskningspropositionen) 2004/05:80, 'Forskning för ett bättre liv'

IVA (2003). 'IVAs underlag till forskningspropositionen'. http://www.iva.se

Granberg, A. and Jacobsson, S. 'Myths or Reality: A Scrutiny of Dominant Beleifs in the Swedish Science Policy Debate', Science and Public Policy, vol. 33, number 5, June 2006.

Kim, L. (2005) 'Bolognaprocessen och dess effekter på svenska universitet och högskolor'.http://www.lu.se/upload/LUPDF/Bologna/Sverige_Bologna/Bologna10maj05_LKim.pdf

Ministry of Industry, Employment and Communications (2005). Innovation Systems – interaction for enhanced knowledge and growth, Stockholm: Government Office

Mowery, D. and Sampat, B.N. (2005). 'Universities in National Innovation Systems' in Fagerberg et al. (eds.) The Oxford Handbook on Innovation, London and New York: Oxford University Press.

Sandström, U. (2002). 'Forskningsdebattens långa vågor' ('The Long Waves of the Research Debate'), in Sandström (ed.) Det nya forskningslandskapet, Stockholm: SISTER.

SCB (2009). Science and Technology Indicators for Sweden 2007 http://www.scb.se/statistik/publikationer/UF0301_2007A01_BR_UF96BR0901.pdf

SCB (2007a). 'Higher Education. Employees in Higher Education 2006' (in Swedish). Sveriges Officiella Statistik, Statistiska meddelanden UF 23 SM 0701.

SCB (2007b). 'Research and experimental development in Sweden 2005. An overview' (in Swedish). Sveriges Officiella Statistik, Statistiska meddelanden UF 16 SM 0701.

SCB (2007c). Students enrolled 1977/78 - 2006/2007 by university/university college and sex' (in Swedish). Accessed October 30, 2007 at http://www.scb.se/statistik/UF/UF0205/2007A01b/Web_GR1_RegUnivKon.xls

Schumpeter, D. (1934, 1996). The Theory of Economic Development, London: Transaction Books.

UNDP (1995). Human Development Report 1995, New York: Oxford University Press.

UNDP (2005). Human Development Report 2005, New York: Oxford University Press.

Visanu (2005). Det nationella programmet för utveckling av innovationssystem och kluster. Slutrapport 6 juli 2005. http://www.nutek.se

Part III
Synthesis

Chapter 16
The Three Missions of Universities: A Synthesis of UniDev Project Findings

Claes Brundenius and Bo Göransson

16.1 Introductory Remarks

This chapter attempts to make some quantitative and qualitative comparisons of the 12 countries that have been involved in the UniDev project, by examining the changing role of academic institutions within the contexts of innovation and economic growth and development. As explained in the introductory chapter of this text, the project has been working with national teams in 12 countries (Brazil, Cuba, Uruguay, Denmark, Germany, Sweden, South Africa, Tanzania, Russian Federation, Latvia, Vietnam, and China). It is interesting to note that in spite of different economic systems (ranging from liberal market economies to socialist economies), different levels of development, and different roles in national innovation systems, the role of higher education (and especially that of universities) has proven to be a hot topic in all the countries.[1]

The country reports presented in this volume provide some in-depth knowledge and analysis of the situation in the 12 countries. This chapter not only draws on these findings but also attempts to provide a quantitative and comparative framework with qualitative inputs from the country studies. The chapter deals with the three missions of universities: (1) teaching, (2) research, and (3) the so-called third mission, that is, what do universities do in order to be relevant for society?

Some basic quantitative information of the 12 countries (plus the World and USA for reasons of comparison) is presented in Table 16.1 below. The table presents latest available data on population, PPP$/capita (as a proxy for level of development), the Human Development Index (HDIS incorporating basic needs satisfaction in the PPP variable), and mobile and Internet penetration (as indicators of linking up capability to the information society).

---

[1] The topic, the changing role of higher education, is addressed in a number of international reports, see e.g. Arocena et al. (2008), Eggins (2009), UNESCO (2009), ESF (2008)

C. Brundenius (✉)
Research Policy Institute, Lund University, Sweden,
e-mail: Claes.Brundenius@fpi.lu.se

B. Göransson and C. Brundenius (eds.), *Universities in Transition: The Changing Role and Challenges for Academic Institutions*, © International Development Research Centre 2011

Table 16.1 UniDev: some basic data

	Population (million) 2007	HDI ranking 2007	PPP (billion.$) 2000 current	PPP (billion.$) 2007 current	PPP per capita 2000 current	PPP per capita 2007 current	Mobile phones per 100 inhabit.	Internet users per 100 inhabit.
Brazil	191.6	75 (8)	1,186.7	1,775.6	6,810 (7)	9,270 (8)	63 (8)	35.2 (5)
Cuba	11.26	51 (6)	61.3	77.4	5,500 (9)	6,876 (9)	2 (12)	11.6 (10)
Uruguay	3.32	50 (5)	25.5	36.6	7,730 (5)	11,020 (6)	90 (6)	29.1 (6)
Denmark	5.46	16 (2)	150.4	201.0	28,180 (1)	36,800 (2)	114 (3)	80.7 (1)
Germany	82.27	22 (3)	2,100.3	2,857.7	25,670 (3)	34,740 (3)	118 (1)	72.3 (3)
Sweden	9.15	7 (1)	243.9	343.0	27,500 (2)	37,490 (1)	113 (4)	79.7 (2)
S. Africa	47.85	129 (11)	284.3	452.3	6,460 (8)	9,450 (7)	88 (7)	8.3 (11)
Tanzania	40.43	151 (12)	25.5	48.7	750 (12)	1,200 (12)	21 (11)	1.0 (12)
Russia	142.1	71 (7)	1,086.3	2,036.5	7,430 (6)	14,330 (5)	115 (2)	21.1 (7)
Latvia	2.28	48 (4)	19.0	35.9	8,010 (4)	15,790 (4)	97 (5)	55.0 (4)
Vietnam	85.15	116 (10)	108.1	215.4	1,390 (11)	2,530 (11)	28 (10)	21.0 (8)
China	1,318.31	92 (9)	2,940.1	7,150.5	2,330 (10)	5,420 (10)	42 (9)	16.1 (9)
WORLD	6,610.26	–	41,825.9	65,752.3	6,887	9,947	51	21.8
USA	301.62	13	9,930.9	13,827.2	35,190	45,840	85	73.5

Sources: World development indicators 2007 (World Bank), Human development report 2009 (UNDP 2009), and Human development index (HDI) world ranking; UniDev ranking within brackets

In terms of level of development, three of the UniDev countries can be characterized as highly developed market economies: Denmark, Germany, and Sweden, with PPP levels considerably higher than that of the others (over 30,000 PPP$/capita). Then follow Russia and Latvia (around 15,000), and after that the Latin American countries and South Africa. China still has a relatively low PPP/capita but is, as known, rapidly catching up. Vietnam and Tanzania are still far behind the others, although they have both experienced rapid growth between 2000 and 2007. The ranking of the countries has not changed very much in the period.

On the contrary, if we look at the HDI, there are some interesting differences in the ranking. Thus, Cuba, Uruguay, China, and Vietnam have higher rankings in HDI than in PPP, while South Africa falls to 11th position from seventh position in the PPP ranking, mainly because of a very skewed income distribution and declining life expectancy (due to high HIV frequencies).

With respect to penetration of information technologies, it is again – not surprisingly – the more developed countries that are ranked the highest. But it is interesting to note that many developing countries are not far behind. This goes particularly for Brazil, Uruguay, and to some extent South Africa (except for Internet penetration). China and Vietnam are also catching up fast. Cuba is catching up on Internet penetration but has still a very low penetration rate of mobile telephone (lowest ranking of all the countries).

16.2   The First Mission: Teaching

The first mission of universities, and still the most important one, is of course teaching. Although investment in higher education is very costly (and it has at times been called a luxury), there is today a growing awareness, also in developing countries, of the importance of higher education and its decisive role for sustained economic growth and development. Tertiary education enrollment has also increased rapidly during the last decade in the UniDev countries, as can be appreciated in Fig. 16.1 below. The figure depicts how enrollment ratios have developed between 1999 and 2007 (see also detailed data in Tables 16.2 and 16.3).

The measurement is the so-called Gross Enrollment Ratio (GER) at the tertiary level, which is really a proxy because it divides total enrollments by the corresponding age group (in this case, the 18–24 cohort). This might seem to be an arbitrary measure because clearly there are many students over 24 years of age in most universities. However, enrollments by age of students are as a rule not readily available, and the GER is considered to be a reasonably usable surrogate.

The data show that enrollments have increased quite fast in many countries. This goes in particular for Cuba, which in 2002 launched a drive for the "universalization" of university studies, which has led to a dramatic increase in tertiary enrollments. This has had the effect that practically all in the age group are enrolled at some tertiary institution in Cuba now, in addition to increased enrollment by older age cohorts. This has, of course, problems that will be mentioned later on. Other countries that have expanded university education impressively are China, Brazil,

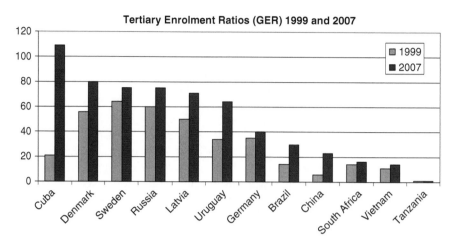

Fig. 16.1 Tertiary enrollment ratios (GER) 1999 and 2007. *Source*: Table 16.3

and Uruguay. But also Denmark, Sweden, Russia, and Latvia have enrollment ratios that are 75 and above.

16.2.1 Which Countries Devote Most Resources to Higher Education?

As mentioned previously, higher education is a costly affair and although unit costs (e.g., cost per student) can vary, if high quality is to be assured there are not many costs in developing countries that can be reduced in relation to costs in rich countries except for one item: teachers' salaries. Teachers as a rule receive much lower salaries in developing countries.

Figure 16.2 below shows the per capita expenditures (PPP$) on higher education in the UniDev countries (see also Table 16.4 for details which also present cost per student data). As expected, it is the three richest countries, Denmark, Sweden, and Germany, which spend most on higher education (between 400 and 600 PPP$/capita in 2007). However, of all the other countries, Cuba is spending most resources per capita on higher education, as a result of its crash universalization program. Russia and Latvia spend just over 100 PPP$/capita on higher education. China, Brazil, and South Africa devote around 75 PPP$/capita to higher education, while Uruguay 51 PPP$/capita, and Tanzania and Vietnam as little as 17 and 13 PPP$, respectively (Table 16.4).

These data as a rule only include public expenditure on higher education. Data on the role of private financing of higher education are not so easy to get, partly due to the rather imprecise definition of what private higher institutions comprise. Private higher education institutions are important, for instance, in Brazil and

Table 16.2 UniDev: tertiary education enrollments, 1999–2007

	1999	2000	2001	2002	2003	2004	2005	2006	2007
Brazil Total	2,369,945	2,694,245	3,030,754	3,479,913	3,887,022	4,163,733	4,453,156	4,676,646	4,880,381
Females	1,318,393	1,515,352	1,705,995	1,966,283	2,193,246	2,346,516	2,488,927	2,605,611	2,680,978
Cuba Total	153,463	158,674	178,021	191,262	235,997	396,516	417,858	681,629	864,846
Females	81,558	84,826	92,824	104,036	132,543	247,063	293,089	414,239	549,670
Uruguay Total	91,275	na	na	na	na	na	na	na	158,841
Females	57,495	na	na	na	na	na	na	na	99,924
Denmark Total	189,970	189,162	192,022	196,204	201,746	217,130	232,255	228,893	232,194
Females	106,957	107,644	108,290	112,698	116,844	125,628	133,376	131,302	133,684
Germany Total	2,087,044	2,054,838	2,083,945	2,159,708	2,242,397	2,330,457	2,268,741	2,289,465	2,278,897
Females	989,271	988,703	1,014,075	1,058,896	1,109,082	1,150,947	1,127,168	1,137,777	1,133,518
Sweden Total	325,124	346,878	358,020	382,851	414,657	429,623	426,723	422,614	413,710
Females	192,961	201,962	211,468	227,682	247,091	255,853	254,325	251,782	247,894
S.Africa Total	623,911	644,763	658,588	675,160	744,489	735,073	741,380	741,024	760,009
Females	340,893	356,631	352,133	362,427	385,857	403,462	401,042	408,519	402,805
Tanzania Total	18,867	na	18,331	23,239	31,772	39,117	41,419	na	55,134
Females	3,970	na	4,775	7,763	9,325	12,861	13,206	na	17,803
Russia Total (000)	4,073.0	na	na	na	8,099.7	8,608.0	9,003.2	9,167.3	9,370.4
Females	na	na	na	na	4,601.9	4,907.4	5,136.9	5,219.5	5,325.6
Latvia Total	82,042	91,237	102,783	110,500	118,944	127,656	130,706	131,125	129,497
Females	50,539	57,850	63,524	67,991	73,403	79,473	82,575	83,010	82,771
Vietnam Total (000)	810.1	899.5	974.1	1,020.7	1,131.0	1,319.8	1,387.1	1,666.2	1,928.4
Females	347.6	374.2	409.1	436.9	486.3	539.8	567.3	na	950.7
China Total (000)	9,019.0	7,979.6	13,629.3	17,730.0	19,782.0	19,898.8	22,631.2	25,742.0	27,195.3
Females	na	na	na	8,325.0	9,325.2	8,183.7	10,866.0	12,588.8	13,536.3

Source: UIS data base (2009) and UniDev updates

Table 16.3 Tertiary education gross enrollment ratios (GER), 1999–2007

	1999	2000	2001	2002	2003	2004	2005	2006	2007
Brazil	14	16	18	20	22	24	25	na	30
Cuba	21	22	26	28	34	55	63	88	109
Uruguay	34	na	na	na	na	na	na	na	64
Denmark	56	58	60	63	67	74	81	80	80
Germany	na	na	na	na	na	na	na	na	40[a]
Sweden	64	67	70	76	82	84	82	79	75
South Africa	14	14	14	15	15	16	15	15	16[a]
Tanzania	1	(1)	1	1	1	1	1	(1)	1
Russia	na	na	na	na	65	69	71	72	75
Latvia	50	56	63	67	71	75	75	74	71
Vietnam	11	9	10	na	na	na	na	na	14[a]
China	6	8	10	13	16	18	20	22	23

Source: UIS data base and UniDev updates

GER = Gross enrollment ratio at the tertiary level, divides total enrollments by the corresponding 18–24 cohort (UNESCO definitions)

aUniDev estimate

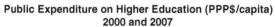

**Public Expenditure on Higher Education (PPP$/capita)
2000 and 2007**

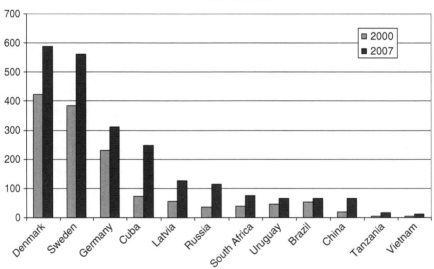

Fig. 16.2 Public expenditure on higher education (PPP$/capita) 2000 and 2007. *Source*: Table 16.4

Latvia, and the data presented here may be greater for some countries if all private institutions were to be included.

But we can also look at higher education expenditures from other angles. How much is spent in relative terms, that is, in terms of percentage of GDP. Here Cuba is at the top with 3.3% of GDP devoted to higher education (and no less than 13.3%

Table 16.4 Public expenditure on education around 2000 and 2007

		Total expenditure on education as % of GDP	Expenditure on higher education as % of GDP	Higher education as % of total education	Public expeditures on higher education per capita (PPP$)
Brazil	2000	3.8	0.8	21.1	54
	2007	4.6	0.7	15.2	65
Cuba	2001	7.8	1.3	16.7	72
	2007	13.3	3.3	24.8	248
Uruguay	1999	2.8	0.6	21.4	46
	2007	3.4	0.6	17.6	66
Denmark	2000	6.4	1.5	23.4	423
	2007	6.8	1.6	23.5	589
Germany	2000	4.2	0.9	21.4	231
	2007	4.1	0.9	22.0	312
Sweden	2000	6.2	1.4	22.6	385
	2007	8.2	1.5	18.7	562
S. Africa	2000	5.3	0.6	11.3	39
	2007	5.3	0.8	15.0	76
Tanzania	2000	2.5	0.5	21.3	4
	2007	5.2	1.4	26.2	16
Russia	1999	2.9	0.5	17.2	37
	2007	3.9	0.8	20.5	115
Latvia	2000	5.4	0.7	12.9	56
	2007	5.1	0.8	15.6	126
Vietnam	2001	4.1	0.4	9.8	6
	2007	5.6	0.5	8.9	13
China	2000	3.4	0.8	23.5	19
	2006	3.8	1.2	31.2	65

Source: UIS data base and UniDev updates

to education in general!). Denmark, Sweden, and Latvia follow suit with around 1.5%, followed by Tanzania 1.4% and China 1.2%. The other countries spend between 0.5% and 0.9% of GDP to higher education.

These two aspects of higher education expenditures are illustrated in the matrix in Table 16.5 below.

16.2.2   What Are the Students Studying?

Although increasing tertiary enrollments are important, there are also other aspects to consider. Thus, there is in many of the UniDev countries a legitimate concern about the orientation of higher studies. In many countries, there is a heated debate about, for instance, the role of humanities and the insufficient interest of students, particularly female students, in natural science and engineering sciences. In other words, what is the purpose of higher education and, being a costly item in government

Table 16.5 Absolute and relative size of public expenditures on higher education – 2007

HE expenditure per capita (PPP$)	Share of HE expenditure as % of GDP		
	Relatively high (more than 1.0%)	Medium (0.5–0.9%)	Low (Less than 0.5%)
High (more than 300 PPP$/capita)	Denmark (1.6%) Sweden (1.5%)	Germany (0.9%)	
Medium high (100–299 PPP$/capita)	Cuba (3.3%)	Latvia (0.8%) Russia (0.8%)	
Medium low (40–99 PPP$/capita)	China (1.2%)	Brazil (0.7%) Uruguay (0.6%) South Africa (0.8%)	
Low (less than 40 PPP$/capita)	Tanzania (1.4%)	Vietnam (0.5%)	

Source: Table 16.4

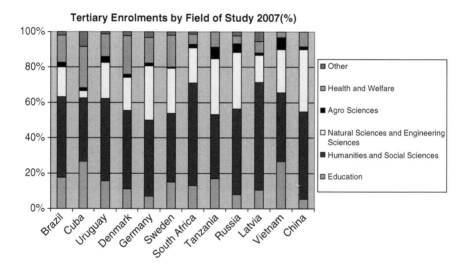

Fig. 16.3 Tertiary enrollments by field of study 2007 (%). *Source*: Table 16.6

budgets, should authorities try to attract students to more "useful" disciplines for society? In many countries, students do not pay tuition fees at public universities and in some (e.g., Uruguay) there is free intake, that is, anybody can enter any field of study. This could lead to disproportionate enrollments in disciplines that are – by some – considered to be "less relevant" than others. Without entering further into this debate, we will here just present the tendencies in the UniDev countries. Figure 16.3 below depicts this situation in 2007 (see Table 16.6 for details).

The data refer to field of study as a percentage of total enrollments. Education (that is, teacher training) has a high priority in especially Cuba and Vietnam, with about 25% of the students enrolled. Humanities is a strong discipline in Denmark, Sweden, Germany, and China with more than 10% enrolled. Enrollments are sizable in social

Table 16.6 UniDev: tertiary enrollments by field of study, 1999 and 2007 (%)

	Edu	Hum	SocSci	Science	Engin	Agro	Health	Other	Total
Brazil 1999	7.2	9.7	43.0	13.5	9.1	2.5	13.6	1.3	100
Brazil 2007	17.6	3.5	42.0	8.4	8.6	2.3	15.4	2.0	100[a]
Cuba 2007	26.4	1.3	34.3	2.3	1.7	1.5	23.2	8.2	100
Uruguay 2007	16.0	4.7	40.2	11.7	9.6	3.2	13.3	1.2	100
Denmark 1999	10.5	17.4	26.6	10.1	9.2	1.8	22.9	1.6	100
Denmark 2007	11.3	15.3	29.0	8.7	10.1	1.5	22.0	2.2	100
Germany 1999	8.0	16.1	26.5	12.3	16.2	1.6	16.2	2.3	100
Germany 2007	7.1	15.5	27.4	15.3	15.5	1.5	14.5	3.1	100
Sweden 1999	12.8	13.4	25.6	11.1	20.5	1.0	17.0	1.8	100
Sweden 2007	15.0	12.5	26.3	9.4	16.1	0.9	17.7	2.0	100
S. Africa 2000	21.2	6.6	47.0	10.6	6.7	1.4	5.3	1.0	100
S. Africa 2006	13.2	4.9	52.9	10.4	9.5	1.8	5.9	1.2	100
Tanzania 1999	14.3	2.5	36.9	3.5	18.1	6.7	5.4	0.4	100
Tanzania 2005	12.9	7.1	20.2	15.2	9.0	4.7	6.6	0.0	100
Russia[b] 2000	8.1	48.1[d]		9.3	23.0	4.7	4.4	2.3	100
Latvia 1999	19.0	8.7	42.8	4.1	16.0	2.7	4.8	1.2	100
Latvia 2007	10.5	7.2	53.7	5.1	10.4	1.1	6.3	5.6	100
Vietnam 1999	25.9	4.9	38.8	17.5[c]		4.0	2.9	0.0	100
Vietnam 2007	26.5	3.8	35.4	24.4[c]		6.8	3.1	0.0	100
China 1999	4.3	14.2	38.9	5.8	27.4	2.3	7.1	0.0	100
China 2007	5.5	15.1	34.3	4.8	30.4	1.7	8.2	0.0	100

Source: UIS data base and UniDev updates
[a]Includes others
[b]Refers to graduates that year
[c]Science + Engineering
[d]Humanities+Social Sciences

sciences (including economics, and law) in all of the countries, varying from a low of 20% in Tanzania to a high of 54% in Latvia. Humanities and social sciences together cover between 25% (Tanzania) and 63% (South Africa) of total enrollments.

As mentioned, there is in many countries a growing concern about lacking student interest in natural sciences, and to some extent also engineering sciences. Natural science studies are strong in Germany (15%) and have increased considerably in Tanzania (from 3.5% to 15% between 1999 and 2005). In most countries, less than 10% of the students are enrolled in natural sciences. Together natural sciences and engineering sciences account for around 30–35% in Russia, China, and Germany. In Sweden, Tanzania, and Vietnam, the figure is around 25%. In the other countries, the percentage is considerably less. In Cuba it is as low as 4.0% (with natural sciences 2.3% and engineering sciences 1.7%). The Cuban government is concerned about this, but it appears that the reason is partly due to the rapid increase in enrollments in general, and partly due to the fact that natural sciences are an expensive discipline with costly equipment that often has to be imported. An additional problem is the deep economic crisis in the 1990s in Cuba, resulting in decapitalization of lots of equipment and also in equipment being obsolete today.

On the contrary, the Cuban government is putting a lot of resources into the health sector (a very expensive sector as well), which is reflected in enrollments.

No less than 23% of the students are enrolled in health education in Cuba (the highest percentage of the UniDev countries), so it may be a question of priorities. In contrast, surprisingly smaller percentages are devoted to health education in some of the other UniDev countries: South Africa (6%), Russia (4%), Latvia (6%), Vietnam (3%), and China (8%).

It is also surprising that agricultural sciences attract so small numbers of students in developing countries: Brazil (2%), Cuba (1.5%), Uruguay (3%), South Africa (2%), and Vietnam (3%). The exception is China where 8% of the students are enrolled in agrosciences.

16.3   The Second Mission: University Research

University research has received a lot of attention because it is seen as building bridges with industry and the society at large. Much attention has been drawn to the need of creating science parks close to universities. Such science parks have mushroomed not only in developed countries but also in China, Brazil, South Africa, and Cuba. These developments are discussed in Prasada Reddy's contribution in this text (Chap. 3). Below we will give some insights into the growth of university research and its increasing importance, especially in developing countries.

16.3.1   Where Is R&D Performed?

Table 16.7 and Fig. 16.4 (see also Table 16.8) show some characteristics of R&D performance in the UniDev countries. If we look at Gross Expenditure on Research & Development (GERD), we see a quite similar pattern with public expenditure on education (cf. Table 16.5). GERD as a percentage of GDP ranges from 3.63 in Sweden to 0.41% in Vietnam. China, however, has an exceptionally high GERD (1.49%) in relation to its income level. The Chinese exception becomes especially noteworthy when we look at Business Expenditure on R&D (BERD), which accounts for 71% of all R&D in China, and places China in company with Sweden, Denmark, Germany, and Russia.

Interesting new patterns appear when we look at University R&D (HERD). Here the situation is in many instances the reverse. For instance, Latvia, Brazil, Cuba, and Uruguay all have higher shares of University R&D (as a percentage of GERD) than the more developed countries, even if the causal relationship is far from clear. It might be that governments in many of the developing UniDev countries give high priority to university research – often as a means of building bridges to industry; on the contrary, this perhaps rather reflects the weak BERD of these countries. University R&D is in contrast quite weak in Russia and China – both in relative terms and in terms of PPP per capita. The weak university research sector in these countries is a reflection of the past (centrally planned) system, where most research was carried out in specialized government research institutes.

Table 16.7   Characteristics of R&D performance – 2000 and 2007

	GERD as % of GDP		GERD (m. PPP)		GERD/cap (PPP)		Performed GERD/cap by sector 2007		
	2000	2007	2000	2007	2000	2007	BUS	GOV	HEI
Sweden	3.62	3.63	8,829	12,451	995	1,361	989	83	287
Denmark	2.18	2.54	3,279	5,105	614	934	606	65	257
Germany	2.40	2.53	50,407	72,300	613	879	615	120	143
China	0.76	1.49	22,344	106,542	18	81	59	15	7
Russia	1.05	1.12	10,727	22,809	74	165	106	48	11
Brazil	1.02	1.11	12,104	19,709	69	103	41	22	40
South Africa	0.73	0.95	2,075	4,297	47	90	52	19	17
Latvia	0.36	0.59	68	158	29	69	22	17	30
Uruguay	0.24	0.44	61	161	18	48	14	16	18
Cuba	0.45	0.41	276	317	25	28	14[b]		14
Vietnam	0.17	0.41	184	883	2	10	1	7	2
Tanzania[a]	na	0.48	na	235	na	6	0.2	2.6	3.2
Memo: USA	2.66	2.68	264,161	370,569	936	1,229	884	132	163

Source: UIS data base
[a]NEPAD/AU (2010)
[b]BUS+GOV

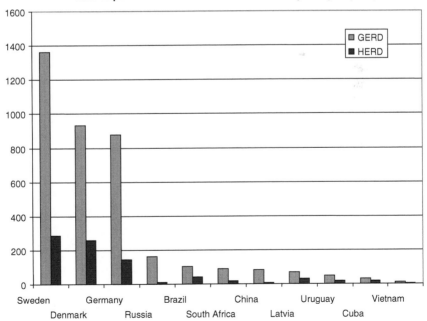

Fig. 16.4   R&D expenditures in 2007: GERD and HERD per capita (PPP). *Source*: Table 16.7

Table 16.8 GERD by sector of performance and source of funding, 2007

	By performance				Source of funding				
	BUS	GOV	HEI	PNP	BUS	GOV	HEI	PNP	Abroad
Sweden	72.7	6.1	21.1	0.1	65.7	23.5	0.6	2.5	7.7
Denmark	64.9	7.0	27.5	0.6	59.5	27.6	–	2.8	10.1
Germany	70.0	13.7	16.3	–	67.6	28.4	–	0.3	3.7
China	72.3	18.5	8.5	–	70.4	24.6	–	–	1.3
Russia	64.2	29.1	6.3	0.4	29.4	62.6	0.6	0.1	7.3
Brazil	40.2	21.3	38.3	0.1	39.9	57.9	2.2	–	–
S.Africa	58.3	20.8	19.3	1.6	43.9	38.2	3.0	1.4	13.6
Latvia	32.5	24.3	43.2	–	36.4	55.2	0.9	–	7.5
Uruguay	28.9	34.5	36.7	–	24.6	60.2	12.9	–	2.3
Cuba	–	50**	50**	–	35.0	60.0	–	–	5.0
Vietnam	14.5	66.4	17.9	1.1	18.1	74.1	0.7	–	6.3
Tanzania[a]	0.1	42.1	54.1	3.8	0	60.6	0	1.0	38.4
Memo:USA	71.9	10.7	13.3	4.2	66.4	27.7	5.8	–	–

Source: UIS data base, *na* not available
[a]NEPAD/AU (2010)

Table 16.9 UniDev: distribution of researchers by sector of employment, around 2000 and 2007 (% of total)

	Around 2000				Around 2007			
	Business	GOV	HEI	Other	Business	GOV	HEI	Other
Brazil	26.7	4.4	72.4	0.4	26.6	3.1	69.8	0.5
Cuba	na	na	na	na	..	20.0[a]	80.0[a]	–
Uruguay	15.7	3.0	81.0	–	27.8	9.0	63.2	–
Denmark	47.9	20.6	30.2	1.2	60.6	7.6	31.0	0.7
Germany	59.0	14.9	26.2	–	60.3	14.3	25.4	–
Sweden	57.2	6.1	36.6	0.1	67.6	5.5	26.4	0.4
S. Africa	20.8	15.0	62.7	1.4	34.0	11.4	53.4	1.2
Tanzania[b]	na	na	na	na	na	21.8	72.6	5.6
Russia	57.2	28.1	14.3	0.4	50.6	32.6	16.3	0.5
Latvia	26.1	17.3	56.5	–	10.9	17.6	71.4	–
Vietnam	11.6	63.3	24.3	0.8	na	na	na	na
China	52.3	25.1	22.6	–	70.0	15.1	14.9	–

Source: UIS data base, *na* not available
[a]Estimate
[b]NEPAD/AU (2010)

16.3.2   How Many Do Research in Universities?

Research thus plays quite different roles in many of the UniDev countries. In the more developed countries, university research does not play such a dominant role as in developing countries. In the developed countries, and also in large economies such as Russia and China, it is the business sector that accounts for the lion's share of performed research as well as financing research (see Table 16.8). It is thus the business sector that is by far the largest contributor to R&D in the developed countries, while it is the government sector that supplies most of the financing in developing countries. The higher education sector plays a minor role in financing of research in developed as well as developing countries.

So, how many are doing research in the UniDev countries, and where? Counting researchers is a tricky business. International organizations such as OECD and UNESCO are devoting a lot of effort to this issue. The problem is that many (perhaps most) researchers (especially in universities) are not doing research full time. That is why statistical manuals (e.g., the Frascati Manual) distinguish between headcounts (HC) and full time equivalents (FTE). Some countries only produce HC statistics and in these cases estimates have to be made in order to arrive at some proxies for FTE, which of course is the most adequate variable for comparisons. It is with this caveat in mind that we present the data for employment of researchers (FTE) in the UniDev countries in Fig. 16.5 and Tables 16.9, 16.10, and 16.11.

Sweden and Denmark have by far the highest density of researchers (over 5,000 per million inhabitants), followed by Germany and Russia (more than 3,000). Then, there is a group of three countries, Latvia, China, and Brazil, with a density ranging between 1,000 and 2,000 researchers per million inhabitants. The other countries, South Africa, Uruguay, and Cuba, have researcher densities below 400. There are no reliable data for Tanzania.

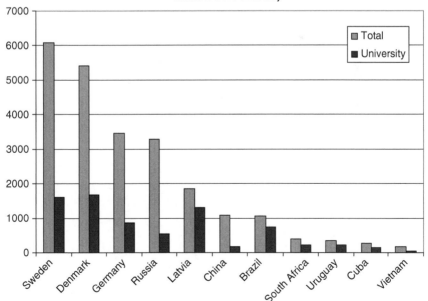

Fig. 16.5 Researcher density (FTE) in 2007: total and at universities (per million inhabitants). *Source*: Table 16.10

Table 16.10 UniDev: number of researchers (FTE), 1999–2007

	1999	2000	2001	2002	2003	2004	2005	2006	2007
Brazil	na	64,002	67,785	71,859	79,301	86,932	109,420	116,669	124,882
Cuba[a]	5,468	5,378	5,849	6,057	5,075	5,115	5,526	5,491	5,236
Uruguay	585	806	na	930	na	na	na	na	1,158
Denmark	18,945	na	19,453	25,547	24,882	26,167	28,179	28,653	na
Germany	254,691	257,874	264,385	265,812	268,942	270,215	277,628	279,800	na
Sweden	39,921	na	45,995	na	48,186	48,784	55,090	55,729	na
S. Africa	na	na	14,182	na	na	na	17,303	18,572	na
Tanzania[ab]	na	na	na	na	na	na	na	na	2755
Russia	497,030	506,420	505,778	491,944	487,477	477,647	464,577	464,357	469,076
Latvia	2,626	3,814	3,497	3,451	3,203	3,324	3,282	4,024	4,223
Vietnam[a]	na	na	na	9,328	na	na	na	na	15,484
China	531,100	695,062	742,726	810,525	862,108	926,252	1,118,698	1,123,756	na

Source: UIS data base
[a]Head Count (HC)
[b]Nepad/AU (2010)

Table 16.11 Number of researchers[a] (FTE), 1999 and 2007[b]

	Number of researchers (FTE)		Researchers per million inhabitants		Employment by sector (%) 2007[b]			
	1999	2007	1999	2007	BUS	GOV	HEI	OTH
Sweden	39,921	55,729	4,501	6,091	67.6	5.5	26.4	0.4
Denmark	18,945	29,572	3,564	5,416	60.6	7.6	31.0	0.7
Germany	254,691	279,800	3,097	3,456	60.3	14.3	25.4	–
Russia	497,030	469,076	3,415	3,303	50.6	32.6	16.3	0.5
Latvia	2,626	4,223	1,096	1,851	10.9	17.6	71.4	–
China	531,100	1,123,756	547	1,080	70.0	15.1	14.9	–
Brazil	64,002	124,882	647	1,053	26.6	3.1	69.8	0.5
South Africa	14,182	18,572	308	395	34.0	11.4	53.4	1.2
Uruguay	585	1,158	177	349	27.8	9.0	63.2	–
Cuba[d]	3,281	3,142	295	279	–	100.0		–
Vietnam[d]	9,328	15,484	115	182	11.6	63.3	24.3	0.8
Tanzania[c,d]	na	2755	na	68	na	21.8	72.6	5.6

Source: UIS data base
[a]Ranked after researcher density 2007
[b]Or closest year
[c]Nepad/AU (2010)
[d]Head Count (HC)

Now, with respect to university researchers, the picture is different. In the case of the top four (Sweden, Denmark, Germany, and Russia) and China, over 50% of the researchers are employed in the business sector. In the other countries, the situation is quite different. In these countries (except in Vietnam), more than 50% of the researchers are employed in the university sector. In Tanzania, foreign donors play an important role in research (Table 16.8). Although university research plays a pivotal role in systems of innovation in all countries, it is in developing countries, where business sector research is weak, that the role of university research is especially crucial.

The research landscape thus differs significantly between primarily the more developed countries and the developing countries. Table 16.12 depicts in an illustrative way these differences among the UniDev countries. High spending per capita does not necessarily mean that countries are investing a lot of R&D in universities, relatively speaking. Thus, university R&D per capita is quite high in Denmark, Sweden and Germany, although the shares in GERD are about 25% or less. On the contrary, there are countries such as Latvia and Brazil that have not only a quite high share of university R&D as a percent of GERD but also a rather high per capita spending. Latvia is an interesting case because, being a former republic in the Soviet Union, its pattern differs quite distinctly from that of the Russian Federation.

In the old Soviet research system, very little research was carried out at universities, but rather at large research institutes linked to the Academy of Sciences. This is the situation to a large extent also in Russia today, where less than 6% of R&D is carried out in universities. In China, the situation is still a reflection of the past with only 9% of research activities taking place in universities. In Latin America,

Table 16.12 Absolute and relative size of university R&D – around 2007

University R&D per capita (PPP$)	Share of university R&D in total R&D spending		
	Relatively high (more than 30%)	Medium (15–30%)	Low (less than 15%)
High (more than 100 PPP per capita)		Denmark (28%) Sweden (21%) Germany (16%)	United States (13%)
Medium high (30–74 PPP/capita)	Latvia (43%) Brazil (38%)		
Medium low (11–29 PPP/capita)	Cuba (50%) Uruguay (37%)	South Africa (19%)	Russia (6%)
Low (less than 11 PPP/capita)	Tanzania (53%)	Vietnam (18%)	China (9%)

Source: Tables 16.7 and 16.8

Africa, and Vietnam, university R&D plays an important role in overall research activities in the countries. In Tanzania, particularly, the lion's share of R&D (over 60%) is carried out at universities.

16.4 Current Debates on the Role of Universities

The country teams organized national workshops to discuss preliminary findings with various stakeholders: universities, government, policy makers, business representatives, and the research community at large. In some of these national workshops, participants discussed the role of universities in society and were asked to rank the 4–5 most critical areas ("hottest issues") from a list, common for all the countries. The result is shown in Table 16.13 below (in some cases, the ranking was made by the national teams). There are many common concerns but there are also interesting country differences.

16.4.1 Financing of Higher Education

On the top of the list in all countries is not surprisingly *financing*. Higher education usually comes from the public budget and there are competing priorities, especially in developing countries. There are thus pressures on universities, especially to prove both their social relevance and cost efficiency of both education and research. A problem in many of the UniDev countries is that education has traditionally been free, also university education. In some of the countries this principle is sacred, and there are no plans to introduce fees in, e.g., Sweden, Denmark, Cuba, and Uruguay. In Uruguay, there is an issue of whether or not foreign students should be able to continue to take advantage of this situation (e.g., in the case of Chilean students). In Sweden there is a similar debate. Any EU student has the right to study in Sweden without paying a fee. So far this is also the case for any other student outside EU. The discussion ranges between those in favor of the "free fee for all"

Table 16.13 The hottest issues in the current university debates in 12 countries

The hottest issues	Sweden	Denmark	Germany	Latvia	Russia	Brazil	Cuba	Uruguay	China	Vietnam	Tanzania	S. Africa
Funding	x	x	x	x	x	x	x	x	x	x	x	x
Allocation of resources		x	x									x
Governance		x	x									x
Quality of teachers	x						x			x	x	x
Low salaries					x		x	x				
Access to higher education	x	x										x
Private vs. public						x		x			x	
Relevance of university R&D	x		x		x	x		x		x		
Social inclusion/relevance	x					x		x	x			
Gender/minorities	x											x[a]
Integration of universities with research					x		x			x	x	
Technology transfer issues			x	x		x			x	x		
Declining interest in S&T		x		x							x	

Source: UniDev: reports from national workshops http://developinguniversities.blogsome.com

[a]Majorities!

system, claiming that this will make Sweden more attractive for foreign students, and those who say that it would be unwise not to make use of this extra source of income to finance the university system.

This debate also goes on in Tanzania where higher education was free until the late 1980s. However, with the rapid population increase and the number of students completing secondary education, it has become increasingly burdensome for the government to provide free quality education.

In some countries the role of private higher education institutions is quite important (e.g., in Brazil). On the one hand, this can be an important means to finance higher education from nongovernment sources. On the contrary, it raises questions about quality control and the unequal access to private institutions that often have quite high fees, making them inaccessible for most students (case of Brazil and South Africa). Another debated issue is that private higher institutions very seldom carry out research. Privatization is a hot issue in Brazil, Uruguay, and Tanzania. In Uruguay, there is so far only one university and that is public, although there are some private initiatives.

16.4.2   The Relevance of University Research

The second hottest issue is not surprisingly the relevance of university research. This is a topic heatedly discussed in all parts of the UniDev spectrum: from Sweden and Germany to Russia, Brazil, Uruguay, and Vietnam, but often from different angles. In some countries, the debate is not so much on what research is relevant, but why should research at all be carried out by universities, when it may be more efficiently – and relevantly – be carried out in the productive sector, or in specialized research institutes. This is the case in, e.g., Russia and China. In other countries, such as Cuba and Uruguay, the debate is rather on the relevance of university research as such.

Social inclusion and social relevance of universities are issues that are being debated in Sweden, Brazil, Cuba, Uruguay, and China. However, it should be emphasized that "social inclusion" can be interpreted in different ways. For some people, it refers to university enrollment policies; in other words, it is almost synonymous with access to higher education. This might explain the difference in this context between Sweden and Denmark. The same goes for gender/minorities that can also be interpreted in terms of inclusion/exclusion. The South African answer is interesting: social inclusion/exclusion is not a minority problem, it is a problem for the (nonwhite) majorities!

In Cuba and Uruguay (and to some extent in Brazil), the concept of social inclusion relates primarily to universities through the research agenda, which aims at taking into account problems that affect the most deprived segments of the population.

16.4.3   The Quality of Teaching and the Importance of Incentives

The quality of education is the third hottest topic, ranging from Sweden to Cuba, Vietnam, Tanzania, and South Africa. Quality of teachers is not surprisingly linked to remuneration. In most of the countries, this is a serious problem. Salaries of university teachers are lagging behind the average salary trend, and in many of the UniDev countries, it is difficult to recruit people to universities, both as teachers and researchers.

But this is not a new phenomenon. Almost a quarter of a millennium ago, the Swedish botanist, physician, and zoologist Carl Linnaeus, father of modern taxonomy, summarized the most pressing issues for the academic community at that time:

> "University professors must be given freedom to practice their profession, receive a decent salary for the work they are devoted to, be given opportunity to fill their students with enthusiasm for the subject and see them gain recognition for the results of their studies, and be promoted on the basis of merits and not merely on seniority or as a result of intrigues and cliquism."[2]

In Cuba, the quality of education has lately become an increasing concern to the government. One reason is the consequences of the massive surge in university enrollments since the beginning of 2000 in a drive toward the "universalization of higher education." There is for understandable reasons a serious lack of qualified university teachers in the initial period – before the system can supply a sufficient number of qualified teachers.

As a consequence, low salaries are related to the issue of quality of education in many countries because it might be difficult to recruit, and to retain, good university teachers and university researchers, if salary levels are low (in relation to other occupations). This is at least the case in Russia, Cuba, and Uruguay.

Governments in some of the countries discussed here are particularly preoccupied with instituting policies for forging closer bonds between university research and the productive sector, either for maintaining or for building up a competitive advantage for industry. This is particularly so not only for the formerly centrally planned economies in Latvia, China, and Vietnam that have an inherited weak university research tradition to compensate for, but also for Germany where the research institute sector is relatively large compared with other developed countries such as Sweden and Denmark. Not surprisingly, issues related to technology transfer and the relation with the productive sector are high on the agenda in the university debate in these countries – perhaps a reflection of policy measures aimed at distilling an entrepreneurial spirit among the university researchers.

16.5   The Third Mission: Toward the Developmental University?[3]

Looking at the country contributions, and also incorporating the outcomes of the workshops, seminars, and international conferences, where project results have been ventilated, there is one topic that stands out: the social relevance of universities, not

---

[2]Carl von Linnaeus, vice chancellor of Uppsala University, 25 September, 1759. Translation by authors, based on a free translation from sixteenth century Swedish by Gunnar Weimarck in *Universitetsläraren* 15/2007

[3]This section builds on UniDev country case studies presented in more detail in *Science and Public Policy* special issue on the Third Mission (March 2009)

only research but also with respect to teaching and above all the "third mission." This is especially a valid observation when it comes to the UniDev countries in the South: Brazil, China, Cuba, Uruguay, South Africa, Tanzania, and Vietnam.

In Cuba, this debate has led to the so-called Universalization of Higher Education, described in the chapter about Cuba. In Uruguay, there is a debate on the "loneliness syndrome," that is, "the lack of social demand for endogenously generated knowledge leaves to a great extent the academic realm on its own." The Uruguayan report says that, "the loneliness syndrome and the current academic reward system shape a sort of schizophrenic situation: research should be useful for different stakeholders that however do not demand its results; according to that, research should be rewarded by its relevance, but the academic system puts a too high a prize on results measured in international rather than in national terms."

So there seems to be a need for a substantially new type of university, at least in the South, the Developmental University (for a further discussion of this concept, see Brundenius et al. 2009). Such a university is defined by its commitment to its third role or mission, to relate to society, be relevant for society, and be part of meeting social needs of society, especially of the poor. We can thus hear voices that ask for more "useful research" in the South (and more useful research in the North to help solving problems in the South).

This call for increased relevance of the universities is embodied in the catch-phrase "third mission" of the universities. The two long-established tasks for the university discussed above – teaching and research – have long worked in conjunction to provide society with certain skills as well as new knowledge and ideas, though not necessarily the skills demanded by the majority of the people. In a sense, universities have always maintained a certain degree of ties with influential segments of society, and not only engaged in obscure l'art pour l'art pursuits as critics have sometimes been fond of maintaining. The medieval universities' religious teaching and "finding God in science" worked toward fulfilling the wishes of the rulers, as did later the Humboldtian university with education and science as instruments for shaping the student's character and perception of the world. It is with the advent of the comprehensive mass education facilities of the late twentieth century, however, that the more precise tasks and obligations of the university have become a concern for broader segments of society.

The result of this development has been that universities are facing a multitude of new demands from a host of stakeholders. Universities are asked to take on a progressively important role in economic and social development. Governments task the universities with providing education for larger and larger shares of age cohorts as well as with developing and transferring state-of-the-art technology to industry. Industry increasingly looks beyond generic engineering education and require universities to deliver new and specialized education as well as research activities in support of their particular needs. Student bodies see education as an investment rather than a personal pursuit, and demand job relevance in education. Furthermore, civil society often looks for guidance from universities for help in addressing all sorts of ills plaguing society, from diseases to human conflicts.

How can universities satisfy such an onslaught of sometimes conflicting expectations? It is clear that the capacity of universities to respond is in general not sufficient and, as the contributions to this book bear out, it is also clear that the crisis of the university to respond to the changing requirements is not confined to the developed world. Better global communications, increasing international trade relations, and commercial ties render any university irrelevant for large segments of society if it cannot respond properly to local demands.

The concept of the third mission encapsulates much of the rising demands on the university. In one sense it is a residual, encompassing all university activities not covered by the first two missions: teaching and research. This makes it a rather amorphous concept. Not surprisingly, the third mission is in general rather vaguely defined in national policy documents, and the interpretation of the mission varies considerably between countries as well as between universities in the same country. However, the common rationale for the third mission is for the university to take on a more visible role in stimulating and guiding the utilization of knowledge for social, cultural, and economic development. For some countries, the definition is quite clear: universities should focus at developing new technological solutions that is transferred to the preferably domestic industry. In other cases, the formulation and interpretation of a third mission is a continuing process and an ongoing debate.

For some countries, the concept of a third mission for universities is quite new. Adhering to the Soviet model of organizing the science and technology system, universities in countries such as Russia, China, Cuba, Latvia, and Vietnam played a limited role in the production of new knowledge and innovations than did their Western counterparts. With the transition from a planned economy toward market orientation, the universities in these countries have taken on broader responsibilities, including activities to reach out to society at large. This does not mean that the interpretation of the third mission, or even the direction of movement of the responsibilities of universities, is uniformly agreed on in these countries. In China, the introduction of the third mission of "serving society directly" has been interpreted by many governing boards to mean that the universities are free to move toward pursuing purely economic benefits to compensate for lowered direct public funding. Consequently, there is a move toward profit seeking by universities that have the capacity and competence to cater to the needs of industry needs. Thus, the focus of the third mission is here placed mainly on transfer of technology to industry. In Vietnam, on the contrary, the third mission for the universities to pursue "activities to reach out to society at large" is intertwined with the second mission (research) and is expected to be responsive to the needs of society.

Also, in Cuba, the interpretation of the third mission requires the universities to broadly "involve in social and economic needs" rather than focusing on the narrow needs of industry. The same understanding permeates the extension programs of the lone university of Uruguay, the University of the Republic. Although the definition of the third mission is still an ongoing process in Uruguay, the university is still mandated to address societal problems at large rather than limiting itself to forging university–industry linkages.

Other countries struggle with striking a balance between these two interpretations of what the third mission should focus on. For Latvia, the third mission for the universities implies not only on merely focusing on economic returns from innovation and technology transfer to industry, but also on "educating the nation" and "influencing society." Russia also has a broad interpretation of the third mission that includes social development, but lacks a clear guiding policy. In the wake of a systemic view on what the third mission should look like, the third mission has in practice centered on technology transfer activities.

The balancing act for the universities caught between the sometimes lofty policy declaration set by the policymakers and the everyday pressures they are facing is also visible in countries as diverse as South Africa, Sweden, and Denmark. In South Africa, the universities are mandated to improve its relationship with society and the productive sector. Although this means "making universities accessible to the community," the emphasis is in practice closely linked to industry and technology transfer. In Sweden, the third mission of "interacting with the surrounding society" more than often leads to activities by the university toward developing patentable technology to be transferred to industry. Also Denmark struggles with what "collaborating with society" should mean in practice and what type of third mission should receive priority. In all of these countries, universities are devoting increasing funds to opening and maintaining technology transfer offices and putting incentive systems in place for encouraging development of new technology for industry.

In Germany, the third mission is more distinctly framed as "activities related to the university's direct contribution to economic development," meaning in practice technology transfer to industry. Other activities do not fall under this definition of the third mission. Also developing countries such Brazil and Tanzania employ a narrow scope to the third mission. In Tanzania, the universities are required by government policy as well as donor pressure to develop university–industry linkages rather than engaging in social innovation. Yet, large segments of society see a broader scope for the Tanzanian university system.

In other words, although some of the countries struggle with balancing a narrowly focused third mission with broader societal involvement, still most of the 12 UniDev countries interpret the third mission in practice to mean transfer of technology to industry. This narrow scope of the third mission is adhered to by nine of the twelve countries (Fig. 16.6). Only Cuba, Uruguay, and Vietnam interpret the third mission of their universities as a broader commitment to include larger segments of society than industry. If we further divide the countries according to the level of national spending on R&D, it is interesting to note that at higher levels of R&D spending, no country is pursuing a broader scope for the third mission. In other words, the more money you spend on R&D, the more it becomes focused on industrial development and competitiveness.

Why is that? One reason might be a tendency of decision makers in government and universities to conform to new theoretical models. New models are being proposed for guiding the evolution of universities toward greater relevance, such as Triple Helix models involving private–public partnerships, the creation of entrepreneurial or specialized universities, and large-scale excellence-driven environments. However, there exists no universal or ready-made model to guide these changes. Each country faces a unique set of economic, social, cultural, and political circumstances that will require stakeholders to engage in a dialog aimed at finding

	Broad Scope: Society at large	Narrow Scope: Transfer of technology to industry
High level of R&D (above 1% of GDP)		Sweden (3.63%) Denmark (2.54%) Germany (2.53%) China (1.49%) Russia (1.12%) Brazil (1.11%)
Low level of R&D (below 1% of GDP)	Uruguay (0.44%) Cuba (0.41%) Vietnam (0.41%)	South Africa (0.95%) Latvia (0.59%) Tanzania (0.48%)

Fig. 16.6 Scope of the third mission and level of national research intensity

an optimal role for universities in a changing national innovation system, particularly in an era of dwindling financial support to the universities.

In spite of this, we find a strong belief among decision makers in the STI sector in all types of countries that the latest imported concepts will be the panacea to the problems at hand. Contrary to this view, one might say that imported, and sometimes untested, systems have a tendency to be inflexible or not suitable when transferred from one environment to clearly differing circumstances. An example is the almost universal belief that universities will benefit economically from setting up technology transfer offices and putting incentive systems in place to encourage their researchers to think business-mindedly. Considerable amounts are spent on these activities although the empirical evidence on a positive outcome is very hard to find in any country. In spite of this, universities all over the world are continuing pouring money into setting up technology transfer offices and creating science parks and business incubators, supported by government policies on intellectual property rights and industrial innovation promotion schemes.

Considerably less effort is devoted to broadening the scope of the outreach activities of universities to focus on knowledge demands in society and social innovation processes that are demand driven and inclusive. Citizens, public authorities, and private enterprises all have different expectations on knowledge production and access. There is a need for better understanding how actors relate and interact, and how "signals" on needs and capacities are communicated, so that broader and more comprehensive "socially driven" innovation may be the outcome. The UniDev network is devoted to exploring these issues, and will continue carrying out case studies on how inclusive perspectives on knowledge lay the ground for welfare gains, improved innovation potential, and poverty reduction.

References

Arocena, Rodrigo (2008). Isabel Bortagaray and Judith Sutz, Reforma Universitaria y Desarrollo, Montevideo: Tradinco S.A

Brundenius, Claes, Bengt-Åke Lundvall and Judith Sutz (2009). "The role of universities in innovation systems in developing countries: developmental university systems – empirical, analytical and normative perspectives", in Bengt-Åke Lundvall, K.J, Joseph, Cristina Chaminade and Jan Vang (eds), *Handbook of Innovation Systems and Developing Countries*, Aldershot: Edward Elgar

Eggins, Heather (ed) (2009). Sharing Research Agendas on Knowledge Systems, Occasional Paper No. 16, Paris: UNESCO

ESF, Higher Education Looking Forward: An Agenda for Future Research, Strasbourg: European Science Foundation, 2008

Göransson, Bo, Rasigan Maharajh and Ulrich Schmoch (eds) (2009). *Science and Public Policy* special issue on the Third Mission

NEPAD/AU (2010). Africal Innovation Outlook 2010. Pretoria: NEPAD/African Union OECD (2009), Main Science and Technology Indicators, Vol. 2009/2, Paris: OECD

UIS Database, Montreal: Unesco Institute of Statistics, http://stats.uis.unesco.org/unesco/ReportFolders/ReportFolders.aspx accessed 20 April 2010

UNESCO (2009). Global Education Digest 2009, Paris: UNESCO

About the Authors

Anda Adamsone-Fiskovica is a researcher and project manager at the Centre for Science and Technology Studies of the Latvian Academy of Sciences. She holds an MSc in Sociology from the University of Latvia and an MA in Science and Technology Studies from the Linkoping University (Sweden). She has also finished doctoral studies in Sociology at the University of Latvia (2003–2007). Her main research interests are related to R&D and innovation policy, development of higher education, and science–society relations in Latvia. She is the Latvian team leader in several international research projects and a member of a number of European innovation and science researchers' networks.
Email: anda@lza.lv

Jan Ågren has a master's degree in Economic History from Lund University, Sweden. He is affiliated as an associate researcher to Research Policy Institute (RPI) at Lund University, where he is also a member of the LEAP4D research group. His main research interests include various topics related to the dynamics between formal and informal institutions in innovation systems or, more particularly, between proprietary knowledge and open science-related attitudes and practices at research universities.
Email: Jan.Agren@fpi.lu.se

Rodrigo Arocena is a full professor of Science and Development in the Faculty of Sciences of the University of the Republic, Uruguay. Currently he is the rector of the University. He holds a PhD in Mathematics and a PhD in Development Studies, both from the Central University of Venezuela. His research work focuses on the interactions between Science, Technology, and Development, with particular attention to the role of universities in underdeveloped countries.
Email: roar@fcien.edu.uy

Mats Benner is a professor and director at the Research Policy Institute (RPI), Lund University, Sweden. He holds a PhD in Sociology from Lund University. His work focuses on research policy and research organization, and deals with the agenda setting and policy priorities in the areas of research and innovation, the management of large-scale research groups, and leadership and organizational change within the academic system. He has been engaged in various evaluation tasks for governments,

universities, and funding organizations, and he has published articles in journals like *Research Policy*, *Science and Public Policy* and *Minerva*.
Email: Mats.Benner@fpi.lu.se

Claes Brundenius is a honorary professor at the RPI, Lund University, Sweden. He holds a PhD in Economic History from Lund University. He has been attached to the OECD Directorate for Scientific Affairs. He has been a guest professor at Pittsburgh University (1984) and Smith College (1987), USA. Between 1997 and 2003, he was research director at the Centre for Development Research in Copenhagen. His current work has focused on policy-based development in developing and transition economies, notably in Latin America and the Caribbean, East Asia, and Southern Africa.
Email: Claes.Brundenius@fpi.lu.se

Tran Ngoc Ca is director of Secretariat for the National Council for Science and Technology Policy and deputy director, National Institute for Science and Technology Policy and Strategy Studies, Hanoi, Vietnam. He has been working on projects on science, technology, and innovation policy and management, information technology and electronics commerce for UNDP, UNIDO, World Bank, European Commission, CIDA, SIDA/SAREC, IDRC, etc. He is involved in various teaching and consulting works. Dr Ca was educated with an engineering degree at Moscow Mining University (former Soviet Union), master's degree in Lund University (Sweden), and PhD at the University of Edinburgh (UK). He spent time in some US universities as UC Davis, UC Berkeley, and Stanford as visiting Fulbright scholar. He has published many articles, chapters in books, and a book by Ashgate Publishing (UK): *Technological capability and learning in firms: Vietnamese industries in transition*. He is member of several professional associations in Vietnam and abroad.
Email: tranngocca@gmail.com

Bitrina D. Diyamett is a senior research officer at the Tanzania Commission for Science and Technology, and a national coordinator for the African Technology Policy Studies Network, Tanzania Chapter. She holds a master's degree in Science and Technology Policy from Lund University, Sweden. Much of her research work, consultancies, and publications focus on systems of innovation in the context of least developed countries. Bitrina is currently in the last stages of her PhD program at the University of Dar es Salaam, Tanzania, where she is investigating innovativeness and inter-organizational linkages in the Tanzanian manufacturing sector.
Email: bdiyamett@costech.or.tz

Aurora Fernández González is a full professor and emeritus professor at the Higher Polytechnic Institute of Havana, and collaborates with the Science, Technology, Society and Innovation (CTS+I) Group of the University of Havana as a part-time professor in the Science, Technology, and Society Master's Degree Program. She holds a PhD in Automatic Control, earned at the Polytechnic University of Poznan, Poland, and a master's degree in Operational Research, from the University of Lancaster, Great Britain. For several years, she was director for

postgraduate education at the Ministry of Higher Education, Cuba. She is the secretary of the Board of the National Council for Postgraduate Studies. Her research work focuses on higher education policies and the role of universities in innovation systems and development.
Email: aurora@reduniv.edu.cu

José Luis García Cuevas is a full professor, Emeritus Academic, and director for Science and Technology at the Ministry of Higher Education, Cuba. He holds a PhD in Electronics. He coordinates a research group on knowledge and innovation management. His research work focuses on how knowledge, science, technology, and innovation, together with the degree and postgraduate systems at the universities, drives social and economic national and local development. Much of his research deals with issues related to science and innovation policies, both at local and national levels, innovation networks, capacity building, and the university support for the development and impact of appropriate new and convergent technologies.
Email: jluis@reduniv.edu.cu

Leonid Gokhberg is a professor and first vice rector of the Higher School of Economics (HSE) – one of the most prominent research universities in Russia – and director of HSE Institute for Statistical Studies and Economics of Knowledge. He has authored over 350 publications in Russia and internationally devoted to S&T and innovation indicators, analyses, and policies; and coordinated dozens of international projects sponsored by the European Commission, World Bank, UNIDO, US National Science Foundation, IIASA, etc. Leonid Gokhberg has served as a consultant to OECD, Eurostat, UNESCO, and other international and national agencies. He is also editor-in-chief of Moscow-based journal "Foresight" and a member of OECD and Eurostat expert groups on indicators for S&T, information society, and education.
Email: lgokhberg@hse.ru

Bo Göransson is a senior research fellow and coordinator of the LEAP4D research group at the Research Policy Institute (RPI), Lund University, Sweden. He holds a PhD in International Economics from Aalborg University, Denmark. His research work focuses on how knowledge and learning systems drive economic development and growth. Much of the research deals with issues related to innovation policies, capacity building, and impact of new technologies in developing countries, particularly in the area of information and communication technologies (ICT). In a related line of research, he studies the role of universities in innovation systems and development.
Email: Bo.Goransson@fpi.lu.se

Birgitte Gregersen is an associate professor in Economics and member of the IKE-Research Group at Department of Business Studies, Aalborg University, Denmark. She has researched and published within the field of technical change and employment, IT in the public sector, public technology procurement, studies of national systems of innovation, university–industry linkages, innovation policy, and sustainable development. Her current research is centered around systems

of innovation with a special focus on institutions and learning capabilities in a sustainable development perspective. She has several years of experience within university governance, including positions as vice dean and study director.
Email: bg@business.aau.dk

Jørgen Gulddahl Rasmussen is a professor in Organisation and Management at the Department of Business Studies, Aalborg University, Denmark. He has for many years done empirical and theoretical studies and published within the fields of business and public sector management, strategy, and organization. University governance and the interaction between universities and their environment have for more than 10 years been one of his main research areas. Previously, he has functioned as Dean and in numerous other university management tasks; currently he is director of the Social Science Research School at Aalborg University.
Email: jgr@business.aau.dk

Nguyen Vo Hung is a researcher and vice head of Innovation Policy and Technology Market Development Division, National Institute for Science and Technology Policy and Strategy Studies (NISTPASS). He holds an MSc in International Trade and Finance from Lancaster University, UK. His main research interests are innovation policy in developing countries focusing on innovation of SMEs, FDI strategy in emerging markets, application of game theory in policy design, and intangible assets management.
Email: hung@ism.ac.vn

Wang Haiyan is an associate research professor at Chinese Academy of Science and Technology for Development, Ministry of Science and Technology, PRC. Her research mainly focuses on the regional development, national innovation system, S&T strategy, and related policies. She has undertaken about 30 international, national, and regional projects in the fields of science and technology strategy, regional development as research director or main researcher, and has published 5 books, about 30 articles in the fields of science and technology strategy, innovation policy research, national innovation system, and regional development.
Email:wanghy@casted.org.cn

Janis Kristapsons is the founder (1991) and head of the Centre for Science and Technology Studies of the Latvian Academy of Sciences and advisor to the President of the Academy. His academic background is in nuclear and solid state physics and sociology. His main research interests currently cover research and innovation policies in the East and Central European countries, R&D and inventing activity, technology transfer and industry–academia linkages, as well as S&T indicators and research evaluation. Together with his Estonian and Lithuanian colleagues, he has written a monograph on the transition of the Baltic R&D systems (2003).
Email: jtk@lza.lv

Tatiana Kuznetsova is the director of the Centre for Science, Innovation and Information Policies (Institute for Statistical Studies and Economics of Knowledge, State University – Higher School of Economics (HSE)). Her research interests cover studies on S&T and innovation policy, its legal environment. She authored over 250

publications; took part in different international projects sponsored by the OECD, NNF, UNIDO, World Bank, etc. She acts as a consultant to various government agencies, scientific centers, and universities. She is a member of Russian team participating in the international project "National Innovation Systems of BRICS Countries."
Email: tkuznetzova@hse.ru

Anne-Marie Maculan is a full professor at Production Engineering Program of COPPE-Federal University of Rio de Janeiro (Brazil). She holds a PhD in Socioeconomics from the University of Quebec at Montreal. She has been a consultant for the Ministry of Science and Technology, World Bank, and Brazilian Federal or State Agencies for research and innovation. Her main areas of academic interest include technology and knowledge transfer, academic entrepreneurship, and the role of the scientific research institutions in the local innovation system with special interest in the science parks and incubators experiences.
Email: amaculan@pep.ufrj.br

Rasigan Maharajh is an activist academic who has worked in nongovernmental organizations concerned with literacy, education, and human development while simultaneously holding elected leadership positions within student and youth formations of the United Democratic Front and in the machinery of the African National Congress. Since 1994, he has been deployed as the national coordinator of the Science and Technology Policy Transition Project, the Head of the Policy Group at the Council for Scientific and Industrial Research and is currently the chief director of the Institute for Economic Research on Innovation.
Email: maharajhr@tut.ac.za

José Manoel Carvalho de Mello is a visiting professor at the Production Engineering Graduate Program and an advisor for the Innovation Agency at the Fluminense Federal University, Brazil. He has a chemical engineering degree and an MSc in Production Engineering, both from the Federal University of Rio de Janeiro. Dr Mello also holds a PhD in Production Engineering (operations research) from the University of Birmingham, England. He was a visiting fellow at the Management Centre, University of Bradford, England (1973); at the Centre Science, Société et Technologie, Conservatoire National de Arts et Métiers, Paris (1984/1985); and at the State University of New York (1997/1998). He is the vice president of the Triple Helix Association and the author of numerous papers on science, technology, and innovation policy, local systems of innovation, triple helix models of innovation, and on entrepreneurial university.
Email: josemello@pq.cnpq.br.

Luis Félix Montalvo Arriete is a senior researcher of the Chair Science Technology Society and Innovation of University of Havana, Cuba. He holds a PhD in Scientific and Technological Policy from University of Campinas (UNICAMP), Brazil. Much of the research deals with issues related to science and technology policies, innovation policies, and innovation systems. His research work focuses on the role of universities in innovation systems.
Email: lfmontalvo@rect.uh.cu

Enver Motala has worked for more than 25 years in a variety of educational environments and fields including adult basic, school-based, further, and higher education. He was a lawyer for the independent trade union movement and played a leading role in the antiapartheid education movement. After the first democratic elections, he was appointed the deputy director general of Education in the Province of Gauteng. He is concurrently an associate of the Education Policy Consortium and the Institute for Economic Research on Innovation; for and with whom he conducts and coordinates research projects on democracy, human rights, and social justice in education in South Africa.
Email: emotala@lantic.net

Burton L.M. Mwamila is an experienced engineering academic, researcher, and consultant. He spearheaded the establishment of the College of Engineering and Technology, for which he served as its first principal from 2005 to 2009. He was the first chairman of the National Council for Technical Education from 1999 to 2007. He is currently the chairman of the Tanzania Commission for Science and Technology (COSTECH). At regional level, he has been a member of the Governing Council of the African Network of Scientific and Technological Institutions (ANSTI) from 2000 to 2009, and at continental level he is the chairman of the Executive Board of the Pan-African Competitiveness Forum (PACF) since 2008. On July 1, 2009, he was appointed the founding vice chancellor of the Nelson Mandela African Institute of Science and Technology in Arusha (NM AIST-Arusha), Tanzania, for the Eastern African region.
Email: mwamila@udsm.ac.tz

Jorge Núñez Jover, studied chemistry, has a PhD in Philosophy, and is director for Postgraduate Studies at the University of Havana (UH). He is the coordinator of the master's and doctoral programs on Science, Technology, and Society. He holds the chair in science, technology, society, and innovation. He has published 10 books and over 100 papers. His research is in the areas of education, science, technology, and society; postgraduate studies in evaluation and accreditation, and university science policy. He is an invited professor in universities in Spain, Germany, Brazil, Mexico, and other countries in Latin America and the Caribbean.
Email: jorgenjover@rect.uh.cu

Isarelis Pérez Ones graduated in sociology in 1997, and also with a master's in science, technology, and society (STS), at the University of Havana (UH). She is now an assistant professor there. She was a graduate student at Roskilde University, Denmark (2002–2003). In 2005 she took a training PhD program, "Globelics Academy," at the Technical University of Lisbon. She is finishing her PhD on STS at the UH. Her main interests are related to the social studies of science and technology and higher education. Her current work has focused on the role of universities in the systems of innovation.
Email: isarelis@rect.uh.cu

Prasada Reddy is a senior research fellow at the Research Policy Institute (RPI), Lund University, Sweden. He has academic qualifications in Economics (PhD),

Science and Technology Policy (MSc), and Law (LLB). He has also worked as an associate professor at the University of Oslo for a couple of years. He held the position of a Senior Economic Affairs Officer at UNCTAD for sometime and has also been a consultant to international organizations such as WIPO, OECD, and UNU. His broad areas of work are foreign direct investment (FDI), technology, and intellectual property rights. In recent years, he has been working in the area of Globalization of R&D and Implications for Innovation Systems, particularly dealing with the issue of location of R&D in developing countries by MNCs and its implications.
Email: PrasadaReddy1@gmail.com

Thiago Borges Renault is a PhD candidate in Federal University of Rio de Janeiro, Brazil. He holds a master's degree in Production Engineering from Fluminense Federal University, Brazil. His research work focuses on university, industry and government relationship, and academic spin-offs formation in Brazilian universities.
Email: thiagorenault@gmail.com

Mario Scerri is a professor of economics in the Faculty of Economics and Finance at the Tshwane University of Technology and a senior research fellow at the Institute for Economic Research on Innovation. For 6 years prior to taking up his post at IERI, he served as the dean of two faculties which eventually evolved into the Faculty of Economics and Finance at the Tshwane University of Technology. His research focus is on the evolution of innovation systems, specifically within Southern Africa. He has written on local innovation systems and on the relationship between the state and the national system of innovation. He has recently published a book on the evolution of the South African System of Innovation since 1916.
Email: mscerri@mweb.co.za

Ulrich Schmoch is a private lecturer at the University of Karlsruhe (Germany), senior researcher at the Fraunhofer Institute for Systems and Innovation Research, and scientific manager at the office of the Expert Commission on Research and Innovation in Berlin (Germany). He received a degree in mechanical engineering, a doctoral degree in social and political sciences at the University of Hannover (Germany), and a state doctoral degree in sociology of science and technology from the University of Karlsruhe (Germany). The focus of his research is systems of innovation, knowledge transfer, innovation indicators, and structures of scientific research.
Email: ulrich.schmoch@isi.fraunhofer.de

Judith Sutz is the academic coordinator of the University Research Council of the Universidad de la República, Uruguay, and full professor of Science, Technology, and Society. She holds a PhD in Socioeconomics of Development from the University of Paris-Sorbonne. Her research work focuses on innovation and the production and social use of knowledge in developing countries. She was part of the Task Force on Science, Technology, and Innovation of the UN Millennium Project, and she is a fellow of WAAS and integrates the Scientific Board of Globelics.
Email: jsutz@csic.edu.uy

Erika Tjunina is a senior researcher at the Centre for Science and Technology Studies of the Latvian Academy of Sciences. She received her diploma in Chemistry from the Riga Technical University and holds a doctoral degree of Engineering Sciences in Polymer Mechanics. Her research work at the Centre primarily deals with the scientometric analysis (quantitative S&T indicators) of the Latvian science and the studies of the inventions and inventors of Latvia. She has also been involved in a range of projects dealing with the role of academic institutions in the national R&D and innovation systems.
Email: erika@lza.lv

Inga Ulnicane-Ozolina was a researcher at the Centre for Science and Technology Studies of the Latvian Academy of Sciences (until 2008), contributing to the studies of research and innovation policies (EraWatch and Trendchart), academic institutions, and science mentoring. She has studied political science and European studies, taught public administration and political economy, and worked for the international initiative EuroFaculty aimed at reforming higher education in social sciences in the Baltic States. Her research interests are related to the internationalization of research and organizations and institutions of science, technology, and innovation.
Email: i.ulnicane-ozolina@utwente.nl

Zhou Yuan holds a PhD in Regional Development, is a research professor and deputy director general, The Administrative Center for China's Agenda 21 (ACCA21), Ministry of Science and Technology, PRC; vice president, China Association of High Technology Industry Development; International Advisory Board Member, Center for Science, Technology & Innovation in China, The Levin Institute, The State University of New York; professor of The University of Science and Technology of China, Xian Jiaotong University, The University of Science and Technology of Beijing, Institute of Nature Science History of Chinese Academy of Science, etc. He has undertaken over 50 international, national, and regional projects in the fields of science and technology strategy, is a research director in regional development, and has published 10 books, over 100 articles in Chinese and English in the fields of science and technology strategy and policy, and regional development.
Email: zhouy@acca21.org.cn

Stanislav Zaichenko is a senior researcher at the Institute for Statistical Studies and Economics of Knowledge (the State University – Higher School of Economics) since 2004. During this period, he took part as expert in several international research programs including GLOBELICS (BRICS and UniDev projects) and TACIS as well as in several tens of national projects initiated by the Russian government bodies and enterprises. The main academic interests, reflected in about a dozen publications, refer to integration of science and education, evaluation of R&D performance, university management reforms, and other S&T policy issues.
Email: szaichenko@hse.ru

Index